THE
DURHAM BOOK

THE
DURHAM BOOK

BEING THE FIRST DRAFT OF
THE REVISION OF THE
BOOK OF COMMON PRAYER IN 1661

Edited with an Introduction and Notes

by

G. J. CUMING

Vicar of Billesdon cum Goadby and Rolleston
Sometime Vice-Principal of St. John's College
Durham

GREENWOOD PRESS, PUBLISHERS
WESTPORT, CONNECTICUT

Library of Congress Cataloging in Publication Data

Church of England. Book of common prayer.
   The Durham book.

   Reprint of the ed. published by Oxford University
Press, London, in series: University of Durham publica-
tions.
   Bibliography: p.
   I. Cuming, G.J. II. Title. III. Series: Durham,
Eng. University. Publications.
[BX5145.A4 1979]   264'.03   79-12674
ISBN 0-313-21481-6

First published in 1961 by Oxford University Press,
London

This reprint has been authorized by the Oxford University
Press

Reprinted in 1979 by Greenwood Press, Inc.
51 Riverside Avenue, Westport, CT 06880

Printed in the United States of America

10 9 8 7 6 5 4 3 2 1

PREFACE

THE last twenty years have seen a great renewal of interest in the Caroline divines, and especially in their use of the Book of Common Prayer and the furnishings of their churches. In Durham, city and county, there is still abundant evidence of the activity of Bishop John Cosin in both these matters: in the woodwork of Brancepeth and Auckland as in the liturgical studies and plans which are presented in this book. Cosin's library still retains its identity, many of the volumes underlined and annotated in his own hand. In the same building there is preserved a mass of manuscript material, including some of the Prayer Books in which he entered the notes on which his reputation as a liturgist chiefly depends. The proximity of so rich a field of research can hardly fail to stimulate interest in the history of our rite.

Although most of Cosin's writings were reprinted during the nineteenth century in editions which are still serviceable, if not entirely trustworthy, there was still one important text which had been reluctantly omitted from the five volumes of works in *The Library of Anglo-Catholic Theology*. It consisted of annotations in a folio Prayer Book of 1619, referred to by liturgical scholars as 'The Durham Book'. Such references were often vague, and sometimes even betrayed confusion with another 1619 Prayer Book, also at Durham, the source of what is now known as Cosin's 'First Series of Notes'. A part of the 'Durham Book' annotations was printed in the Surtees Society's edition of Cosin's correspondence, but the only attempt at a complete transcription, published in 1877 by James Parker, failed to do justice to the extreme complexity of some of the entries, and was accompanied by a misleading account of their genesis. Later, J. T. Tomlinson demonstrated Parker's shortcomings with two or three carefully chosen facsimiles, but did no more to provide a better transcription. Up to the present day, therefore, scholars who wished to be certain of what Cosin actually wrote have had to journey to Durham to consult the manuscript. F. E. Brightman, for example, evidently did so in the preparation of his *magnum opus*, *The English Rite*, a massive piece of scholarship which provided the first inspiration of the present edition, the model for its layout, and some of its material. Brightman was less encyclopaedically versed in the seventeenth century than in earlier periods, and some of the notes below will reveal disagreement with his judgement, but the present work has no higher aim than to be regarded as a worthy supplement to *The English Rite*.

The relative inaccessibility of the manuscript and the lack of a wholly reliable edition have prevented scholars from giving these annotations their due importance in the history of the Book of Common Prayer. They reveal to us the aims and aspirations of the two most prominent followers of Archbishop Laud still surviving at the Restoration, John Cosin and Matthew Wren. Their object was to restore the characteristic elements of the 1549 Prayer Book without alienating a House of Commons which would have been content to revive that of 1604. This task was then further complicated by the attempt to reconcile the Presbyterians to using the Prayer Book at all. In these annotations can be traced the gradual modifying of the proposals made by Cosin and Wren until something approaching the final compromise of 1662 is already taking form. The drafting and redrafting of the crucial passages illustrate the bishops' clear understanding of the situation in which they were working, and their painstaking search for perfection in the smallest detail.

Many of their suggestions are relevant at the present time, when Prayer Book revision is once more in the air. They were faced by a problem similar to that which confronts us today, though we see it in terms of the reconciliation of catholic and evangelical attitudes to the Prayer Book, complicated by the pressure of the Ecumenical Movement towards wider union. Their solution, though not wholly acceptable in 1661, may well now command the most general support. Their arrangement of the Communion Service, for example, has been closely followed by both the American and South African Prayer Books, and would make an excellent starting-point for a revision today. Though in some ways our hands are freer than theirs were, and we can draw on a wider and more accurate knowledge of the ancient liturgies, yet the problem that faced them was inherent in the very nature of the Church of England, and their solution has an abiding value.

This text, then, is offered as a document of both historical and topical importance. It forms part of the ecclesiastical and political history of our nation; it gives us a fascinating glimpse into the workshop of two great liturgists trying to seize the opportunity of a lifetime; and it deals with problems which, *mutatis mutandis*, are our problems also.

G. J. C.

Billesdon, 24 July 1961

ACKNOWLEDGEMENTS

I WOULD like to express my gratitude to Mr. D. S. Ramage, Librarian of the University Library, Durham, for his generous provision of facilities for transcribing the 'Durham Book'; and to Dr. A. I. Doyle, Assistant Librarian, for his unvarying courtesy and assistance in making available the riches of the Cosin and Routh libraries at Durham, which contain, with very few exceptions, every printed book of the period that I wished to consult. I am also grateful to the Keeper of Western Manuscripts, Bodleian Library, for permission to print two manuscripts in his keeping, Wren's 'Advices' and Sancroft's 'Fair Copy'.

Parts of the Introduction and the Appendixes appeared as an article in *The Journal of Ecclesiastical History*, vol. vi, No. 1 (1955), and I am grateful to the editor and publishers for permission to reprint them.

I am also indebted to Professor E. C. Ratcliff for his friendly help and encouragement.

G. J. C.

CONTENTS

INTRODUCTION

I. THE BACKGROUND OF THE DURHAM BOOK

THE Reformation in England was the reformation of the national Church, not the creation of a reformed church within the nation; and so the Church of England contained in its composition elements of various character. There were those who still remained faithful to the Roman allegiance; there were those who accepted the new ways, but only under protest; there were moderate reformers; and there were thorough-going reformers of every shade of doctrinal colour. The simultaneous existence of these strands is revealed by the successive revisions of the Book of Common Prayer, of which even the brief reign of Edward VI produced two editions: the first a moderate, though extensive, adaptation of the Sarum service-books, the second a decided step towards the doctrinal standpoint of the continental reformers. Even the latter did not go far enough for one section of opinion, for the exiles who fled from the return of Popery under Mary were divided into those who continued to use the Prayer Book at Frank-fort, and those who went off to Basle or Geneva to find a more Calvin-istic type of service. At the accession of Elizabeth I there was revealed the existence of a third group, those who wished to return to the book of 1549; among them, it is suggested, the Queen herself.[1] But that book was too little reformed in character to be acceptable at that juncture, and the Elizabethan Prayer Book is the book of 1552, with one or two significant concessions to the supporters of 1549. No concessions were made to the Romish recusants or to the followers of Master Calvin. Both these latter parties attempted to impose their methods of worship upon the Church of England, the former by force of arms, the latter by gaining control from within. The hundred years from 1560 were largely occupied in maintaining the precarious equilibrium expressed in the Elizabethan Prayer Book, and in determining whether those who desired further reform were to be accommodated within the Establish-ment, to gain control of it, or to be excluded from it.

On the Puritan side, the chief objective in liturgical matters was freedom from the compulsory use of various ceremonies, notably the sign of the cross in Baptism, the ring in the Marriage Service, and kneeling at the Communion.

[1] Neale, J. E., *Elizabeth I and Her Parliaments, 1559–1581*. London, 1953.

These, with the 'popish' surplice, formed the core of the Puritan complaints.[1] Though the Book of Common Prayer was far from congenial to them, its text did not at first draw their fire to a comparable extent. When it became clear that the Establishment was not prepared to shift its ground one inch, the battle widened to include the text of the Prayer Book. The archbishops of Elizabeth's early years were too hard-pressed in maintaining the position laid down by the Queen to consider any kind of alteration. Their Injunctions,[2] Advertisements,[3] and Interpretations[4] were concerned with points of ceremonial and church furnishing: their liturgical work took the form of frequent occasional services, whose fulsome and prolix style shows the direction which any revision at this time would have taken.[5] The Puritans, for their part, either mutilated the Prayer Book services or ignored them; they made repeated efforts, all unsuccessful, to have the Act of Uniformity repealed; and published their own forms of service,[6] which lacked all authorization.

It was left for James I to attempt to meet the Puritan demands for textual revision, at the Hampton Court Conference of 1604. The results fell far short of what the Puritans desired, but did add a slight Puritan flavour to the book: the section on the Sacraments was added to the Catechism, the rules for Private Baptism were made more strict, some Apocryphal lessons were removed, and the Thanksgivings were inserted.[7] Almost simultaneously, the promulgation of the new Canons in 1604, embodying many of the Elizabethan directives mentioned above, and adding new material of a similar character, strengthened the hands of those who wished to maintain or even emphasize the ceremonies allowed and enforced under Elizabeth. Thus the fourth edition of the Book of Common Prayer, taken together with the Canons, shows King James trying to maintain the balance as before. Neither Puritans nor ceremonialists were satisfied.

In the years following the conference the text of the Prayer Book was subjected to minute examination and detailed criticism in such works as the *Petition of the Lincolnshire Ministers*,[8] which became an arsenal for Puritan controversialists, and was still in use at the Restoration; and the anonymous

[1] e.g. Frere, W. H., and Douglas, C. E. (eds.), *Puritan Manifestoes*. London, 1954.
[2] Cardwell, *Documentary Annals*, i. 178 ff.
[3] Ibid. 287 ff.
[4] Kennedy, W. H., The *'Interpretations'* of the Bishops. London, 1908.
[5] Examples in *Liturgical Services of the Reign of Queen Elizabeth*. Parker Society, 1847.
[6] Procter and Frere, *A New History of the Book of Common Prayer*, 131.
[7] A complete list, ibid. 141–3. [8] London, 1605.

Survey of the Book of Common Prayer.[1] In these, the Puritan case against the Prayer Book is now fully stated. The more important criticisms reappear in the proceedings of the Lords' Committee of 1641[2] and in the Presbyterian *Exceptions*[3] at the Savoy Conference twenty years later. The Puritans had taken up their position, and it was almost wholly unfavourable to the Book of Common Prayer. Their criticisms were intended less as serious proposals for its revision than as providing grounds for its complete abandonment.

At the same time a counter-movement was developing, initiated by men who not only loved the Prayer Book as it was, but wished to enrich it by the restoration of those elements which were retained in 1549 but omitted in 1552. This strain of thought had lain dormant since 1559, but began now to emerge among the younger divines under the leadership of John Overall (1560–1619) and Lancelot Andrewes (1555–1626). Overall left few writings behind, but evidently exercised great influence upon his chaplain, John Cosin, and thus indirectly upon the revision of 1661. It is probable that the so-called 'First Series' of annotations on the Prayer Book attributed to Cosin[4] are in reality a collection made by Overall himself, or selections made from it by his nephew, J. Hayward, which Cosin copied out for his own edification. They are extremely anti-Puritan in tone, dealing with the objections of the *Survey* point by point, and drawing extensively upon Roman writers such as Maldonatus. An important feature is their insistence that the Prayer of Oblation should be said *before* the Communion, to which Cosin adds a note that this was Overall's invariable practice. Andrewes's influence, on the other hand, was widespread both as a preacher and as a man of great sanctity, but as far as the Prayer Book is concerned, it was concentrated in a set of notes[5] which appear to describe the ceremonial used in his private chapel, with occasional illuminating comments on the text. These notes were widely circulated in manuscript: Cosin incorporated them into the 'First Series'; and the Scottish bishops used them in the Scottish Book of 1637.[6] The ceremonial envisaged is too elaborate to be adopted into the Prayer Book as it stands, but its ethos, however diluted, permeates Cosin's suggestions for revision throughout his lifetime.

A much more direct influence was exerted upon the text of the Prayer Book by the next generation of leaders, whose desire for ceremonial benefited from the reputation of Andrewes and was supported by the legal authority of the 1604 Canons, while their desire for revision was stimulated

---

[1] London, 1606.   [2] Cardwell, *Conferences*, 270 ff.   [3] Ibid. 303 ff.
[4] *Works*, v. 1–176.   [5] *Minor Works* (LACT).   [6] e.g. no. 219 in the text.

by their study of older liturgies. The group takes its usual name from William Laud (1573–1645), who as Archbishop of Canterbury had the widest opportunity of putting his views into practice. The temper of his time did not permit him to attempt much more than the enforcement of the Prayer Book rubrics, and that with only partial success. His chief object was to secure that the Holy Table should be placed altarwise against the east wall of the church and fenced with rails. Although frequently (and baselessly) accused of tampering with the text of the Prayer Book, he in fact initiated no attempts at revision; and at his trial, though he fully admitted to approving the Scottish Book of 1637, he was at pains to show that he was in no way responsible for its departures from the familiar text as revised in 1604.[1]

Next to Laud in the eyes of the Puritans came Matthew Wren (1586–1667), uncle of Sir Christopher, who was certainly the chief agent in the execution of Laud's policy. After having been chaplain to Bishop Andrewes, he held in succession the bishoprics of Norwich and Ely, both widely affected by Puritanism; and it was his rigid enforcement of outward conformity in these dioceses that earned him the hatred of the Puritans, and led ultimately to his committal to the Tower of London, where he was imprisoned from 1641 until 1660. This enforced leisure he employed in compiling a mass of annotations on the Bible and on the Prayer Book: while the former seem to have perished, the latter played a prominent part in the revision of 1661. Despite his notoriety in the 1630's, Wren's name is barely known to the present generation. This is due in part to the extreme paucity of his literary remains. It was not until 1874 that Bishop Jacobson published the Prayer Book annotations,[2] and by then the credit for the 1661 revision had been given entirely to Cosin, so that Wren's share in the work has only been recognized by specialists. He was a typical 'Laudian' in ceremonial matters: his *Particular Orders* for the diocese of Norwich[3] show only very moderate additions to the rubrics; and his enemies cannot find anything more damaging to bring against him than the charge that he adopted the eastward position and was accustomed to elevate the chalice.[4] Likewise, as will appear, he desired only a conservative revision of the text.

Associated in the popular mind with Laud and Wren was a slightly younger man, John Cosin (1594–1672), whom we have already met as chaplain to Bishop Overall. He early incurred Puritan enmity by his attempts

[1] *Works*, iii. 356. [2] In *Fragmentary Illustrations of the Book of Common Prayer*, 43–109.
[3] Cardwell, *Documentary Annals*, ii. 200 ff.
[4] Baillie, R., *A Large Supplement of the Canterburian Self-conviction* (1641), 109.

to improve the conduct of worship in Durham Cathedral, and by his compilation of a book of Devotions for the ladies of the Court. His continued
introduction of ceremonies in Cambridge, where he followed Wren as
Master of Peterhouse, led eventually to his impeachment in 1641 and going
into exile in 1643. From early youth he had been a great student of the
Sarum liturgy and the Roman ritualists, and was all his life a diligent anno-
tator of the Prayer Book (Vol. V of his *Works* contains three distinct series
of Notes) with an especial admiration for the 1549 book. Up to his exile he
leant decidedly towards the Roman Church, but his experience of life in a
Roman Catholic country and his discovery of continental Protestantism led
to a marked change in his position, and he returned to England in 1660 a
central churchman. Unlike Wren, he left a mass of material behind him: five
volumes of *Works* in the LACT, and two of *Correspondence* published by the
Surtees Society, besides the annotations edited here and other unpublished
papers. He was regarded by the Anglo-Catholic party of the later nineteenth
century as their apostle, and his early 'extreme' practice and writings were
cited as authority for all manner of corrupt following of Rome; and because
the first draft for the revision of 1661 was in his writing, he was believed to
be the author of all the changes proposed. Thus his influence as a liturgist has
been overestimated, and his churchmanship misrepresented. Yet he remains,
with Wren, the most copious contributor to the Prayer Book since Archbishop Cranmer.

   With the existence of so able and influential a group within the Church of
England, there would doubtless have been sooner or later an attempt to
revise the Book of Common Prayer. But before this could be undertaken,
the Scottish bishops submitted a draft of a proposed Scottish edition, a
reproduction of the book of 1604 with a few minor alterations designed to
commend it to the Presbyterian Scots.[1] Laud would have wished it to be
identical with the English book, but the bishops insisted upon the changes.
Printing had already begun when Bishop Wedderburne of Dunblane submitted some further suggestions consisting mainly of passages from the 1549
book which had been omitted in 1552, now more cautiously phrased. Laud
and Wren were appointed to consider these suggestions and approved them;
Cosin may possibly have been concerned at some stage. The Scots, however,
immediately and decisively rejected the book in its final form, the 'Scottish
Liturgy' of 1637 already referred to (SL below); and this rejection was due
in no small part to the suggestions of Wedderburne. The prospects for a

---

[1] Donaldson, G., *The Making of the Scottish Prayer-Book*, 43–49.

similar revision in England were now far from bright, though the Scottish book came to be much esteemed by the High Church party. Any revision with a hope of success would have had to be acceptable to the Puritans, and in 1641 the House of Lords appointed a committee to work in this direction. A group of nine divines produced some recommendations which were too moderate to have a chance of acceptance at that moment, though they were not lost sight of by the Presbyterians in 1661. In a list of innovations condemned is included 'putting to the Liturgy printed secundo, tertio Edwardi sexti, which the Parliament hath reformed and laid aside'.[1] Evidently the 1549 book was now becoming generally recognized as the clearest expression of the views of High Churchmen. The immediate fate of the Book of Common Prayer, however, was not revision, but total proscription, which befell it in 1645. The pendulum had swung from the norm of 1552, not towards 1549, but towards the Presbyterian ideal of worship. Under the Commonwealth, worship by the Prayer Book services, though officially forbidden, was carried on in Royalist houses all over the country, where the dispossessed clergy were given shelter as chaplains, and educated the young gentry in the ways of Laudian churchmanship. Jeremy Taylor and Robert Sanderson drew up their own forms of service;[2] two full-length commentaries on the Prayer Book were printed, Anthony Sparrow's *Rationale* in 1655, and Hamon L'Estrange's *Alliance of Divine Offices* in 1659,[3] the latter including complete texts of 1549 and SL; and on the Continent the exiles celebrated the Prayer Book service of Holy Communion with as much ceremony as they could muster.

II. THE COMPILATION OF THE DURHAM BOOK

In 1660 the tide turned: in March Bishop Wren was released from the Tower, and at the end of May Dean Cosin returned with the King from exile. The status of the Book of Common Prayer immediately appeared at the centre of political controversy. On 10 July the Presbyterians asked for a committee of 'learned, godly, and moderate divines', to compile a new liturgy, 'or at least to revise and effectually reform the old'; and the bishops replied that they were 'not against revising of the Liturgy' by a Royal Commission.[4] On 25 October the King issued a Declaration in which he promised to appoint some 'learned divines of different persuasions to review the Book

---

[1] Cardwell, *Conferences*, 270 ff.
[2] *Works*, xv. 237 ff. *Fragmentary Illustrations . . .*, 1–40.   [3] LACT, Oxford, 1846.
[4] Gould, G. (ed.), *Documents Relating to the Act of Uniformity*, 17, 35.

of Common Prayer, and to make such alterations as shall be thought most necessary, and some such additional prayers as shall be thought fit for emergent occasions'.[1] Wren was already prepared for this situation. In the months immediately preceding the King's return, he had arranged his annotations on the text of the Prayer Book in a paper of definite and detailed recommendations.[2] The manuscript of this has been damaged by fire, and the title is no longer fully decipherable, but as Wren later speaks of 'these Advises', the document is referred to below as the *Advices*. Wren begins by suggesting a royal proclamation inviting all men of quality to submit proposals for revision, and then sets forth his own. He is greatly, and professedly, concerned with the removal of Latinisms and archaisms, with the explanation of obscurities, and with the defence of the monarchy against sedition. Though a very large number of changes is suggested, nearly all are of small individual significance. The wording tends to the pedantic, and the phrasing is clumsy; he exhibits a partiality for giving chapter and verse, underlining the scriptural origin of much of the Prayer Book text. Some of his suggestions are repeated from his own *Particular Orders* (1636), the Scottish Liturgy (1637), and the Lords' Committee (1641). The *Advices* reveal no desire for large-scale alteration, the most drastic suggestion being the removal of the Exhortations from the Communion Service.

It is highly probable that Cosin saw the *Advices* soon after his return to England. On regaining contact with his former colleague and fellow-sufferer, he would naturally be given the document to read and would easily be led to produce a similar document for himself. His paper[3] probably derives its title, *Particulars*, from a phrase of Wren's, and likewise his method of giving the reasons for each change (see p. 287). Unlike the *Advices*, Cosin's suggestions are more concerned with the rubrics than with the text, though the latter is not by any means neglected. The former archdeacon and future bishop lays monotonous stress on legality and uniformity, and the avoiding of disputes and questions. Exactitude of statement and the removal of ambiguity are his chief concerns. Some of his points are so trivial as to be hardly worth making; others, such as the position of the Prayer of Oblation, are of far-reaching significance. He constantly cites the 1549 book as an authority of the highest worth. In preparing the *Particulars* he evidently consulted his three series of *Notes*, making especial use of the Third.

At some time during the winter of 1660–1, perhaps encouraged by the

---

[1] Ibid. 73, note.   [2] See above, p. xvi, note 2.   [3] *Works*, v. 502 ff.

Declaration of 25 October, Cosin began to enter suggestions for revision into a folio Prayer Book of 1619 now known as 'The Durham Book' (DB below), which is preserved in the Cosin Library at Durham (as are also the manuscripts of the *Particulars* and the first two series of *Notes*). As far as can be deduced from internal evidence, he had before him both the *Advices* and the *Particulars*, and also the Scottish Liturgy. The latter had not been quoted explicitly by either Cosin or Wren in their papers, though they had frequently borrowed its ideas; but now it was used, often verbatim, to formulate the changes which Wren and Cosin wished to make. Wren does not appear to have shared Cosin's whole-hearted admiration for 1549, and possibly suggested SL as a practical means of realizing Cosin's ideals. The proposed changes were written in the margin or between the lines, and were often rewritten, sometimes three or four times. By no means the whole of either *Advices* or *Particulars* is entered, and other material is freely used.

SL was drawn on chiefly for improved rubrics and the restoration of 'High Church' ideas in a form suitable to the situation. Its most frequent use was in the Communion Service, where it influenced the rubrics on the furniture of the Holy Table, the Collect for the King, the oblation of the alms and the elements, the position of the celebrant when about to consecrate, the manual acts, reconsecration, the veiling of the elements, the use of wafers, the consumption of the elements, and the use of the collection; it provided the actual words of the thanksgiving for the dead in the Prayer for the Church, and of the *epiclesis*; it gave precedent for the use of the words 'Church' and 'sacrifice', the position of the Prayer of Oblation and some of its wording, and the *Amen* after reception. Outside the Communion Service it contributed the assimilation of February to the other months in the saying of the Psalms, several improvements in the Proper Lessons, rubrics about congregational saying of prayers, the printing of the 'State Prayers' at the end of Matins and Evensong, the second Ember Collect, the Collect for Easter Even, the rubric about Trinity XXV, and the formula for blessing the water in the font.

These three sources, *Advices*, *Particulars*, and SL, were combined with the greatest attention to detail. An excellent example of the process is to be found in the rubric preceding the Prayer of Consecration (no. 239 in the text). The first revision of this ran:

When the Priest hath so ordered the Bread and Wine placed upon the Table, as that he may with the more ease & decency take them into his hands, standing up he shall say . . .

In this sentence 'the Priest . . . standing up . . . shall say' is retained from the existing rubric; 'so ordered the Bread and Wine', 'the Table', and 'take' come from the *Advices*; 'with the more ease & decency' is from SL.

The rubric is then recast thus:

> When the Priest standing before yᵉ Table, hath so ordered the Bread & Wine, that he may with the more readines & decency break the Bread & take the Cup into his hands, he shall say, as followeth . . .

Here 'before', 'break the Bread', and 'take the Cup into his hands' are from Particular 57; 'readines' may be either from Wren, who has 'readily', or from Cosin's *Second Series of Notes*: 'with yᵉ more readines'; 'as followeth' is from the existing rubric.

Finally, the words 'before the people' are added from Particular 57. This procedure is paralleled many times over.

These three main sources were supplemented by several other authorities. The most important of these is the Prayer Book of 1549: throughout DB, many passages which had been omitted in 1552 are restored. As has been said, much of its influence is felt through its use in SL, which is always followed in preference to the original version of 1549. As with SL, its chief contributions are to the Communion Service. Here it contributes the idea of a deacon as gospeller, phrases in the rubrics about oblation of the elements and about the manual acts, and in the Prayer of Oblation; of greatest importance, the passage on the theology of the Holy Communion now restored to the Second Exhortation, the *Agnus Dei* and Postcommunions, and (ultimately) much of the material taken from SL. Outside the Communion Service are to be noted the title of the book ('Rites and Ceremonies of the Church, according to the use of the Church of England'), the idea that the daily Offices begin with the Lord's Prayer, the Easter Procession Collect, several minor changes in Baptism and Matrimony, and the rules for the Communion of the Sick. Some 1549 practices which had remained in use are once more authorized in rubrics.

Another important source is the Book of Common Prayer itself: many entries in DB are remodellings of material from elsewhere in the book, or the turning of a rubric into a form of words. Many restorations of the true text are made, for the 1619 edition used had a large number of errors, many of which had already been corrected in subsequent editions. Further interpretations and directions, such as the Canons of 1604, and occasionally the *Injunctions* and *Advertisements*, are quoted in the rubrics, and thereby made more effective. Cosin's *Devotions* provide rules about the Church Year, details in the Kalendar and Tables, two introductory sentences, the titles of the Canticles, the paragraphing of the Creed, the first Ember Collect, the Rogation Collect, and some phrases in the Prayer of Oblation.

The influence of the Sarum books is confined to the rules for the saying of Collects, and such additions as the suggested proper for Epiphany IV, the third Easter Anthem, and the form of banns. Cosin's *Notes*, in addition to their use in the *Particulars*, provide material chiefly for the introductory section and the Communion Service, after which they disappear almost entirely. Many of the entries drawn from the *First Series* are quotations from the *Notes* of Lancelot Andrewes, whose influence is thus felt in DB at second hand. The Lords' Committee of 1641 and Wren's *Particular Orders* provide little of importance beyond what Wren included in the *Advices*. Several entries seem to be prompted by the compiler's pastoral experience.[1]

Little use is made of contemporary writers: L'Estrange's *Alliance of Divine Offices* had appeared in 1659, and Cosin had allowed the author to draw on his *Third Series of Notes*,[2] but it is impossible to prove beyond doubt that it is utilized anywhere. Sparrow's *Rationale* supplies five possible points of contact, all trivial and none proved, though there is a presentation copy of the 1655 edition in the Cosin Library at Durham inscribed by Sparrow: 'For my R[nd] Freind, Deane Cos.' The forms drawn up by Robert Sanderson and Jeremy Taylor under the Commonwealth each coincide with DB at a dozen points; but in spite of superficial similarities, in no case can dependence be proved, the changes being such as would be prompted by common sense or contemporary practice. Sanderson's part in the changes made later by Convocation is of obvious importance,[3] and it is unlikely that his contribution to DB would have been so slight if he or his work had been consulted at all. The points at which use of the last four writers appears possible are nearly always those about which there was evidently a general consensus of opinion; two or more are often found together with language similar to that of DB, but not close enough to prove verbal dependence. In almost every case there is an equally close resemblance to one of the sources which can be proved to have been in use.

A detailed examination of the entries does not reveal any consistent order of using the sources: it cannot be said, for example, that the *Particulars* were

---

[1] See, for example, Cosin's comment at no. 375.
[2] Cf. *Alliance* (LACT ed.), 277, 445, 477 with Cosin, *Works*, v. 467, 493, 500.
[3] *Journal of Ecclesiastical History*, viii, no. 2 (1957), 188–92.

always drawn upon before the *Advices*, or vice versa. Nor can any source be connected with any particular type of Cosin's handwriting, widely though this varies: there is, for example, no 'SL hand'. The most that can be said is that sometimes two or three entries from the same source were obviously made at the same time.

The preparations of the bishops for revision of the Book of Common Prayer were thus far advanced when, on 25 March 1661, the King issued the Warrant for the long-promised conference, to be held at the Savoy. After three months of unprofitable negotiation, the concessions extorted from the bishops, few and insignificant, were quickly entered into DB by Cosin's chaplain, William Sancroft, who took over the book when Cosin went north in August for his enthronement as Bishop of Durham. Sancroft's entries were not confined to the Savoy concessions. Many of the rubrics were redrafted after he took over, without any change in content, but with greater precision of language; and others were inserted by analogy with suggestions entered by Cosin. Instructions to the printer were added, and fair copies were provided of various lists which had become almost undecipherable. This much may have been done by Sancroft on his own initiative or under general instructions; but there is another large group of entries which seems to represent a reversal of the general trend of DB. Alterations, additions, and omissions are suppressed on such a scale that it is difficult to believe that Sancroft was solely responsible for it. Possibly it was due to the influence of Wren asserting itself more strongly in Cosin's absence. This process may provide the basis of Clarendon's remark about making the book 'more grateful to the dissenting brethren'.[1] The Prayer Book had been held up at the Savoy Conference as so unsusceptible of improvement that it was now difficult to bring forward the very numerous changes of DB without an appearance of considerable inconsistency. Again, the Commons were eager for the reintroduction of the 1604 book unaltered.[2] Thus it may well have seemed prudent to remove all avoidable alterations, and this task would fall to Sancroft. At this stage the policy seems to have been to sacrifice as many minor changes as possible in order to increase the chances of acceptance of the really important ones, those in the Communion Service. Few of the suggestions seem to have been withdrawn for doctrinal reasons. It is also possible that this process may have been carried out at a meeting between Wren, Cosin, and Gilbert Sheldon, Bishop of London, who was in charge of

---

[1] Clarendon, *Life* (1827 edn.), ii. 118.   [2] Parker, *Introduction* . . ., lxxxv.

ecclesiastical policy. The three bishops met at the beginning of November 1661, three weeks before the opening of Convocation, when the revision was to be carried through.[1]

The incorporation of second thoughts completed, DB had become at many points extremely difficult to read; and Sancroft copied out the entire mass of entries in their latest state into a folio Prayer Book of 1634 (the 'Fair Copy'—FC below), in all probability to be used for reading out the proposed changes to Convocation. The same process of quiet improvement of the wording is still visible, and there is one important change: whereas DB proposes quite definitely to rearrange the Canon, FC leaves it as it stands, and gives the proposed rearrangement as Paper B, '& both left to censure'. This change must be due either to Wren or to the three bishops together: Cosin by himself would never have left the question open. But it seems clear that much of the wording of our present book is due to Sancroft, though his share in the revision was editorial rather than constructive. This agrees with Isaak Walton's estimate of Sancroft's contribution:[2] he was, says Walton, 'in these imployments diligently useful, especially in helping to rectifie the *Kalendar* and *Rubrick*'.

III. CHARACTER AND SUBSEQUENT HISTORY OF DB

We have now reached the end of the stage of revision contained in DB and FC, and before tracing the further fortunes of the proposals made in the two volumes it will be well to consider briefly the doctrinal position and churchmanship which inform them. Though both Cosin and Wren were, at any rate by 1660, 'Central Churchmen', DB envisages a more generous attitude towards ceremonial than is to be found in the book that eventually emerged from Convocation. This attitude is to be seen chiefly in the Communion Service. According to DB, the Table is always to stand in the upper part of the chancel (no. 206 in the text); there is to be an Epistoler and a Gospeller, in accordance with the Canons; and, in the first draft, the Gospeller may be a deacon (no. 212); the collection is to be presented by the celebrant at the altar; and the elements likewise (no. 220). The latter are also to be 'ordered' (no. 239) in a position convenient for the manual acts, which are now recognized once more (no. 245). The deacon is to administer the chalice (no. 257); and wafers may be used if desired (no. 277). The remnant of the consecrated elements is to be consumed in church after the blessing

---

[1] Cosin, *Correspondence*, ii. 31, 36.   [2] *Life of Dr. Robert Sanderson*, f. l. 5.

(no. 278). These directions taken together suggest a very moderate increase in ceremonial; even the Laudian altar-rails do not appear; and the result falls far short of what the young Cosin would have wished. Even so, it went too far to be wholly acceptable to Convocation.

Outside the Communion Service, the chief changes of this kind are the blessing of the font, the 'tokens of spousage', the phrase 'the outward reverence of my body' in the Catechism, and the direction that Confirmation is to be administered at the Lord's Table. Only the last of these survived the process of drafting long enough to be included in FC.

Apart from changes aiming at greater reverence and decency, there are a number of alterations in the Communion Service which indicate a particular doctrinal standpoint. First, in the bidding of the Prayer for the Church, the words 'militant here in earth' are omitted (no. 221), and in the conclusion of the Prayer, the prayer and thanksgiving for the dead are restored (no. 224). The significant point here is that DB does not reproduce 1549, but the modified version in SL, thus avoiding the reference to the Blessed Virgin Mary, and the commendation of those who 'rest in the sleep of peace', misliked by Bucer and Calvin as unscriptural and tending to superstition.[1] The prayer for their welfare 'at the day of the generall Resurrection', common to 1549 and SL, did not pass Convocation.

Secondly, mention of the death of Christ is frequently coupled with an allusion to his sacrifice (nos. 223, 226, 242, 263, 264). This is a concept on which Cosin lays great emphasis, while always insisting that Christ's sacrifice cannot be repeated, and that 'we only make a commemoration, or a representation' of it at each celebration. The Eucharist is essentially an offering of Christ's death.[2] With this may be linked the position of the Prayer of Oblation immediately after the Prayer of Consecration (no. 250). This arrangement was adopted in SL, and Laud at his trial strongly denied that it had any 'popish meaning', claiming that it was 'better and more agreeable to use in the primitive Church'.[3] Cosin learnt the practice of saying it here from his 'Lord and Master Dr. Overall', but there is no evidence that he ever followed it himself. Overall regarded it as the offering to God of the consecrated sacrament, 'the true public sacrifice of the Church'; Cosin contents himself with calling it 'more Consonant both to former precedents, and the Nature of this holy Action'.[4]

---

[1] Cosin, *Works*, v. 477 (S III).
[2] This position is set out at length in *Works*, v. 106–21 (S I, mostly from Maldonatus) and 332–55 (S II, mostly from Calixtus).   [3] Laud, *Works*, iii. 343–5.   [4] Cosin, *Works*, v. 114, 517.

Thirdly, the consecrated bread and wine are described as the Sacrament of the Body and Blood of Christ (nos. 228, 251, 257, 265). Cosin maintained that the Body and Blood of Christ are 'sacramentally and really', but not 'sensibly', present,[1] a position which he elaborates in his *History of the Papal Transubstantiation*.[2] In this sense must be understood the reinsertion of the 1549 phrase 'in these holy Mysteries' (no. 240), and of the *Agnus Dei* (no. 259), both of which were later omitted once more, presumably for fear of appearing to countenance the 'Papal' doctrine.

Fourthly, an *epiclesis* is inserted (no. 243); it is based on those in 1549 and SL, and follows them in including the words 'that we receiving them . . . may be partakers . . .', though it omits the suspect phrase found in both, 'that they may be unto us'.

Wren's sole contribution to the doctrinal changes in DB (apart from his very limited responsibility for those deriving from SL) is the theory that 'in remembrance of me' means 'To put me in mind of you, Christ of us, and not, us in mind of Christ' (nos. 230, 244, 251, 254), a notion to which he attaches undue importance.

Lastly, the consumption of the consecrated elements (no. 278) is probably to be regarded as directed in the interests of reverence, and as expressive of a mediating position between the Roman and Puritan theories of the Presence.

In general, the position is less 'High Church' than that of Andrewes, Laud, or Thorndike, and may be compared with that of Morley and Pearson, of Robert Sanderson and Jeremy Taylor. As we shall see, these doctrinal changes were entirely eliminated in Convocation. To this stage of revision we must now turn.

Whether FC was prepared for the meeting of Wren, Cosin, and Sheldon, or was the result of their scrutiny of DB, it came before Convocation on 21 November 1661, when a committee was appointed to carry on the work of revision between the formal sittings of the whole body.[3] The final result of Convocation's deliberations was entered in the 'Convocation Book' and differs in only a few small particulars from the book annexed to the Act of Uniformity of 19 May 1662, the '1662 Prayer Book'. The departures from the text of FC may be summarized under three heads: first, the Book is enlarged by the addition of further *Prayers and Thanksgivings*, of extra prayers to be said at the *Visitation of the Sick*, and of the form which Sancroft calls

---

[1] Cosin, *Works*, v. 345.   [2] *Works*, iv.   [3] Selborne, *Notes* . . ., 45 ff.

'The Sea Service'.[1] Secondly, improvements are made in the Kalendar and Lectionary; several Collects are retouched; in the Communion Service, the notices are placed before the sermon, and the second Exhortation before the first; the order of the service of Private Baptism is altered; and the Burial Service is extensively remodelled. Besides many minor emendations throughout the book, the Ordinal, which received only sketchy treatment in FC, is now thoroughly revised.

These additions and alterations continue and supplement the revision of DB already carried out in FC. The third class, however, runs counter to the original intentions of DB; but it can be seen as the logical continuation of the policy already observable in DB and FC of reducing the number of changes. Without completely surrendering to Parliament's demand for the restoration of the 1604 book, the Convocation revision swings back even further in that direction. The axe falls most heavily upon the Communion Service, where the changes were both numerous and important. Cosin's cherished rearrangement of the Canon after the Scottish pattern was rejected, and even the compromise put forward by 'My LL. the BB.' (no. 268) was further modified. Every change that suggested the introduction of 'High Church' ideas or resort to SL was abandoned. The thanksgiving for the dead in the Prayer for the Church was further toned down; all references to Christ's sacrifice and our 'representation' of it were removed, as were the *epiclesis*, the *Agnus Dei*, and the Postcommunions; even the congregational responses before and after the Gospel (no. 212) were omitted; finally, at a very late stage the old bidding of the Prayer for the Church was restored, and the rubric on kneeling at the Communion was revived.

Outside the Communion Service, changes of similar purpose included the dropping of the rubric permitting the Lessons, Epistle, and Gospel to be sung (no. 28); of the direction for antiphonal singing (no. 75); of the prohibition of marriages at certain times (nos. 41, 368); and of the proper for the Rogation Days (no. 181). To give one example in detail, in the Churching of Women, the woman is not now required to be 'decently vayled', but merely 'decently apparelled'; the service need not now precede the Communion, nor need it take place 'before the Holy Table'. These are small changes, but typical. In short, most of the alterations that give DB its special character of a Prayer Book for 'Central Churchmen' are suppressed, and what emerges, after a general tidying-up and modernization, is still recognizably the book

---

[1] Note by Sancroft in the Convocation Book.

of 1604. Although Cosin and Wren must have been glad of the numerous minor improvements, to Cosin at least the rejection of the most important changes must have been a severe disappointment after a lifetime of work upon the Prayer Book and the labour spent on compiling DB.

Any hope of subsequent adoption of the rejected changes was greatly diminished, if not destroyed, by the secession of the non-jurors; and though the latter might have adopted the Scottish Canon in their own Prayer Book, their interest turned further back, first to 1549, and then to the primitive liturgies. This orientation was shared by the Episcopalians in Scotland, whose liturgy has followed a rather different path from that blazed by Maxwell and Wedderburne, and pursued by Cosin and Wren. In the Church of England itself, interest in Prayer Book revision, such as it was, took a different turn, but the existence of the entries in DB was never lost sight of. Archdeacon Sharp, a Prebend of Durham from 1732 to 1758, quotes from them as evidence for the interpretation of the rubrics of the 1662 book.[1] The editor of Vol. V of Cosin's *Works* wished to include them in that volume, but was prevented by lack of space.[2] The rejected entries only were printed in 1872 in the second volume of the *Correspondence*, and almost the entire contents of DB and FC in Parker's *Introduction to the History of the Successive Revisions of the Book of Common Prayer* (1877). In the end, the suggestions of DB have been given effect in several Prayer Books: for instance, the South African alternative form of 1929, the American rite of 1935, and the *Holy Eucharist* in the proposed Indian book (1951). All these follow the main outline of the SL–DB Canon, though with variations in detail, such as the position of the *epiclesis*; while the English revision of 1928 differs mainly in the position of the Prayer of Humble Access. The churchmanship of Cosin and Wren may have been rather too advanced for the majority of their contemporaries, at any rate as expressed in a liturgy which had to be passed by Parliament; but it is thoroughly acceptable in several parts of the Anglican Communion three hundred years later. This posthumous fulfilment echoes Isaac Basire's choice of text for the sermon he preached at Cosin's funeral, Heb. xi. 4: *By it, he, being dead, yet speaketh.*

---

[1] Sharp, T., *The Rubric in the Book of Common Prayer* (London, 1753), 35, 37, 46, 78, 82.
[2] Op. cit. xxi.

BIBLIOGRAPHY

I. MANUSCRIPTS

(a) Cosin Library, Durham

	Reference
Prayer Book, folio, 1619, with annotations by Cosin and Sancroft (the 'Durham Book')	..
Catalogue of the Library, folio, c. 1669–70	..
Prayer Book, folio, 1619, with annotations by Cosin (the *First Series* of Notes)	SR. 5. F. 3
Particulars to be considered, explayned & corrected in y *Book of Coṁon Prayer* (Cosin). 14 pp. Bound up with the above	SR. 5. F. 3
Prayer Book, folio, 1636, with annotations by Cosin (the *Second Series* of Notes)	SR. 5. F. 9
Visitation Articles . . ., 1626 (Cosin)	MS. B. II. 13

(b) Bodleian Library, Oxford

Prayer Book, folio, 1634, with annotations by Sancroft and Cosin (the 'Fair Copy')	Auct. V. 3. 16
'Advices' (Wren)	MS. Add. A. 213
Directions to the Chancellor of the Diocese of Norwich, 6 March 1635 (Wren)	MS. Tanner 68
Particular Orders, Directions, & Remembrances given in y *Diocese of Norwich . . . 1636* (Wren)	MS. Tanner 68
Some particulars to be added & amended in y *Booke of Comon Prayer*, before it be signed (Cosin)	MS. Tanner 48.1

II. PRINTED BOOKS

ANDREWES, L., *Notes on the Book of Common Prayer* (ed. J. Bliss). Oxford, 1854.

BAILLIE, R., *Ladensium Αυτοκατακρισις, The Canterbvrians Self-Conviction.* [Amsterdam,] 1640.

—— *A Parallel of the Liturgy with the Mass-Book, the Breviary, the Ceremonial, and other Romish Rituals.* 2nd edn., London, 1661.

BAKER, R., *A Chronicle of the Kings of England.* London, 1674.

BOSHER, R. S., *The Making of the Restoration Settlement*. London, 1951.

BRIGHTMAN, F. E., *The English Rite*. 2 vols., London, 1915.

BURNET, G., *The History of the Reformation of the Church of England*. 3 vols., London, 1679, 1683, 1715.

B[URTON,] H., *A Tryall of Private Devotions. Or, A Diall for the Houres of Prayer*. London, 1628.

CALAMY, E., *An Abridgement of Mr. Baxter's History of his Life and Times*. London, 1713.

CARDWELL, E. (ed.), *Documentary Annals of the Reformed Church of England*. 2 vols., Oxford, 1839.

—— *A History of Conferences and other Proceedings*. Oxford, 1841.

—— *Synodalia*. 2 vols., Oxford, 1842.

CLARENDON, EARL OF, *The Life of Edward, Earl of Clarendon*. 2 vols., Oxford, 1827.

COOPER, J. (ed.), *The Book of Common Prayer . . . for the use of the Church of Scotland. . . .* Edinburgh, 1904.

COSIN, J., *Correspondence* (ed. G. Ornsby). Surtees Society, vols. 52 and 55, Durham, 1869 and 1872.

—— *A Collection of Private Devotions*. London, 1627.

—— *Works*, Vol. V (ed. J. Barrow). Oxford, 1855. (Contains the three *Series of Notes* and the *Particulars*.)

DONALDSON, G., *The Making of the Scottish Prayer Book of 1637*. Edinburgh, 1954.

D'OYLY, G., *The Life of William Sancroft*. 2 vols., London, 1821.

DUGMORE, C. W., *Eucharistic Doctrine in England from Hooker to Waterland*. London, 1942.

FULLER, T., *The Church-History of Britain; From the Birth of Jesus Christ, Untill the Year MDCXLVIII*. London, 1656.

GAUDEN, J., *Considerations touching the Liturgy of the Church of England*. London, 1661.

GOULD, G. (ed.), *Documents relating to the Settlement of the Church of England by the Act of Uniformity of 1662*. London, 1862.

GRISBROOKE, W. J., *Anglican Liturgies of the Seventeenth and Eighteenth Centuries*. London, 1958.

HALL, P. (ed.), *Fragmenta Liturgica*. 7 vols., London, 1847.

HATTON, C., *The Psalter of David*. 15th edn., London, 1724. (Probably by Jeremy Taylor.)

JACOBSON, W. (ed.), *Fragmentary Illustrations of the History of the Book of Common Prayer . . .* London, 1874. (Contains Sanderson's *Liturgy in the Times of Rebellion* and Wren's *Advices*.)

KENNETT, W., *A Register and Chronicle Ecclesiastical and Civil*. London, 1728.

LATHBURY, T., *A History of the Book of Common Prayer*. 2nd edn., London, 1859.

—— *A History of the Convocation of the Church of England*. London, 1842.

LAUD, W., *Works*, Vol. III and Vol. VI, Part II (ed. J. Bliss). Oxford, 1853 and 1857.

LEGG, J. W., *English Church Life from the Restoration to the Tractarian Movement*. London, 1914.

—— *English Orders for Consecrating Churches*. London, 1911. (Includes three by Cosin.)

L'ESTRANGE, H., *The Alliance of Divine Offices*. London, 1659.

NICHOLLS, W., *A Comment on the Book of Common-Prayer*. London, 1710. (The primary source for Cosin's *Third Series of Notes*.)

OSMOND, P. H., *A Life of John Cosin*. London, 1913.

PARKER, J., *An Introduction to the History of the Successive Revisions of the Book of Common Prayer*. Oxford, 1877.

[PEARSE, E.], *The Conformists Plea for the Nonconformists*. London, 1682.

PRIDEAUX, H., *The Validity of the Orders of the Church of England*. London, 1688.

PRYNNE, W., *A Briefe Survey and Censure of Mr Cozens His Couzening Devotions*. London, 1628.

SELBORNE, LORD, *Notes on some Passages in the Liturgical History of the Reformed English Church*. London, 1878.

SHARP, T., *The Rubric in the Book of Common Prayer and the Canons of the Church of England, as Far as it Relates to the Parochial Clergy, Considered*. London, 1753.

SPARROW, A., *A Rationale upon the Book of Common Prayer of the Church of England*. London, 1655.

SYLVESTER, M. (ed.), *Reliquiae Baxterianae*. London, 1696.

TAYLOR, J., *A Collection of Offices or Forms of Prayer in Cases Ordinary and Extraordinary*. London, 1658.

TOMLINSON, J. T., *The Prayer Book, Articles, and Homilies*. London, 1897.

WALTON, I., *The Life of Dr. Robert Sanderson*. London, 1678.

WREN, C., *Parentalia: or, Memoirs of the Family of the Wrens*. London, 1750.

Breviarium ad usum insignis Ecclesiae Sarum (ed. F. PROCTER and C. WORDSWORTH). 2 vols., Cambridge, 1882.

Missale ad usum Sarum (ed. F. H. DICKINSON). Oxford, 1883.

Iniunctions geuen by the Queenes Maiestie. [London,] 1559.

Aduertisments partly for due order . . . London, [1565].

Constitutions and Canons Ecclesiasticall. London, 1604.

The Booke of Common Prayer . . . for the use of the Church of Scotland. Edinburgh, 1637.

A Suruey of the Booke of Common Prayer. London, 1606.

A Copie of the Proceedings of some worthy and learned Divines, appointed by the Lords . . . Together with considerations upon the Common Prayer Book. London, 1641.

An Account of all the Proceedings of the COMMISSIONERS of both PERSWASIONS ... London, 1661.

The Grand Debate between the most Reverend the BISHOPS, and the PRESBYTERIAN Divines. . . . London, 1661.

Facsimile of the Black-letter Prayer-book containing Manuscript Alterations and Additions Made in the Year 1661. . . . London, 1871. (The 'Convocation Book').

Facsimile of the Original Manuscript of the Book of Common Prayer. . . . London, 1891. (The 'Annexed Book'.)

NOTE

Standard works of reference on the Book of Common Prayer and the history of the period have not been included above; neither have a large number of seventeenth-century publications of only general relevance. The list is confined to sources of information bearing on the text of DB.

NOTE

I N the present edition, the first column of the left-hand page is devoted to the text of the Book of Common Prayer as printed in the 1619 edition which Cosin used. It has not been thought necessary to reproduce the text in its entirety, as there are long portions, notably among the Epistles and Gospels, where no corrections are made at all. For the most part, the text is identical with that of the book of 1552, which is readily available in modern editions.

The second column on the left-hand page contains the proposals of the revisers: alterations, additions, and omissions. Each entry is described in the conventions used in lists of *errata*: 'Read', 'Add', 'Delete', and so forth. The successive stages of drafting at each point are distinguished by the numbers *i, ii, iii.* . . . This notation is not intended to suggest that any period of time elapsed between the stages so distinguished, or that all entries marked '*i*', for example, were entered at the same time. Entries in Cosin's hand are printed in this type: **Plantin**; those in Sancroft's in this: Gill.[1] Variant readings in the Fair Copy and certain other points are recorded in the footnotes. Marginal numbers are added for ease of reference. Where entries are frequent and complicated, the whole passage has been printed as the revisers intended it to read, so that the second column sometimes includes words from the text in the first column. This has been done in the interests of clarity, since the student's chief concern is with the text as amended, rather than with the precise means by which the changes were indicated.

On the right-hand page are printed the sources from which the proposals are derived, with editorial comment where necessary. They are arranged in the following order:

> Wren's *Advices*
> Cosin's *Particulars*
> The Scottish Liturgy
> The Presbyterian *Exceptions* & the Bishops' *Reply*
> The 1549 Prayer Book
> Other sources.

---

[1] It is not usually possible to tell which hand has effected a crossing-out; the phrase (*crossed out*) is therefore printed in the most convenient type, and without implication of authorship, though this can sometimes be deduced from the context.

In view of their special importance, *Adv.* and *Part.* are printed in their entirety at the appropriate places, whether entered in DB or not. The page-references in *Adv.* (to a 1639 quarto Book of Common Prayer) have been suppressed, as tending to confusion: there is never any difficulty in identifying the passage Wren is referring to. The later *Particulars*, which Cosin did not number, are given numbers in inverted commas. The spelling is, wherever possible, that of the manuscript or the first edition.

ABBREVIATIONS

(For the full titles, see the Bibliography)

Adv.	Wren's *Advices*, 1660.[1]
Andrewes	Lancelot Andrewes, *Notes on the Prayer Book.*[1]
BCP	Editions of the Book of Common Prayer previous to 1619 (including 1549 and 1552).
Bishops	The Bishops' *Reply* to the Presbyterian *Exceptions*, 1661.[2]
Brightman	F. E. Brightman, *The English Rite*, 1915.
Canons	*Constitutions and Canons Ecclesiasticall.*[3]
Conc.	Concession (in the Bishops' *Reply*).
DB	The Durham Book.[1]
Devotions	Cosin's *Devotions*, 1627.[2]
Exceptions	The Presbyterian *Exceptions* to the Book of Common Prayer, 1661.[2]
FC	Sancroft's Fair Copy of DB.[1]
LACT	Library of Anglo-Catholic Theology.
L'Estrange	H. L'Estrange, *Alliance of Divine Offices*, 1659.[2]
Lords	Proceedings of the House of Lords' Committee, 1641.[2]
Parker	J. Parker, *Introduction to the . . . Revisions of the Book of Common Prayer*, 1877.
Part.	Cosin's *Particulars*, 1660.[1]
S	Sancroft's hand in DB.
S I, II, III	Cosin's *First*,[1] *Second*,[1] and *Third*[2] *Series of Notes on the Prayer Book.*
Sanderson	R. Sanderson's *Liturgy in the Times of Rebellion. . . .*
Sarum	The Sarum Breviary, Missal, &c.
SL	The Scottish Liturgy, 1637.[2]
Sparrow	A. Sparrow, *Rationale upon the Book of Common Prayer*, 1655.[2]
Taylor	Jeremy Taylor, *Collection of Offices*, 1658.[2]
Tomlinson	J. T. Tomlinson, *The Prayer Book, Articles, and Homilies*, 1897.

[1] Quoted from the manuscript.
[2] Quoted from the first edition.
[3] Quoted from a copy of the 1633 edition in the Cosin Library.

1 O Lord who at thy first comming didst
send thy Messenger to prepare thy way before
thee; Grant that yᵉ Ministers & Stewards of thy
Mysteries may likewise so prepare & make ready
thy way, by turning yᵉ hearts
of the disobedient to yᵉ wisdome
of the just, that at thy second
comming to judge the world, wee
may be found an acceptable people
in thy sight, who
livest & reignest
with yᵉ father &
the holy Spirit
ever one God,
world without end.
Amen.

i.Cor.4.

A table of all yᵉ Feasts, yᵗ are to be observed in
yᵉ Church of Engld ~~throughout~~ thᵉ yeare:

All Sundaies in the yeare.

The daies of yᵉ Feasts of
the Circumcision of oᵘ ld Jesus Christ.
The Epiphanie.
The Conversion of S. paul.
The purification of yᵉ Bl. Virg.
S. Matthias yᵉ Apostle.
The Annunciation of yᵉ Bl. Virg.
S. Marke yᵉ Evangelist.
S. philip, & S. Jacob yᵉ Apostles.
The Ascension of oᵘ ld Jesus Christ.
S. Barnabas.
The Nativitie of S. John Baptist.
S. peter yᵉ Apostle.
S. James yᵉ Apostle.
S. Bartholmew yᵉ Apostle:

Specimens of the hands of (a) Cosin and (b) Sancroft
(a) Signature B 9 V; no. 145 in text.   (b) Preliminary MS. folio 3 R; no. 48 in text

The Communion.

The prayer of Consecration.

Then the Priest standing vp, shall say as followeth.

Lmighty God, our heauenly Father, which of thy tender mercy diddest giue thy onely Sonne Iesus Christ to suffer death vpon the Crosse for our redemption, who made there (by his one oblation of himselfe once offered) a full, perfect, and sufficient sacrifice, oblation, and satisfaction for the sins of the whole world, and did institute, and in his holy Gospel command vs to continue a perpetuall memory of that his precious death, vntill his comming againe: heare vs, O mercifull Father, we beseech thee, and grant that wee, receiuing these thy creatures of Bread and Wine, according to thy Sonne our Sauiour Iesus Christs holy institution, in remembrance of his death and passion, may be partakers of his most blessed Body and Blood: Who in the same night that hee was betrayed, tooke Bread, and when he had giuen thankes he brake it, and gaue it to his disciples, saying, Take, eat, this is my Body which is giuen for you, Doe this in remembrance of mee. Likewise after Supper he tooke the Cup, and when hee had giuen thankes he gaue it to them, saying, Drink ye all of this, for this is my Blood of the new Testament, which is shed for you and for many for the remission of sinnes: Doe this as oft as ye shall drinke it, in remembrance of me. *A men.*

Immediatly after shall follow thy Memoriall or prayer of Oblation

Then shal the Minister first receiue the Communion in both kinds himselfe, and next deliuer it to other Ministers (if any be there present) that they may helpe the chiefe Minister, and after, to the people in their hands, kneeling. And when he deliuereth the Bread, he shall say,

He Body of our Lord Iesus Christ, which was giuen for thee, preserue thy body and soule into euerlasting life: And take and eate this in remembrance that Christ dyed for thee, and feed on him in thine heart by faith, with thankesgiuing.

N 3

And here each person receiuing shall say [Amen.] Then shall the priest adde, Take & Eate &c.

If there be a ~~deacon or~~ another priest, or a Deacon, to assist ye chief Minister, then shall he follow with the Cup. & as ye chief Minister giveth ~~as they p~~ the Sacrament of the Body, so shall he give ye Sacrament of the Blood, in forme before prescribed.

In the Communion time shall be sung (where there is a Quire) O Lamb of God that takest away the sins of the world ... &c. or some or all these Sentences of holy Scripture following

[illegible]

And where there is no Quire let ye Communicants make use of the same at their owne private & devout meditations.

The Communion.

And when he delivereth the Cup to any one he ~~the Minister delivereth the Cup,~~ shall say.

THE Blood of our Lord Jesus Christ which was shed for thee, preserve thy body and soule into everlasting life. ~~and~~ Drinke this ~~in~~ remembrance ~~that~~ Christs ~~blood was~~ shed for thee, and be thankfull.

He that receiveth shall say Amen. Then the priest shall adde

~~Then shall the Priest say the Lords prayer, the people repeating after him every petition. After shall be said as followeth.~~

Wherefore O Lord & heavenly Father according to ye institution of thy dearly beloved Sonne our Saviour Jesus Christ wee thy humble servants doe celebrate & make here before thy divine majestie with these thy holy gifts the Memoriall wch thy Sonne hath willed & commanded vs to make; having in remembrance his most blessed passion & sacrifice his mighty Resurrection & his glorious Ascension into Heaven; rendring unto Thee most heartie thanks for the innumerable benefits procured vnto vs by the same; & wee entirely &c.

O ~~Lord and heavenly Father, we thy humble servants~~ entirely desire thy Fatherly goodnesse, mercifully to accept this our sacrifice of praise and thankesgiving, most humbly beseeching thee to graunt, that by the merites and death of thy Sonne Jesus Christ, and through faith in his Blood, we and all thy whole Church may obtaine remission of our sinnes, and all other benefits of his Passion. And here we offer and present unto thee, O Lord, our selues, our soules and bodies, to be a reasonable, holy, and liuely sacrifice unto thee, humbly beseeching thee, that ~~all we which be~~ whosoever shall be partakers of this holy Communion, may worthily receive ye most precious Body & Blood of thy Sonne Jesus Christ, & be fulfilled with thy grace and heavenly benediction. And although we be unworthy, through our manifold sinnes, to offer unto thee any sacrifice: yet we beseech thee to accept this our bounden duty and service, not weighing our merits, but pardoning our offences, through Jesus Christ our Lord, who maketh intercession for vs at thy right hand, by whom, and with whom, in the unity of the holy Ghost, all honour and glory be unto thee, O Father Almighty, world without end. Amen.

Then shall ye priest adde

As our Saviour Christ hath taught & commanded vs wee are bold to say,

Our Father which &c (as printed out at large) Amen

Then shall ye priest kneeling downe at God's Board say in the name of all them that are to receive ye Communion this prayer following.

Wee doe not presume &c, as in the 3 page before.

~~Or this.~~

ALmighty and everliving God, we most heartily thanke thee, for that thou ~~doest~~ vouchsafe to feede us, ~~which~~ who have duely received these holy mysteries, with the spirituall food of the most precious body and blood of thy Sonne our Saviour Jesus Christ, and doest assure us thereby of thy favour and goodnes toward us, and that wee be very members incorporate in

When all have communicated, he that celebrateth shall returne to the Lords Table, & reverently place upon it what remaineth of ye consecrated Elements, covering the same with a faire linen cloth, & then say ~~[struck through]~~

The Lord be with you

Answere

And with thy Spirit

Priest

Let vs pray. Almighty & ever living &c.

Signature N 3 R & V; nos. 241–269 in text

ayer fhalbe vfed in the accuftomed
, or Chauncell, except it fhall be o-
Ordinarie of the place: And the
ue done in times paft.
nifter at the time of the Communi-
iftration, fhall vfe fuch ornaments
authoritie of Parliament, in the fe-
ard the fixt, according to the Acte
g of this Booke.

ning Prayer dayly
be yeere.

The Ornaments Rubric. Signature A 1 R; no. 57 in text

THE
DURHAM BOOK

Directions to be given to ye Printer.[1]

1. To page ye whole Booke
2. Not To adde, leave out or alter any thing, in any volume wherin it shalbe printed hereafter.
3. Not to print any Capitall Letters with profane Pictures in them.
4. Asmuch as may be to compose so that ye Leafe be not to be turned over in any Collect, Creed or verse of a Psalme.
5. A faire frontispiece at ye begiñing of ye Booke, & before the Psalter, to be cutt in brasse, & designate as direction shalbe given by ye A.Bp.
6. Print all ye Creeds allw. in 3 Paragraphs
7. Printed by ye K. Prints.
In all the Epistles, & Gospells follow the new translation. & in ye Gosp. at Baptisme, ye Lesson at ye Buriall, ye Exhort'on at Marriage.
Never cutt of the Lords praier, Creed, or any Collect wth an &c. but when ever they are repeated, print them out at large.
Nevr print ye Lord's prayer beyond — evill. Amen.

(all crossed out)

Directions to be given to ye Printers.[2]

Set a faire Frontispiece at ye beginning of ye Booke, & another before the psalter, to be design'd, as ye Arch-B. shall direct, & after to be cutt in Brasse.
Page the whole Booke.
Adde nothing. Leave out nothing. Alter nothing, in what Volume soever it be printed. Particularly; never cut of ye Lord's prayer, Creed, or any Collect &c with an &c. but wherever they are to be used, print them out at large; & adde [Amen] to ye end of every prayer.
Never print ye Ld's prayer beyond — deliver us from evill. Amen.
Print ye Creeds allwaies in three paragraphs, relating to ye 3 persons &c.
Print noe Capital Letters with profane pictures in them.
In all ye Epistles, & Gospels follow ye new translation.
As much as may be, compose soe, yt ye Leafe be not to be turn'd over in any Collect, Creed, Verse of a psalm, middle of a sentence &c.
Sett not your owne Names in ye Title-page, nor elsewhere in ye booke: but only,
Printed at London by ye printers to ye King's most Excellent Maty. such a yeare:
Print [Glory be to ye Father &c] at ye end of every psalme, & of every part of ye cxix psalme.

In this Booke,

Where a line is drawne through ye words, that is all to be left out.
Where a line is drawne under ye words, yt is to be printed in ye Romane letter.
Where a prickt line is drawne under ye words, yt is not part of ye booke; but only a direction to ye printer, or Reader.
Where this note] is sett, a breake is to be made, or a new line begun.
Where a double line is drawne under any words, they are to be printed in Capitals.

---

[1] Written on the first fly-leaf of the book; nos. 1–5 are in Cosin's hand, the rest in Sancroft's.
[2] Written on the second fly-leaf; all in Sancroft's hand.

Adv.: It is needfull, that ye Printer be so charged, as not to dare,

1. To add any thing, but what is directed in his Originall Copy.
2. Not to leave out any thing: Not [Amen] at the end of every prayer; Not [Glory be to the Father,] at the end of every Psalm.
3. Not, for sparing of his labour or papyr, to cutt of the Lds Prayer, or the [Glory be to] or any thing else, wth his &c.
4. Not to sett [For thyne is ye Kingdome] but where it is appointed.
5. To set the Number of his Pages through the whole book.
6. To compose so, as that no Prayer have part of it set, to turn over a Leaf to it. And that every Order, doe begin upon a New page.
7. It would also be for the Reverence of this holy Book, that he and his fellowes, justle not so, in naming themselves, in the Title page of it.

THE
BOOKE
of Common Prayer,
and Administration of
the Sacraments.
And other Rites and Ceremo-
nies of the Church of

ENGLAND.

1. *i. After* Church *add*: after the use of
    the Church
    ii. For after *read*: accordg to
2. *i. Add*: Together with the psalmes
    ii. Read: Together with the PSALMES
    of DAVID
    And the Booke of Consecrating &
    Ordeyning of Bps, Priests &
    Deacons.
    iii. Read: Together with the PSALTER
    or PSALMES of DAVID, as they
    are appointed to be sung or said
    in Churches,
    And
    The Forme or Manner of Making,
    Consecrating, & Ordeyning of
    Bishops, Priests & Deacons.
    iv. For appointed *read*: pointed
    For Consecrating, & Ordeyning
    read: Ordeyning & Consecrating

Imprinted at London by
Robert Barker, and Iohn Bill,
Printers to the Kings most
Excellent Maiestie.

3. *i. For* Robert . . . Maiestie *read* the Kings
    Printers
    ii. Read: the Printers to the King's most
    excellent Maiestie.

ANNO DOM. 1619.

Cum priuilegio.

1. **1549:** The booke of the common prayer and administracion of the Sacramentes, and other rites and ceremonies of the Churche: after the vse of the Churche of England.

2. **Adv.:** To ye very Title Page, towards the bottome thereof would be added, Wth ye Psalter, or Psalmes of David, *as they are to be read in Churches.*

  BCP (Title-page of the Ordinal): The forme and manner of making and consecrating Bishops, Priests and Deacons.

On the addition of the Ordinal, see Cosin's letter to Laud:
It was grounded upon ye Statute, An Act of Parliamt made 8º. Elizab. cap. 1. (Correspondence, i. 139.)
For the text of the Act, see Parker, op. cit., li.
The addition of the Ordinal to the title is an innovation; 'Consecrating' is placed before 'Ordeyning', under the influence of Adv. (see p. 289). iii assimilates the title to the title-pages of the Psalter and Ordinal. iv improves the order.

3.   *See* Directions . . ., *above, and cf. no. 420. An example of S incorporating Adv.*

The contents of this Booke.

4. **Adv.:**   The *1.* page is in a manner needless, and very much of it is wrong; Let therfore the first
10 Heads be quite left out, as being very broken, false, & disordered.

The tother part to be placed rather for the *40th* Page, & to be set down thus,

    1. The Order for Morning Prayer.   pag.
    2. The Order for Evening Prayer.   ·
    3. The Confession of Fayth, cald Quicunque Vult.
    4. The Publike Supplication, cald ye Letany.   ·
    5. The Collects, Epistles, and Gospells.   ·
    6. The Order for Administring the Holy Communion.   ·
    7. The Order for Baptism, Publike & Private.   ·
    8. The Order for Confirmation, wth the Instruction, cald the Catechism.   ·
    9. The Order for Holy Matrimony.   ·
  10. The Prayers in Publike for ye Sick.   ·
        [Yf any shall be appointed.]
  11. The Visitation of the Sick.   ·
  12. The Communion of the Sick.
  13. The Order for Buriall.   ·
  14. The Thancksgiving after Childbirth.   ·
  15. The Denouncing of Gods Judgments agaynst Sinners, cald ye Cõmina-
      tion.   ·

SL: 1.   A Proclamation for the authorising of the booke of Common Prayer.

        Cf. the titles in the text at the appropriate points: nos. 8, 16, 29, 32, 34, 36, 42, 54, 108,
        139, 202, 283, 335, 366, 384, 396, 409, 416, 420.
        The first correction of 'The Table for the order of the Psalmes' follows the printed title
        of this section (no. 32); the second follows the first correction of the title (no. 32. i).
        No. 32. ii is not represented here.

    The entry on the Litany is closer to Adv. than to that in the text (no. 108. iii).

    Holy Communion, Baptism, Matrimony, Visitation of the sick, and Burial are brought
    into line with the headings in the text as printed.

    The first correction of Confirmation follows the printed text, and is therefore earlier than
    no. 335, to which ii conforms.
    It appears that Cosin corrected these titles before beginning the revision of the main body
    of the book, so that most of them had to be altered again afterwards. He may well have
    done this many years before 1661.

16 Matrimonie.

17 Visitation of the sicke.
18 The Communion of the sicke.
19 Buriall.

20 The thankesgiuing of women after childbirth.
21 A Commination against sinners, with certaine
   prayers to be vsed diuers times in the yeere.

Read: 18. The Forme of solemnizing
holy Matrimony.
Read: 19. The Order for . . .
For 18 *read*: 20
Read: 21 The Order for ye Buriall of
the dead.
Read: 22. *For* of *read*: for.   Stet
Read: 23.
Delete to be vsed . . . yeere.
Add: 24. The Psalter to be sung
or said at Morning & Evening
Prayer, with ye Table before it,
in what order the Psalmes are to
be said.
25. The Forme and Manner of
Making Ordeyning & Consecrat-
ing Bishops, Priests, & Deacons.

5.   *A loose sheet*[1] *bound at the beginning of the
book, entirely in Sancroft's hand, reads:*
An Act for ye Uniformitie of Cõmon
prayer.
A proclamation for ye authorizing ye
same.
A preface concerning ye Service of ye
Church.
Another preface, Of Ceremonies.
The Order how ye Psalter is appointed
to be read.
The Order how ye rest of Holy Scripture
is to be read.
The Table of proper Lessons, & psalmes.
Tables, & Rules for ye Feasts, & Fasts
through the yeare.
The Kalendar, with ye Table of psalms,
& Lessons.
The Order of Morning, & Evening
prayer through ye yeare.
The Litanie.
Prayers, & Thanksgivings upon severall
Occasions.
The Collects, Epistles, & Gospels
throughout ye yeare.
The Order for ye Ministration of ye
Holy Cõmunion.
The Ministration of publick Baptisme of
Children.
The Ministration of private Baptisme in
houses.
The Order of Baptizing such, as be of
yeares of Discretion.[2]

---

[1] FC *follows this sheet.*   [2] FC *originally:* . . . be of perfect Age.

5.   *'A Proclamation . . .' is closer to SL than in no. 4.*

'The Litanie' returns to the earlier version, corrected as at no. 108. ii.

'Collects . . .': S finally restored 'to be vsed' at no. 139.

The Baptism titles are close to those now suggested, q.v.

The Catechisme.

The Order of Confirmation.

The forme of Solemnization of Matrimonie.

The Order for ye Visitation of ye Sick.

The Comunion of ye Sick.

The Order for ye Buriall of ye dead.

The Thanksgiving of Women after
Childbirth.

A Comination against sinners, with certain prayers, &c.

The Psalter, or Psalms of David; with ye
Table, in what Order they are every
Month to be read.

The Forme, & Manner of Making,
Ordeyning, & Consecrating of Bishops,
Priests, & Deacons.

An acte for the vniformitie of Common prayer, and Seruice in the Church, *and administration of the Sacraments.*

Where at the death of our late Soueraigne Lord King Edward the sixt . . .

. . . . . .

And for the authoritie in this behalfe, . . all and singular the same Archbishops, Bishops, and all other their Officers, exercising Ecclesi-asticall iurisdiction . . . shall haue full power and authoritie by this Acte, to reforme, cor-rect, and punish by censures of the Church, all and singuler persons, which shall offend . . . against this Acte and Statute; and other Law . . . notwithstanding.

. . . . . .

Prouided alwayes . . . That all and singuler Archbishops and Bishops . . . shall haue full power and authority by vertue of this Act . . .

. . . . . .

Prouided alwayes, and be it enacted, that whatsoeuer person offending in the premises, shall for the first offence receiue punishment of the Ordinary . . . shall not for the same offence eftsoones be conuicted before the Justices: and likewise, receiuing for the said first offence punishment of the Justices,

6. *Add*: made in the first yeere of the Reigne of Q. Eliz.

7. *Before* full *add*: ye use & exercise of their (*crossed out*) q

 After against *add*: anything in any (*crossed out*) q

 Before full *add*: ye exercise of their (*crossed out*) q

 And likewise . . . Ordinarie *bracketed* q

The sheet as a whole gives a careful reproduction of the titles, fuller than that to be found above.
Cf. nos. 125, 315, 334.

Adv.:   Name the yeare, wherein this Act was made: And so *pag. 22* for that Preface.

7.

The insistence on the 'exercise' of full power may be a reaction against the Presbyterian proposals to limit the authority of the Bishops; see e.g. the Declaration of 25 October 1660, sections IV and V (Cardwell, Conferences, 292–4).

he ſhall not for the ſame offence eftſoones receiue puniſhment of the Ordinarie: any thing conteined in this Act to the contrary, notwithſtanding.

Prouided alwayes, & be it enacted, that ſuch ornaments of the Church, and of the miniſters thereof, ſhall be reteined, and be in vſe, as was in this Church of England by the authority of Parliament in the ſecond yeere of the reigne of King Edward the ſixt, untill other order ſhall bee therein taken by authority of the Queenes Maieſtie, with the adviſe of her Commiſſioners, appointed and authorized under the great ſeale of England, for cauſes Eccleſiaſticall, or of the Metropolitane of this Realme.

For Queenes *read*: King's
After Maieſtie *add*: his Heyres & successors (*So also later in the sentence.*) (crossed out) q

. . . . . .

By the King.
A Proclamation for the authorizing and Vniformitie of the Booke of Common Prayer to be vsed throughout the Realme.

Although it cannot bee unknowen . . . Although wee had no reaſon to preſume that things were ſo farre amiſſe, as was pretended, becauſe we had ſeene the Kingdome vnder that forme of Religion which by Law was eſtabliſhed in the dayes of the late Queene of famous memorie, bleſſed with a Peace and Proſperitie, both extraordinary and of many yeeres continuance (a ſtrong euidence that God was therewith well pleaſed,) . . .

because we had seene . . . well pleaſed,) *bracketed*. q

. . . . . .

God saue the King.

The reference to the King's 'Heyres & successors' is intended to refute the Puritan theory that the Queen's authority died with her (see e.g. A Suruey of the Booke of Common Prayer, *1606*).

Part. I.: *The Proclamation* lately added to ye Booke after ye Conference at Hampton Court, is no legall Part therof, & were better omitted; for ye Act of Parliamt prefixed to ye Booke forbids any Addition thereunto.

The Preface

There was neuer any thing . . .
such as were Ministers of the Congregation . . .

should continually profit more and more . . .
But these many yeres passed, this godly and
decent order of the Fathers hath been so altered,
broken, and neglected by planting in vncertaine
Stories, Legends, Responds, Verses, vaine repe-
tions,[2] Commemorations, and Synodals,

that commonly when any booke of
the Bible was begun, before three or foure Chapters were read out, all the rest were vnread . . .
These inconueniences therefore considered, here
is set forth such an order, whereby the same shall
be redressed. And for a readinesse in this matter,
here is drawn out a Kalender for that purpose
which is plaine and easie to be vnderstanded
wherein (so much as may be) the reading of holy
Scriptures is so set forth, and all things shall be
done in order . . . So that here you haue an order
for prayer (as touching the reading of holy Scripture) much agreeable to the minde and purpose
of the old Fathers, and a great deale more profitable and commodious then that which of late was
vsed. It is more profitable, because here are left
out many things, whereof some be vntrue, some
vncertaine, some vaine and superstitious, & is
ordained nothing to be read, but the very pure
word of God . . . Furthermore, by this order the
Curates shall neede none other bookes for their
publike seruice, but this booke and the Bible. By
the meanes whereof, the people shal not be at so
great charges for bookes, as in time past they haue
beene . . . And if any will iudge this way more
painefull, because that all things must be read
vpon the booke, whereas before, by the reason of
so often repetition they could say many things by
heart: if those men will weigh their labour, with
the profit and knowledge which daily they shall

8.   *Read*: A Preface, concerning the
         Service of ye Church.[1]

9.   *i. Read*: . . . Ministers of God in ye
         Church.
         ii. Read: Ministers of ye Church.
             For more and more *read*: &
             increase   Stet

         i. For vncertaine . . . Synodals *read*:
             vncertaine Stories & Legends, with
             multitudes of Responds & Verses;
             besides many other vaine repeti-
             tions & Commemorations
         ii. Read: vncertaine Stories & Legends,
             Responds & Verses, vaine repeti-
             tions, Commemorations, & Syno-
             dals[3]

For before *read*: after
For vnread *read*: omitted.   Stet.

10.   *For* vnderstanded *read*: understood.
             (*So also lower down.*)
         For and *read*: that
         Read: Here therefore you haue . . .
             Stet
         For as touching *read*: and for
         Delete brackets.

For be *read*: are
For & is ordained nothing *read*: &
         nothing is ordeyned
11.   Omitted: Furthermore . . . they
         haue beene.

Omitted: And if any . . . ensue
         thereof.

---

[1] *New paragraphs at* But these many yeres. . . . And moreouer. . . . And furthermore. . . . Yet
because. . . .   [2] *Sic.*
[3] FC: vncertaine Stories & Legends, wth multitudes of Responds. & Verses. . . .

8.   *Cf. the Elizabethan Act of Uniformity (definition of 'open prayer'): commonly called the Seruice of the Church.*

9.   *The alteration of 'Congregation' to 'Church' is almost invariably made.*

10.   'that': BCP.

            The other alterations are typical of a large group made for stylistic reasons, which are not hereafter commented upon in these notes.

11. **Cf. S I:** I cannot see what kind of cõmendation this can be, sure ye more books, ye more solemne wold Gods service be. But it seems the people began even then to desire yt their divine service might be quickly dispatched, and yt they might be put to no grt charges for ye maintenaunce of it, or els these 2 argumts wld never have bin thought of.

obtaine by reading vpon the booke, they will not
refuse the paine, in consideration of the great
profit that shall ensue thereof . . .
Though it be appointed . . . when men say
Morning and Euening prayer priuately, they
may say the same in any language that they
themselues doe vnderstand.

12.   *i.* Alter ye Character & set it on ye
          other side.
      ii. After Character *add*: to faire Italick
      i. Add: especially in ye Colledges of
          either University, & in yẹ Schooles
          of Westminster, Eaton, & Win-
          chester.
      ii. After Colledges *add*: & Halls

And all the Priests and Deacons shall be bound to
say daily the Morning & Euening prayer, either
priuately or openly, except they be let by preaching, studying of Diuinity, or by some other
vrgent cause.

13.   *i.* Omitted.   (*crossed out*)
      ii. Alter ye Character to Italick.
          Read: And all Priests . . .
14.   *i. For* preaching . . . cause *read*: sick-
          nes, or some vrgent & unfeyned
          cause, wch ye Bp. of ye dioces
          shall approve.
      ii. Read: sicknesse or some other vrgent
          cause.

And the Curate that ministreth in euery Parish
Church or Chappell, being at home, and not
being reasonably letted, shall say the same in the
Parish Church or Chappell where he ministereth,
and shall toll a bell thereto a conuenient time
before he begin, that such as be disposed, may
come to heare Gods word, and to pray with him.

15.   *i.* Omitted   (*crossed out*)

      ii. After letted *add*: as before   (*crossed
          out*)
      iii. Before reasonably *add*: otherwise[1]
          For toll a bell *read*: cause a bell to be
          tolled
          After begin *add*: (wch may be any
          houre betweene six & ten of ye
          clock in the Morng & betweene
          Two & six of ye clock in the
          Evening,) (*crossed out*)
          For such as be disposed *read*: the
          parishioners

---

[1] FC *in text.*

12. **Adv.:** It would be sayd, from whence this came, that it may be known, By what Authority. In the first Line, it would be sayd, [though it be intended in the].

Part. 2: In ye order betwixt ye Preface & ye Treatise of Ceremonies it is allowed to all men *to say ye Morning & Evening Service Privately in any language* (besides ye English) *wch they understand.* Here an Explanation is wanting, whether this word Privately may not be extended to Colledges in either of ye Universities, & some other places, (as Westminster, Eaton, & Winchester Schooles) for whose use Q. Elizab. in ye 2d yeere of her Reigne caused the Comon Prayer Booke to be sett forth in Latin, as being ye most proper Language for them.

> *The Letters Patent of 1560 allow the Colleges of Cambridge, Oxford, Winchester, and Eton the privilege of praying* publicly *in Latin. This entry, though clearly derived from Part. 2, is perhaps also influenced by Canon 17 ('Halls', 'either University').*

13. **Adv.:** In the *8th* line, say, [are bound]. But what Warrant for those Exceptions?

'all priests': BCP.

14. **Part. 3:** In ye same order, *every Curate* is injoyned to *say ye Morning & Evening Prayer daily in ye Church, unlesse he be otherwise reasonably letted;* wch requires an Explanation (agst them yt accompt themselves reasonably letted by any comon & ordinary affaires of their owne,) whether any thing but sicknes or necessary absence abroad shall be sufficient to excuse ym from this duty.

SL: of which cause, if it bee frequently pretended, they are to make the Bishop of the Diocesse, or the Archbishop of the Province, the Judge and Allower.

> *S I quotes the Council of Venice, Canon xiv: . . . sine probabili excusatione aegritudinis . . .*
> *S II quotes Lyndwood: Puta Infirmitatem.*

15. **Adv.:** In the *12*th line, the word [Curate] now in England is grown into quite another sense. It is here put, to signify every one, upon whom doth lye the duty of Administration in that Church, or Chapell.

In the *13*th line, these words [and not being otherwise reasonably let] are no very good sense; but they would be left out, as letting it rest at his own perill, yf wthout good reason he do at any time omitt it.

In the *15th* line, Let the hours for tolling of the bell be named, [at some time, betwixt *10 and 12*, and agayn betwixt *2 & 4.*

Part. 19: In ye Rubrick before Morning & Evening Prayer, there is no order what Houre ye Service for Morning or Evening shall begin. For want wherof in most places, when ye Morning is past & when ye Evening is not yet come, those Services are comonly begun. Wch in ye Morng is crosse to those words in ye 3d Collect for Grace where wee say to God, *Who hast safely brought us to ye Beginning of this day, defend us in ye same &c.*

'otherwise': BCP.

> *This entry is modelled on Adv., though Wren's times are altered. Part. 19 goes back to a note in S I, on the third Collect at Morning Prayer:*
> *Wch shews when ye Morning Prayer shold regularly be said, at ye first houre of ye day, wch is 6 a clock in ye morning & not towards high noone day or after nine when ye morning is past.*

Of Ceremonies, why some be abolished, and some reteined.

𝕺𝖋 𝖘𝖚𝖈𝖍 𝕮𝖊𝖗𝖊𝖒𝖔𝖓𝖎𝖊𝖘 𝖆𝖘 𝖇𝖊 𝖇𝖘𝖊𝖉 𝖎𝖓 𝖙𝖍𝖊 𝕮𝖍𝖚𝖗𝖈𝖍 . . . 𝖎𝖓 𝖉𝖎𝖚𝖊𝖗𝖘 𝖈𝖔𝖚𝖓𝖙𝖗𝖊𝖞𝖘.

16.   *Add*: Another Preface,

No alterations.

The Table and Kalender, expressing the order of the Psalmes and Lessons to be said at Morning and euening prayer throughout the yeere, except certaine proper feasts, as the rules following more plainely declare.

The order how the Psalter is appointed to be read.

The Psalter shall be reade thorow once euery Moneth.

17.   *i.* Sett this as a Title by it self in ye page before. (*crossed out*)
 ii. *Delete the whole Title.*

For order *read*: Order

 i. *Add*: as is there in order appointed both for Morning & Evening prayer.
 ii. *Read*: (except February) every day as it is there . . .
 iii. *Delete* (except . . . day
 Add: but in February only 28 or 29 daies shalbe read.
 vi. *Read*: only in February it shalbe read to ye 28, or 29 day day of ye Month.

And because that some Moneths bee longer then some other be, it is thought good to make them euen by this meanes.

To euery moneth shall be appointed (as concerning this purpose) iust xxx. dayes.

And because Ianuary and March haue one day aboue the said number, and February, which is placed betweene them both, haue onely xxviij. dayes: February shall borrow of either of the moneths (of Ianuary & March) one day: And so the Psalter which shall bee read in February, must begin at the last day of Ianuary, and end the first day of March.

And whereas May, Iuly, August, October, and December haue xxxj dayes a piece; It is ordered that the Psalmes shalbe read the last day of the said moneths which were read the day before, so that the Psalter may begin againe the first day of the next moneth ensuing.

18.   Omitted.

Omitted.

Delete the whole paragraph.

19.   *After* whereas *add*: January, March

Before Psalmes *add*: same

16. **Adv.:** The Date of this would not be omitted.

    Cf. S III: . . . this Preface of Ceremonies . . .

17. **SL:** save Februarie, and in that Moneth so far as the Psalms are appointed for xxviii. or xxix. daies in the leap year.

        i is editorial; ii and iii are based on SL.

18. **Adv.:** Upon this Page, here are *6* paragraphs. The *2* first, (the first line onely excepted,) would be omitted: for that Order for ye Psalmes is not observed; And it makes such a strange disturbance, so long together, the people jeering now at the Ministers for it, as yf they were mistaken, or worse; that it cannot be used.

19.   *The addition of January and March is necessitated by the abandonment of the arrangement set out in the previous paragraph, whereby their extra days were incorporated into February.*

    'same': BCP.

20.   *i. Add*: And in February when it hath
      but xxviii. dayes, let all the Psalmes
      appointed for ye 27th. day of the
      Month be read that day at Morn-
      ing Prayer, and all ye psalmes
      appointed for ye 28. day, be read
      the same 27. day at Evening
      prayer; And on ye xxviiith day,
      Let ye usuall Psalmes of ye whole
      29th day, be read at Morning, &
      the psalmes appointed for ye whole
      30th day, be read at Evening.
      And when it hath xxix. dayes,
      Let all ye psalmes usually ap-
      pointed for that 29th day be read
      at Morning, & all ye psalmes of ye
      next day, at Evening: that so ye
      whole Psalter may be read tho-
      rough on that Month also.
      ii. Delete the whole new paragraph.

Now to know what Psalmes shall be read euery day: Looke in the Kalender the number that is appointed for the Psalmes, and then find the same number in this table. and vpon that number, you shall see what Psalmes shall be said at Morning and Euening prayer.

And where the Cxix. Psalme is divided into xxij. portions, and is ouerlong to bee read at one time: it is so ordered, that at one time shall not be read aboue foure or fiue of the said portions, as you shall perceiue to be noted in this table following.

21.   Omitted.

      For where *read*: whereas
      For and is *read*: being

      For foure . . . following *read*: foure
      at Evening prayer, & five at
      Morning, as in the Psalter is
      appointed.

22.   *Add*: And at ye end of every Psalme,
      & of every such part of the 119.
      psalme, shall be repeated this
      Hymne
      Glory be to the Father &c
      As it was in ye begiñing &c.

And here is also to be noted, that in this table, and in all other parts of the seruice where any Psalmes were appointed, the number is expressed after the great English Bible, which from the ix. Psalme, vnto the Cxlviij. Psalme (following the diuision of the Hebrewes) doth vary in numbers from the common Latine translation.

23.   *i. Omitted.*
      ii. Read: Note, that the Psalter fol-
      loweth the division of the
      Hebrews, & the Translation of
      the Great English Bible, set forth
      & used in the time of K. Edw. VI.
      iii. Read: . . . of K. Hen. VIII. & Edw.
      VI.

20.   *This idea may well be Cosin's own, but does not appear in any of his works; neither has it been traced in any other writer.*

21. **Adv.:** Also the *4th* paragraph is in vayn, and would be omitted.

22. **Part. 25** (quoted at no. 76, q.v.).

    This entry is transferred to this point from Morning Prayer.

23. **Adv.:** In the *6th* paragraph, name the yeare of the Edition of the great English Bible.

    S II: this great English Bible was set forth in the time of K. Hen. 8. by Cuthbt Tunstall Bp of Duresme, & Nicholas Heath Bp of Rochester, Ao. 1540. & Ao. 1541. used in all churches in ye time of K. Edw. the VI. And out of this Bible were ye Epistles and Gospells, and ye Psalmes taken yt are in this Book of Comon Prayer.

    Brightman (I. ccxi) criticizes the phrase 'set forth & used in the time of K. Hen. VIII. & Edw. VI'. As the quotation from S II shows, the meaning is that it was set forth in the time of K. Hen. VIII. and used in the time of K. Edw. VI.

    Bishops: 3. That the Psalms be collated with the former Translation, mentioned in *Rubr.* and Printed according to it.

The order how the rest of holy Scripture
(beside the Psalter) is appoynted to bee
read.

Delete (beside the Psalter)

The old Testament is appointed for the first
Lessons at Morning and Euening prayer, and
shall bee read through euery yeere once, except
certaine Bookes and Chapters, which be least
edifying, and might best bee spared, and therefore
are left vnread.

24. *i. Delete* except . . . vnread.
   Before shall bee read *add*: except
   certaine Bookes & Chapters
   ii. Read: the most part therof
   iii. Stet: except . . . vnread (*crossed out*)
   After once *add*: as in ye Kalendar is
   appointed.

The New Testament is appointed for the second
Lessons at Morning and Euening prayer, and
shalbe read ouer orderly euery yeere thrise, besides the Epistles and Gospels: except the Apo-
clypse, out of the which there be only certaine
Lessons appointed vpon diuers proper Feasts.

   i. Delete besides . . . Feasts.
   ii. Stet: except . . . Feasts
   For diuers *read*: some
   iii. Stet: besides . . . Gospels *in brackets.*
   Read: . . . certaine proper Lessons appointed vpon diuers Feasts.

And to know what Lessons shalbe read euery day,
find the day of the Moneth in the Kalender following, and there ye shall perceiue the Bookes
and Chapters that shall be read for the Lessons
both at Morning and Euening prayer.

   For find . . . Moneth *read*: looke
   After following *add*: & in the Table
   of proper Lessons
   Delete Bookes and

And here is to be noted, that whensoeuer there
be any proper Psalmes or Lessons appointed for
the Sũdayes, or for any Feast, moueable or vn-
moueable: then the Psalmes & Lessons appointed
in the Kalender shalbe omitted for that time.

   Read: And note that whensoever
   proper Psalmes or Lessons are
   appointed; the Psalmes & Lessons
   of ordinary course appointed in
   the Psalter & Kalender, if they be
   different, shalbe omitted for that
   time.

Ye must note also, that the Collect, Epistle, and
Gospel, appointed for the Sunday, shall serue al
the weeke after, except there fal some Feast that
hath his proper.

25. *Delete* Ye must
   Before serue *add*: where it is not in
   this Booke otherwise ordered.
   Delete except . . . proper.
   Add: And ye Collect wch is appointed for every Sunday, or any
   Holyday yt hath a Vigil, shalbe
   said ye Eve before. (*crossed out*)
   Where ye second Lesson & the
   Gospel appointed upon any day
   happen to be coincident, then so
   much of the Lesson as the Gospel
   conteyneth shalbe left unread, &
   likewise (*crossed out*) q

When the yeeres of our Lord may be diuided into
foure euen parts, which is euery fourth yeere:
then the Sunday letter leapeth, and that yeere the
Psalmes & Lessons which serue for the xxiij. day
of February, shalbe read againe the day following,

26. *i. Read*: When the yeere of our Lord
   which begins upon the Annunciation day may be diuided into
   foure euen parts (as it hapneth
   euery fourth yeere) . . .
   Delete Psalmes &

24. **Adv.:** The 2 first Paragraphs here also would be omitted: For those words [least aedifying, and might best be spared] are not so satisfactory, but that they will rather incite the quarrelsome to a comparison, betwixt these Parts of Scripture omitted, and those of the Apocrypha, wch are appointed to be read.

Part. 4: In ye order how ye rest of ye H. Scripture besides ye Psalter is appointed to be read, it is said, *That ye Old Testamt shalbe read thorow every yeere once, except &c* wch in King Edw. first Service Book was accordingly done; but afterwards since ye Lessons were interposed for Sundayes & Holydayes, this order cannot be observed, & therfore ought to be amended . . .

> *A note in S III points out that the Old Testament is not in fact read through, no book being 'entirely read or continued on, without Interruption'. Cosin wants the Order amended to take account of this fact, Wren wants the Order omitted to conceal it!*

Part. 4, cont.: In ye order how ye rest of ye H. Scripture besides ye Psalter is appointed to be read, it is said, *That whensoever any proper Lessons are appointed for ye Sundayes or for any feast day, then shall ye Lessons appointed in ye Calendar for yt day of ye Month be omitted.* But here is no provision made for ye feast dayes yt fall upon a Sunday, whether ye Lessons appointed for ye Sunday or yt feast day shalbe taken. For want of wch provision, in some places they read one Lesson, and in othersome another, according to ye Curate's choyce, wch breeds diversitie in ye Service, & is agt ye Uniformitie intended in it by ye Act of Parliamt, & ye Prefaces before named.

Part. 5: In ye same order, there wants ye like provision for ye Collect, Epistle, & Gospell, when a feast day falls upon a Sunday, wch of them shalbe taken.

> *The question raised in these two Particulars was not dealt with in DB.*

25. **Adv.:** To the 5th paragraph add, thus, [Except in that week, there be some Feastday, wch hath a Proper Collect, Epistle, & Gospell].

Sarum Breviary: Si illud festum habeat Vigiliam, non dicitur Oratio de Vigilia, sed Oratio de die dicitur.

> *The rubric about Eves was transferred to the Collects, Epistles, and Gospels (no. 140). Wren notes three instances of the Second Lesson and the Gospel coinciding (Good Friday, Easter I, and Trinity IV). Cf. nos. 43, 171, 178, and 185.*

26. **Adv.:** The 6 paragraph is lyable to a Quarrell, unless it be put, thus, [When the yeares of our Lord upon the Annunciation day may be divided into.] for in our Church the yeare begins not till then; But the Leap is in February. This Rule therfore counts the beginning of the yeare from Xtmas, At wch time indeed the Golden Number, and the Dominicall Letter doe chang.
'St. Matthias': cf. no. 43 (Sarum).

except it be Sunday, which hath proper Lessons of the Testament, appointed in the Table seruing to that purpose.

Read: (except it be Sunday, the first proper Lessons wherof of the Old or New Testament, appointed in the Table seruing to that purpose). And then ye feast of St. Matthias shall be ye xxv. day.

ii. Delete the whole paragraph.

Also wheresoeuer the beginning of any Lesson, Epistle, or Gospel is not expressed, there ye must begin at the beginning of Chapter.

Omitted.

And wheresoeuer is not expressed how farre shalbe read, there shall you read to the end of the Chapter.

Omitted

Item, so oft as the first Chapter of Saint Matthew is read either for Lesson or Gospel, ye shall begin the same at (𝕿𝖍𝖊 𝖇𝖎𝖗𝖙𝖍 𝖔𝖋 𝕵𝖊𝖘𝖚𝖘 𝕮𝖍𝖗𝖎𝖘𝖙 𝖜𝖆𝖘 𝖔𝖓 𝖙𝖍𝖎𝖘 𝖜𝖎𝖘𝖊, &c.) And the third Chapter of Saint Lukes Gospel, shall bee read vnto, 𝕾𝖔 𝖙𝖍𝖆𝖙 𝖍𝖊 𝖜𝖆𝖘 𝖘𝖚𝖕𝖕𝖔𝖘𝖊𝖉 𝖙𝖔 𝖇𝖊 𝖙𝖍𝖊 𝖘𝖔𝖓𝖓𝖊 𝖔𝖋 𝕵𝖔𝖘𝖊𝖕𝖍, &c.

27.   *Delete* Item
Delete or Gospel   Stet
After at *add*: v. 18

After vnto *add*: these words v. 23.

28.   *Add*: And, to the end the people may the better heere & understand in such places where they doe sing, the Lessons, Epistle, & Gospel, shalbe sung or pronounced in a plaine tune, after the manner of distinct reading.

27. **Adv.:** In the last Paragraph, let the Verses be set down, [To begin the same at *the 18 v.* and the other, [Shall be read to *ye 23 v.*]

    Part. 6: In ye last Clause in yt order, ye first word there *Item* seemes to contradict ye former clause, wch com̃andeth all Chapters to be read from ye beginning to ye ending, where it is not otherwise expressed. This Item therfore should rather be Excepted only, That &c.

        Cf. nos. 153 and 31.

28.   *This entry has been transferred to this point from Morning Prayer (no. 79), with the addition of the words '& understand'.*

Proper Lessons to be read for the first Lessons both at Morning and Euening prayer on the Sundayes throughout the yeere, and for some also the second Lessons.

29. *i. Read*: Proper Lessons at Morning and Euening prayer for Sundayes & other Holydaies.

 ii. Read: Proper Lessons to be read at Morning and Euening prayer on Sundayes & other Holy dayes thoroughout ye whole yeare.

 Add subtitle: Lessons proper for Sundayes.

Sundayes of Aduent.[1]

30. *i. Read*: Sundayes before ye Coming of Christ, commonly called th Aduent.

 ii. For Coming *read*: Nativity
 iii. Stet as printed.

Sundayes after Christmas.

 Read: Sundayes after the Birth of Christ, comonly called Christmas.

Sundayes after the Epiphanie.

 Read: Sundayes after the Manifestation of Christ to ye Gentils, called the Epiphanie.

Septuagesima.

 Add: or the Third Sunday before Lent.

Sexagesima.

 Add: or the Second Sunday before Lent.

Quinquagesima.

 Add: or the next Sunday before Lent.
  (*all the above crossed out*)
The ix. of Genesis is to be read unto ye 20. v.[2]

Lent. 𝔉irst sunday

The xix. of Genesis is to be read vnto the 30. v.

  vi

 1. Lesson Exod. ix | x
 2. Lesson Matth. xxvi. | Hebr. V.
 to v. 11 Seeing ye are, &c.

Easter day.

Acts ii. (upon Easter day at Eveng is to begin at ye 22. v. & read to the end of the chapter.

Sundayes after Easter.

Upon ye 2d. Sunday after Easter, for ye first Lesson at Morng read ye xxiii. & xxiiii. Chapters of Numbers.

Whitsunday.

On Whit Sunday at Morng read Deut. xvi. unto ye 18. vse.

ii. 𝔏esson. 𝔄cts. x 𝔗hen 𝔓eter ...

 Add: v. 34. vnto the end of the Chapter. (*crossed out*)

  𝔄cts xix.

    v. 1 (unto) v. 21.

---

[1] *Only those days are quoted to which some alteration is made.*
[2] *This and the following marginal notes are crossed out and the entries in the Table corrected accordingly.*

29. **Adv.:** To keep to the Rule of Expounding every Word, instead of [Mattens & Evensong] set it, [Morning and Evening Prayer.]

> *Wren's comment refers to the headings of the columns.*

30. **Adv.:** Sundayes before the Comming of Xt, cald The Advent.

Sundayes after the Birth of Xt, cald Xtmas.

Sundayes after the Manifesting of Xt to the Gentiles, cald th'Epiphany.

For Septuagesima, Sexagesima, and Quinquagesima, to expound them, and to give the Reason (What use soever they have bin in,) is so gross and unreasonable, that it will be better quite to omitt them. For howe're Quadragesima was never amiss, bycause that first Sunday in Lent is just the *40th* day before our Saviours Passion; yet from any Analogye thereunto, the Sunday before it to be cald Quinquagesima, wch is but *47* daies, and Sexagesima, wch is but *54* dayes, and Septuagesima, wch is but *61* dayes before, how great soe're the Devotion of those times was, yet the blindnes was greater. Will it not be best now to style thē, [The Third, The Second, and The Next Sunday before Lent?]

Rather let the *VI* Sunday in Lent have the xxvith Chap. of St Matthew set to it for a Proper Second Lesson. Bycause that, and *27th* Chap. joyned together do make the Gospell for that Day (in divers regards) overlong.

Easter Day, Evening Prayer, Exod. xiiii.
Also Acts the IId, to begin at the *22 v*.

Whitsunday, Of both the *2d* Lessons set down the Verse. *Act. 10. 34*, and *Act. 19, to the 23 v*. And thus set down the Verse, in all places here following.

¶Trinitie Sunday.   i. **Lesson.**
                                                    On Trin. Sund. at Morn. read
                                                      Gen. 1. & at Evg Gen. 18.
                        ii. **Lesson.**
                                                    On Trinitie Sunday, for ye 2d
                                                      Lesson at Eveng, read 1. John. v.
Sundayes after Sundayes.
                                                    Read: Sundayes after Trinity (*al-*
                                                      tered to Trinitie)
ѵi.   ii. **King. xxi.**   xix.
ѵii.   xxii.   xxiii to ye 24 v.   (*crossed out*)
xѵi.   **Eʒech.** xiiii.   xiii.
xѵii.   xѵi.   xiiii.

⟜ᴢLessons proper for holy dayes.

Natiuitie of Christ. i. **Lesson.**   31.   Esay. ix. [v. 2] unto the 8. v.
                                                    Esay. vii. v. 10. unto ye 9th. v.
                        ii. **Lesson.**   Luke ii unto v. 15
                                                    Titus iii v. 4. unto ye 9th. v.
S. Steuen.   i. **Lesson.**   **Eccles.**   Ecclesiastes. (*so also below*)
                     ii. **Lesson.**   Acts vi. v. 8. unto ch. vii. v. 30
                                                    Acts vii. v. 30. unto. v. 55.
Innocents day.   Jerem. xxxi. v. 1. unto v. 18.
                              Wisedome iii   ii
Circumcisiō.   Deut. x. v. 12. unto the end of the
                                                      chap.
Epiphanie.   **Esay. xl.**   lx.
                     ii. **Lesson.**   Luke iii. v. 1. unto v. 23
So yt he was supposed . . .   Being as was supposed . . .
                                                    Acts xxii. v. 1. to v. 22
Conuersion of S. Paul.   Ecclesiasticus. (*so also below*)
S. Matthias.   **Eccle.**   *Read*: . . . of our Lord to the blessed
Annunciatiō of our Lady.   Virgin Mary. (*crossed out*)
                                                    2. Lesson   John xi. v. 45 to ye end.
Wednesday afore Easter.   (Mattens)   2. Lesson   John xiii.
Thursday afore Easter.   (Mattens)   1. Lesson   Gene. xxii. v. 1. unto
Good Friday.   v. 20.
                                                                Esay liii.
Easter Euen.   2. Lesson.   S. John. xviii.
                                                                1 Pet. 2.[1]
Tuesday in Easter weeke. ii. Lesson.   2. Lesson.   Luk. xxiii. v. 50 to the
                                                                  end.
                                                                Hebr. iiii.
                                                    Luk. xxiiii. v. 1. unto v. 13.
Philip and Jacob.   *Read*: S. Philip and S. Jacob.

---

[1] ? Sancroft.

For Trinity Sunday here wants a *2d* Lesson at Evening Prayer. Take the *1. Ioan. 5.*

On ye VII Sunday after Trinity, the first Lesson at Morng: is *2. Sam. 22.* Now that being the *17* Psalm, and thereby is read every Moneth, and falleth sometimes to be read among the Psalmes for that day, rather let the Lesson be *2 Sam. 23* unto the *24th vs.*

31. **Adv.:** Add here in every place, the Number of the Verse, at which to beginne, or end.
The Manifesting of Xt to the Gentiles, calld th'Epiphany.
The Presenting of Xt in the Temple, calld the Purification of the Virgin Mary.
Lessons are here wanting for the First Day of Lent. There would be also a second Lesson proper for Good-fryday, for when it falls on ye last of March, the Second Lesson is the Gospell.
Adding here also the Note of ye verses, where to begin & end.
It would be, [S. Phil. and Iac.] S. Iohn Bapt.] S. Peter and Paul.] Note the verses also. [S. Simon & Iude. Here also note the Verses.

Part. 7: In ye Lessons proper for Holydayes there are divers appointed to be read out of *Eccle.* (as upon St. Stephen's day, St. John's day, Annuntiation, St. Mark, St. Ph. & Jacob, & St. Barnabe, besides S. Peter, St. James, St. Barth., St. Matth, St. Mich, & St. Luke,) but whether it be Ecclesiastes or Ecclesiasticus, it is not there specified at large, wch hath occasioned much diversity in reading those Lessons; & therfore this would be explayned, for better uniformity to be therein observed.

Part. 8: Upon ye Feast of Circumcision for the first Lesson at Evensong is appointed *Deut. 10. unto—And now Israel.* whereas it ought to be, *Beginning at, And now Israel,* unto ye *End.* For so it was ordered in the first Edition of this Booke, wch since that time the Printers Negligence hath thus disordered, & appointed ye first pt of yt chapter to be read, that hath no relation to ye day, (as all ye latter part of ye Chapter hath,) & ye Lesson to end, where it should begin.

Part. 9: Upon ye feast of ye Epiphany for ye first Lesson at Morning prayer is appointed *Esay xl,* wch is a Lesson yt hath no Relation to the day; It should be (as it was at first printed) *Esay lx,* wch altogether referrs to ye Calling of ye Gentiles that day Remembred. But this mistake also came from the Printers negligence by putting the x here before ye L, wheras it ought to follow it.

Part. 10: Upon Good Friday, for ye first Lesson at Morng Prayer is appointed *Genes. 22.* concerning ye Sacrifice of Isaac; wch is all yt referrs to yt day. & therfore it would be advised, whether it were not fitt here to order ye End of that Lesson at the 19th verse of that chapter, unto—*And it came to passe after these things &c* all wch following verses are not proper for that day.

Ascention day.

On Ascension day at Morng read for ye 2d Lesson Luk. xxiiii. v. 44. to ye End. And at Eveng Ephes. iiii. v. i. to ye 17. v.

Munday in Whitson-weeke. i. Lesson.

Gen. xi. v. i. unto v. 10.
Num. xi. v. 16. unto v. 30.
On Monday in Whitsunweek, read for ye 2d. Less. at Eveng 1 Cor. xiiii. to ye 26. v.

Tuesday in Whitsun-weeke. i King. xix.

1 Sam. xix. v. 18. unto the end.
On Tuesday in Whitsunweek, read for ye 2d. Less. at Morng 1. Thess. 5. v. 12. to ye 24. v. & at Evening 1. Joh. iiii. to ye 14. v.

S. Barnabe.
S. Joh. Bap.   ii. Lesson. Matth. iii.

Acts. xv. v. i. unto v. 36.
On S. Joh. Bap. day 2d Lesson at Morng read Matth. iii.
Matth. xiiii unto v. 13.

S. Bartholomew.   Ecclus. xxv.

xxiiii.

Part. 11: Upon St. John Baptist's day, for the 2d Lesson at Matins is appointed S. Matth xiii. wch is an Error comitted by the Printer's Negligence since the first edition of this Booke, where it was S. Matth. iii. for this is proper to St. John ye Baptist, wheras ye other referrs nothing to him at all.

Upon St. Barth. day. ye Lessons appointed out of Ecclus agt women have bin so offensive yt they were better to be changd for others.

Part. 12. Upon All Saints day, for ye 2d Lesson at Morng Prayer is appointed Hebr. 11. & 12. beginning at these words *Saints by faith*. wch referre us to the Old English Bible (comonly called ye Bps. Bible) & named in ye Order, before, how ye Psalmes ought to be read. For in ye New Translation These words are not to be found, wch causeth many Curates to begin some at one verse, & some at another. That therfore there may be a uniformity observed aswell in this Lesson as in some others before (upon ye day of St. Paul's Conversion 2d Lesson at Matins, &c) either ye verse where to begin ought to be specified, or ye Bps. Bible only used, wch seemes here to be only autorized for ye Publick Lessons of ye Church, by ye Act of Parliamt prefixed before ye Book of Comon Prayer.

SL: Nativitie of Christ.

    i. Lesson. Esay vii. from verse 10 unto the end.

    ii. Lesson. Luke ii. unto verse 15.

        Titus iii. from verse 4. unto 9.

S. Steven.

    ii. Lesson. Acts vi. from verse 8. to chap. 7. verse 30.

        Acts. vii. from vers. 30. unto 55.

Innocents' day.

        Jer. xxxi unto v. 18.

Circumcision day.

        Deut. x. from vers. 12. unto the end.

Epiphanie.

    i. Lesson. Esay lx.

    ii. Lesson. Luke iii unto verse 23. Being as was supposed the sonne of Joseph.

Conversion of S. Paul.

    ii. Lesson. Acts xxii. unto verse 22.

Munday in Whitsun-weeke,

    i. Lesson. Gen. xi. unto verse 10.

        Numb. xi. from vers. 16. unto 30.

Tuesday in Whitsun-weeke.

    i. Lesson. 1 Sam. xix. from vers. 18 unto the end.

S. Barnabe.

    ii. Lesson. Acts xv. unto verse 36.

S. John Baptist.

    ii. Lesson. Matt. xiii. unto vers. 13.

S. Michael.	**Ecclus.** xx xix.	On St. Mich. day. I. Less. at Morn. Gen. xxxii.
	xliiii.	at Even Dan. x. v. 5. to ye End.
		II. Lesson at Morn. Act. xii. v. 5. to the 18. & at Even Coloss. ii v. 8. to the end.
		For Coloss . . . *read*: Jude v. 6. to the 16.
Simon and Jude.		*Read*: S. Simon and S. Jude.
All Saints.	**i. Lesson.**	Wisdome 3. unto v. 10.
		Wisdome 5. unto v. 17.
	ii. Lesson.	Hebr. xi v. 33 unto chap. 12. v. 7.
		Apocal. 19. unto v. 17.

¶ Proper Psalmes on certaines dayes.

· · · · · ·

Whitsunday. Mattens. xlv. xlvii.

32.   *i. Read*: . . . certaine feasts & dayes of ye yeere.

    ii. Read: . . . certaine dayes.

    Read: xlviii. lxvii.

33. *Add*:

  Epiphany

    Mattins. 2. 67.

    Evensong. 72. 97.

  Ashwedensday

    Mattins.   *i.* 25. 32.

         ii. $\psi\psi$ penit. 6. 32. 38.

    Evensong. *i.* 69.

         ii. $\psi\psi$ penit. 102. 130. 143.

All Saints.
    i. Lesson. Wisedome 3. unto verse 13. Wherefore blessed is the barren.
        Wisedome 5. unto verse 17.
    ii. Lesson. Hebr. xi. unto chapt. 12. verse 7.
        Apocal. 19. unto verse 17.

The entries in this section are mainly derived from SL, supplemented by the suggestions of Parts. 7–12. The latter are based upon a note in **S III**:

The second Lesson at Evensong [upon Christmas Day] Tit. 3. was appointed both in the first and second Edition, to proceed no further then unto these Words, *Foolish Questions* . . . On Ascension Day, there were two second Lessons, and here be none . . . Upon All Saints, the second Lesson at Morning Prayer is ordered to begin at these Words in Hebr. xi.: *Saints by Faith subdued Kingdoms*; and so should it be printed in our Books, where for want of the Words, *subdued Kingdoms*, since the Old Bible was out of use, (I know not by what Authority left off, seeing these References of the Beginnings and Endings of Proper Lessons, relate to that old Translation which was in use 5. Edw. VI.) they commonly begin at the first Verse of the Chapter, and read it through; and sometimes also (for want of printing this Table exactly according to the first Copy) they leave off where they should begin; and sometimes, instead of the true proper Lesson, read another, that is nothing to the purpose of the Day: so that for the first Lesson upon the Circumcision Day at Evensong, they commonly begin the Chapter, Deut. x. and leave off at the Words, *And now Israel &c.* where they should begin, and read out from thence to the end of the Chapter. And upon Epiphany Day, usually for the first Lesson at Matins, they read Esay xl. (which is nothing to the Day,) instead of Esay lx. which is proper to it. And upon St. John Baptist's Day, the second Lesson at Morning Prayer is printed Matth. xiii. when it should be Matth. iii. and all this, and more, through the Carelessnes of the Printer, and the Negligence of them who should have the oversight of these Books, and be better acquainted with them then they are.

The alterations on The Circumcision and The Epiphany are also referred to in Cosin's letter to Laud (p. 294), and that on The Epiphany is also made in S I. They are typical of Cosin's respect for the 1549 Book. Cf. also no. 27.

32. Part. 13: The proper Psalmes for Morning Prayer upon Whitsunday are in some Books 45. & 47. in others 47. & 68. wch numbers are mistaken by the negligence of ye printer; for in ye first Edition of this Booke, ye Psalmes appointed & ye true numbers are. 48. 67.

Sparrow comments upon Psalms 45 and 47, without apparent sense of incongruity.

33. Adv.: Also here would be proper Psalms set, for the

		Mor.	Even.
First day of Lent.	Psal.	vi	cii
		xxxii	cxxx
		xxxviii	cxliii
Good Fryday.	Psal.	xxii	xciiii
		lxxxviii	cxliii

Good Friday
   Mattins.   *i.* 3. 22. 23. 40.
             ii. 22. 40. 54.
   Evensong. *i.* 54. 69.
             ii. 69. 88.
Rogation Monday
   Mattins.   *i.* 12. 13. 107.
             ii. 86. 90.
   Evensong. (*blank*)
Rogation Tuesday
   Mattins.   *i.* 86. 122.
             ii. 28. 42. 46. 70.
   Evensong. (*blank*)
Rogation Wednesday
   Mattins. 8. 19. 33. 103. 104. 144.
   Evensong. (*blank*)
Ember (*crossed out*) (*blank*)
S. Michael & all Angels day
   Mattins. 34. 80. 91.
   Evensong. 103. 104. 148.
All Saints day
   Mattins. 1. 15. 84. 91.
   Evensong. 112. 113. 119. 1st part.
           145. 149.
(*All except Ash Wednesday and
Good Friday crossed out.*)

The Table for the order of the Psalmes, to be said at Morning and Euening Prayer.

Dayes of the Moneth.	❡ Psalmes for Morning Prayer.	❡ Psalmes for Euening Prayer.
1	i. ii. iii. iv. v.	vi. vii. viii.
. . . . . .		
30	cxliiii. cxlv. cxlvi.	cxlvii. cxlviii. cxlix. cl.

34.
For The *read*: A
Before said *add*: sung or
Put this table before ye Psalter & omitt it here. (*crossed out*)

35. *i. Add*: Note, that upon the 19th day, ye 95. psalme here appointed in order is not to be said or repeated, after ye Venite exultemus (wch is ye same psalme) at Morng pr.
    ii. Read:... is not to be repeated, being the same with Venite exultemus.
    iii. Delete the whole entry.
    Add: Note also, yt upon ye 12th day the 67. psalme, & upon ye 19th day ye 98. psalme are not to be said or repeated after ye first or second Lesson at Evg. pr.[1] (*crossed out*)

---

[1] FC: ... are not to be repeated as Hymns after ye Lessons at Evening Prayer.

Ps. xxii is appointed as Introit on Good Friday in 1549. S I has a note from St. Augustine: Psalmus vicesimus primus omni anno legitur in novissimâ Hebdomadâ, intento universo populo.

Ps. 149 is appointed as Introit on All Saints' Day in 1549.
The Sarum Breviary includes the following proper psalms:

Epiphany.	2. 72. 97.
Good Friday.	22. 88.
Michaelmas.	103.
All Saints'.	84. 113. 145. 149.

34. **Adv.:** There is no need, or use at all of this Table. It is transplaced also. It should stand *pag. 28,* next under that Title; for there it is promised, and there's none.

     Cf. no. 35. Wren's 'pag. 28' refers to 'The Table and Kalender' (no. 17).

35. **Part. 24:** In ye Rubrick after ye *Venite Exultemus* wch is the 95th Psalme, ye Psalmes in order are appointed to be said for every day of ye Month, as they are set downe in a Table before; where, upon ye 19th day of ye Month are appointed ye 95. 96. & 97. If this order be strictly observed, ye 95th Psalme will be twice said over wthout any intermission. Wherefore it were not amisse yt an Exception were here made of yt Psalme for ye 19th day.

     FC rightly transfers this note, together with the Table, to the head of the Psalter (no. 416). The latter part of the note is given effect at nos. 98 and 100; hence its deletion here.

An Almanacke for xxxix. yeeres

(*Not reproduced here*)

36.   *i.* This Almanake is to be renewed[1]

  ii. Read: A Table for fortie yeeres shewing the Moveable Holydayes of every yeere.

  This Table is to be renewed.[1]

  iii. Read: A Table of the moveable feasts.

  iv. Add at end of Almanack: TABLES & RULES For the moveable & immoveable feasts, together with the dayes of Fasting & Abstinence, through ye whole yeere.

  v. Read: RULES for the moveable Feasts & Fasts & Dayes of abstinence in the yeere.

  vi. Read: RULES to know wn the moveable Feasts & holy Dayes begin.

37.   *Add*: Easter day (upon all wch all ye rest depend) is allwaies ye 4th Sunday after ye New Moone, wch happens upon, or next after ye Nones of March. And if ye new Moone happeneth upon a Sunday, reckon yt inclusively for one of ye fower.

38. *Add*: ADVENT Sunday is always the neerest Sunday to the feast of St. Andrew, whether before or after.

Septuagesima			9. weeks
Sexagesima	is		8. weeks
Quinquagesima	before	Easter	7. weeks
Quadragesima			6. weeks

(before Easter *crossed out and placed after* weeks)

Rogations			5. weeks
Ascension day	is		40. dayes
Whitsunday	after	Easter	7. weeks
Trinity Sunday			8. weeks

(*For* Rogations *read*: Rogation Sunday)

To finde Easter for euer.

(*Not reproduced here*)

39.   *Read*: A Table to finde . . .

  Add: Easter day is always the first Sunday (*crossed out*)

  A TABLE of all the Feasts that are to be observed in the yeere.

  After in *add*: the Church of England thorough

  All the Sundayes in ye yeare &c ut infra post Kalendariũ.

  (the *crossed out*)

---

[1] *In the margin.*

36. **Adv.:** Make a new One, for this is neer to an End.
Put in also the Rule of the Golden Number, or leave out the Name of it, at the bottome
of this page.

Devotions: A Table of the moueable Feasts . . .
Rules to know when the moueable Feasts and Holydaies begin.

As also in nos. 37 and 41, S transcribes from the Devotions.

37. **Devotions:** Easter day (on which the rest depend) is alwaies the first Sunday after the Full
Moone, which beginneth next the Equinoctiall of the Spring in *March.*

38. **Devotions:** *Septuagesima Sunday* is Nine weekes before EASTER . . . (*verbatim*)
Rogation Sund. is 5. weeks after EASTER . . . (*verbatim*)
Advent Svnday is always the neerest Sunday (whether before or after) to the Feast
of S. Andrew . . .

The first sentence is from the Devotions; *the rest is transferred to this point from no. 44,
and assimilated (by S) to the order in the* Devotions.

39.   *Cosin began to enter no. 37 at this point.*
For the text of the 'Table of all the Feasts', see no. 48. iv.

40.   *Add*: A Table of ye vigils, fasts, & dayes of Abstinence to be observed in the yeere.

The Evens or Vigils before 1. The Nativity &c. ut infra, ibm. The Dayes of Fastg or Abstinence. The 40 dayes of Lent &c. ibm.

41. *i. Add*: The Kalendar, wth ye table &c ut sequitur

    ii. Read: By ye Ecc'ticall Lawes of this Realm, there be some times in ye year, wherein Marriages are not usually solemnized; as—

from $\begin{cases} \text{Advent} \\ \text{Septuagesima} \\ \text{Rogation} \end{cases}$ Sunday untill

$\begin{cases} \text{8 daies after ye Epiphanie.} \\ \text{8 daies after Easter.} \\ \text{Trinitie Sunday.} \end{cases}$

The Kalendar, wth ye table &c. p. seq.

42.   *Before the Kalendar add*: The Kalendar, wth ye Table of Psalmes, & Lessons.

40. *For the full text, see nos. 50–53.*

41. *Verbatim from the* Devotions. *The rules are those of Sarum, as quoted in S II:*

Ordo Sarum. In certis Anni temporibus prohibetur Solennitas Matrimonij, non tamen Consensus: tamen si Solennitas adhibeatur, non retractetur Matrimonium. A Solemnizatione abstinendum est, a 1a. Dñica Adventus usque ad 8m. diem post Epiphaniam, inclusivè; a Dñica Septuages. usque ad 8m. diem post Pascha inclusivè, id est, usque in crastinũ, & vocatur ille dies, Dñica in Albis. Item, a die lunae in 2a. feria in Rogationibus usque in crastinum Trinitatis.

42. *Cf. no. 17 (text).*

Adv.: The *2d* Page, and the *11* wch follow are the Kalendar. In all wch, The first Note about the Sunnes Rising, and Falling, (the Setting, is a fitter word) is very false, in the most of them.

Also the word [Psalmes] set in redd letters over the first Colum. is in vayn. Leave it out.

Then there are *8* distinct Colums: Of wch the Third is of no use now, as to our Divine Service. If it must stand, let it be formed in every one, thus:

Kalendas Ian: | Nonas Ian: | Idus Ian: | xix Kalend: Februari. so that the word [Februarii] run not into ye next Colum. And so in ye rest.

The *4th* Colum would be well considered of. Stand it must: For there is ne'er a moneth but hath some day in it, of God, or of the Holy Apostles of Xt.

As for ye rest, though it hath bin truly sayd, That in the Reformation, to avoyd so great a Number of Sts in generall, one day (calld All Sts') was set out, and became a great Feast, And yet some few were then retayned, unto whom our people were most affected, and wth whom they were best acquainted, This very Reason (taken from the times, as then they were,) is sufficient, why there should now be some alteration; And none but of our own Nation, or such as in some particular respect do concern our Nation (for we formerly had a great hold in France,) be retayned, and sprinckled into that Colum: And the Choyse of these, or of any other, to be recommended by the Church, to the King and his great Counsell. Also whosoever shall be left in, it will be very meet, that who they were, and the time when they lived, bee breefely expressed.

Part. 14: In ye Ends of ye Months of August, October, & November, there be 3 severall directions to alter certaine Lessons formerly appointed in Q. Elizab. time; wch seemes to be agt the Act of Parliamt yt forbiddeth any Alteration to be made in the Booke. And these Alterations were made only by ye Kings order Ao. *1604*, at ye instance of Dr. Chadderton & Mr. Knewstubbs, &c. in the Conference at Hampton Court: where they tooke Exceptions agt ye Reading of Tob. 5. & got ye King's consent to change it into Exod. 6. (a Lesson altogether sett out of order) upon ye first day of October, &c. But this was not legally chang'd.

Part. 15: In ye months throughout ye whole Calendar, the Printer hath set ye Names of *Februarij*, *Januarij*, &c at ye 14. 15. or 16. day of every month, among the Names of ye Saints,

[*The Kalendar.*]¹

Jan.	25	**Conuers. Paul.**	43.		red lr̃es.
	30	**Exod. vii**			q
Feb.	1–28				*All psalms altered to correspond with the day of the month.*
	2	Purifi. of Mary			*Read*: Presentation of Christ, com̃only called The Purification of ye virg. Mary (*crossed out*)
					q
	10	**Leui. 18**			*Add*: Note, yt in every leap yeere St. Matthias is to be set & observed on ye 25. day. (*crossed out*)
	24	S. Matthias			
	28				*Add*: 29. And in leap yeere
					Deut. xiiii Luk. xi.
					Deut. xv Ephes. v.
					(29. And *crossed out*)
March	24	In. reg. Iaco.			*crossed out*
	25	Annun. of Mary			*After* Annun. *add*: Christ to ye virg. (*crossed out*)
April	3	**Richard**			*crossed out* Stet
	19	**Alphege**			*crossed out* Stet
May	6	**John Euang.**			*Add*: ante port. Lat.
	19	**Dunstane**			*crossed out* Stet
	21	**1. Esdr. 2**			Ezr. 1.
	25	**2. Esdr.**			Nehem.
	26	**Augustine**			*Add*: sent to convert ye Saxons
June	11	**Barnabe**			Barnabas In red letters
	19	Nati. K. Iames			*crossed out*
	24	**John Baptist**			*Add*: S.
	29	**S. Peter Apost.**			*After* S. Peter *add*: & St. Paul (*crossed out*)
July	6	**Dogdayes.**			*crossed out*

¹ *Throughout the year, the names of the months (in the Roman dating) have been removed from among the names of saints. Only those days are quoted to which some alteration is made.*

wthout any distinction of letter or other note of difference from them. Wch hath occasioned many to aske what those Sts (Januarius & Februarius &c. were;) wheras they are to be only Notes of ye old Roman Accompt, & put into a severall character from ye rest, as ye Solstices & Equinoctials are.

Part. 16. In those Months there be some Sts put downe, wherof question is made, whether there were ever any such persons or no, (as *St. Katherine* & *St. Faith,*) & the Conception of ye Virgin Mary is mentioned, wch was first put in by yt partie among ye Papists, who believed her to be Conceived wthout originall Sin; a thing offensive to some other partie of the Papists themselves, aswell as to all Protestants. And therfore it would be considered, whether these particulars were not better left out of ye Calendar.

Part. 17. The Addition of ye Kings Birthday, or ye Begiñing of his Reigne, is not authorized to be put there by Act of Parliamt.

Devotions: *The Conversion of St. Paul and S. Barnabas are in red letters.*

S. IOHN Euang. boyled in a Caldron of hot oyle before *Port Latin*, in *Rome*.
S. PETER, Apost. & Martyr, with S. PAUL.

43. Adv.: On the *xxv* day, let [Convers. of Paul] be in a Rubrick, inasmuch as our Church observes it, though ye Statute overslipt it.
The *2d* day would rather be styled [Presenting of Xt] and so the six day, on ye Page before, [Xt manif. to Gent:] for Epiphany.
There would be also Lessons set for the *xxix* day in Leap-yeares | Deut. xiii | Deut. xiiii |
On the first Day, that Second Lesson should be, Luc. xii. The *xxv* Day to be cald [Annunc. of Xt to Mary.] for, by our Lawyers leave, [Annunc. of Mary] is a Soloecisme.
The *xxxi* day, The 2d Lesson was ye Gospell in *Ao. 1648.* and so will be agayn ere long. Let there be a Rubrick to direct, what to doe in that Case.
The iid Lesson April. 30. ii and iii. Iohn.
[Barnab. Ap.] on the *xi* day would be in a Rubrick, for our Churches sake, though it was scattered out of the Statute: And it is to be wished the Statute were a little amended.
The *xxix* day should be, [Peter and Paul Ap.]
Out wth [Doggdayes] from among the Saynts.
Yf Lammas stand, let it be expounded, from Laf'en; Bycause of the Oblations, & Divine Service, for ye New corn, thẽ in use.
The Notes for ye Lessons on the xxv day, and the xxix, and the xxx, are disordred: Let them be set right.
Put in ye first Lesson at Morn: on ye first day, *Exod. vi.* And yf the note of ye Sunnes Progress do stand in every moneth, put here, [Sol in Scorp.]

> *These notes of Wren's apply to the successive months in the Kalendar. The coincidence of 2nd Lesson and Gospel on March 31 was actually due to recur in 1670.*

> *The restoration of the Conversion of St. Paul and St. Barnabas to red-letter status is a commonplace at this period: besides the sources above, see SL, S I, S III, and Taylor's Collection of Offices.*

> *Exod. vii is queried because Exod. vi is transferred to 1 Oct., q.v.*
> *The alteration of the Psalms is occasioned by the omission of the rubric at no. 18.*
> *Leui. 18 is queried as being unedifying.*

Sarum: Si bissextus fuerit, quarta die a cathedra Sancti Petri fiat festum Sancti Mathiae.
> *This rule is revived by Taylor.*

Sept.	5	**Dogdapes end.**	*crossed out*
	28	**Tob. 1**	q
Oct.	1	1. Lesson the 6. of Exodus	q
	6	**Judit. 1**	q
Nov.	7	**Eccle. xxb**	*Add*: to v. 13

Note that the beginning of the 24. Chapter of Ecclesiasticus (vnto) But when one is, &c. **must be read with the 25. Chapter.**
Note that the 46. Chapter of Ecclesiasticus, is to be read vnto these words, After this he told, &c.

Read: Note that the 25. Chapter of Ecclesiasticus must be read to ye 13 v.

After these words *add*: v. 20

Dec.	8	**Conc. of Mary**	*crossed out*

Septuagesima
Sexagesima
Quinquagesima
Quadragesima $\Big\}$ **before Easter** $\begin{pmatrix} \text{ix} \\ \text{viii} \\ \text{vii} \\ \text{vi} \end{pmatrix}$ **weekes.**

44. *Crossed out (and placed after the Almanacke).*

Rogations
Whitsunday
Trinitie Sunday $\Big\}$ **after Easter** $\begin{cases} \text{vi} \\ \text{vii} \\ \text{viii} \end{cases}$ **weekes.**

Cf. S II: *Añun. Dñica. Miss. Sarum.*
Richard, Alphege, and Dunstan were omitted from the Kalendars of 1549 and 1552: hence their cancellation here, though they were restored in 1561. Cf. S III:
In this Kalendar . . . there is some difference between this Edition and that of Edw. VI. to which the Act of Uniformity referreth. . . . In April, Richard and Alphage are omitted.
St. John ante Port. Lat. is also revived by Taylor, and is the subject of notes in S I and S II, adequately summarized by the entry in the Devotions, *quoted above.*

S I: Augustine: Angl. Ap. The first Bp. of Canterbury sent hither by St. Greg. ye great, to convert ye Saxons from Paganisme.

Once more, Taylor agrees in reviving the ascription to St. Paul. Cf. S II: Ord. Sarū. habet Petri & Pauli.

Lords: 1. Whether the names of some *departed Saints* and others should not be quite expunged the Calender.

Footnote: See also Cosin's letter to Laud (p. 294).

44. *See no. 38.*

These to be obserued for Holy dayes, and
none other.

45.   *Add*: according to the Act of Parliamt set forth Aº. 5º. & 6º. Edw.
cap. 3. (*crossed out*)[1]

That is to say: All Sundays in the yeere.
The dayes of the feastes of the Circumcision
of our Lord Jesus Christ. Of the Epiphanie.
Of the Purification of the blessed Virgin. Of
S. Matthias the Apostle.

Of the Annuncia=
tion of the blessed Virgin. Of S. Marke the
Euangelist. Of S. Philip and Jacob the
Apostles. Of the Ascension of our Lord
Jesus Christ. Of the Natiuitie of S. John
Baptist. Of S. Peter the Apostle. Of S.
James the Apostle. Of S. Bartholomew the
Apostle. Of S. Matthew the Apostle. Of
S. Michael the Archangel. Of S. Luke
the Euangelist. Of S. Simon and Jude the
Apostles. Of All Saints. Of S. Andrew the
Apostle. Of S. Thomas the Apostle. Of
the Natiuitie of our Lord. Of S. Steuen the
Martyr. Of S. John the Euangelist. Of the
holy Innocents.

46.   *Delete* That is to say:

Add: Of the Conversion of St. Paul.
Read: Of the Presentation of Christ,
comonly called the . . .
(*crossed out*)
Read: Of the Annunciation of
Christ, comonly called the . . .
(*crossed out*)
Read: . . . St. Jacob . . .
Add: Of St. Barnabas.
Read: Of St Peter & St Paul the
Apostles. (*crossed out*)

Read: Of St Michael and all angels.
Read: . . . St. Jude . . .

Add: Monday & Tuesday in Easter
week; & Monday & Tuesday in
Whitsunweeke. (*crossed out*) Stet

47.   *i*. The Conversion of S. Paul. & S.
Barnaby's day are appointed in
the Kalender.

---

[1] *In FC the whole page is crossed out.*

45. **Adv.:** Name the yeare, and the Act. And it were to be wisht, it might be altred, as we sayd before.

S I: I suppose this whole Page to bee but the Printers work, no order of the Church, as appeares by the sequent declaration of ye beginning & ending of ye Lawyers Termes, for what had Churchmen to doe wth them? And so here for Holydaies I never cold see where it was appointed that these here shold only be observd and no other. Which are Holydaies and which are not according to the purpose & intent of our Church appeares by the Lessons appointed before as proper for Holydaies, where are many more dayes accompted holy then here are by the ignoraunce of the printer. In the statute 5. Ed., ca. 3. these indeed were appointed & none other: but yt statute being repealed 1. Mar. 1. cap. 2. & being not since revived, we are to stick rather to the autoritie of this service Book in the Catalogue of Lessons proper (as before) rather then to the printers pleasure and ignoraunce. I cannot tell it seemes the printer was loth to loose the work of his servants so many Holy dayes of the yeare, as he saw proper Lessons appointed for before, and therfore he comes stealing in with this lay direction, wch the peoples indevotion & carelesnes of observing any day was ready enough to take hold on, & to make a rule of, though it be no more a pt of ye Service Booke established by the Church, then yt the Lawyers Termes shold have their beginning & ending, as here is noted.

46. **Part. 18:** In ye order, what dayes are to be observed for Holydayes, & No other, there is no mention made of St. Paul's Conversion, & St. Barnabe's day; wch nevertheless are numbered before among ye Holydaies in this Booke, where Proper Lessons are appointed for ym as Holydaies; and ye like may be said for Good Friday & other dayes in ye Passion Weeke, all set under that Title of Holydayes. So yt there is some Explanation here wanting to Reconcile these Two Places of ye Booke together.

SL includes The Conversion of S. Paul and S. Barnabas in this list.

47. **S I** (at no. 31): In the Title to all these dayes we read, *Lessons proper for Holydaies.* It seems those P'liament men who made the Act, (These to be Holydaies & no other.), forgat to mend this Title as they did to put out the Epistles & Gospells upon all the weeke before Easter & upõ St. Barnabes & St. Paul's Day, wch we are comãnded by ye Rubrick at ye end of ye Comũnion to read only upon Holydaies. I cannot reconcile them.

S III has a similar note.

Cosin, *Visitation Articles, 1626:* 6. . . . upon the whole *week before Easter,* together with Ash Wedensday, & the dayes wherin St. *Paul* & St. *Barnabie* are commemorated . . .

ii. Read: Upon The Conversion of St.
Paul, Ashwedensday, the week
before Easter & St. Barnaby's day
are peculiar services appointed in
the church. (*crossed out*)

48.   *i.* There is also an Act made for the
keeping of ye fift day of Novem-
ber & for divine Service to be celebrated on that day as likewise on
ye 30th day of January, besides
Rogation & Ember dayes.

ii. Read: Ye fift day of November,
being the Papists Conspiracie &
the 29. of May, being the day of
the Kings birth & Returne.

iii. Read: The v. day of November being ye
day of ye Papists Conspiracy. &
The xxix day of May, being ye day of ye
King's Birth, & Return.

*iv. A loose sheet bound at the beginning of the
book, entirely in Sancroft's hand, reads:*
A table of all ye Feasts, yt are to be
observed in ye Church of Engld
through the yeare:
All Sundaies in the yeare.
The daies of ye Feasts of
    The Circumcision of our Ld Jesus
      Christ.
    The Epiphanie.
    The Conversion of S. Paul.
    The Purification of ye Bl. Virg.
    S. Matthias ye Apostle.
    The Annunciation of ye Bl. Virg.
    S. Marke ye Evangelist.
    S. Philip, & S. Jacob ye Apostles.
    The Ascension of our Ld Jesus
      Christ.
    S. Barnabas.
    The Nativitie of S. John Baptist.
    S. Peter ye Apostle.
    S. James ye Apostle.
    S. Bartholmew ye Apostle.
    S. Matthew ye Apostle.
    S. Michäel, & all Angels.
    S. Luke ye Evangelist.
    S. Simon, & S. Jude ye Apostles.
    All Saints.
    S. Andrew ye Apostle.
    S. Thomas ye Apostle.
    The Nativitie of our Lord.
    S. Stephen ye Martyr.

Wren, Particular Orders: 6. . . . that ministers forget not to read ye Collects Epistles & Gospells appointed for ye Conversion of St Paule & all ye holy week before Easter, & St. Barnabies day, & on Ashwednesday . . .

48.
An Act for a Publick Thanksgiving to Almighty God every year on the fifth day of November was passed on 30 January 1606.

A Committee of Convocation was appointed on 16 May 1661:

de et super precibus specialibus pro die nativitatis domini nostri regis, necnon pro felicissima restauratione ejus ad et in regna sua, viz. 29 die mensis jam instantis Maii . . .

necnon etiam de et super precibus specialibus et particularibus in 30 diem mensis Januarii in quolibet anno publice peragendis et perlegendis . . . (Cardwell, Synodalia, ii. 640.)

The form for 29 May was prepared forthwith; the form for 30 January was not published until 7 January 1662.

S. John ye Evangelist.
The Holy Innocents.
Monday & Tuesday in Easter weeke.
Monday & Tuesday in Whitsun weeke.
The 5th day of November, being ye
   day of ye Papists conspiracy.
The 29th day of May, being ye day of
   ye King's Birth, & Returne.

A briefe declaration when euery Terme
beginneth and endeth.

49. *This title and the whole paragraph following crossed out.*

Be it knowne . . . nor vpon any Sundayes.

50. *i. Add*: These to be observed for
         Fasting Dayes.
     ii. Read: A Table of ye Vigils, Fasts and
         dayes of Abstinence to be ob-
         served in the yeere.   (*crossed out*)
         Stet
51. *i. Add*: The Even or day before
         1. ye Nativitie of our Lord.
         2. Easter day.
         3. Ascension day.
         4. Pentecost.
         5. Purification of ye virg. M.
         6. Annunciation of our Lord.
         7. All Saints.
         8. All ye feasts of ye Apostles,
            except St John ye Evangelist,
            & Phillip & Jacob.

49. **Adv.:**   To what end this here? Away wth it.

    S I: What has this to doe in so holy & divine a Book? There are Almanaks enough to hold it.

    S II: This declaration of ye Termes which is here annexed to ye Observation of Holydaies, was first made & set forth by the Injunctions of K. Hen. 8. & the Convocation of the Clergie Ao. *1536*: where it was ordered, that the people might freely goe to their worke upon all such Holydaies (as were usually before kept) wch fell either in ye time of Harvest, (compted from ye 1. day of July to ye 29. of September,) or in any time of ye 4 severall Termes, when ye King's Judges sate at Westminster. But yet These Holydaies (here in our Booke mentioned) are specially excepted by those Injunctions of K. Hen. 8. & his Clergy-Convocation, & comanded to be kept solemne & holy by every man, ye Harvest time, & ye Terme time notwithstanding. And therfore I see no use of this Declaration when ye Termes begin & end, to be added to our Holydaies in this place. For neither was it permitted in K. Hen. 8. time, nor is it in ours, that any man should goe to his worke upon these dayes appointed to be kept sacred, whether they fall in Terme-time, or no.

        SL omits the Declaration entirely.

50. **Part. 49:** In ye Rubrick following ye Nicen Creed, ye Curate is ordered to *Bid ye Fasting dayes*; wch being not so usually knowne to every Curate, it would be here specified, *what dayes* are appointed to be *Fasted* by the Lawes of ye Kingdome & Church of England, throughout ye yeare.

        Cf. nos. 36 and 40.

51.   *S I has a note in Latin, attributed to Andrewes, but not found in the other manuscripts of his Notes, giving the reasons why some Feasts (e.g. St. John the Evangelist) do not have Vigils.*

    ii. Read: The Evens or vigils before
      1. ye Nativitie of our Lord.
      2. Purification of ye virg. M.
      3. Annunciation of our Lord.
      4. Easter day.
      5. Ascension day.
      6. Pentecost.
      7. St. Matthias.
      8. St. John Baptist.[1]
      9. St. Peter.[2]
     10. St. James.
     11. St. Bartholomew.
     12. St. Matthew.
     13. St. Simon & St. Jude.
     14. St. Andrew.
     15. St. Thomas.
     16. All Saints.
   iii. Crossed out. Stet

52. *i. Add*: Note, yt if any of those feast
    dayes fall upon a Monday, then
    ye fast day shalbe kept upon ye
    Saturday & not upon ye Sunday
    before it.
    ii. After then ye *add*: Vigil or
    After Sunday *add*: next
    iii. All crossed out. Stet

53. *i. Add*: Days of fasting or abstinence.
    1. The 40 dayes of Lent.
    2. The Ember weeks at the 4
      Seasons, being ye Wedensday
      Friday & Saturday after ye 1. day
      of Lent, Pentecost, ye Exaltation
      of ye Cross (Sept. 14) & St.
      Lucia's day (Dec. 13).
    3. The 3 Rogation dayes, yt is
      Monday Tuesday & Wedensday
      before holy Thursday or ye
      Ascension of our Lord.
    4. All the Fridayes in ye yeere
      except those yt fall in the time of
      Christmas.
    5. The 30th. of January being the
      day of the Martyrdom of King
      Charles the first.
    ii. After the title add:
    Ashwedensday & good Friday &
    all ye passion week before Easter.
    (*crossed out*)

---

[1] *First written as* St. Peter & Joh; *this is crossed out, and* St. Peter & St. Paul *substituted; then this is crossed out, and* St. John Baptist *inserted.*   [2] *Originally* St. Peter & St. Paul.

53. **Devotions:** The Fasting Daies of the Chvrch, or Dayes of speciall Abstinence and Deuotion.
The fortie daies of LENT.
  2. The *Ember* weekes at the foure Seasons, being the Wednesday, Friday, and Saturday after the first Sunday in *Lent*.
the Feast of *Pentecost*.
Holy Crosse. Septemb. 14.
S. Lucies day. Decemb. 13.

  3. The three *Rogation daies*, which be the *Munday*, *Tuesday*, & *Wednesday* before *Holy Thursday*, or the *Ascension* of our Lord.

  4. The Euens, or Vigils before
The Natiuity of *Christ*.
The Purification of the blessed *Virgin*.
The Anuntiation
The Natiuity of S. *Iohn Baptist*.
S. *Matthias*
S. *Peter*
S. *Iames*
S. *Bartholomew*
S. *Matthew*   } day.
S. *Simon* & *Iude*
S. *Andrew*
S. *Thomas*, and
All Saints

  5. It hath been also an ancient religious custome to fast *All the Fridaies* of the yeere, expect those that fall within the Twelue dayes of *Christmas*.

iii. After The 40 dayes of Lent *add*:
especially the week before Easter.
(*crossed out*)
Delete ye Exaltation of ye Cross *and*
St. Lucia's day

iv. For Ember weeks *read*: Ember daies
Before Pentecost *add*: ye feast of
For yt is *read*: being ye
For in the time of *read*: in ye 12 daies of
Before Martyrdom *add*: Murder &

v. The whole entry crossed out.   Stet

*vi. A loose sheet bound at the beginning of the
book, entirely in Sancroft's hand, reads:*
A Table of ye Vigils, Fasts, & daies of
Abstinence to be observed in ye yeare.
The Evens, or Vigils before
   The Nativitie of our Lord.
   The Purification of ye Virg. Marie.
   The Annunciation of ye Bl. Virg.
   Easter day.
   Ascension day.
   Pentecost.
   S. Matthias.
   S. John Baptist.
   S. Peter.
   S. James.
   S. Bartholomew.
   S. Matthew.
   S. Simon, & S. Jude.
   S. Andrew.
   S. Thomas.
   All Saints.

Note, That, if any of these feast daies
fall upon a Monday, then ye Vigil, or
Fast day shall be kept upon ye
Saturday, & not upon ye Sunday
next before it.

Daies of Fasting, or Abstinence.
1. The 40 daies of Lent.
2. The Ember weekes/daies[1] at ye
4 seasons; being
  the Wedensday,⎫
     Friday,   ⎬after
  & Saturday,⎭
    ⎧the first Sunday in Lent.
    ⎪the feast of Pentecost.
    ⎨Sept. 14.
    ⎩Dec. 13.
3. The 3 Rogation daies, being ye
Monday, Tuesday, & Wedensday.

---

[1] daies *is written above* weekes.

before Holy Thursday, or ye Ascension of our Lord.

4. All the Fridaies in ye yeare; except those, yt fall within ye twelve daies of Christmas.

5. The 30. of Januarie; being the day of ye Murther, & Martyrdome of King CHARLES ye first.

By ye Ecc'ticall Lawes of this Realme, there be some times in the yeare, wherein Marriages are not usually solemnized; as,

From $\begin{cases} \text{Advent} \\ \text{Septuag.} \\ \text{Rogation} \end{cases}$ Sunday untill

$\begin{cases} \text{8 daies after ye Epiphanie.} \\ \text{8 daies after Easter.} \\ \text{Trinitie Sunday.} \end{cases}$

The Kalendar, with ye Table &c.

The Times wherein Marriages *are not vsually solemnized.* From *Aduent* Sunday . . . *Trinity* Sunday. (*verbatim*)

> *The first draft of the list follows that in the* Devotions *fairly closely: S makes it closer still, also adding the rules about marriages (no. 41). The latter should be compared with* Wren's *remarks at no. 383.*

Detached Note: The Order of the Tables
In the 1619 Prayer Book the Tables were arranged in the following order:

1. *The Almanacke.*
2. *To find Easter for euer.*
3. *The Kalendar.*
4. *These to be obserued for Holy dayes.*
5. *A briefe declaration [of the Terms].*

Throughout the process of revision, the Almanack (under different titles) and 'To find Easter for ever' remain in the first and second place respectively. In the first stage of DB, they continue to be followed by the Kalendar and the Table of Holy days, but the Declaration of the Terms is replaced by the Table of Fasting days. In the second stage (represented by the directions to the printer which comprise nos. 39–41, and by Sancroft's sheets inserted at the beginning of the book, nos. 5 and 53. vi), the Tables of Feasts and of Fasts are brought forward before the Kalendar. This order (1, 2, 4, 5, 3) is retained in FC, and thenceforward.

The order where Morning and Euening
prayer shall be vsed and said.

54.   *i. Read*: The order for Morning and
          Euening prayer daily to be vsed
          and said, throughout the yeere.
          Set this on the other side.
      ii. For Set . . . side *read*: Set this first
          Title & ye 2 orders following on
          the other side, retro, wth a fayre
          compartemt before it.

      iii. Add: & in Italick letters

The Morning and Euening prayer shalbe vsed in
the accustomed place of the Church, Chappell,
or Chauncell, except it shall be otherwise determined by the Ordinarie of the place: And the
Chancels shall remaine as they have done in
times past.

55.   *After* Chancels shall *add*: be divided
          from ye body of the Church, &
          (*crossed out*)

56.   *i.* & adde this Title here
          Of Ornaments to be used in ye
          Church.
      ii. Read: An Order for Ornaments . . .
          (*all crossed out*)

And here is to be noted that the Minister in the
time of the Communion, and at other times in
his Ministration, shall vse such Ornaments in
the Church, as were in vse by authoritie of Parliament, in the second yeere of the Reigne of
Edward the sixt, according to the Acte of Parliament set in the beginning of this Booke.

57.   *i. Before* other *add*: all
          Before Edward *add*: K.
      ii. Omitted: the Minister . . . this
          Booke.
          Read: Such ornaments of the
          Church, & of the ministers
          therof at all times of their minis-
          tration shalbe reteyned & be in
          use, as were in this Church of
          England by the Authority of
          Parliament in the Second yeere of
          ye Reigne of K. Edw. VI. that is
          to say—A Surplice &c.

      iii. Delete that is to say—A Surplice &c *and
          add*: these are ye words of ye Act
          itself. v. supr.[1]

---

[1] FC: . . . of the Act itselfe § penult. ut suprà.

54. Adv.: Set down, when this Order was made.
But who can now tell, wch place, when this Order was made, was the Accustomed place?

55. Adv.: Also, who knows how the Chancels were in those times past, so many having since then bin demolished, and many disused?
But what is now fit to be ordred herein, and to preserve those, that are still in use, It would be set down in express words, wthout these uncertayneties wch breed nothing, but debate, and scorn.

S II: That is, distinguished from ye Body of ye Church by a frame of Open Worke, & furnished wth a Row of Chayres or Stalls on either side; & if there were formerly any steps up to ye place where ye Altar or Table stood, that they should be suffered to continue so still, & not to be taken downe or layd levell with ye lower ground, as lately they have bin by violence & disorder, contrary to Law & Custome.

56. *Attention to titles is characteristic of DB.*

57. Adv.: The very words also of that *Act. 2º. Edw. VI* for the ministers Ornaments, would be sett down, or, to pray to have a New One made; For there is somewhat in that Act, that now may not be used.

Part. 19: And in the same Rubrick, ye *Minister is appointed to use such ornamts in the Church, & at all times in his Ministration, as were in use in the Second yeere of King Edward ye Sixt, according to ye Act of Parliamt.* But what those Ornamts of the Church & of the Ministers were, is not here specified, & they are so unknowne to many, yt by most they are neglected. Wherfore it were Requisite that those Ornamts used in the 2d yeere of K. Edward, should be here particularly named & sett forth, that there might be no difference about ym.

Lords: 3. Whether the Rubrique should not bee mended, where all Vestments in time of divine Service are now commanded, which were used 2 Ed. 6.
'all': see the note in S II quoted on p. 293. The omission of the word might be held to justify disuse of the surplice.
Cosin deals with the question of what ornaments are referred to by this rubric in all three Series of Notes, the fullest treatment being found in S II (Works, V. 230 ff.). There he concludes that the 'second year' refers to the 1549 Book, and quotes the rubrics of that Book which order an alb or surplice with a vestment or cope at the Communion; and 'Certain Notes', as ordering a surplice for other services. He then glosses the words of the Act as follows:
Provided alwayes, & be it enacted, that Such Ornaments of the Church, (whereunto the adorning & decent furniture of the Comunion-Table relate,) & of the Ministers therof (as the Albe or Surplice, the Vestment or Cope, with the Rochet & Pastorall Staffe before mentioned,) shall be reteyned & be in use, as was in this Church of England by Autority of

¶ An Order for Morning Prayer dayly *throughout the yeere.*

At the beginning both of Morning prayer, and likewise of Euening prayer, the Minister shall reade with a loude voice some one of these Sentences of the Scriptures that follow. And then he shall say that which is written after the said Sentences.

𝔄t what time soeuer a sinner . . . sayth the 𝔏ord.   Ezek. 18.[2]

    .   .   .   .   .   .

58.   Place at ye end herof on the other side a fleuron.

59.   i. *After* Prayer *add*: & Evening
       (*crossed out*)
   ii. *Delete whole title and read:*
       The Beginning of Morning and Evening Prayer.
       Place here a fayre Compartement.

60.   *Read*: At the beginning of Morning, and Euening prayer . . .
       After Minister *add*: (yt is, he who at that time ministreth or cele-brateth divine Service)
       (*crossed out*)
       After some one *add*: or more
       For Scriptures *read*: Scripture[1]
       Omittd: And then . . . Sentences.
       Stet

61.   *Add*: Esay. 55. v. 6. Seek yee the Lord while he may be found, Call yee upon him while he is neere.
       v. 7. Let ye wicked forsake his way, & the unrighteous man his thoughts, & let him returne unto ye Lord, & he will have mercy upon him; & to our God, for he will abundantly pardon.
       (*crossed out*)

---

¹ FC: *no alteration.*   ² *Verse numbers are added to the reference at the end of each Sentence.*

Parliamt, *in the Second* (not the fift) *yeere of the Reigne of King Edward the Sixt; untill other Order shalbe therein taken by the Autority of the Queene's Majestie, with the Advise of her Commissioners appointed & autorised under the Great Seale of England, for Causes Ecclesiasticall, or of the Metropolitan of this Realme.* Wch other Order so qualified, as here it is appointed to be, was never yet made.

> *His conclusion is, therefore, that the vestments mentioned are still legal, despite anything to the contrary in the* Advertisements *or* Canons. *S III repeats the evidence and the conclusion. S I originally reached the same conclusion, but Cosin later added a note which shows him beginning to have doubts:*
>
> But ye Act of parlt (*I see*) refers to ye Canon, & untill such time as other order shall be takē.
>
> *The choice of 'A Surplice &c' to exemplify the ornaments of the minister clearly has Canon 58 in mind, and therefore may be regarded as a concession to general practice and feeling, rather than as Cosin's own interpretation of the Act. The later deletion of the words leaves the interpretation open.*
>
> *It is not by any means clear from the original that the words 'that is to say' were added later, nor that they were originally followed by dots, which were later made into a dash, as Tomlinson asserts (op. cit. 148).*
>
> *The insertion of 'K.' restores the correct text.*

58. }
59. }   *Characteristic examples of directions to the printer. Cosin is always anxious to distinguish the various sections of the Book.*

60. **Adv.:** Leave out of ye Rubrick those words, [and likewise of Evening Prayer,] for it is more then is in the Title above it, It thwarts also the Rubrick for Evening prayer.

> *DB instead corrects the Title (no. 59).*

> *'one or more': cf. the similar rubrics in the Communion Service, nos. 217 and 260 (Offertory and Communion Sentences).*
>
> *'And then . . . Sentences' was to be replaced by no. 63. When that was dropped, this direction was restored.*

61. **Adv.:** The first Sentence should be set, *Ezech. 18. 21.* Examine all the rest also; For my book is torn.

> *The 'Esay' Sentences are quoted from the A.V. They are also to be found in Taylor.*

If we say that wee haue no sinne, wee de=
ceiue our selues, and there is no trueth in vs.
1 Iohn 1.

62.   *Add*: v. 9. If wee confesse our sins
       he is faithfull & just to forgive us
       our sins, & to cleanse us from all
       unrighteousnes. (*crossed out*) Stet

63.   *Add*: Then shall he say this Exhorta-
       tion. (*crossed out*)

Dearly beloued brethren . . . saying after me.   64.   Omittd: after me.   Stet

A generall Confession to be said of the whole
Congregation after the Minister, kneeling.

       For after *read*: with   (*crossed out*)
       Before kneeling *add*: all

Almighty and most mercifull Father, wee
haue erred and strayed from thy wayes like
lost sheepe, wee haue followed too much the
deuices and desires of our owne hearts . . .
spare thou them, O God, which confesse
their faults . . . to the glory of thy holy Name.
Amen.

65.   Omittd: too much   Stet

       For which *read*: that[1]

The absolution or remission of sinnes to be pronounced by the Minister alone.

66.   *i. Add*: standing.
      ii. Read: standing, & all the people
          still kneeling.

Almighty God, the Father of our Lord Jesus
Christ . . . through Jesus Christ our Lord.

---

[1] Which *is normally corrected to* that *or* who; *this correction has not been noticed hereafter, except in special cases.*

62.   *Also from the A.V. The addition is made also in the* Devotions *(as an Exhortation*
           before the Communion), in Taylor, and in Sanderson. This consensus probably reflects
           general contemporary practice, rather than interdependence.

63. **Adv.:** In the Exhortation there are needless multiplying of words, [acknowledg and confess]
           humble and lowly] Assemble and meet together] requisite, and necessary] pray and
           beseech.]
           Sanderson begins his Liturgy with a section entitled Exhortations.

64. **Adv.:** Those words [saying after me] would be well considered of. They came in here,
           after the Reformation had bin admitted, but it was a time of great aversnes from
           making any Confession, but Auricular, and of great ignorance in people, of that,
           wch was to be sayd. Secondly it hath now bin much disused, and layed aside, expe-
           cially in Cathedrall Churches, (wch should be the Pattern to other Churches, as a
           Mother to hir Daughters:) and in the Ks Chappells and in Colledges. Thirdly it gives
           some countenance to another uncough & senseles custome, not long since brought
           in by some Factions, One to read a line of a Psalm, and then all the rest, to sing it.
           Will it not be better therfore, though not to set down anything to the contrary, yet
           to leave out those 2 words, [after me] and so in the Rubrick also?
   SL: A generall Confession to be said by all that are present after or with the Deacon or
           Presbyter, all humbly kneeling.
           The suggested alteration of 'after the Minister' to 'with' depended on the omission of
           'after me'.

65. **Adv.:** *In the Confession,* [Erred, and straied] is of the former strayn. Especially seing that in
           David, from whence it is taken, *Psal. 119. 176,* it is onely, [I have gone astray.]
           [We have followed tomuch the devices. etc] This is very improper: As though there
           were a Proportion, How farr to follow that, wch it is unlawfull to follow at all. Put
           it home rather here, and make it, [We have onely followed the devises, & desires of
           our own harts.]
           'which' : see no. 69.

66. **Adv.:** Add unto the first Rubrick, [By the Preist alone standing up, and the people all still
           kneeling.]
           In the Absolution, the word [Wch] is 3 times: the last onely is right, and that shewes,
           the other two should be [Who.]
   Part. 20: After ye Confession is appointed *The Absolution,* wch some Ministers read Standing &
           some Kneeling. For uniformitie herin, it should be declared what posture he ought
           to use, & ye Posture of Kneeling is not agreeable to it, because it is no prayer to God,
           but a pronouncing of so many words to the people.

The people shall answere.
Amen.

67.   *After* answere *add*: heere, & at the end of
       all other Prayers,

       Place here a fleuron.
       Add: An order for Morning Prayer
       (*crossed out*)
       Set here a fayre Compartement
       before this Title.

Then shall the Minister begin the Lords prayer
with a loude voice.

68.   *i. Read*: The Priest shall kneele & say
       the Lords prayer with an audible
       voice, & the people shall say the
       same after him.
       ii. Read: . . . voice, ye people repeating
       it after him both here, & wherever
       els it is used in Divine Service.[1]
       iii. Read: . . . ye people also kneeling
       & repeating every petition after
       him . . .
       iv. Read: . . . repeating it with him . . .
       v. For The Priest . . . voice *read*: The
       Minister shall kneele & begin the
       Lords prayer with a loud voice

---

[1] FC: . . . in the Divine Service.

Part. 21: The words there (in the Rubrick) *Or Remission of Sins*, were added at ye instance of the Ministers[1] in the Conference at Hampton Court; but it is no legall Addition, for ye Act of Parliament forbiddeth it.

SL: The Absolution or Remission of sinnes to be pronounced by the Presbyter alone, he standing up and turning himself to the people, but they still remaining humbly upon their knees.

Cf. S I (from Andrewes): & because he speaks it autoritativè, in ye name of Xp̄ & his Church, he must not kneele, but stand up.

67. **Adv.:**   At the end of every Prayer, all the People shall audibly answer, [Amen].

> *An example of an entry from Adv. made by S.*
> *The insertion of a fleuron, the title 'An order for Morning Prayer', and a 'fayre Compartement' is explained by this note from S I:*

Here begins ye Service; for that which goes before is but a preparation to it, and is newly added to K. Edwards first Book in imitation of ye Liturgie & Masse of ye Ch. of Rome. But as their Houres begin with the Lds Prayer, so begins our Mattins, and our High Service at ye Altar.

> *We need not follow the author of S I in imputing to the revisers of 1552 a desire to imitate the Church of Rome. Cosin clearly intends to return to the structure of 1549, and indicates it by separating the Lord's Prayer from what goes before by a fleuron, a compartment, and a title. The erroneous transcription in Vol. V (not in Nicholls) 'newly added in K. Edwards first Book' has led to Cosin (or the anonymous author) being charged with gross ignorance, while the editor alters the text to 'second Book'.*

68. **Adv.:**   To the next Rubrick, add, [begin the Lords prayer, wth an audible voyce, all kneeling and saying wth him, Our Father].
This note was put in at first, bycause in ye Latine Service, they were to say it to themselves.

Part. 22: In ye Rubrick before ye Lord's Prayer, ye Minister is appointed to begin it, but ye people are not appointed to say after him, as in Cathedrall Churches & most Places besides they use to doe. To prevent all diversitie herin, there wants here an Explication to that purpose.

1549:   The Priest . . . shall begynne with a loude voyce the Lordes prayer . . .

> *Part. 22 is partly based on a note in S I ('Cathedrall Churches', 'explicated').*
> *Five stages are distinguishable in the drafting of this rubric. The first owes something to 1549 ('The Priest'), to Part. 22 ('the people shall say the same after him'), and to Adv. ('with an audible voice'). The second extends the rubric to all occurrences of the Lord's Prayer. The third makes 'after him' more explicit ('every petition'). The fourth adopts Wren's suggestion 'with him' (cf. no. 64). Lastly, S restores as much as possible of the existing rubric.*

---

[1] *Originally Puritans.*

𝔒ur 𝔉ather 𝔴hich art in heauen . . . but   69. *Read*: Our Father, who art . . .[1]
deliuer us from euill.

                                                      Add: Amen.

Then likewise he shall say.   70.   *Read*: Then all standing up the
                                                              priest shall say or sing
                                                              (*crossed out; stet as printed*)
𝔒 𝔏ord open thou our lips.   *Add*: Psal. 51. 15.[2]

                   Answere.

𝔄nd our mouth shall shew forth thy praise.

                   Priest.

𝔒 𝔊od make speed to saue us.   Psal. 70. 1.[2]

                   Answere.

𝔒 𝔏ord make haste to helpe us.

                   Priest.   71.   i. *Read*: All Heere stand up, the Priest
                                                              shall say
                                                         ii. *Read*: Heere all standg up, the Priest
𝔊lory be to the 𝔉ather, and to the 𝔖onne, &c.   sayth

                                                     72.   *Add*: Answere.

                                                              Add: Priest
𝔄s it was in the beginning, is now, &c.
                                                              Add: Answere
𝔓raise ye the 𝔏ord.   The Lord's name be praised.
                                                              (*all crossed out*)

───

                [1] FC: . . . which art. . . .   [2] FC *omits*.

69. **Adv.:** And here let be added [For thyne is ye kingdome the power, etc] though the Church of England did then use to omitt it, as appeares by the Catechism, and in the Letany: And now it may be omitted in other places of ye Divine Service, except it be at larg printed.

BCP: Amen.

The correction to 'that' or 'who' is made throughout the Book. At this point, which Wren regarded as crucial, it was finally discarded. For the full statement of Wren's views upon the use of 'which', see the preface to the Advices *(p. 288).*

70. **Adv.:** Then the Minister alone shall say, [O Lord, open Thou our Lipps.] &c.
To the first word there [Answer] let be adjoyned, [By all present] and so to be observed through this whole Book, where there is this generall Direction, [Answer.]

'Then all standing up . . .' is possibly entered here in error. Cf. no. 71.
The insertion of references may be due to Wren (cf. nos. 61, 234, and 385), though Adv.
does not suggest it at this point.

71. **Adv.:** Then all shall stand up, and the Preist shall say, [Glory be to the Father, and to the Sonne and to the Holy Ghost.

SL: Then, all of them standing up, the Presbyter shall say or sing . . .

i is from Adv.; ii may show influence of SL (stronger at no. 70); both are entered by S.
It seems that Cosin entered the relevant SL rubric at the wrong place; Sancroft filled
the gap with a rubric derived from Adv., then crossed out Cosin's entry, and conflated
the two. Since, however, the same process is observable at this point in Evening Prayer,
Cosin may really have meant that all should stand at 'O Lord, open thou our lips.'

72. **Adv.:**   *Answer*
[As it was in the beginning, is now, and ever etc.

                  The Preist
[Prayse yee the Lord.

                  Answer
[The Lds name be praysed.

SL: Answer.
As it was in the beginning . . . Amen.
Praise ye the Lord.

                  Answer.
The Lords Name be praised.

Part. 23: *see no. 75.*
This arrangement was already found in SL, but DB is slightly closer to Adv.

Then shall be said or sung this Psalme following.

73. *Add*: And upon every Sunday or Lords day this Com̃emoration of his Rising from the dead shalbe sd or sung

Priest

Christ is risen againe &c.

And upon ye feast of Easter

Christ our Passeover is offred up for us, Therfore let us keep ye feast &c ut in die Pasch.

Then shalbe said or sung,

(*crossed out*)

74. *i. Add*: (except upon ye feast of Easter, when another Antheme is appointed).

ii. For another *read*: a proper

iii. Read: (except on Easter day, wn another Antheme is appointed).

75. *i. Add*: one verse by the Priest, & another by the people; And the same order shalbe observed in all Psalmes & Hymnes throughout this Booke. But where there is a Quire, ye same shalbe sung by sides, as hath bin accustomed.

ii. Before where *add*: in Colledges &

𝕺 **come, let ᵇs ᵴing ᵇnto tꜧe 𝕷orꝺ . . . ꞔorlꝺ ꞔitꜧout enꝺ. Amen.**

Then shall follow certaine Psalmes in order, as they be appointed in a Table made for that purpose, except there be proper Psalmes appointed for that day.

And at the end of euery Psalme throughout the yere, and likewise in the end of *Benedictus, Benedicite, Magnificat*, and *Nunc dimittis* shall be repeated.

𝕲**lorꝑ be to tꜧe 𝕱atꜧer &c.**

As it ꞔas in tꜧe, &c.

76. *i. For* certaine *read*: the

Omitted: in a Table . . . that day.

Read: And at the end of euery Psalme, & of every part of the cxix Psalme throughout the yere, and likewise in the end of Te Deum, Benedicite, Benedictus, Magnificat, and Nunc dimittis shall be repeated this Hymne. . . .

ii. Delete Te Deum *and* this Hymne

iii. Delete And at the end . . . As it was in the &c.

iv. Frō hence stet.

Stet: this Hymne[1]

Before As it was . . . *add*: Answer

---

[1] FC omits

73. *The first Sentence is 1 Cor. xv. 20, in the earlier translation: Christ is risen agayne, the fyrste fruytes of them that slepe . . . The second is 1 Cor. v. 7, first added to the Easter Anthems in DB (no. 174). The source of this suggestion of weekly repetition has not been identified.*

74. **Adv.:** This being the first Psalm that is read in the Divine Service, it is meet, that here it be well considered, and resolved, what Translation of the Psalmes shall be followed, through the whole book of Common Prayer.

75. **Adv.:** Also a Rubrick would here be set, that [Throughout the Divine Service, whensoever any Psalm, or Hymn is begun by the Preist, He saying the first verse thereof, the Clarks, and the people that can, are to answer the next verse, and so by courses to the end thereof.

   Part. 23: The *Gloria Patri*, & ye *Venite Exultemus* are appointed next to be Said or Sung; but whether by the Minister alone, or by him & ye people *alternatim*, there is not here nor elswhere (in ye Hymnes and Psalmes following besides ye *Quicunque vult*,) any Order given; wch for an uniformitie herin ought in this place to be added.

   Cf. S III: . . . so that our manner of singing by Sides, or all together, or in severall parts, or in the People's answering the Priest in repeating the Psalms and Hymns, is here grounded . . .

   S I collects a number of patristic precedents for antiphonal singing. Cf. no. 105 ('by sides').

76. **Adv.:** The first Rubrick, is to be divided, and the last part of it to be set formost, thus,
   At the end of every Psalm that is read, and likewise, at the end of the Benedictus, Benedicite, Magnificat, and Nunc dimittis, the Preist shall say,
   Glory be to the Father, and to] etc.

   Answer

   As it was in the beginning, is now, and etc.
   [Here shall follow the Psalmes that are appointed for this day of ye Moneth, except there be some Proper Psalmes appointed for it.]

   Part. 25: In ye same Rubrick ye *Gloria Patri* &c is appointed to be said at ye End of Every Psalme throughout the yeere. There is a difference betweene many, whether it ought to be said by vertue of this order at ye End of every portion of ye 119th Psalme, wch are appointed for so many Psalmes upon ye 24. 25. & 26. dayes of the Moneth; for if it shall not be said before ye whole Psalme bee ended, it will not be said during three whole dayes together. To avoyd this doubt, an Explanation of ye Rubrick is here needfull.

Then shall be read two Lessons distinctly with a loude voice, that the people may heare. The first of the olde Testament. The second of the New, like as they be appointed in the Kalender, except there bee proper Lessons assigned for that day. The Minister that readeth the Lesson standing and turning him so, as hee may best be heard of all such as be present.

And before euery Lesson, the Minister shall say thus, The first, second, third, or fourth chapter of Genesis, or Exodus, Matthew, Marke, or other like, as is appointed in the Kalender. And in the end of euery Chapter he shall say, 𝕳𝖊𝖗𝖊 𝖊𝖓𝖉𝖊𝖙𝖍 𝖘𝖚𝖈𝖍 𝖆 𝕮𝖍𝖆𝖕𝖙𝖊𝖗 𝖔𝖋 𝖘𝖚𝖈𝖍 𝖆 𝕭𝖔𝖔𝖐𝖊.

And to the end the people may the better heare, in such places where they do sing, there shall the Lessons be sung in a plaine tune, after the mañer of distinct reading: and likewise the Epistle and Gospel.

After the first Lesson, shall follow *Te Deum laudamus* in English, dayly throughout the whole yeere.

𝖂𝖊 𝖕𝖗𝖆𝖎𝖘𝖊 𝖙𝖍𝖊𝖊, 𝕺 𝕲𝖔𝖉:

   •   •   •   •   •   •

77. *i. Read*: Then shall the two Lessons appointed be read distinctly & audibly. He that readeth so standing and turning him self, as hee may best be heard of all such as be present.

ii. Read: Then shall be read the two Lessons appointed distinctly & with a loud voice, yt ye people may heare: he that readeth . . .

78. *i. Read*: And before every Lesson he shall say [Here begiñeth,] & after every Lesson, [Here &c such a Chapter (or verse of that Chapter) of such a Booke. & after the same, Here endeth the First, (or the Second) Lesson.

ii. Read: And before every Lesson he shall say [Here begiñeth,] such a Chapter (or verse of such a Chapter) of such a Booke. & after every Lesson, Here endeth the First, (or the Second) Lesson.

79. Omittd.

80. *i. Read*: After the first Lesson, shall be said or sung this Hymne of S. Ambrose (Te Deum laudamus), as followeth.

ii. Read: . . . shall be sung, or said *Te Deū laudamus in English daily throughout ye whole yeare, as followeth.
*Italick.

Part. 26: And it is as needfull to name the *Jubilate* after ye *Benedictus*, & ye *Cantate Dño* after ye
Magnificat, & ye *Deus misereatur* after ye *Nunc dimittis*; for els some men shall be in
doubt, whether they may repeat ye *Gloria Patri* &c after these Psalmes or no.

SL: . . . And the people shall answer. As it was . . .

> *Again S enters Adv. rather than SL (cf. no. 71).*
> *For the addition of* Te Deum, *cf. no. 81.*

77.   *Stylistic improvements.*

78.   *Cf. nos. 211 and 212 (Epistle and Gospel).*

79. **Adv.:**   The last Rubrick of this Page, the most of it is to be left out, for now the Lessons, Epistle,
and Gospell are nowhere sung.

Lords: 6. Whether the Rubrique should not bee mended, where it is (that the Lessons should
bee sung in a plaine tune) why not (read with a distinct voice.)

Cf. S I: For in the Church of Rome they were wont to sing them modulatè, & so they use to
doe still; wch how ancient a custome it is I cannot tell, but sure it cannot boast of
many yeeres . . . So singing of Lessons (what com̃endation soever it may have, as I
my self mislike it not) is not so ancient as the plaine Reading of them according to this
Rubrick & appointment of our Church.

> *The rubric is transferred to no. 28, q.v.*

80. **Adv.:**   [After the First Lesson, the Preist standing up, shall say, Let us now give Prayse unto
Almighty God, and say,]

> We prayse Thee, O God, We, etc.

> *Answer*

> All the earth doth worship. etc.

and so by course unto ye end of that Hymn calld Te Deum: Very requisite it is that
some such words of Exhortation be appointed, wherewth to stirr up the People to
Thanksgiving after every Lesson; Bycause very many are not quick enough of themselves to mark, How ye Church passeth from Reading to Praysing; and it hath bin
a Cavill against the Liturgy, as though it were wanting in this Duty of Prayse.
[Holy, Holy, Holy, Lord God of Tsebaoth,] or, of Hosts.] not [Sabbath.]

SL: After the first Lesson, shall be said or sung *Te Deum laudamus.*

. . . let me neuer be confounded.

Or this Canticle. Benedicite omnia opera, &c.

O Al ye works of the Lord:

    .   .   .   .   .

. . . world without end. Amen.

And after the second Lesson, shall be vsed and said Benedictus in English, as followeth.

81.   *Add*: Glory be to the Father, &c.
As it was &c. (*crossed out*)

82. *i. After* said *add*: or sung
After Benedictus *add*: (the Song of Zachary)
After followeth *add*: But when ye 2 Chapt. of St. Luke is read for ye Lesson, that day this Benedictus is not to be used, said or repeated over againe: but ye 100 Ps. following is to be said after ye Lesson.

  ii. Read: . . . ye first Chapt . . . Benedictus is not to be repeated over againe: but ye 100 Ps. in that case is alwayes to be used.

  iii. Read: And after the second Lesson (except, when it is the first chapter of St. Luke, or the latter part of it) shall be sung, or said Benedictus* (the song of Zachary) in English, as followeth. *Italick

Blessed be the Lord God of Israel:

    .   .   .   .   .

As it was in the beginning, is now, &c.

Add: S. Luke i. 68.[1]

Or this C. Psalme.

O be ioyfull in the Lord . . .

    .   .   .   .   .

As it was in the beginning, is now, &c.

83. *i. Delete* C. *Add in margin*: Psal. 100.
  ii. Add: *Jubilate Deo.
*Italick

Then shall be said the Creede by the Minister and the people, standing.

84. *i. Before* said *add*: sung or
Before Creede *add*: APOSTLES

---

[1] *Originally* S. Luke 2. 68.

Devotions: The Song of S. Ambrose.

> *'As followeth' disallows metrical psalms (so S III, on the rubric before the* Benedictus).
> *S, as usual, restores the original text.*

81. **S I:** The Puritan asks why Gloria Patri is not repeated here as well as at ye end of Benedicite, q. 9.

> *The reference is to the anonymous* Survey of the Book of Common Prayer, *1606.*

82. **Adv.:** After the Second Lesson, the Preist shall say,

> Let us now bless God, as holy Zachary did,

and so he shall begin in English that Hymn, wch was cald The Benedictus, The people
Answering every other verse.

Devotions: The Song of Zachary the Priest, called Benedictvs.

> *1549 gives the reference 'Luc. i', so it was probably not before Cosin when he made the*
> *first entry here. The source of the suggestion embodied in this entry has not been*
> *traced. Luke i was read in its entirety on June 17, and in two parts on Feb. 18 and 19.*

83. **SL:** Jubilate Deo.
BCP: Jubilate.

84. **Adv.:** The last Rubrick thus,

> [Then shall be said the Confession of Fayth, calld the Apostles Creed, by the Minister
> and the people, all standing up.]

SL: Then shall be said or sung the Creede . . .

> *i is a combination of Adv. and SL; ii is based on no. 106; iii is an editorial improvement*
> *by S.*

ii. Add: (except certaine daies on wch ye
Creed of S. Athanasius is to be used in
stead of it, as it is after appointed.)

iii. Read: (except only some few daies in ye
yeare; on wch ye Creed of S. Athanasius
is after appointed to be used in stead
of it.

𝕴 𝕭𝖊𝖑𝖊𝖊𝖚𝖊 𝖎𝖓 𝕲𝖔𝖉 𝖙𝖍𝖊 𝕱𝖆𝖙𝖍𝖊𝖗 𝕬𝖑𝖒𝖎𝖌𝖍𝖙𝖞,
𝖒𝖆𝖐𝖊𝖗 𝖔𝖋 𝖍𝖊𝖆𝖚𝖊𝖓 𝖆𝖓𝖉 𝖊𝖆𝖗𝖙𝖍: 𝖆𝖓𝖉 𝖎𝖓 𝕵𝖊𝖘𝖚𝖘
𝕮𝖍𝖗𝖎𝖘𝖙 𝖍𝖎𝖘 𝖔𝖓𝖊𝖑𝖞 𝕾𝖔𝖓𝖓𝖊 𝖔𝖚𝖗 𝕷𝖔𝖗𝖉; 𝖜𝖍𝖎𝖈𝖍 𝖜𝖆𝖘
𝖈𝖔𝖓𝖈𝖊𝖎𝖚𝖊𝖉 𝖇𝖞 𝖙𝖍𝖊 𝖍𝖔𝖑𝖞 𝕲𝖍𝖔𝖘𝖙, 𝖇𝖔𝖗𝖓𝖊 𝖔𝖋 𝖙𝖍𝖊
𝖁𝖎𝖗𝖌𝖎𝖓 𝕸𝖆𝖗𝖞; 𝖘𝖚𝖋𝖋𝖊𝖗𝖊𝖉 𝖚𝖓𝖉𝖊𝖗 𝕻𝖔𝖓𝖈𝖊 𝕻𝖎𝖑𝖆𝖙𝖊,
𝖜𝖆𝖘 𝖈𝖗𝖚𝖈𝖎𝖋𝖎𝖊𝖉, 𝖉𝖊𝖆𝖉 𝖆𝖓𝖉 𝖇𝖚𝖗𝖎𝖊𝖉, 𝖍𝖊𝖊 𝖉𝖊𝖘𝖈𝖊𝖓𝖉𝖊𝖉
𝖎𝖓𝖙𝖔 𝖍𝖊𝖑𝖑. 𝕿𝖍𝖊 𝖙𝖍𝖎𝖗𝖉 𝖉𝖆𝖞 𝖍𝖊𝖊 𝖗𝖔𝖘𝖊 𝖆𝖌𝖆𝖎𝖓𝖊 𝖋𝖗𝖔𝖒
𝖙𝖍𝖊 𝖉𝖊𝖆𝖉. 𝕳𝖊𝖊 𝖆𝖘𝖈𝖊𝖓𝖉𝖊𝖉 𝖎𝖓𝖙𝖔 𝖍𝖊𝖆𝖚𝖊𝖓, 𝖆𝖓𝖉
𝖘𝖎𝖙𝖙𝖊𝖙𝖍 𝖔𝖓 𝖙𝖍𝖊 𝖗𝖎𝖌𝖍𝖙 𝖍𝖆𝖓𝖉 𝖔𝖋 𝕲𝖔𝖉 𝖙𝖍𝖊 𝕱𝖆𝖙𝖍𝖊𝖗
𝕬𝖑𝖒𝖎𝖌𝖍𝖙𝖎𝖊. 𝕱𝖗𝖔𝖒 𝖙𝖍𝖊𝖓𝖈𝖊 𝖍𝖊𝖊 𝖘𝖍𝖆𝖑𝖑 𝖈𝖔𝖒𝖊 𝖙𝖔
𝖎𝖚𝖉𝖌𝖊 𝖙𝖍𝖊 𝖖𝖚𝖎𝖈𝖐𝖊 𝖆𝖓𝖉 𝖙𝖍𝖊 𝖉𝖊𝖆𝖉. 𝕴 𝖇𝖊𝖑𝖊𝖊𝖚𝖊 𝖎𝖓 𝖙𝖍𝖊
𝖍𝖔𝖑𝖞 𝕲𝖍𝖔𝖘𝖙, 𝖙𝖍𝖊 𝖍𝖔𝖑𝖞 𝕮𝖆𝖙𝖍𝖔𝖑𝖎𝖖𝖚𝖊 𝕮𝖍𝖚𝖗𝖈𝖍, 𝖙𝖍𝖊
𝕮𝖔𝖒𝖒𝖚𝖓𝖎𝖔𝖓 𝖔𝖋 𝕾𝖆𝖎𝖓𝖙𝖘, 𝖙𝖍𝖊 𝖋𝖔𝖗𝖌𝖎𝖚𝖊𝖓𝖊𝖘𝖘𝖊 𝖔𝖋
𝖘𝖎𝖓𝖓𝖊𝖘, 𝖙𝖍𝖊 𝖗𝖊𝖘𝖚𝖗𝖗𝖊𝖈𝖙𝖎𝖔𝖓 𝖔𝖋 𝖙𝖍𝖊 𝖇𝖔𝖉𝖞, 𝖆𝖓𝖉 𝖙𝖍𝖊
𝖑𝖎𝖋𝖊 𝖊𝖚𝖊𝖗𝖑𝖆𝖘𝖙𝖎𝖓𝖌. 𝕬𝖒𝖊𝖓.

85.   *New paragraph.*
Read: who   Stet

Read: Pontius Pilate . . .
Read: . . . buried: Hee . . .

Read: . . . dead: Hee . . .

New paragraph.
Read: . . . Ghost; the *and so to the
end.*

Add: Upon these feasts, Christmas
day &c. ut infra to ye end of S.
Athanasius Creede.   (*crossed out*)

And after that, these prayers following, as well
at Euening prayer, as at morning prayer, all
deuoutly kneeling, the Minister first pronouncing
with a loud voice.

86.   *Delete* as well . . . morning prayer.

𝕿𝖍𝖊 𝕷𝖔𝖗𝖉 𝖇𝖊 𝖜𝖎𝖙𝖍 𝖞𝖔𝖚.
                    Answere.
𝕬𝖓𝖉 𝖜𝖎𝖙𝖍 𝖙𝖍𝖞 𝖘𝖕𝖎𝖗𝖎𝖙.
                    Minister.
¶ 𝕷𝖊𝖙 𝖚𝖘 𝖕𝖗𝖆𝖞.
𝕷𝖔𝖗𝖉 𝖍𝖆𝖚𝖊 𝖒𝖊𝖗𝖈𝖞 𝖚𝖕𝖔𝖓 𝖚𝖘.
Christ haue mercy vpon vs.
𝕷𝖔𝖗𝖉 𝖍𝖆𝖚𝖊 𝖒𝖊𝖗𝖈𝖞 𝖚𝖕𝖔𝖓 𝖚𝖘.

Add: Answ. Lord &c.
        Answ. Christ &c.
        Answ. Lord &c.
(*crossed out*)

Then the Minister, Clerkes, and people, shall say
the Lords prayer in English, with a loude voice.

Delete in English[1]
For which *read*: who   Stet, *and so passim*

𝕺𝖚𝖗 𝕱𝖆𝖙𝖍𝖊𝖗 𝖜𝖍𝖎𝖈𝖍 𝖆𝖗𝖙 𝖎𝖓 𝖍𝖊𝖆𝖚𝖊𝖓, &𝖈.

Then the Minister standing vp, shall say.

Print it on at large as before.[2]

For Minister *read*: Priest[2]

---

[1] FC: *no alteration.*   [2] FC: *in text.*

85. **Adv.:** In the Creed,

     [His onely Sonne, our Lord, Who was conceived, etc.]

Devotions: Pontius Pilate. *The Creed is divided into three paragraphs.*
     The rubric at the end refers to nos. 105 and 106. It is in accordance with no. 106. ii, but is
     cancelled by no. 106. iii.

86. **Adv.:** After, Let us pray, the Minister, Clarks, and people shall all say together,

     [Lord, have mercy] etc.
     [Our Father, who art in Heaven, hallowed] &c.

     The words 'as well . . . morning prayer' are omitted as being not strictly true, since the
     Collects at Evening Prayer are different from those that follow here.

     The six-fold Kyrie (as in the Litany) is often suggested in DB, though it is not to be
     found in any of the usual sources, but it is nowhere finally retained.

✠ **Lord shew thy mercy vpon vs.**

    Answere.

And grant vs thy Saluation.

    Priest.

✠ **Lord saue the King.**

    Answere.

And mercifully heare vs when we call vpon thee.

    Priest.

Indue thy Ministers with righteousnesse.

    Answere.

And make thy chosen people ioyfull.

    Priest.

✠ **Lord saue thy people.**

    Answere.

And blesse thine inheritance.

    Priest.

Giue peace in our time, ✠ Lord.

    Answere.

Because there is none other that fighteth for vs, but onely thou, ✠ God.

    Priest.

✠ **God make cleane our hearts within vs.**

    Answere.

And take not thy holy Spirit from vs.

Then shall follow three Collects. The first of the day, which shalbe the same that is appointed at the Communion. The second, for peace. The third for grace to liue well. And the two last Collects shall neuer alter but daily be said at Morning prayer throughout all the yere, as foloweth.

The second Collect for peace.

✠ **God, which art Authour of peace . . . through the might of Jesus Christ our Lord, Amen.**

The third Collect for Grace.

---

87. *Read*: Let thy Priests be clothed with righteousnesse.

And let thy chosen ministers be ioyfull. *Stet as printed.*

Read:
  i. For there is none other that can help us,
  ii. . . . that helpeth us . . .
  iii. . . . that saveth us from our enemies,
  iv. Stet

88. *i. Read*: Then shall be said the Collect of the day, which shalbe the same that is appointed at the Communion. And these two Collects folowing.
  ii. Stet totū.

89. *Delete* second   Stet
  Add: & defence. (*crossed out*)
  Before Authour *add*: the (*crossed out*)

90. *Delete* third   Stet
  Add: to live well (*crossed out*)

87. **Adv.:** In the last line of that Page, the word [People] should be left out, thus,

Answer.
And make Thy Chosen joyfull.
The text suggested in DB is that of the A.V., not of the BCP.

88. **Devotions:** Then the Collects proper for the week, with these Prayers following.

Part. 27: Before the Collects at Morng & Eveng Prayer, it is appointed that the first Collect shalbe that of the day wch is appointed at ye Comūnion: & ye Collect for Peace to be always ye Second. But when a feastday falls upon a Sunday, it is not said here, wch of the Collects appointed for either of those dayes shalbe read; or whether they may both be read one after another. Somewhat therfore is wanting to settle an uniformitie herein. q

When ye Comūnion Service is read, this Collect is repeated ye second time. Wch were fitt to be so ordered yt at one & ye same Service, or assembly of the Church, it should be said but once, at ye Comūnion Service only.

89. **Adv.:** The title of that second Collect would be

[For Peace, and Defense.]
[O God, Who art]

Devotions: O God, Which art the Author . . .

90. **Adv.:** At ye third Collect, a Rule in ye margen, yf it be after Nine of the clock in the morning, to read it,

[Who hast safely brought us through the beginning of this day, defend us in the same,]
'to live well': BCP (at no. 88).

𝖔 𝕷𝖔𝖗𝖉 𝖔𝖚𝖗 𝖍𝖊𝖆𝖚𝖊𝖓𝖑𝖞 𝕱𝖆𝖙𝖍𝖊𝖗 . . . 𝖙𝖍𝖗𝖔𝖚𝖌𝖍
𝕵𝖊𝖘𝖚𝖘 𝕮𝖍𝖗𝖎𝖘𝖙 𝖔𝖚𝖗 𝕷𝖔𝖗𝖉, 𝕬𝖒𝖊𝖓.

91. *i. Add*: In places & Quires where they
          sing, here followeth ye Antheme.
    ii. Read: In Quires & places . . .

92. *i.* Here print ye Collects for the King
          Queene & Clergy.[1] with this
          prayer
          Prevent us O Lord in &c.
          The Grace of our Lord. &c.
          Place here a fleuron.
          And after that print here Athana-
          sius's Creed & ye Rubrick before
          it.
    ii. For with this prayer
          Prevent us O Lord in &c.
      read: with this finall prayer
          Almighty God, who hast promised
          to heare ye petitions &c.
   iii. After Here print *add*: at large
      For promised to heare ye petitions *read*:
      given us grace

¶ An order for Euening prayer throughout the yeere.
The Priest shall say.

Place this Title on the other side.

93. *i. Read*: After the Sentences of Scrip-
          ture, Exhortation &c as is before
          appointed, the Priest & ye people
          with him (all kneeling) shall say
          the Lord's prayer.[2]
    ii. For &c *read*: Confession, & Absolution

𝖔𝖚𝖗 𝕱𝖆𝖙𝖍𝖊𝖗 𝖜𝖍𝖎𝖈𝖍 𝖆𝖗𝖙 𝖎𝖓 𝖍𝖊𝖆𝖚𝖊𝖓, &𝖈.

94.   *For* which *read*: who
      Print it out at large to — from Evill.
      Amen.[3]

---

[1] FC *gives the opening words of each Collect.*   [2] FC *omits the Lord's prayer.*   [3] FC *in text.*

91.   *This rubric rests on the Elizabethan Injunction permitting a hymn 'in the end of the common prayers'. Cf. S II (referring to no. 79):*

           As in Cathedrall & Collegiate Churches, or where there be many Priests and Clerks together, yt are skilfull to doe it.
        The correction to 'Quires & places' must have been made at once, as it alone is found at no. 104. Cf. no. 79: 'places where they do sing'.

92. **SL:**   After this Collect ended, followeth the Letany: and if the Letany be not appointed to be said or sung that morning, then shall next be said the prayer for the Kings Majestie, with the rest of the prayers following at the end of the Letany, and the Benediction.

    S III: ... by virtue of the Queen's Injunctions, allowing an Anthem to be sung after Morning and Evening Prayer, and the Collect for the Queen to be daily said after the Anthem: So that this, and the other that follow before St. Chrysostom's Prayer ... are ... to be said after an Anthem or Psalm, in the end of Morning and Evening Service.

        The practice of SL and S III had evidently become general: it is confirmed by Sparrow:
        Then the Prayers for the King and Bishops and the whole Church ...
        and L'Estrange (see no. 104); and it is now only regularized. Similarly, the use of 'Almighty God, who hast promised to hear the petitions . . .' is paralleled in the Devotions, where it ends the Litany, and in C. Hatton's Psalter of David (1644; attributed with much probability to Jeremy Taylor), in both of which it is called 'A Prayer wherewith to conclude all our Devotions'; and in Adv., which recommends the use here of all the Collects at the end of the Communion Service (see no. 272); the latter is presumably responsible for the choice of 'Prevent us, O Lord . . .'. By 'the Benediction', SL means what is now usually called 'the Grace', a usage in which it is supported by Taylor (see no. 402).

93. **Adv.:**   A first Rubrick here let be,
        The Preist beginning the Lds Prayer, all shall kneel down, and say it wth him.

    Part. 28: At ye beginning of Evening Prayer, ye Rubrick only is that ye Priest shall say — Our Father &c. wch gives occasion to divers Curates, to begin this Eveng Prayer wth ye *Pater nr*, & to omitt what is before appointed to be said at ye Beging both of Morng & likewise of *Eveng Prayer daily throughout ye yeere.* That therfore ye Sentences, ye Exhortation, & ye Confession with the Absolution following, (wch are all but preparatory both to Morng & Eveng Service,) be never omitted, it is requisite that in this place some word of direction or Reference were given to ye former Rubrick.

    SL: After the sentences, exhortation, confession, and absolution, as is appointed at morning prayer, the Presbyter shall say or sing.

        The point made by Part. 28 is already found in S I and S III. The new rubric is a combination of SL and Adv., giving effect to Part. 28. It is noteworthy that here 'with him' appears at once, whereas at no. 68 it only appeared at the fourth stage of drafting. This suggests that the various stages followed each other at once in Morning Prayer, before the revisers went on to Evening Prayer.

94.   *Cf. no. 69.*

Then likewise he shall say.

95.   *i. Read*: Then shall all stand up, & the
                 Priest shall say
         ii. Read: Then the Preist shall say
         iii. Stet as printed.

✠ **Lord open thou our lips.**   Psal. 51. 15.[1]

       Answere.
And our mouth shall shew forth thy praise.

       Priest.
✠ **God make speed to saue vs.**   Psal. 70. 1.[1]

       Answere.
✠ **Lord, make haste to helpe vs.**

       Priest.   **96.**   *Read*: All heere stand up, & the Priest sth
Glory be to the Father, and to the Sonne: *(crossed out)*
and to the Holy Ghost.

                                                        Add: Answere.

As it was in the beginning, is now, and euer
shall be: world without end. Amen.
                                                        Add: Priest.
Praise ye the Lord.   Answ. The Lords Name be praised.
                                                        (crossed out)

Then the Psalmes in order as they be appointed   **97.**   *i. After* Then *add*: shalbe said or sung
in the Table for Psalmes, except there be proper   *ii. Read*: shalbe sung or said
Psalmes appointed for that day. Then a Lesson of   *Delete* in the Table . . . that day.
the olde Testament, as it is appointed likewise in   *For* Then *read*: And   Stet Then
the Kalender, except there be proper Lessons ap-   *For* except . . . day *read*: or in ye
pointed for that day. After that, *Magnificat* in   Table for proper Lessons.
English, as followeth.   *Before* After *add*: And
                                                                  After Magnificat *add*: (ye Song of
My soule doth magnifie the Lord . . . world   the blessed Virgin Mary)
without end. Amen.   *Delete* in English   Stet

Or else this Psalme.   **98.**   *i. Add*: except it be on ye 19th day of
                                                                  ye month, because it is then said
✠ **sing vnto the Lord a new song: . . .**   in ye course of ye Psalter.
As it was in the beginning, is now, &c.   *ii. For* because it is then said *read*:
                                                                  when it is said
                                                                  Bracket the clause.

---

[1] *FC omits.*

95.   *Cf. no. 70.*

96. **Adv.:** A second Rubrick, after [Make haste to help us], here shall all stand up, and the Preist
              shall say,
              [Glory be to the Father, and to the Sonne, and] &c.
                          Answer.
              As it was in the beginning, is now, and, &c.

                          Preist.
              Prayse ye the Lord.

                          Answer.
              The Lord's Name be praysed.

SL: Glory be to the Father . . . world without end. Amen.
              All standing up, as often as it is repeated.

                          Presbyter.
              Praise ye the Lord.

                          Answer.
              The Lords Name be praised.
                          Cf. nos. 71 and 72.

97. **Adv.:** Then this Rubrick,
              After the Psalmes for the day be sayd, the first Lesson shall be read, and then shall
              follow in English the Hymn cald the Magnificat, the Preist first distinctly saying,
              [Let us give Prayse to God, wth the same words that the Blessed Virgin did.
              It is very requisite to express this Exhortation thus, bycause of those words spoken of
              Hirself, [All generations shall call Mee blessed.]

Devotions: The Magnificat of the blessed Virgin Marie.

98. **Adv.:** Or, Let us prayse God, and say the *98th* Psalm of David.
                          Cf. no. 35.

Then a Lesson of the New Testament. And after that, Nunc dimittis in English, as followeth.

𝕷𝖔𝖗𝖉 𝖓𝖔𝖜 𝖑𝖊𝖙𝖙𝖊𝖘𝖙 𝖙𝖍𝖔𝖚 . . . 𝖜𝖔𝖗𝖑𝖉 𝖜𝖎𝖙𝖍𝖔𝖚𝖙 𝖊𝖓𝖉. 𝕬𝖒𝖊𝖓.

99. *After* Testament *add*: as it is appointed
     After dimittis *add*: (ye Song of Simeon)
     Delete in English   Stet
     Nunc dimittis   Italick

Or else this Psalme.

𝕲𝖔𝖉 𝖇𝖊 𝖒𝖊𝖗𝖈𝖎𝖋𝖚𝖑𝖑 𝖛𝖓𝖙𝖔 𝖚𝖘 . . . 𝖜𝖔𝖗𝖑𝖉 𝖜𝖎𝖙𝖍𝖔𝖚𝖙 𝖊𝖓𝖉. 𝕬𝖒𝖊𝖓.

100. *Add*: (except it be on ye 12th day of the Month.)

Then shall follow the Creed with other prayers, as is before appointed at Morning prayer after Benedictus, and with three Collects. First of the day. The second for peace. The third for aide against all perils, as hereafter followeth: which two last Collects shall be daily said at Euening prayer without alteration.

101. *i. Read*: Then shall follow three Collects. The First of the day. And these two Collects following.
      ii. Add: Print here againe (as at Morning prayer)
      Then shalbe said &c
      I Believe in God &c   unto & these two Collects following.
      iii. After prayer) *add*: (except ye mention of Athanasius Creed)
      iv. Delete & these two Collects following (*ii*) *and read*: & take not thy H.Sp. frō us.
      For (i) *read*: Then shall follow three Collects. The first of the day . . . Stet frō hence.[1]

The second Collect at Euening prayer.

𝕺 𝕲𝖔𝖉, 𝖋𝖗𝖔𝖒 𝖜𝖍𝖔𝖒 𝖆𝖑𝖑 𝖍𝖔𝖑𝖞 𝖉𝖊𝖘𝖎𝖗𝖊𝖘 . . . 𝖙𝖍𝖆𝖙 𝖇𝖔𝖙𝖍 𝖔𝖚𝖗 𝖍𝖊𝖆𝖗𝖙𝖘 𝖒𝖆𝖞 𝖇𝖊 𝖘𝖊𝖙 . . . 𝕵𝖊𝖘𝖚𝖘 𝕮𝖍𝖗𝖎𝖘𝖙 𝖔𝖚𝖗 𝕾𝖆𝖚𝖎𝖔𝖚𝖗. 𝕬𝖒𝖊𝖓.

102. *Read*: The Collect for peace & defence.   Stet
      For that both *read*: both that[2]
      Add:
      The Collect for Grace & protection.
      O almighty Lord & everlasting God, vouchsafe wee beseech thee to direct sanctifie & governe both our hearts & bodies in ye wayes of thy Laws, & in the works of thy comdmts, yt through thy most mighty protection both here & ever wee may be preserved in body & soule, through our Lord and Saviour Jesus Christ. Amen. (*crossed out*)
      Print here ye Collects for ye King &c as before at Morning prayer. (*crossed out*)

---

[1] FC: Then shalbe sung or said ye Apostle's Creed by ye Min'r, & ye people standing.
I Beleeve in God &c.
Print it out at large wth all the Rubricks Prayers, & Suffrages after it, to — thy Holy Spirit from us.
Then read: Then shall follow three Collects. The first of the day . . .
[2] FC: *no alteration.*

99. **Adv.:** Then shall be read the 2d Lesson; And after it shall be sayd in English, the Hymn, cald Nunc dimittis, the Preist first saying,

[Let us give Prayse unto God, as old Symeon did.]

Devotions: The Song of Simeon, called Nunc Dimittis.

100. **Adv.:** or Wth the *67th* Psalm of David.

Cf. no. 35.

101. **Adv.:** Leave out the last words of the first Rubrick, [wthout alteration.]

ii corresponds with no. 88. i; iii is an afterthought of Cosin's; iv, like no. 88. ii, is the restoration of the original by S.

102. **Adv.:** In the Second Collect for Peace, it is Nonsense, and abominable falssation to say, [That both our harts,] either leave the word [Both] quite out, or read it, [Both that our harts may be set,] &c.

'*& defence*': *cf. no. 89.*
'*The Collect for Grace and protection*' *inserted before the third Collect is the second of the* '*Collects to be said after the Offertory*' *printed at the end of the Communion Service. The rubric permits these to be said after the Collects of Morning and Evening Prayer, and is amended by no. 272 to* '*before ye finall Collect*' (*cf. no. 103*). '*Print here . . .*' *is surely an error.*

The third Collect for aide against all perils.   103.   *Read*: The finall Collect for defence . . .   Stet

𝕷ighten our darkenesse we beseech thee, ☧
𝕷ord, and by thy great mercy defend vs from
all perils and dangers of this night, for the
loue of thy onely Sonne our Sauiour Jesus
Christ. Amen.

Read: Lighten the darkness of our
hearts, we beseech thee, O Lord,
by thy gracious visitation, and of
thy great mercy defend vs from
all terrours & dangers of the night,
for the loue . . .[1]

104.   i. *Add*: In Quires & places where they
sing here followeth ye Antheme.
Here print the Collects for ye King,
Q. & Clergy, wth this prayer
Prevent us O Lord &c
&
The Grace of our Ld &c
(*crossed out*)
ii. *Read*: In Quires &c as at M. pr. & yn ye
prayers for ye K. Q. BB. yt of Chrysost.
the grace of our Ld at large as before.[2]
Thus endeth ye Order of Ev. pr. thr. ye
yeare.
Ital. lett.

Place here a faire fleuron.

In the Feasts of Christmas, the Epiphanie, Saint   105.   i. *Read*: Upon these Feasts; Christmas
Matthie, Easter, the Ascension, Pentecost, Saint   Day, the Epiphanie, Saint Mat-
Iohn Baptist, Saint Iames, Saint Bartholomew,   thias, Easter Day, the Ascension,
Saint Matthew, Saint Simon and Iude, Saint   Whitsunday . . . Saint Simon and
Andrew, and Trinity Sunday shall be sung or   S. Iude, Saint Andrew, and upon
said, immediately after *Benedictus*, this Confession   Trinity Sunday shall be sung or
of our Christian faith.   said, at Morning prayer, in stead
of the Apostles Creed, this Con-
fession of our Christian faith,
(comonly called The Creed of
St Athanasius.) one vse by ye
Priest & another by ye people; or
in Colledges, & where there is a
Quire, by sides.
ii. *Delete* or in Colledges . . . by sides.

---

103. **Adv.:** In the Third Collect, [Perils and Dangers] is idem per idem.

That this Prayer also is to be sayd in the afternoons in Summer, is but very improper, unles it shall be thought fit to say it, thus,

Lighten the Darknes, we beseech thee, ô Lord, that the Night will bring upon us, and by Thy great Mercy defend us from all Dangers of the same, for the Love of thy onely Sonne our Saviour Jesus Xt. Amen.

BCP (Collect for Advent III): Lord, wee beseech thee, giue eare to our prayers, and by thy gracious visitation, lighten the darkenesse of our hearts, by our Lord Jesus Christ.

'*finall*': *cf. no. 272 (quoted at no. 102).*

The Collect is conflated with that for Advent III, now to be replaced by a new one composed by Cosin. The incongruity of saying 'this night' in the afternoon is easily remedied by altering it to 'the night'. This achieves the same result as Wren's cumbrous phrase.

104. **SL:** Then shall follow the prayer for the Kings Majesty, with the rest of the prayers at the end of the Letany, to the Benediction.

L'Estrange comments on the SL rubric:

A very necessary Rubrick. For though use and custome had stated in our Churches a practice conformable to it, annexing those Prayers to the Morning and Evening service, yet the want of expresse rule for its establishment, left our Liturgy, in this point, not altogether inobnoxious to exceptions.

Cf. nos. 91 and 92: i corresponds to no. 92. i; ii to no. 92. iii. 'Thus endeth ...' is taken from no. 107. Wren's suggestion (at no. 272, referred to at no. 92) may be responsible for the addition of 'Prevent us, O Lord'.

105. **Adv.:** In the great Rubrick there following, chang the Epiphany, and for [Pentecost] read [Whitsunday.]

Add to the end of the Rubrick,

[This Confession of the Christian Fayth, cald Quicunque vult, in ye place of th' Apostles Creed.]

Part. 48: . . . *Athanasius his Creed* . . .

Wren, *Particular Orders:* 6. . . . in stead & place of ye Apostles Creed.

Cosin, *Regni Angliae Religio Catholica, 1656:* . . . in quibusdam vero festis Symbolum quod dicitur S. Athanasii.

S III: And though it be not here set down, yet I believe the meaning was, that the Apostles Creed should be omitted that Day, when this of Athanasius was repeated.

L'Estrange, followed by Brightman (I. ccxv), points out that the attribution to Athanasius had been challenged by Gerard Voss in 1642, followed by Archbp. Ussher in 1647. Hence, perhaps, the insertion of 'commonly called'.

106. i. Leave out this here & print it out at
        morning prayer.
     ii. *Read*: . . . at the Aples Creed.
    iii. *Read*: . . . before the Aples Creed at
        M.pr.
     iv. *Read*: . . . att the end of Morng prayer.[1]

Quicunque vult.

𝔚𝔥𝔬𝔰𝔬𝔢𝔲𝔢𝔯 𝔴𝔦𝔩𝔩 𝔟𝔢 𝔰𝔞𝔲𝔢𝔡 . . . 𝔚𝔥𝔦𝔠𝔥 𝔉𝔞𝔦𝔱𝔥,
𝔢𝔵𝔠𝔢𝔭𝔱 𝔢𝔲𝔢𝔯𝔶 𝔬𝔫𝔢 𝔡𝔬𝔢 𝔨𝔢𝔢𝔭 𝔥𝔬𝔩𝔶 𝔞𝔫𝔡 𝔲𝔫𝔡𝔢𝔣𝔦𝔩𝔢𝔡
. . . 𝔅𝔲𝔱 𝔱𝔥𝔢 𝔴𝔥𝔬𝔩𝔢 𝔱𝔥𝔯𝔢𝔢 𝔭𝔢𝔯𝔰𝔬𝔫𝔰 . . . 𝔄𝔰 𝔦𝔱
𝔴𝔞𝔰 𝔦𝔫 𝔱𝔥𝔢 𝔟𝔢𝔤𝔦𝔫𝔫𝔦𝔫𝔤, 𝔦𝔰 𝔫𝔬𝔴, &𝔠.

Thus endeth the order of Morning and Euening
prayer throughout the whole yeere.

107.   *Read*: At Morning Prayer.

       For holy *read*: whole
       For the whole *read*: all the   Stet

       Read: Thus endeth the Order of Morn.
          Pr. throughout ye yeare.[2] Ital. lett.

       Here sett a fayre fleuron.

---

[1] FC: Print this Rubric, & the Creed following at ye end of Morning Prayer.   [2] FC *omits*.

106.   *ii is carried out by no. 84, iv by no. 92.*

107. **Adv.:**   Leave out yt Latin Title, Quicunque vult.

    SL: . . . whole and undefiled . . . (**Sarum:** integram inviolatamque)

¶ Here followeth the Letanie, to be vsed vpon Sundayes, Wednesdayes, and Fridayes, and at other times when it shalbe commanded by the Ordinarie.

108. *i.* *Add*: The Litanie   (*crossed out*)
      For Letanie *read*: Litanie
      For vsed *read*: said or sung after Morning prayer
      Bracket and at . . . Ordinarie.
   ii. *After* Litanie *add*: or publick Supplication
      For said or sung *read*: sung or said

109. *i.* *Add*: The Priest (or Clarks) kneeling in ye midst of ye Quire, & all the people kneeling & answering, as followeth.
   ii. *For* Clarks *read*: Minister   Stet

Ⓞ God the Father of heauen . . .

.   .   .   .   .   .

From all sedition and priuie conspiracie, from all false doctrine and heresie, from hardnesse of heart, and contempt of thy word and Commandement.

Good Lord deliuer vs.

.   .   .   .   .   .

110. *i.* *Read*: From all open Rebellion & Sedition, from secret Conspiracie & all Treason, from all false Doctrine, Heresie & Schisme, from hardnesse . . .
   ii. *For* from secret . . . Treason *read*: from all Conspiracie & Treason

By thine agonie and blood Sweat . . .

.   .   .   .   .   .

111.   *For* blood *read*: bloody[1]

thy holy Church vniuersally . . .

.   .   .   .   .   .

For universally *read*: universall

thy seruant James . . .

For James *read*: Charles

_____

[1] FC *in text*.

108. **Adv.:** That Rubrick, thus,

> Here followeth the Publike Supplication, cald the Letany, to be sayd next after the 3 Collects, on Sundayes, Wednesdayes, & Frydaies, and at other times, when the Ordinary appointeth it.

Chang the Title, into [The Publike Supplication] and so to the end of it.

Part. 29: In ye Rubrick before ye Litany there is no Appointmt at what time of ye day, or after what part of the Service it ought to be said; so yt a contentious man may take his libertie to say it after Evening prayer or at any time of ye day upon Sundayes, Wedensdayes, & Fridays &c, at his owne choyce, unlesse an order be here added to confine him.

SL: . . . to be used after the third Collect at Morning prayer . . .

Cf. S III: By the Position of it in this place (though it be not specified after what part of the Service it shall be used) it seems that they intended it to follow the Morning Prayer.

109. **Part. 29, cont.:** Nor is ye place of ye Church here specified, where it shall be said; though in ye Rubrick before ye Comination it is presumed yt a peculiar place is appointed for it, and in Q. Elizab. Injunctions, yt appointed place is said to be in ye Midst of ye Quire, as in Cathedrall & many other Churches hath bin accustomed.

Injunctions: 18. . . . The Pryestes with other of the Quyre, shall kneele in the myddes of the Churche, and syng or say playnely and distinctly the Letany . . .

> *Cosin's copy of the Injunctions is preserved at Durham; in it he has underlined the words 'kneele in the myddes of the', but not the word 'Churche', which begins the next line. It will be noticed that the word 'Quyre' occurs just before the words underlined. Thus it is just possible that the substitution of 'Quire' for 'Church', which has earned Cosin much criticism, was accidental; especially as in S I he has copied from Andrewes the words:*
> *The Letanie to be said or sung in ye midst of ye church. Iniunct. Eliz.*

110. **Adv.:** [O God the Father from Heaven.]

Also.

> [From all Rebellion, Treason, Sedition and Conspiracy, from all fals Doctrine Haeresy, and Blasphemy, from Schism, and Faction, from hardnes of hart, and contempt of Thy Word & Comandment.]

111. **Adv.:** Also, [By thyne Agony and Sweat, as drops of Bloud, by thy Cross and Passion], &c

> [for bloudy sweat is a phrase much quarrelled at.]

Also [. . . holines of life, thy Servant Charles, our Soveraygn Lord the King.

> [To say, [King and Governour] is a Diminution of the former by the latter: Advantages also for Treason have bin pretended to, out of that phrase.

BCP: bloody

Part. 29, cont.: In ye Letanie, where wee pray for the Catholick Church, ye word *universally* is falsely printed: for it ought to be universall, as it is in the Latin *Catholicam.*

1549: universall

That it may please thee to blesse and preserue our Noble Prince Charles, Fredericke
the Prince Elector Palatine, and the Lady
Elizabeth his wife.

We beseech thee to heare vs good Lord.

· · · · ·

112.   i. Here such names as ye King shall
          appoint (yt is) ye Q. & Q. mother[1]
          & ye Heyre apparent. our gracious
          Queene N. &c. & all the Royall
          familie.

      ii. Read: Here such names as ye King shall
          appoint shall be inserted & all the
          Royall familie. & to yt purpose a blanck
          space is to be left between preserve
          -&- (???)[2]

     iii. Read: Here such only are to be named as
          ye King shall appoint & all the Royall
          familie. Leave therfore a blanck space
          between preserve -&- & all the Royall
          familie.

That it may please thee to illuminate all
Bishops, Pastours, and Ministers of the
Church . . .

113.   i. Read: That . . . all Bishops, Priests,
          and Ministers . . .

      ii. Read: That . . . all the Pastors,
          Bishops, and Ministers . . .

     iii. Stet as (i.)

That it may please thee to blesse and keepe
the Magistrates . . .

· · · · ·

114.   i. Before Magistrates add: all the
          subordinate

      ii. For subordinate read: inferior   Stet

Our Father which art in heauen, &c.
And leade vs not into temptation.
But deliuer vs from euill. Amen.

The Versicle.

O Lord deale not with vs after our sinnes.

Answere.

Neither reward vs after our iniquities.

¶ Let vs pray.

O God mercifull Father . . . which the craft
and subtiltie of the deuill or man worketh
against vs . . . through Jesus Christ our
Lord.

115.   Add: Then shall the Priest & the
       people with him say the Lords
       Prayer.
       Print it out at large, as before.

116.   Read: Priest.

       Print it in ye Roman letter.
       (crossed out)
       Add: Priest.
       Read: which the craft of the deuill
       or the subtiltie of man worketh
       against vs   Stet

[1] & Q. mother added later.   [2] Indecipherable.

112. **Adv.:** Leave a space for the Third Petition upon this Page, wth this Rubrick in it,

           [Here to be put in, as by ye Soveraygn shall be appointed, from time to time.

           The King did appoint on 8 November 1661 (Cosin, Correspondence, ii. 38), and repeated his instructions on 20 May 1662 (Parker, dviii).
           There was no Queen Mother from 1619 to 1649, and no Queen from 1649 to 1662; possibly the entry was made after Charles II's betrothal to Katherine of Braganza in May 1661. Cf. no. 122.

113. **Adv.:** Also [That it may please thee to illuminate all Pastors of Thy Church, cald the Bishops, and all other Ministers thereof, wth true knowledge, and, &c.

    Part. 29, cont.: In ye Petition for ye Clergy there is distinction betweene Bpps. & Pastors, wch are all one. Inferior priests were never anciently called pastors.

    SL: ... all Bishops, Presbyters and Ministers of the Church ...
        i is from SL, ii from Adv., or Part.

114. **Adv.:** [That it may please thee to endue the Lords of his Counsell, and all his Nobles with grace, Wisdome, Understanding, and Courage.]
           [That it may please thee to bless all that are in Office, and Magistracy under him, giving, &c.]

    Part. 29, cont.: In ye Petition for ye *Magistrates*, that word would be altered or explayned; for ye *Magistrate* (as wee now understand ye word) is properly None but ye *King*.

    Cf. S II: Those that are subordinate, & have no autoritie but from the King: of ancient time The Word Magistrate had no other Signification; howsoever of late dayes they use it & take it commonly for the Chief Governor in a kingdome, contra Latinae vocis usum; Nam Romanis Magistratus minorum semper potestatū nomen est; as here it is. The Magistrates are here but the Ministers or Servants under the King for Secular affayres.

115.   *Cf. no. 68. iv.*

116. **Adv.:** Leave out ye word [The Versicle] and set in place of it,
           Preist.
    O Lord deale not wth us according to our sinnes.
           Answer.
    Neither reward us according to our iniquities.

    [The craft, and subtilty] are both the same. Will it not goe better, thus, [Wch the subtilty of the Devill, or the craft of man worketh against us,]

    SL: Presbyter. O Lord deal not with us after our sinnes.

O Lord, arise, helpe vs, for thy Names sake.

𝕺 God, wee haue heard . . . before them.

O Lord, arise . . . for thine honour.

Glory be to the Father . . .
As it was in the beginning . . . world without
end. Amen.
From our enemies defend vs, 𝕺 Christ.

Graciously looke vpon our afflictions.

.   .   .   .   .

The Versicle.
𝕺 Lord let thy mercy be shewed vpon vs.

Answere.
As we doe put our trust in thee.

¶ Let vs pray.

We humbly beseech thee . . . for the glory of
thy Names sake, turne from vs all those
euils that wee most righteously¹ haue de=
serued . . . Jesus Christ our Lord. Amen.

¶ A Prayer for the Kings Maiestie.

𝕺 Lord our heauenly Father . . . that hee
may banquish and ouercome . . . through
Jesus Christ our Lord. Amen.

¶ A Prayer for the Prince, and other the Kings
children.

Almighty God, which hast promised to bee a
Father of thine Elect, and of their seed: We
humbly beseech thee to blesse our Noble
Prince Charles, Fredericke the Prince Elector
Palatine, and the Lady Elizabeth his wife
. . . through Jesus Christ our Lord. Amen.

117. *Add*: Ans.   (*crossed out*)
      Pr.   „   „
      Answ.   „   „
      Pr.   „   „
      i. Answ.   *ii.* Answer
      Print it in ye Roman letr.
      Pr.   (*crossed out*)
      Ans.   „   „

Crossed out.   Stet

Crossed out.   Stet
Print it in ye Roman letr.
(*crossed out*)

118. *Read*: . . . of thy Name, turne . . .

119. Leave these 3 prayers unprinted
      here, & sett them after Morning
      & Evening prayer, as before is
      ordered there.²

120. *For* ouercome *read*: subdue   Stet

121. *i. Read*: A Prayer for the Q. & ye
      Royall familie
      where such are only to be named as
      ye King shall appoint.
      ii. Delete the Q. &
      For are only *read*: only are
      Leave therfore a blanck space betw.
      blesse, &— & all ye royall

122. *For* which . . . seed *read*: the foun-
      taine of all goodnes³
      i. For Noble . . . his wife *read*: gracious
      Q. &c
      ii. Read: & all ye Royal family

123. *i. Add*: A prayer for the Clergie, &
      their charge.
      ii. Delete & their charge

---

¹ FC: *delete* most righteously.   ² FC: Leave out this prayer, & the two next heere.   ³ FC *in text*.

117. **Adv.:** Let there be a distinct letter, for [As it was in the beginning &c] thereby to make it an Answer, as all the others are.

Leave out here, [Let us pray.] and so, on ye Page before.

118. **Adv.:** [For the Glory of Thy Names sake.] Is absurd. Leave out ye word [sake.] Some quarrell at [Righteously have deserved] and would have it [Rightly.] But inasmuch as all our righteousnes, is but filthiness, let the Church judg, how it shall be read.

FC deletes 'most righteously', which seems to show that Sancroft was capable of independent action.

119. *Cf. no. 92. Also S III:*

This, and the other that follow before St. Chrysostom's Prayer . . . are no part of the Litany, but only Additionals to be said after an Anthem or Psalm, in the end of Morning and Evening Service.

120. **Adv.:** The first word [Wch] should be, [Who.]

[Vanquish, and overcome] is a vayn & childish Repetition.

121. **Adv.:** Instead of yt Prayer following, let a Rubrick be, To put in such Names, as the Soveraygn shall from time to time appoint, and so to use it.

Part. 30: The Prayer for ye Queene & ye Royall Progeny is not autorized by Act of Parliamt, but first added by ye Order & Comdmt of K. James, & since continued by K. Charles wth some variation agreeable to his owne time & condition. Wch, to free it from any Exception yt a Parliamt might take agt it, were not amisse to be here noted by a speciall Rubrick in ye margin.

BCP (edition of, e.g., 1636): A Prayer for the Queen, Prince CHARLES, and the rest of the Royall progenie.

Cf. no. 112.

122. *'The fountaine of all goodnes' first appeared in the BCP in 1627; it was dropped in 1632, after the birth of an heir, but was reintroduced, for good, in 1633.*

On 8 November 1661 the King commanded this Collect to be read in all churches: Almighty God, the fountaine of all goodness, we humbly beseech thee to bless our most gracious Queen Katherine, Mary the Queen Mother, James Duke of York, and the rest of the Royall Progeny. Endue them . . . (Cosin, Correspondence, ii. 38).

123. **SL:** A Prayer for the holy Clergy.

Almighty and euerlasting God, which onely workest great marueiles, send downe vpon our Bishops, & Curates, and all Congregations committed to their charge, the healthfull Spirit of thy grace, and that they may truely please thee, powre vpon them the continuall dew of thy blessing: Grant this O Lord, for the honor of our Aduocate and Mediatour Jesus Christ. Amen.

⁋ A Prayer of Chrysostome.

Almighty God . . . life euerlasting. Amen.

2. Corinth. 13.

The Grace . . . vs all euermore. Amen.

⁋ For raine if the time require.

O God heauenly Father . . . through Jesus Christ our Lord. Amen.

⁋ For faire weather.

O Lord God, which for the sinne of man diddest once drowne all the world, except eight persons, & afterward of thy great mercie diddest promise neuer to destroy it so againe:

we humbly beseech thee, that although wee for our iniquities haue worthily deserued this plague of Raine and waters, yet vpon our true repentance, thou wilt send vs such weather, whereby wee may receiue the fruits of the earth in due season . . . through Jesus Christ our Lord. Amen.

---

i. *Read*: Almighty . . . God, who didst powre out upõ thy Apostles the great & merveilous Gifts of thy H. Spirit, & from whom all spirituall graces & gifts doe proceed, send downe vpon our Bishops, the Pastors of thy Church, & all others that have cure of Soules under them, together with all Congregations . . .

ii. *For* thy H. Spirit *read*: the H. Ghost
Delete & gifts
For all others . . . under them *read*: such others under them as have cure of Soules

iii. *Stet as printed.*

124.   i. *Read*: The finall Collect, & Prayer of S. Chrysostome.

ii. *Read*: A Prayer of S. Chrysostome.

Read: The Blessing.[1]
1. Cor. 13. (*sic*)

125.   *Add title*:[2]

i. Prayers & Thanksgivings upon severall occasions to be used before ye finall Collect of the Litanie, or of Morning & Evening Prayer, if the time require.

PRAYERS.

ii. *For* Collect *read*: praier

Delete if the time require.

126.   i. *Read*: O Almightie Lord God, though for the sinne of man thou diddest once drowne all the world, except eight persons, yet afterward of thy great mercie thou diddest promise . . .

ii. *Stet as printed, with the addition of* Almightie.

i. *Read*: deserued a plague of Raine & unseasonable weather, yet . . . thou wouldst send us such moderate & seasonable weather, as that wee may receiue . . .

ii. *Read*: . . . Raine & unseasonable showers . . . moderate & kindly weather . . .

---

[1] FC omits.   [2] *For the page-heading* The Letanie *read*: Prayers.

Adv.: Next to that, thus,

> Almighty and everlasting God, from whom proceedeth all Grace, and who onely workest great marvayles, send down upon the Pastors of thy Church, the Bishops, and upon all that stand charged wth Cure of soules, and upon all Congregations committed to their charge, the healthfull Spirit of Thy Grace: And that they may all truly please thee, poure upon them all the continuall Dew of thy blessing; Grant this, ô Lord, for the Honour of our Advocate, and Mediator Jesus Christ. Amen.

Lords: 10. In the Prayer for the Clergy, that phrase perhaps to be altered, *which only worketh great marvails.*

> '*from whom all spirituall graces & gifts doe proceed*': cf. *the second Collect at Evening Prayer* ('*from whom all holy desires . . .*').

124. **Adv.:** After this, leave out ye Rubrick, [A Prayer of Chrysostome.]

Cf. 1552: And the Letany shal euer ende with thys Collecte folowyng.

SL: . . . the Benediction . . .

Sparrow (on Mattins): We end our Service with a BLESSING, which is to be pronounced by the Bishop, if he be present.

> *Cf. nos. 92 and 104.*

125. **S III:** These in the Second of King Edward are set in the end of the Collects after the Offertory, being then only two for Rain and Fair Weather. After in the 5th yeere of King Edw. they were augmented to that number which we have now; but they were placed between the Collects, *We humbly beseech thee*, &c. and St. Chrysostom's Prayer; which is a Direction for us, where to read them, when need is.

126. **Adv.:** Let the second Title be, [For fayre, & seasonable weather,]

> O Lord God, howe're for the sin of man thou didst once drown all the world, except 8 persons, yet afterward of Thy great mercy thou didst promise never to destroy it so agayn: Upon Thy blessed pleasure, ô Lord, depende the gracious influences of Heaven, and the goodnes of every season comes from thee; We humbly beseech thee therfore, that although we for our iniquities have worthily deserved a plague of rayne and of all unseasonable weather, yet upon our true Repentance, and for the meritts of our blessed Redeemer, thou wouldst send us weather so moderate, and kindly, as that we may receive the fruits of the earth in due season, and learn both &c.

Sanderson (Prayers for Fair Weather):

> . . . but yet didst afterwards . . .
> . . . by the long continuance of the late sad and unseasonable weather . . .
> . . . to send us such comfortable and kindly weather . . .

> > *Sanderson's prayers are both free adaptations of the BCP prayer, and the resemblance between some of his additions and Wren's may be regarded as coincidental, and indeed difficult to avoid, granted the subject. In any case, DB is always closer to Wren than to Sanderson.*

In the time of dearth or famine.

𝕺 𝕲𝖔𝖉 𝖍𝖊𝖆𝖚𝖊𝖓𝖑𝖞 𝕱𝖆𝖙𝖍𝖊𝖗 . . . 𝖇𝖊 𝖆𝖑𝖑 𝖍𝖔𝖓𝖔𝖚𝖗, &𝖈.

            i. Add: Amen.
           ii. Read: honour & glory now, & for ever. Amen.

127.   *Add*:   or This

O God mercifull Father who in the time of Elisha the prophet didst suddenly in Samaria turne great scarcetie & dearth into plenty & cheapnes; have mercie upon us, who are now for our sins punished with like adversitie; increase the fruits of ye Earth by thy heavenly Benediction, & grant that wee receiving thy bountifull liberality, may use the same to thy glory, ye relief of those that be needy, & our owne comfort, through Jesus Christ our Lorde. Amen.

In the time of Warre.

𝕺 𝕬𝖑𝖒𝖎𝖌𝖍𝖙𝖞 𝕲𝖔𝖉, 𝕶𝖎𝖓𝖌 𝖔𝖋 𝖆𝖑𝖑 𝖐𝖎𝖓𝖌𝖘, 𝖆𝖓𝖉 𝖌𝖔𝖚𝖊𝖗𝖓𝖔𝖚𝖗 𝖔𝖋 𝖆𝖑𝖑 𝖙𝖍𝖎𝖓𝖌𝖘 . . . 𝕵𝖊𝖘𝖚𝖘 𝕮𝖍𝖗𝖎𝖘𝖙 𝖔𝖚𝖗 𝕷𝖔𝖗𝖉.

128. *i. Read*: In the time of any Warre, or Tumults.
      ii. Read: In the time of Warre, & Tumults.
      For things *read*: men   Stet
      Add: Amen.

In the time of any common Plague or sickenesse.

𝕺 𝕬𝖑𝖒𝖎𝖌𝖍𝖙𝖞 𝕲𝖔𝖉, 𝖜𝖍𝖎𝖈𝖍 𝖎𝖓 𝖙𝖍𝖞 𝖜𝖗𝖆𝖙𝖍

129.   *After* wrath *add*: didst send a plague upon thyne owne people in the wildernes for their obstinate Rebellion against Moses & Aaron, And also

              𝖎𝖓 𝖙𝖍𝖊 𝖙𝖎𝖒𝖊 𝖔𝖋 𝕶𝖎𝖓𝖌 𝕯𝖆𝖚𝖎𝖉, 𝖉𝖎𝖉𝖉𝖊𝖘𝖙 𝖘𝖑𝖆𝖞 𝖜𝖎𝖙𝖍 𝖙𝖍𝖊 𝖕𝖑𝖆𝖌𝖚𝖊 𝖔𝖋 𝖕𝖊𝖘𝖙𝖎𝖑𝖊𝖓𝖈𝖊 𝖙𝖍𝖗𝖊𝖊𝖘𝖈𝖔𝖗𝖊 𝖆𝖓𝖉 𝖙𝖊𝖓 𝖙𝖍𝖔𝖚𝖘𝖆𝖓𝖉, 𝖆𝖓𝖉 𝖞𝖊𝖙 𝖗𝖊𝖒𝖊𝖒𝖇𝖗𝖎𝖓𝖌 𝖙𝖍𝖞 𝖒𝖊𝖗𝖈𝖞, 𝖉𝖎𝖉𝖉𝖊𝖘𝖙 𝖘𝖆𝖚𝖊 𝖙𝖍𝖊 𝖗𝖊𝖘𝖙: 𝖍𝖆𝖚𝖊 𝖕𝖎𝖙𝖎𝖊 𝖚𝖕𝖔𝖓 𝖚𝖘 𝖒𝖎𝖘𝖊𝖗𝖆𝖇𝖑𝖊 𝖘𝖎𝖓𝖓𝖊𝖗𝖘, 𝖙𝖍𝖆𝖙 𝖓𝖔𝖜 𝖆𝖗𝖊 𝖛𝖎𝖘𝖎𝖙𝖊𝖉 𝖜𝖎𝖙𝖍 𝖌𝖗𝖊𝖆𝖙 𝖘𝖎𝖈𝖐𝖊𝖓𝖊𝖘𝖘𝖊 𝖆𝖓𝖉 𝖒𝖔𝖗𝖙𝖆𝖑𝖎𝖙𝖎𝖊, 𝖙𝖍𝖆𝖙 𝖑𝖎𝖐𝖊 𝖆𝖘 𝖙𝖍𝖔𝖚 𝖉𝖎𝖉𝖘𝖙 𝖙𝖍𝖊𝖓 𝖈𝖔𝖒𝖒𝖆𝖓𝖉 𝖙𝖍𝖎𝖓𝖊 𝕬𝖓𝖌𝖊𝖑 𝖙𝖔 𝖈𝖊𝖆𝖘𝖊 𝖋𝖗𝖔𝖒 𝖕𝖚𝖓𝖎𝖘𝖍𝖎𝖓𝖌: 𝖘𝖔 𝖎𝖙 𝖒𝖆𝖞 𝖓𝖔𝖜 𝖕𝖑𝖊𝖆𝖘𝖊 𝖙𝖍𝖊𝖊 𝖙𝖔 𝖜𝖎𝖙𝖍𝖉𝖗𝖆𝖜 𝖋𝖗𝖔𝖒 𝖚𝖘 𝖙𝖍𝖎𝖘 𝖕𝖑𝖆𝖌𝖚𝖊 𝖆𝖓𝖉 𝖌𝖗𝖎𝖊𝖚𝖔𝖚𝖘 𝖘𝖎𝖈𝖐𝖊𝖓𝖊𝖘𝖘𝖊, 𝖙𝖍𝖗𝖔𝖚𝖌𝖍 𝕵𝖊𝖘𝖚𝖘 𝕮𝖍𝖗𝖎𝖘𝖙 𝖔𝖚𝖗 𝕷𝖔𝖗𝖉. 𝕬𝖒𝖊𝖓.

      Delete plague of   Stet

      For command thine Angel *read*: accept of an Atonement, & didst command the destroying Angel

130. *i. Add*: In the Ember dayes
      ii. Read: On the Ember dayes
      For those that are to be admitted into holy Orders.
      iii. Read: In ye weeke before any Ordination comonly cald the Ember dayes
      For those . . .
      iv. Read: In the Ember weekes.
      For those . . .

127.   *This prayer was added in 1552 and omitted in 1559. The 1552 text has the following*
              differences from DB:
              . . . didst suddynly turne in Samaria . . .
              . . . cheapnes, and extreme famine into abundance of vyctuall: have pietie upon us that
              nowe bee punished for our sinnes . . .
              . . . thy glorye, oure comforte, and reliefe of our nedy neyghbours . . .

128. **Adv.:** Make the Title of the first Prayer here,
              [In the Time of any Warre, or Tumults.]
              O Almighty God, King of all Kings, and Governor of all the World, whose power &c.
              to glorify thee, who art ye onely &c.

129. **Adv.:** In the *2d* Prayer, thus,
              O Almighty God, Who in thy wrath in the Wildernes didst send the first Plague upon
              thyne own people, for the Obstinacy of their Rebellion against Moses, & Aaron, and
              also in the time of King David, didst slay wth &c. Have pitty, we humbly beseech thee,
              upon those parts of our Land, that now are visited wth sicknes and mortality, that, like
              as thou didst then accept of an Atonement, and didst command the destroying Angell
              to cease frõ punishing, so it may &c.
              The topicality of Wren's introduction of Moses and Aaron is obvious.

130. **SL:**   A Prayer to be said in the Ember weeks, for those which are then to be admitted into
              holy Orders: and is to be read every day of the week, beginning on the Sunday before
              the day of Ordination.
              This practice appears to be peculiar to the Church of England.

131.   i. *Add*: Almighty God, our heavenly
        father, who hast purchased to thy
        self an universall Church by the
        precious bloud of thy deare Sonne;
        mercifully looke upon the same,[1]
        & at this time so rule & governe
        the Minds of thy Servants the
        Bishops & Pastors of thy flock,
        that they may lay hands suddenly
        on no man, but faithfully & wisely
        make choyse of fitt persons, to
        serve in ye sacred ministery of thy
        Church; & to those yt shalbe
        Ordeyned to any holy function
        give thy grace & heavenly bene-
        diction, that both by their life &
        doctrine they may set forth thy
        glory, & set forward ye Salvation
        of all men, to the glory of thy
        Sonne our Saviour, the great
        Shepperd & Bishop of our Soules,
        Jesus Christ our Lord. Amen.

       ii. *For* rule *read*: guide
        For to the glory . . . of our Soules *read*:
        through

132.   i. *Add*: Or. yt of the Scottish Liturgie.
        vid. ĩf.

       ii. *Read*: Or this.
        Alm. G. ye giver of all good gifts who of
        thy div. provid. hast appointed divers
        Orders in thy Church; Give thy grace,
        we humbly bes. thee, to all those, wch
        are to be called to any Office, &
        Administration in ye same: And so
        replenish ym wth ye truth of thy
        Doctrine, & Iñocency of life, yt they
        may faithfully serve before thee, to ye
        glory of thy great Name, & ye benefit
        of thy holy Church, through J. X. our
        Ld. Amen.

133.   *Add*: For ye Parliamt & Convoca-
        tion   during   their   Sessions
        (*crossed out*) q

134.   *Add title*: A Prayer that may be said
        after any of ye former.
        (*crossed out*) Stet
        Delete tied and   Stet

        For Christs sake *read*: Christ

𝕺 𝖌𝖔𝖉, 𝖜𝖍𝖔𝖘𝖊 𝖓𝖆𝖙𝖚𝖗𝖊 𝖆𝖓𝖉 𝖕𝖗𝖔𝖕𝖊𝖗𝖙𝖎𝖊 𝖎𝖘 𝖊𝖚𝖊𝖗
𝖙𝖔 𝖍𝖆𝖚𝖊 𝖒𝖊𝖗𝖈𝖞, 𝖆𝖓𝖉 𝖙𝖔 𝖋𝖔𝖗𝖌𝖎𝖚𝖊, 𝖗𝖊𝖈𝖊𝖎𝖚𝖊 𝖔𝖚𝖗
𝖍𝖚𝖒𝖇𝖑𝖊 𝖕𝖊𝖙𝖎𝖙𝖎𝖔𝖓𝖘: 𝖆𝖓𝖉 𝖙𝖍𝖔𝖚𝖌𝖍 𝖜𝖊𝖊 𝖇𝖊 𝖙𝖎𝖊𝖉 𝖆𝖓𝖉
𝖇𝖔𝖚𝖓𝖉 𝖜𝖎𝖙𝖍 𝖙𝖍𝖊 𝖈𝖍𝖆𝖎𝖓𝖊 𝖔𝖋 𝖔𝖚𝖗 𝖘𝖎𝖓𝖓𝖊𝖘, 𝖞𝖊𝖙 𝖑𝖊𝖙
𝖙𝖍𝖊 𝖕𝖎𝖙𝖎𝖋𝖚𝖑𝖓𝖊𝖘𝖘𝖊 𝖔𝖋 𝖙𝖍𝖞 𝖌𝖗𝖊𝖆𝖙 𝖒𝖊𝖗𝖈𝖎𝖊 𝖑𝖔𝖔𝖘𝖊 𝖚𝖘,
𝖋𝖔𝖗 𝖙𝖍𝖊 𝖍𝖔𝖓𝖔𝖚𝖗 𝖔𝖋 𝕵𝖊𝖘𝖚𝖘 𝕮𝖍𝖗𝖎𝖘𝖙𝖘 𝖘𝖆𝖐𝖊, 𝖔𝖚𝖗
𝕸𝖊𝖉𝖎𝖆𝖙𝖔𝖚𝖗 𝖆𝖓𝖉 𝕬𝖉𝖚𝖔𝖈𝖆𝖙𝖊. 𝕬𝖒𝖊𝖓.

---

[1] *Originally* looke upon thy whole.

131.   *This prayer is taken from the* Devotions, *where the text differs only at the following points:*
mercifully looke vpon thy whole Congregation . . .
. . . ordained to that holy Function . . .
. . . of all men. Grant this O Lord for his sake, who is the great Shepheard . . .
Cosin, in copying it, began to write 'thy whole Congregation', but stopped in the middle of the phrase, and substituted 'the same'.

132.   *This prayer is taken from SL, verbatim. It is a recasting of the Collect at the end of the Litany in the Ordering of Priests.*

133.   *'A Prayer for the High Court of Parliament, to be read during their Session' had appeared in 1625. On 24 May 1661 the Archbishop of Canterbury's chaplains were commissioned to make 'a prayer or collect for the Parliament sitting, and one for the Synod'. It was produced on 31 May, and printed on 12 June (Cardwell, Conferences, 374). It is hard to account for the deletion of this entry from DB. As it was subsequently placed after 'O God, whose nature . . .', it may have been crossed out with the intention of transferring it to that place, though the intention was not carried out in DB or in FC. The inclusion of Convocation suggests that this entry was prompted by the commission of 24 May, as the prayer produced on 31 May contains no reference to that body.*

134. **Adv.:**   In the third Prayer, [We be tyed, and bound] put out [tyed, &]
and [for the honour of Jesus Xts sake] put out [sake.]

Lords: 33. In the Collect next unto the Collect against the Pestilence, the Clause perhaps to be
mended, *For the honour of Jesus Christs sake.*

The title seems to have been added simply because all the other Prayers and Thanksgivings had titles.

❡ A Thankesgiuing for Raine.

☉ **God our heauenly Father . . . in Jesus Christ our Lord. Amen.**

❡ A Thankesgiuing for faire weather.

☉ **Lord God, who hast iustly . . . Jesus Christ our Lord. Amen.**

❡ A Thankesgiuing for plentie.

☉ **Most mercifull Father . . . Jesus Christ our Lord. Amen.**

❡ A Thankesgiuing for Peace and Victory.

135.   *Add*: THANKSGIVINGS[1]
        Read: For Raine.

        Read: For faire weather.

        Read: For plentie.

136.   *i. Read*: For Peace and Victory.
       ii. Read: For Victory over Rebells, & Restoring of Publick Peace at home.
     iii. Read: For Restoring . . . at home.

137.   *i. Add*: O eternal God our heavenly father, who alone makest men to be of one mind in a house, & stillest the madnes of a raging & unreasonable people; wee blesse thy holy Name that it hath pleased thee to appease ye seditious tumults, wch[2] have bin raised up among us, most humbly beseeching thee to grant us all grace that wee may hereafter live in obedience peace & unitie, walke in thy holy Comandments, & live a quiet & peaceable life in all godlines & honestie, may continually offer up unto thee our Sacrifice of praise & thanksgiving, for these thy mercies towards us, through Jesus Christ our Lord. Amen.
       ii. Read: . . . stillest the outrage of a violent & unruly people . . . grace that wee may henceforth obedientlie walke in thy holy Comandments, & leading a quiet . . .
    iii. Before raised up *add*: lately

138.   *Add new title*: For Deliverance from Forraine Invasion.

☉ **Almightie God . . . Jesus Christ our Lord. Amen.**

❡ A Thankesgiuing for deliuerance from the Plague.

☉ **Lord God . . . Jesus Christ our Lord. Amen.**

          Or this.

Wee humbly acknowledge . . . Jesus Christ our Lord. Amen.

        Read: For deliuerance from the Plague.

        Sett here a large fleuron.

---

[1] *For the page-heading* The Letanie *read*: Thanksgivings.   [2] *Written with a different pen from this point.*

135. **Adv.:** In the first Prayer, thus,

    [O Lord God, Who hadst justly humbled us,] &c.

    In the second Prayer, thus,

    [O most mercifull Father, Who of Thy gracious] &c.

Part. 31: The like ought to be added at the Thanksgiving for Raine, Fayre Weather, Plenty, Peace & Victory, wth those Two for deliverance from ye plague; all wch are here inserted wthout any legall [1]Act of Parliamt (at ye instance of those men yt excepted agt the Booke for want of these Thanksgivings, in the Conference at Hampton Court,) only by ye permission of K. James.

        Cf. Part. 30, at no. 121.

136. **Adv.:** Add here another Prayer, wth this Title,

    A Thanksgiving for the Restoring of Publike Peace:

        The words 'Victory over Rebells' are less suitable to the thanksgiving in its amended form.

137. **Adv.:** O Æternall God, our Heavenly Father, Who alone makest men to be of one mind in an house, and art the God of peace and unity in every Nation, we bless thy holy name for this gracious chang among us, and that it hath pleased thee with so high a hand to appease those seditious Tumults, wch by the subtilty of the Devill were raysed up, and long fomented among us, and so to subdue the Oppositions of men of evill minds, as that, through thy Grace, we may now assemble in peace and safety to offer up unto thee this our Sacrifice of prayse and thanksgiving, through Jesus Xt our Lord. Amen.

        Wren's draft is drastically altered, probably by Cosin, and the new version is then further improved. The process could still have been continued.

138. **Adv.:** Let the Title of the third Prayer, be,

    A Thanksgiving for Deliverance from Invasion of Enimies.

    [O Almighty God, Who art a strong Tower of] &c.

    [O Lord God, Who hadst wounded us for our sinnes, and consumed us for] &c.

---

[1] *Originally* Autority or Act.

The Collects, Epistles, and Gospels, to
be vsed at the celebration of the *Lords
Supper, and holy Communion* through the
yeere.

139. *i. For* through the yeere *read*: for the
whole yeere.
ii. For to be vsed ... yeere *read*: to be used
throughout the yeare.[1]

140. *i. Add*: The Collect wch is appointed
for every Sunday, or any Holyday
that hath a vigil shalbe said at ye
Eveng service before.
ii. Read: Note that The Collect appointed ...
iii. After or *add*: for

The first Sunday in Aduent.

141. *i. After* first *add*: Dominicall or[2]
ii. Read: Lord's Day or (*crossed out*) q

The Collect.

𝔄lmightie 𝔊od, giue vs grace ... now and
euer. 𝔄men.

142. *i. Add*: And this Collect is to be repeated every day after ye other
Collects here appointed untill
Christmas Even.
ii. For here appointed *read*: appointed
in Advent

The Epistle.

𝔒we nothing to any man ... to fulfill the
lustes of it.

143. *Add*: Rom. 13. 8.
In all the Epistles, & Gospells follow ye
new translation.

---

[1] FC: throughout *in text.*
[2] *This addition is made to all the Sundays until* the Sunday next before Easter, *and has not been repeated below.*

139. **Adv.:** In the Title ... leave out those words, [at the Celebration of the Lds Supper, and Holy Communion.] inasmuch as there is direction elsewhere for the using of them then, and also they are to be used, though there be no Communion.

Adv. entered by S.

140.   *Brought here from no. 25.*

141. **Adv.:** Let the Title for ye first Collect be,

[The first Sunday for the Comming of Christ, cald Advent.]

Exceptions: XI. . . . that instead of the Word (Sunday) the word (Lords day) may be every where used.

Bishops: The word *Sunday* is antient. *Just. Mart.* Ap. 2. And therefore not to be left off.
Sarum: Dominica ...

'Dominicall' is perhaps an attempt to satisfy the Puritans while maintaining a link with Sarum. The substitution and, later, cancellation of 'Lord's Day' may well be closely related to the receipt of the Presbyterian Exceptions and the composition of the Bishops' Reply during the Savoy Conference.

142. **Adv.:** lett it be added, [This Collect to be used every day after, untill Xtmas day.]

Wren's suggestion, and also the DB modification, 'untill Christmas Even', may be derived from the Sarum Breviary:
Et dicatur haec praedicta Antiphona ad Memoriam de S. Maria usque ad vigiliam Nativitatis Domini.

143. **Adv.:** Being now come unto the Epistles and Gospells, It must here be well considered and determined, in what Translation they shall now be read: For the Old Translation in very many places is much amiss: The last Translation also was but tumultuarily made, and is full of mistakes.

Exceptions: VIII. That in regard of the many defects which have been observed in that Version of the Scriptures which is used throughout the Liturgy, (manifold instances whereof may be produced) . . . we desire instead thereof the Translation allowed of by Authority may alone be used.

Bishops: Conc. 1. We are willing that all the Epistles and Gospels be used according to the last Translation.

The most important of the alterations resulting from the Savoy Conference. Wren's opinion of the Authorized Version is interesting.
Editions of the BCP up to 1604 had 'Rom. 13.' in the margin; thereafter 'Rom. 13. 8.'; and so throughout the Epistles and Gospels.

The second Sunday in Aduent.
                    The Collect.

𝕭𝖑𝖊𝖘𝖘𝖊𝖉 𝕷𝖔𝖗𝖉 . . . 𝕲𝖗𝖆𝖓𝖙 𝖛𝖘 𝖙𝖍𝖆𝖙 𝖜𝖊𝖊 𝖒𝖆𝖕 𝖎𝖓   144.   *Delete* vs
𝖘𝖚𝖈𝖍 𝖜𝖎𝖘𝖊 . . . 𝖔𝖚𝖗 𝕾𝖆𝖚𝖎𝖔𝖚𝖗 𝕵𝖊𝖘𝖚𝖘 𝕮𝖍𝖗𝖎𝖘𝖙.   *Add*: Amen.[1]

The third Sunday in Aduent.
                    The Collect.

𝕷𝖔𝖗𝖉, 𝖜𝖊𝖊 𝖇𝖊𝖘𝖊𝖊𝖈𝖍 𝖙𝖍𝖊𝖊 𝖌𝖎𝖚𝖊 𝖊𝖆𝖗𝖊 𝖙𝖔 𝖔𝖚𝖗   145.   *Read*: O Lord who at thy first
𝖕𝖗𝖆𝖞𝖊𝖗𝖘, 𝖆𝖓𝖉 𝖇𝖞 𝖙𝖍𝖞 𝖌𝖗𝖆𝖈𝖎𝖔𝖚𝖘 𝖛𝖎𝖘𝖎𝖙𝖆𝖙𝖎𝖔𝖓 𝖑𝖎𝖌𝖍𝖙𝖊𝖓   coming didst send thy Messenger
𝖙𝖍𝖊 𝖉𝖆𝖗𝖐𝖊𝖓𝖊𝖘𝖘𝖊 𝖔𝖋 𝖔𝖚𝖗 𝖍𝖊𝖆𝖗𝖙𝖘, 𝖇𝖞 𝖔𝖚𝖗 𝕷𝖔𝖗𝖉   to prepare thy way before thee;
𝕵𝖊𝖘𝖚𝖘 𝕮𝖍𝖗𝖎𝖘𝖙.   Grant that ye Ministers & Stew-
                                                        ards of thy Mysteries may like-
                                                        wise so prepare & make ready
                                                        thy way, by turning ye hearts of
                                                        the disobedient to ye wisedome
                                                        of the just, that at thy second
                                                        Coming to judge the world, wee
                                                        may be found an acceptable peo-
                                                        ple in thy sight, who livest &
                                                        reignest with ye Father & the
                                                        holy Spirit ever one God world
                                                        without end. Amen.

The iiij. Sunday in Aduent.
                    The Collect.

𝕷𝖔𝖗𝖉, 𝖗𝖆𝖎𝖘𝖊 𝖛𝖕 (𝖜𝖊 𝖕𝖗𝖆𝖞 𝖙𝖍𝖊𝖊) . . . 𝖆𝖓𝖉 𝖜𝖎𝖙𝖍   146.   *Read*: . . . with thy[2] great might . . .
𝖌𝖗𝖊𝖆𝖙 𝖒𝖎𝖌𝖍𝖙 𝖘𝖚𝖈𝖈𝖔𝖚𝖗 𝖛𝖘 . . . 𝖜𝖔𝖗𝖑𝖉 𝖜𝖎𝖙𝖍𝖔𝖚𝖙 𝖊𝖓𝖉.   *Add*: This Collect is to be said only
                                                        untill Christmas Even.
                    The Gospel.   (*crossed out*)

𝕿𝖍𝖎𝖘 𝖎𝖘 𝖙𝖍𝖊 𝖗𝖊𝖈𝖔𝖗𝖉 𝖔𝖋 𝕵𝖔𝖍𝖓 . . . 𝖜𝖍𝖊𝖗𝖊 𝕵𝖔𝖍𝖓   *Add*: This Collect, Ep'le, & Gospell shall
𝖉𝖎𝖉 𝖇𝖆𝖕𝖙𝖎𝖟𝖊.   serve only untill X̃pmas Even.
                                                        Set here a fleuron.

⚜Christmas day.   147.   i. *Read*: The NATIVITIE of our
                                                           LORD, comonly called Christ-
                                                           mas day.
                                                           Print this Title on ye next page,
                                                           with a faire Compartemt before it.
                                                        ii. *After* LORD *add*: or The Birth of Christ

                    The Collect.

𝕬𝖑𝖒𝖎𝖌𝖍𝖙𝖞 𝕲𝖔𝖉, 𝖜𝖍𝖎𝖈𝖍 𝖍𝖆𝖘𝖙 𝖌𝖎𝖚𝖊𝖓 . . . 𝖆𝖓𝖉 𝖙𝖍𝖎𝖘   148.   i. *For* this day *read*: at this time
𝖉𝖆𝖞 𝖙𝖔 𝖇𝖊 𝖇𝖔𝖗𝖓𝖊 . . . 𝖜𝖍𝖔 𝖑𝖎𝖚𝖊𝖙𝖍 𝖆𝖓𝖉 𝖗𝖊𝖎𝖌𝖓𝖊𝖙𝖍   ii. *Read*: this day (or as about this time)
𝖜𝖎𝖙𝖍 𝖙𝖍𝖊𝖊, &𝖈.

---

[1] *And at the end of all the other Collects.*   [2] FC omits.

144. **Adv.:** The Second Sunday for the Coming of Xt.
[O blessed Lord, Who hast caused all,] &c.
accordingly chang the Title of all the rest.

SL: . . . Grant that we may . . .

Cf. no. 67. 'Amen' is added throughout the Book.

145. *This Collect is usually ascribed to Cosin: it is very close in style to that for Epiphany VI (no. 162), which is in all probability his. Like that Collect, it draws on both Epistle and Gospel, a point to which Cosin attached importance (cf. Part. 46, at no. 209). The parallel between John the Baptist and the ministers of Christ's mysteries is underlined by a neat quotation from Luke i. 17.*

146. **Adv.:** The fourth Sunday for ye Coming of Xt, thus, [. . . by our sinnes we are sorely hindered,
thy bountifull grace & mercy &c.
[. . . wth Thee and the Holy Ghost be all Honour and glory, world wthout end. Amen.

'Thy' is not in the Latin: FC omits it.
The rubric is the first of a series intended to exclude any possibility of doubt about the correct proper on any day. Cf. nos. 154, 156, 158, 164, 180, 182, 189.

147. **Adv.:** On the Birth of Christ, cald Xtmas Day.

Devotions: The Natiuity of our LORD.

Sarum: Nativitas Domini.

148. **Adv.:**
[Almighty God, Who hast given us thy onely begotten Sonne, to take our nature upon Him, and at this time to be born of a pure Virgin, Grant] &c.
It cannot be sayd [This day] bycause it is to be used till New-yeares day, and after.

Part. 32: It is likewise here ordered, yt the same Collect shalbe used upon every day unto ye Circumcision. But how can it be used in *ijsdem Terminis,* & that said to be done upon *This day,* wch those following dayes are not?

Exceptions: We desire that in both collects the words (this day) may be left out, it being according to vulgar acceptation a contradiction.

149.   *For* &c. *read*: & the holy Ghost, one God world without end. Amen.[1]

❡ S. Steuens day.

150.   *Read*: S. Stephen's day.

The Collect.

𝔊rant ꝰs, ☉ 𝔏or𝖉, to learne to loue our enemies, b𝔂 t𝔥e example of t𝔥𝔂 𝔐art𝔂r 𝔖. 𝔖teuen, w𝔥o pra𝔂e𝖉 for 𝔥is persecutors, to t𝔥ee w𝔥ic𝔥 liuest, &c.

Read: Grant Lord, that in all our Sufferings here upon Earth for the Testimonie of thy Truth, wee may stedfastly looke up to heaven, & by faith behold ye glory that shalbe revealed; and being filled with the Holy Ghost may learne to love & blesse our persecutors by ye Example of thy first Martyr St. Stephen, who prayed for his Murderers to Thee ô blessed Jesus, who standest at the right hand of God, to succour all yt suffer for thee, our only Mediator & Advocate. Amen.

Then shall follow the Collect of the Nativitie which shall be said continually unto New-yeeres day.[2]

The Epistle.

151.   *Read*: For the Epistle.[3]

❡ S. Iohn Euangelists day.

152.   *After* Iohn *add*: the

.   .   .   .   .   .

❡ Innocents day.

i. Read: The Innocents day.
ii. Before Innocents *add*: Holy   (crossed out)

.   .   .   .   .   .

❡ The Sunday after Christmas day.

The Collect.

𝔄lmig𝔥tie 𝔊o𝖉, &c. As ꝰpon Christmas day.

Print it out at large.

---

[1] *And elsewhere.*   [2] FC: . . . New-yeeres Even.
[3] *And elsewhere when the Epistle is not from one of the New Testament Epistles.*

Bishops: Conc. 4. That the words (this day) both in the Collects, and Prefaces, be used only upon the day itself, and for the following dayes, it be said (as about this time.)

SL: . . . but in stead of the words [and this day to be born] the Presbyter shall say [at this time to be born.]

Sanderson (Collects Adventual): . . . and as at this time to be born . . .

> *This was a long-standing Puritan 'exception', but one with which Cosin, Wren, and Sanderson (and probably many others) were in sympathy.*

149. **Adv.:** [. . . Who liveth and reigneth with Thee and the Holy Ghost ever one God world wthout end. Amen.

> *The traditional ending, implied by the '&c.' in the text.*

150. **Adv.:** On St. Stevens Day.

> . . . Who prayed for his Persecutors to thee, Who livest, and reygnest wth the Father, and the Holy Ghost, ever one God, world wthout end. Amen.

> *Another Collect that may be confidently ascribed to Cosin: it draws freely on the Epistle, and also quotes Rom. viii. 18. It is difficult not to see an allusion to Cosin's own 'sufferings here upon earth'.*

151. **Exceptions:** XIV. That no portions of the Old Testament, or the Acts of the Apostles be called Epistles; or read as such.

> **Bishops:** Conc. 2. That when any thing is read for an Epistle, which is not in the Epistles, the superscription be, [for the Epistle.]

152. **Adv.:** On Innocents day.

> for [mortify, and kill] read it, [mortify we beseech Thee all vices in us,] &c.

BCP: The Innocents day.

> *'The Holy Innocents' is the title given in the BCP list of Holy dayes (no. 46); it is also found in Sarum.*

Adv.: On the Sunday after Xtmas.

> for this day, and for Xtmas day, let it be well weighed, wch is most proper to say, [to take our Nature upon Him] or rather [to take our Nature unto Him] for that is [ἐπιλαμβάνεσθαι, Assumere] the manhood into God.

The Gospel. Matt. 1. 1.

𝕿𝖍𝖎𝖘 𝖎𝖘 𝖙𝖍𝖊 𝕭𝖔𝖔𝖐𝖊 𝖔𝖋 𝖙𝖍𝖊 𝖌𝖊𝖓𝖊𝖗𝖆𝖙𝖎𝖔𝖓 . . .   153.   Omit ye printing of all this to The
𝖋𝖔𝖚𝖗𝖊𝖙𝖊𝖊𝖓𝖊 𝖌𝖊𝖓𝖊𝖗𝖆𝖙𝖎𝖔𝖓𝖘.   Birth &c.
𝕿𝖍𝖊 𝖇𝖎𝖗𝖙𝖍 𝖔𝖋 𝕵𝖊𝖘𝖚𝖘 𝕮𝖍𝖗𝖎𝖘𝖙 . . . 𝖈𝖆𝖑𝖑𝖊𝖉 𝖍𝖎𝖘   Matth. 1. 18. Here begin ye Gospel.
𝕹𝖆𝖒𝖊 𝕵𝖊𝖘𝖚𝖘.

154.   *i. Add*: This Collect is to be said only till the
                 Circumcision.
          ii. Read: This Collect, Epistle, & Gospel are
                 to be used only till the Circumcision.

¶ The Circumcision of Christ.   155.   *Add*: or New Yeere's day.[1]
              The Collect.

𝕬𝖑𝖒𝖎𝖌𝖍𝖙𝖎𝖊 𝕲𝖔𝖉 . . . 𝕲𝖗𝖆𝖓𝖙 𝖚𝖘 . . . 𝖙𝖍𝖆𝖙 𝖔𝖚𝖗
𝖍𝖊𝖆𝖗𝖙𝖘 . . . 𝖇𝖊𝖎𝖓𝖌 𝖒𝖔𝖗𝖙𝖎𝖋𝖎𝖊𝖉, 𝖒𝖆𝖞 𝖎𝖓 𝖆𝖑𝖑 𝖙𝖍𝖎𝖓𝖌𝖘   *Read*: being mortified, wee may . . .
𝖔𝖇𝖊𝖞 𝖙𝖍𝖞 𝖇𝖑𝖊𝖘𝖘𝖊𝖉 𝖜𝖎𝖑𝖑 . . . 𝖔𝖚𝖗 𝕷𝖔𝖗𝖉.

              .   .   .

If there be any Sunday betweene the Epiphanie   156.   *Read*: And the same Collect, Epistle
and the Circumcision, then shall be vsed the   & Gospel shall serve for every day
same Collect, Epistle and Gospel, at the Com-   after untill the Epiphanie.
munion, which was vsed the day of Circumcision.

The Epiphanie.   157.   *i. Add*: or, The Manifesting of Christ
                                                                 to the Gentils.
              .   .   .   .   *ii. Read*: or, The Manifestation of
                                                                 Christ.

              The Gospel.

𝖂𝖍𝖊𝖓 𝕵𝖊𝖘𝖚𝖘 𝖜𝖆𝖘 𝖇𝖔𝖗𝖓𝖊 . . . 𝖆𝖓𝖔𝖙𝖍𝖊𝖗 𝖜𝖆𝖞.   158.   *Add*: And the same Collect, Eple &
                                                          Gospel shall serve till ye Sunday
                                                          next following.

The first Sunday after the Epiphanie.

              .   .   .   .

              The Gospel.

𝕿𝖍𝖊 𝖋𝖆𝖙𝖍𝖊𝖗 𝖆𝖓𝖉 𝖒𝖔𝖙𝖍𝖊𝖗 𝖔𝖋 𝕵𝖊𝖘𝖚𝖘 𝖜𝖊𝖓𝖙 𝖙𝖔
𝕳𝖎𝖊𝖗𝖚𝖘𝖆𝖑𝖊𝖒 𝖆𝖋𝖙𝖊𝖗 𝖙𝖍𝖊 𝖈𝖚𝖘𝖙𝖔𝖒 𝖔𝖋 𝖙𝖍𝖊 𝖋𝖊𝖆𝖘𝖙 𝖉𝖆𝖞   159.   *After* Hierusalem *add*: every yeere
. . . 𝖜𝖎𝖙𝖍 𝕲𝖔𝖉 𝖆𝖓𝖉 𝖒𝖆𝖓.   at the Feast of the Passeover.
                                                          And when he was twelve yeeres
                                                          old, they went up to Jerusalem

---

[1] FC *omits.*

153. **Adv.:** The first half of this Gospell should (By former Directions) be omitted, and it to begin at the *18th vs.*

> *Wren's 'former Directions' are the rubric at no. 27, first added in 1561. S II quotes*
> *Grotius:*
> *Ebionitae haeretici deleverunt totam Genealogiam . . .*

154. **Part. 32:** In ye Rubrick upon ye Sunday after Christmas, ye same Collect is appointed to be read, wch was used upon Christmas day: But if ye Feast of Circumcision & this Sunday fall together, it will be a question wch of ye Collects ought to be read; & for resolution herin some direction would here be added; because both cannot be used, being inconsistent together.

> *This is an acute case of the difficulty already raised by Part. 5 (at no. 24) in general terms.*

155. **Adv.:** On the Circumcision of Xt.

> [O Almighty God, Who madest Thy Blessed Sonne] &c.
> [. . . from all worldly and carnall lusts, we may in,] &c.

Sparrow: *Feast of* CIRCUMCISION, *or Newyears-day.*

> *'New Year's Day' is more probably derived from the St. Stephen's Day rubric, or from common usage, than from Sparrow.*

156. **Part. 33:** In ye Rubrick after ye Circumcision, it is ordered, that if there fall any Sunday betweene yt day & ye Epiphany, ye same Collect, Eple, & Gospel shalbe read, wch was used upon ye day of Circumcision. This defect may be otherwise supplyed by appointing both a Collect Eple & Gospel more proper for yt Time.

SL: If there be any Sunday . . . which was used the day of the *Circumcision*; and so likewise upon every other day from the time of the *Circumcision* to the *Epiphany.*

> *Cosin's suggestion was not followed until 1928.*

157. **Adv.:** The Manifesting of Xt unto the Gentils.

> [O God, Who by the leading of a starre, didst] &c.
> . . . through Jesus Xt our Lord. Amen.

S I: This Epistle & The Collect ruñe all upon ye calling of ye Gentiles . . .
The offices of ye Sundayes wch follow ye Epiphanie untill Septuagesima Sunday, are of ye same argument wth ye Epiphanie itself, all belonging to the Manifestation of Christ.

> *Cosin's title supplants Wren's.*

158. **Part. 34:** For if ye Epiphany shall fall upon Monday or Tuesday &c, what Collect must be used for all the dayes of ye week after? It is a great incongruitie to use ye Collect of ye Circumcision after ye Epiphanie is past. Therfore there wanteth an order here either to continue ye Collect of ye Epiphanie all the dayes of the week following, or to make a new Collect for ye Sunday before.

159. **Adv.:** On the first Sunday after the Manifesting of Xt to the Gentils.
The beginning of that Gospell is but brokenly set down here: Let it begin at the 41th vs. [Now His parents went, &c.

> *DB, like SL, retains the BCP opening, 'The father and mother of Jesus', in preference to the AV text recommended by Wren.*

The second Sunday after the Epiphanie.
The Collect.

𝕬𝖑𝖒𝖎𝖌𝖍𝖙𝖎𝖊 𝖆𝖓𝖉 𝖊𝖚𝖊𝖗𝖑𝖆𝖘𝖙𝖎𝖓𝖌 𝕲𝖔𝖉 . . . 𝖉𝖆𝖞𝖊𝖘 𝖔𝖋
𝖔𝖚𝖗 𝖑𝖎𝖋𝖊.   160.   *Add*: through Jesus Christ our Lord.
·   ·   ·   ·   ·   ·   Amen.

The third Sunday after the Epiphanie.
·   ·   ·   ·   ·   ·

The fourth Sunday after the Epiphany.

The Epistle. Rom. 13. 1   161.   *Add*: or rather
·   ·   ·   ·   ·   ·   2 Pet. 1. 15 to ye 20. v.

The Gospel. Matth. 8. 23.   or rather
·   ·   ·   ·   ·   ·   Matth. 17. 1 to ye 6. v.
The fift Sunday after the Epiphanie.   (*both crossed out*)
·   ·   ·   ·   ·   ·

                              162.   Omit.   *Add*:
The sixt Sunday (if there be so many) shall haue   The Sixt Sunday after ye Epiphany.
the Collect, Epistle and Gospel, that was vpon
the fift Sunday.   The Collect
                                         O God, whose blessed Sonne was
                                         manifested, yt he might destroy
                                         the works of the divel, & make us
                                         the Sons of God and heyres of
                                         eternall life; Grant wee beseech
                                         thee that having this hope in us,[1]
                                         wee may purifie our selves even
                                         as he is pure: that when he shall
                                         appeare againe with power & great
                                         glory, we may be made like unto
                                         him in his eternall & glorious
                                         kingdome where with Thee ô
                                         Father & ye Holy Ghost he liveth
                                         & reigneth[2] one God world with-
                                         out end. Amen.

                                         The Epistle
                                         1 S. John.[3] 3. v. 1. to v. 9.
                                         The Gospel

                                         S. Matth. 24. v. 23. unto v. 32.
                                         Add: Print it out at large.

---

[1] FC *omits* in us   [2] FC: . . . ever one God . . .   [3] *Originally* 1 Peter.

160. **Adv.:** On the Second Sunday.

> [. . . God, Who doest govern all things in heaven and earth, mercifully hear the Supplications of Thy people, and grant us thy Peace all the dayes of our Life, through Jesus Xt our Lord. Amen.

SL: . . . through Jesus Christ our Lord. (*no Amen.*)

> *Adv. rather than SL.*

Part. 35: In the Gospel upon ye 2d Sunday after ye Epiphany there is a Translation of some words, comonly spoken in old time wthout offence, but now in our dayes not so fitt to be used. The words therfore, — *And when men be drunk* — would be now rendered — *And when men have drunk well* — according to ye later Translation of our Bible.

161. **Adv.:** On the fourth Sunday.

> O God, Who knowest us to be set in the midst of so many and great Dangers, that for mans fraylnes, we cannot alway stand in that integrity, we ought to do; Grant to us the health &c. and overcome, through Jesus Xt our Lord. Amen.

> *The Epistle and Gospel suggested are those of Sarum for The Transfiguration, chosen here as an example of Christ's manifestation, though not to the Gentiles. This suggests Cosin's influence (cf. no. 157).*

162. **Part. 36:** After ye fifth Sunday there, it is appointed, That if there be a sixth, ye same Collect Eple & Gospel shalbe used, wch was read upon ye fifth. But it were both fitt & easie, rather to supply the day wth Collect Eple & Gospel proper to it self, then to suffer this defect to stand still wthout need.

Part. 37: And if there be but Three or fower Sundayes after the Epiphanie (as sometimes it will happen), ye Eple Gospel & Collect upon ye fifth, referring to ye Great Epiphanie of our Saviour at ye End of ye world, wilbe more proper for yt Third or Fourth Sunday, then those wch are appointed. There wants a provision here to be made in that Case.

> *As Cosin suggested the addition of a Collect here, its authorship is usually ascribed to him. Like those for Advent III and St. Stephen's Day, it is almost entirely made up of phrases from the Epistle and Gospel (cf. note on no. 145).*

¶ The Sunday called Septuagesima.

The Collect.

𝕺 **Lord, we beseech thee . . . who liueth and reigneth world without end.**

. . . . . .

¶ The Sunday called Sexagesima.

. . . . .

¶ The Sunday called Quinquagesima.

The Gospel.

Jesus took vnto him . . . gaue praise vnto God.

¶ The first day of Lent.

The Collect.

Almighty and euerlasting God . . . through Jesus Christ.

. . . . . .

¶ The first Sunday in Lent.

. . . . .

¶ The second Sunday in Lent.

. . . . .

¶ The third Sunday in Lent.

. . . . .

¶ The fourth Sunday in Lent.

. . . . .

163. *Add*: And if there be fewer Sun-
      dayes then Six, yet the Collect,
      Ep. & Gosp. of ye Sixt Sunday
      shalbe ye last. (*crossed out*)
      Set here a fleuron.

164. *Add*: or the Third Sunday before
      Lent.

   i. *After* reigneth *add*: with thee O
      Father & the holy Ghost
  ii. *After* Ghost *add*: ever one G.

      Add: or the Second Sunday before
      Lent.

      Add: or the next Sunday before
      Lent.

      Add: This Collect, Epistle, & Gospel shall
      serve only till the Weddensday fol-
      lowing.
      Set here a fleuron.

165. *Add*: comonly called Ashwedensday.

      Add: our Lord.

166.   i. *Add*: And this Collect is to be re-
          peated every day in Lent after
          the Collect hereafter appointed
          for that time.
      ii. *Read*: . . . after each Collect ap-
          pointed during that time.
     iii. *Read*: And this Collect wth ye Eple, &
          Gosp. is to be said untill ye Sunday
          following & the Collect is to be re-
          peated . . .
      iv. *Read*: And this Collect (wth ye Eple, &
          Gosp. following) shall serve untill ye
          Sunday . . .

163.   *Cf. Part. 37 (see no. 162). Cf. nos. 188 and 189 (Trinity XXV).*

164. **Adv.:** Touching the Sundayes cald Septuagesima, Sexagesima, and Quinquagesima, hath
           enough bin sayd. *Vide pag. 8.*
           On the Third Sunday before Lent.
           [. . . our Saviour, Who liveth and reygneth wth thee, and the Holy Ghost, ever one
           God, world wthout end. Amen.
           On the Sunday next before Lent.
           [. . . for thyne onely Sonnes sake, Jesus Christ our Lord. Amen.
                'pag. 8' refers to no. 30 in DB.
                The rubric 'This Collect . . .' is based on Sarum practice.

165. **1549 and SL:** The first day of Lent, commonly called Ash-Wednesday.

166. **Adv.:** That Collect for the First Day of Lent, [Almighty and Everlasting God, Who hatest
           nothing, that thou hast made] &c.
           let it be appointed to be read every day, wth the other Collects for the Day, untill Good
           fryday.

     SL: From Ashwednesday to the first Sunday in Lent shall be used the same Collect, Epistle
           and Gospel which were used on Ashwednesday.
                Adv. before SL. Wren's suggestion of repetition throughout Lent may be based on Sarum:
                (Missal) Ab hac die usque ad cenam domini, in omnibus missis de ieiunio fiat memoria
                pro penitentibus.
                (Breviary) Haec praedicta Antiphona . . . Responsorium . . . Hymnus . . . dicantur
                quotidie ad Completorium usque ad Passionem Domini.

     Adv.: On the First Sunday in Lent.
           [O Lord, Who for our sakes didst fast,] &c.
           . . . to thy honour and glory, Who livest, and reygnest wth the Father and the Holy
           Ghost, ever One God, world wthout end. Amen.
           On the Second Sunday in Lent.
           [Almighty God, Who doest see, that we have no,] &c.
           . . . through Jesus Xt our Lord. Amen.

❡ The fift Sunday in Lent.

.   .   .   .   .

❡ The Sunday next before Easter.

The Gospel. Mat. 26. 1.   167.   *For* 26 *read*: 27

Anð it came to passe . . .   ☞ Leave out ye 26. Chapter (wch is
                                                    appointed for ye 2. Lesson of
                                                    this day) & print only ye 27.
.   .   .   .   .   .   chap.[1]

anð wept bitterly. When the morning was   When &c. here begin ye Gospel.
come . . .   *Add*: Matth. xxvii.
Truely this was the Sonne of God . . . Zebe=   Here end ye Gospel.
ðees childen.   *Delete the last two verses.*

❡ Munday before Easter.

.   .   .   .   .

❡ Tuesday before Easter.

The Gospel.

Anð anon in the dawning . . .
the Sonne of God . . . where he was laiðe.   Here end ye Gospel.
                                                    Delete the last 8 verses.
❡ Wednesday before Easter.

.   .   .   .   .

❡ Thursday before Easter.   168.   *Add*: comonly called Mandie Thurs-
                                                    day. (*crossed out*)

The Gospel. Luk. 23. 1.   169.   *Add*: or rather S. John. 15. 1. unto
The whole multituðe of them   v. 26 They hated me without a
                                                    cause. v. 25. (rather *and* v. 25
.   .   .   .   .   .   *crossed out*) q

beholðing these things . . . accorðing to the   Here end ye Gospel.
Commanðement.   *Delete the last 7 verses.*

❡ On good Friday.

The Collects.

Almightie anð euerlasting God . . . in thy
holy Congregation . . . in his uocation anð   170.   *For* Congregation *read*: Church
ministery . . . through Jesus Christ our   *For* uocation *read*: profession
Lorð.   (*crossed out*)
Mercifull God . . . who liueth anð reigneth,
&c.   *Add*: with thee & thy holy Spirit,
                                                    one God world without end. Amen.

---

[1] FC: This cap. is ye second Lesson for this day, & therefore heere omitted.

167. **Adv.:**   On the Sunday next before Easter.
> O Almighty, and everlasting God, Who of Thy tender &c.
> The Gospell for this day is made overlong. Rather, let the *26th* Chapt. of St Matthew, (wch is the first half of it,) be appointed to be the Second Lesson, Proper for this Sunday.

> > *The transfer of ch. 26 to Mattins probably suggested the similar treatment of the Gospel for Good Friday (no. 171, q.v.), originally desired for a different reason. The removal of the last two verses may be due to Cosin (cf. Part. 10, quoted at no. 30); here the purpose is presumably to secure a more effective ending. In the case of the other three Gospels, the verses removed contain accounts of the burial of our Lord. 1549 had taken the first step towards commemorating this on Easter Even, by transferring St. Matthew's account to that point: the present change brings the other Gospels into line with Palm Sunday's and restricts the commemoration of the burial to Easter Even.*

168. **Devotions:** Maundy Thursday.

> **Sparrow:** Hence it is called *Dies mandati*, Mandate or *Maunday Thursday*.

169. **Adv.:**   Let it be considered, yf on the Thursday before Easter, in our Church, where the King observes Xts Washing of Feet, the Gospell should not rather, be *Ioan. 13. 1.*

> > *The suggestion of John xv seems to be without precedent; though appropriate, it is less so than John xiii. It seems scarcely possible that Cosin can have misread Wren's '13' as '15'.*
> > *For the shortening of the Gospel, cf. no. 167.*

170. **Adv.:**   On Good Fryday. In the middle Collect,
> [wch we offer before thee, for all Estates of Men in thy holy Church, that every member of the same in their Christian Vocation and Ministry, may truly and Godly serve Thee, through our Lord Jesus Xt. Amen.]

SL: ... in thy holy Church ...

> > *Cf. also Part. 69, at no. 307 (substitution of 'Church').*

The Gospel. Ioh. 18. 1.

𝔚𝔥𝔢𝔫 𝔍𝔢𝔰𝔲𝔰 𝔥𝔞𝔡 𝔰𝔭𝔬𝔨𝔢̈ 𝔱𝔥𝔢𝔰𝔢 𝔴𝔬𝔯𝔡𝔰 . . .

. . . 𝔅𝔞𝔯𝔞𝔟𝔟𝔞𝔰 𝔴𝔞𝔰 𝔞 𝔪𝔲𝔯𝔡𝔢𝔯𝔢𝔯. 𝔗𝔥𝔢𝔫 𝔓𝔦𝔩𝔞𝔱𝔢 𝔱𝔬𝔬𝔨𝔢 𝔍𝔢𝔰𝔲𝔰 . . .

𝔥𝔦𝔪 𝔴𝔥𝔬𝔪 𝔱𝔥𝔢𝔶 𝔥𝔞𝔲𝔢 𝔭𝔦𝔢𝔯𝔠𝔢𝔡 . . . 𝔴𝔞𝔰 𝔫𝔦𝔤𝔥 𝔞𝔱 𝔥𝔞𝔫𝔡.

¶ Easter Euen.

171.　For 18 *read*: 19

☞ Leave out ye 18. Chapter (wch is appointed for ye 2. Lesson of this day) & print only ye 19. Chapter.[1]
Here begin[2] ye Gospel.
S. John. xix.

Here end ye Gospel.
Delete the last 5 verses.

2.　*Add*:　The Collect.
Grant ô Lord, that as wee are baptised into the death of thy blessed Sonne, our Saviour Jesus Christ, so by continuall mortifying our corrupt affections, our Sins may be buried with him; & that through the grave & gate of death wee may passe to our joyfull Resurrection, for his merits who dyed, & was buried, & rose againe for us, ye same Jesus Christ our Lorde. Amen.
For ye same read: thy Sonne

The Epistle.

𝔍𝔱 𝔦𝔰 𝔟𝔢𝔱𝔱𝔢𝔯 . . . 𝔪𝔦𝔤𝔥𝔱𝔰 𝔰𝔲𝔟𝔡𝔲𝔢𝔡 𝔲𝔫𝔱𝔬 𝔥𝔦𝔪.

The Gospel.

𝔚𝔥𝔢𝔫 𝔱𝔥𝔢 𝔢𝔲𝔢𝔫 𝔴𝔞𝔰 𝔠𝔬𝔪𝔢 . . . 𝔞𝔫𝔡 𝔰𝔢𝔞𝔩𝔢𝔡 𝔱𝔥𝔢 𝔰𝔱𝔬𝔫𝔢.

Set here a fayre fleuron.
Set here a fayre Compartemt.

Easter day.

At Morning prayer, in stead of the Psalme, 𝔒 𝔠𝔬𝔪𝔢 𝔩𝔢𝔱 𝔲𝔰, &c. these Anthemes shall be sung or said.

173.　i. *After* prayer *add*: from this day
　　ii. *For* At Morning . . . vs, &c. *read*: upon this day & ye two following
　　　　Stet

174.　i. *Add*: Christ our Passeover is sacrificed for us, therfore let us keep the Feast. Not with old Leven, nor with ye Leven of Malice & Wickednes; but wth the unlevened Bread of Sincerity & Truth. 1 Cor. 5. v. 7. & 8.
　　ii. *For* sacrificed *read*: offered up

𝔠𝔥𝔯𝔦𝔰𝔱 𝔯𝔦𝔰𝔦𝔫𝔤 𝔞𝔤𝔞𝔦𝔫𝔢 . . . 𝔠𝔥𝔯𝔦𝔰𝔱 𝔍𝔢𝔰𝔲𝔰 𝔬𝔲𝔯 𝔏𝔬𝔯𝔡.[2]
𝔠𝔥𝔯𝔦𝔰𝔱 𝔦𝔰 𝔯𝔦𝔰𝔢𝔫 𝔞𝔤𝔞𝔦𝔫𝔢 . . . 𝔟𝔢 𝔯𝔢𝔰𝔱𝔬𝔯𝔢𝔡 𝔱𝔬 𝔩𝔦𝔣𝔢.[3]

175.　i. *Add*: Glory be to the Father &c. As it was in ye begiñing &c.
　　ii. *Delete* Glory be . . . Father &c.
　　iii. Stet.
　　Before As it was . . . *add*: Answer.

---

[1] FC: This cap. is ye 2d Lesson for the day, & therfore heere omitted.
[2] *Originally* end.
[3] *The reference is added in the margin.*

171. **Adv.:** Now the Gospell for Good Fryday was the *2d* Lesson in *Ao 1648*. It will fall out so agayn in other yeares. A Rubrick therfore would now be put, as a Rule, How either the Lesson, or the Gospell shall be changed, when it so happeneth.

> *This difficulty is overcome by the simple expedient of appointing the first half of the Gospel (John xviii) as Second Lesson, as had been done on Palm Sunday. For the ending at v. 37, see no. 167. The choice of this verse may have been influenced by Sarum, which ended the reading of the Passion here, vv. 38–42 being read as the Gospel.*

172. **SL:** O Most gracious God, look upon us in mercy, and grant that as we are baptized into the death of thy Sonne our Saviour Jesus Christ; so by our true and hearty repentance all our sins may be buried with him, and we not fear the grave: that as Christ was raised up from the dead by the glory of thee, O Father, so wee also may walk in newnesse of life, but our sins never bee able to rise in judgment against us, and that for the merit of Jesus Christ that died, was buried, and rose again for us. Amen.

> *The adaptation of the clumsy SL Collect is probably Cosin's work: it borrows a phrase from the Easter Day Epistle, and introduces 'the gate of death' (possibly from Ps. ix. 13) in contrast to 'the gate of everlasting life' in the Easter Day Collect.*

173.

> *No precedent for the extension of the Easter Anthems to Monday and Tuesday in Easter week has yet been traced.*

174. **S II:** Epla in ord. Sarū. 1. Cor. 5. *Expurgate vetus ferm.* usque ad *in azymis sinceritatis & veritatis.*

> *This reference suggests that the Sarum Epistle is the source of the new Anthem, rather than the Sarum Communion, as Brightman suggests (I. 392). The latter, it is true, starts at Pascha nostrum, but it diverges from the biblical text.*
> *The translation is that of the A.V., except 'offered up'. The latter is indicative of Cosin's eucharistic doctrine (cf. note on no. 250).*

175. **Part. 38:** At Easter day, it is appointed, yt in stead of ye *Venite Exultemus*, ye Two Anthemes (*Christ Rising, & Christ is Risen,*) shalbe used. But there is no *Gloria Pr̄i* sett to follow either of ym, as after ye *Venite* is ordered before. Therfore ye question is, whether *Glory be to ye Father &c.* should not be here added after either or both of these Anthemes.

> Cf. no. 76.

❡ Munday in Easter weeke.

The Collect.

𝔄lmighty 𝔊od, which through thy onely begotten 𝔖on 𝔍esus 𝔆hrist hast ouercome death, and opened vnto vs the gate of euerlasting life: wee humbly beseech thee, that as by thy speciall grace preuenting vs, thou doest put into our mindes good desires: so by thy continuall helpe wee may bring the same to good effect, through 𝔍esus 𝔆hrist our 𝔏ord, who liueth and reigneth, &c.

· · · · · ·

176.   *i. Read*: O God, who for our Redemption didst give thy only begotten Son to the death of ye Crosse, & by his glorious Resurrection hast delivered us from ye power of our ghostly Enemies; Grant us so to die daily from Sinne, yt wee may evermore live with him in ye joy of his Resurrection, through the same Christ our Lord. Amen.

     ii. Read: O God, who for our Redemption didst suffer thy only begotten Son to dye upon ye Crosse . . . *Delete* the same

     iii. Delete the whole Collect   Stet *as printed.*

❡ Tuesday in Easter weeke.

The Collect.

𝔄lmightie 𝔉ather, which hast giuen thine onely 𝔖onne to die for our sinnes, and to rise againe for our iustification: graunt vs so to put away the leauen of malice and wickednesse, that wee may alway serue thee in purenesse of liuing and trueth, through 𝔍esus 𝔆hrist our 𝔏ord.

· · · ·

177.   *i. Delete the whole Collect.*
Almighty God; as on Easter day. Print this for the next Sunday.

     ii. For Print . . . Sunday *read*: Omitt this Collect here, & print it for ye Sunday following.

❡ The first Sunday after Easter.

The Collect.

𝔄lmightie 𝔊od, which, &c. (𝔄s at the 𝔆ommunion on 𝔈aster day.)

178.   *i.* Print it out at large.   (*crossed out*)
     ii. Delete Almightie . . . day.) *and read*: O God, who for our Redemption.
     iii. Read: Almighty F. who hast given thine only Sonne &c. as on Easter Tuesday.
     q

The Gospel. Ioh. 20. 19.

· · · ·

❡ The ij. Sunday after Easter.

· · · ·

❡ The iij. Sunday after Easter.

· · · ·

176. **Adv.:** On Easter day.
 [Almighty God, Who through thy onely begotten Sonne Jesus Xt hast subdued
 Death, and opened unto us the Gate of everlasting Life; we humbly beseech thee,] &c.
 The like again, on Easter Munday.

 The DB Collect comes from the 1549 Easter Day Procession. DB reproduces it verbatim,
 except for altering 'enemy' to 'ghostly Enemies'. This departs from the Latin, which is
 'inimici' (gen. sing.). ii, on the other hand, is closer to the Latin ('subire voluisti').
 iii agrees with nos. 177 and 178.

177. **Adv.:** That Collect for Easter Tuesday, [Almighty Father, Who hast given thyne onely Sonne,
 to dye] &c. would be reserved, for the Sunday after Easter, and the Collect for Easter
 Day to serve for all this week.

 Cf. no. 178.

178. **Adv.:** The Gospell for the First Sunday after Easter, was the Second Lesson for that Day, in
 Ao 1654. A Rule therfore now to be set, What the Alteration shall be, yf it so fall
 agayn.

 1549: Almighty Father, &c. as at the second Communion on Easter day.

 i is very early, before any change was contemplated at all. ii follows Sarum, which re-
 peated the Procession on the Octave; it is presumably not earlier than no. 176. iii, as
 a Collect would hardly be said from Monday to Sunday. iii at last adopts the suggestion
 of Adv. at no. 177, which follows 1549.

 Adv.: On the Second Sunday after Easter.
 O Almighty God, Who hast given thyne onely Sonne
 . . . most holy Life, through the same Jesus Xt our Lord. Amen.
 On the III and IIII Sundayes after Easter.
 Let it be [Who] instead of [Wch] and through Jesus Xt our Lord. Amen.

¶ The iiij. Sunday after Easter.

The Collect.

𝔄lmighty 𝔊od which doest make the minds
of all faithfull men to be of one wil . . . our
𝔏ord.

179.   *Read*: Almighty God who doest
make all faithfull men to be of
one mind . . .

·   ·   ·   ·   ·

¶ The fift Sunday after Easter

The Gospel.

𝔙erily, verily, 𝔍 say vnto you . . . 𝔍 haue
ouercome the world.

180.   *i. Add*: This Collect Eple, & Gospell shall
serve only for this day.
ii. Read: . . . shall be used only upon this day.

181.   *i. Add*: The Three Rogation dayes.

The Collect.

Almighty God, Lord of Heaven &
Earth, in whom wee live, & move,
& have our Being; who dost good
unto all men, making thy Sunne
to rise on ye evill & on the good,
& sending Raine on ye just, & on
ye unjust; Favourably behold us
thy people, who call upon thy
Name, & send us thy Blessing
from Heaven in Giving us fruitfull Seasons, & filling our Hearts
with food & gladnes, that both
our hearts & mouths may be
continually filled with thy praises,
giving thanks to thee in thy holy
Church through Jesus Christ our
Lord. Amen.

The Epistle.

S. James. 5. 13.[1] to ye 19. v.

The Gospel.

S. Luke. 11. 1. to ye 11. v.

A fleuron.

ii. Read: The Rogation dayes . . .
Delete the Epistle and the Gospel.

iii. Stent.
Print ym out at large.

---

[1] *Originally* 16.   FC: James. V. v. 15. to ye 19.

179. **Exceptions:** We desire that these Collects may be further considered and debated, as having in them divers things that we judge fit to be altered.

Bishops: We do not find, nor do they say, what is to be amended in these Collects; therefore to say anything particularly, were to answer to we know not what.

> *Nevertheless, some of the Collects were altered, some in DB, some not until the Convocation Book. The Collects excepted against were those for St. John, the Innocents, Ash Wednesday, Easter IV, Trinity Sunday, Trinity VI, Trinity XII, St. Luke, and Michaelmas.*
> *'of one mind': cf. no. 137 (Wren).*

180.
> *Sarum had propers for Monday and Wednesday; for Tuesday a Mass of the Blessed Virgin. On Friday and Saturday the Ascension Day propers were repeated. This rubric, which arises from the provisions of nos. 181 and 182, thus follows Sarum practice.*

181.
> *The Collect comes from the Devotions ('Prayers for the Fovre Ember Weekes: IV. For the Fruits of the earth'), and is a typical product of its author. The Epistle and Gospel are adapted from Sarum, which had James v. 16–20 and Luke xi. 5–13. The Epistle could reasonably begin at v. 16 (Sarum, and DB's first thought), or v. 13 (DB's second choice), but not at v. 15 (FC), which must be a misreading.*

The Ascension day.

The Collect.

𝕲rant we beseech thee . . . world without end.   182.

The Gospel.

𝕵esus appeared unto the eleuen . . . with miracles following.

⸿ Sunday after Ascension day.

.   .   .   .   .

⸿ Whitsunday.

The Collect.

𝕲od which as vpon this day taught the hearts   183. of thy faithfull people . . . world without end.

.   .   .   .   .

⸿ Munday in Whitsun weeke.

The Collect.

𝕲od which . . . faithfull, &c. As vpon Whitsunday.

.   .   .   .   .

⸿ Tuesday in Whitsun weeke.

The Collect.

.   .   .   .   .

The Gospel.

𝖁erily, verily . . . more abundantly.

⸿ Trinitie Sunday.

The Collect.

𝕬lmighty and euerlasting 𝕲od . . . we be=   184. seech thee, that through the stedfastnesse of this faith, we may euermore be defended from all aduersitie . . . world without end. 𝕬men.

.   .   .   .   .

⸿ The first Sunday after Trinitie.   185.

The Collect.

𝕲od, the strength . . . our 𝕷ord.

.   .   .   .   .

⸿ The ij. iij. iiij. Sundays after Trinitie.

.   .   .   .   .

⸿ The fift Sunday after Trinitie.

The Collect.

𝕲rant 𝕷ord . . . that thy 𝕮ongregation . . .   186. our 𝕷ord.

Add: And this Collect is to be repeated till ye Sunday following. (*crossed out*)

Add: This Coll. Eple, & Gosp. shall serve to the Sunday following.

A fleuron. A fayre Compartement.[1]

i. Read: God who as vpon this feast didst teach the hearts . . .

ii. For feast *read*: day (or as about this time)

As above. Print it out at large.

As above.

A fleuron. A fayre Compartement.

Read: . . . we beseech thee, that thou wouldst keep us stedfast in this faith, & euermore defend us from all aduersitie . . .

After first *add*: Dominicall, or and so print it throughout all ye Sundays followg. (*crossed out*) *Read*: O God, the strength . . .

For Congregation *read*: Church[2]

---

[1] FC *in text.*   [2] *Also on Trinity XVI.*

182.   *See no. 180.*

   Adv.:   On the Sunday after Ascension.
        [O God the King of Glory, Who hast exalted thyne onely Sonne Jesus Xt, wth great,]
        &c.
        . . . Who liveth and reygneth wth thee and the holy Ghost, ever one God, world
        wthout end. Amen.]

183. **Adv.:**   On Whitsonday.
        [O God, Who as upon this Feast didst teach] &c. putting it thus, it will be fitt for all
        the week after.

   Part. 39. Upon Monday & Tuesday in Whitsun-weeke the same Collect is appointed, wch was
        read upon Whitsunday it selfe: but upon those Two dayes, & all ye week following
        wee cannot say — *As upon this day*: therfore there is a direction here wanting for ye
        change of that word (*This day*) into some other.

Exceptions and Bishops: *See no. 148.*

        Adv. *before Exceptions, therefore probably entered before the Savoy Conference ended.*

184. **Adv.:**   On Trinity Sunday.
        Almighty and everlasting God, Who hast given unto us thy Servants grace, by the] &c.
        . . . we beseech Thee to keep us stedfast in this fayth, and evermore to defend us from
        all adversity, Who livest and reygnest ever One God world wthout end. Amen.

Exceptions and Bishops: *See no. 179.*

185.   *Cf. no. 141.*

   Adv.:   On the *2d* Sunday after Trinity.
        [. . . Grant this, O Heavenly Father, for Jesus Xts sake, our Lord. Amen.
        On the *4th* Sunday after Trinity.
        This Gospell was the 2d Lesson for the same Day, in *Ao 1651. Jun. 22º.* Let Order now
        be set down about it.

186. **Adv.:**   On the *5th* Sunday after Trinity.
        [. . . governance, that thy Church may joyfully serve thee, in all, &c.

   SL: (Trinity V): . . . that thy people may joyfully serve thee . . .
        'Church': cf. also Part. 69 (at no. 307).

¶ The vi. vij. viij. ix. Sundays after Trinitie.

¶ The x. Sunday after Trinitie.
                    The Collect.

𝕷et thy merciful eares . . . make them to   187.   *Read*: grant them grace to aske.
aske . . . through Jesus Christ our Lord.   Stet

¶ The xi.–xxiiij. Sundays after Trinitie.

    .   .   .   .   .   .

¶ The xxv. Sunday after Trinitie.   188.   *i. Add*: Which when there be fewer or
                                                         moe shall always be the last next
                                                         before Advent.
                                                      ii. Read: And whether there be fewer
                                                         or moe Sundayes after Trinity,
                                                         this Collect, Eple & Gospel shall
                                                         alwayes . . .
                                                      iii. Delete the whole Rubric.

If there be any moe Sundayes before Aduent   189.   *i. For* moe *read*: more
Sunday, to supply the same, shall be taken the   *Before* shall be taken *add*: upon ye
seruice of some of those Sundayes that were   24. or 25. Sunday
omitted betweene the Epiphany and Septua-   *ii. Read*: If there be any more Sun-
gesima.   dayes before Aduent Sunday,
                                                         the seruice of some of those
                                                         Sundayes that were omitted after
                                                         the Epiphany shalbe taken in to
                                                         supply so many as are here want-
                                                         ing. And if there be fewer, then
                                                         shall ye 25. or 24. or both be
                                                         omitted. But whether more or
                                                         fewer, this last Collect, Epistle,
                                                         & Gospell, shall always be used

Adv.: On the 6th Sunday after Trinity.

[O God, Who hast prepared for them that love thee such good things, as pass] &c.
On the VIIth Sunday after Trinity.

[O God, the Lord of all Power and might, and the Author and giver of all good things, graff in our hearts the Love of thy name, increase] &c.

187. **Adv.:** On the 10th Sunday after Trinity.

[. . . theire Petitions, by the inspiration of thy grace make them such, as shall ever please thee, through Jesus Xt our Lord. Amen.

On the XI Sunday after Trinity.

[O God, Who declarest Thy Almighty Power most] &c.
On the XII Sunday after Trinity.

[Almighty and everlasting God, Who art alwayes more ready to heare, then we to pray, and delightest to give more then we either deserve, or desire, poure down upon us the] &c.
On the XVI Sunday after Trinity.

[. . . pity cleanse, and defend Thy Church, and] &c.
On the XXIIIth Sunday after Trinity.

[O God our refuge and Strenght, the Author of all Godlines be pleased to hear the devout prayers] &c.
On the XXIIIIth Sunday after Trinity.

[O Lord, we beseech thee grant thy people Absolution frō all their Offenses, That through thy bountifull goodnes, We may be delivered from the Bands of all those Sinns that we have committed against Thee. Grant this we beseech thee for Jesus Xts sake our Lord. Amen.

SL (Trinity XVI): cleanse, and defend thy Church

188. *Incorporated into no. 189.*

189. **Adv.:** The Rubrick that stands before St Andrewes day, to be rectified as hath bin already advised.

Part. 40: In ye End of ye 25th Sunday after Trinity it is ordered, That if there be any more Sundayes before Advent, ye Office omitted in the Sundayes after ye Epiphanie shall be taken in to supply ye same. But it will be easie & more fitt to appoint Collects Eples & Gospels peculiar to this time, when ye Sundayes after Trinitie exceed ye Number of 25. And because ye last words of the Gospel appointed upon yt 25th Sunday referre to the *Advent* or *Cõming of Christ* into ye world next to follow & to be remembered in the Church Service, therfore it were requisite that here a Rubrick should be added, to make this Eple & Gospel of ye 25. Sunday to be the *last* of them all, both when there be more, & when there be fewer Sundayes after Trinitie.

SL: If there be any moe Sundayes . . . Septuagesima. But the same shall follow the xxiiii. Sunday after Trinity. And if there be fewer Sundayes then xxv. before Advent, then shall the xxiii. or xxiiii. or both be omitted: so that the five and twentieth shall never

upon ye Sunday next before
Advent.

Set here a faire fleuron.

iii. For shall *read*: may

iv. For ye 25. or 24. *read*: ye 24. or ye 23.
after Trin.

For But whether more or fewer *read*:
Provided that

For may *read*: shall

¶ S. Andrewes day.   A fayre Compartement.

. . . . .

¶ S. Thomas the Apostle.

. . . . .

¶ The conuersion of S. Paul

. . . . .

¶ The Purification of Saint Mary the Virgine.   190.   *Read*: The Presentation of Christ
in the Temple, comonly called the
The Epistle.   Purification . . .

The same that is appointed for the Sunday.   191.   *Read*: Malach. 3. to ye 6. v.
Print it at large.

The Gospel.

𝔚𝔥𝔢𝔫 𝔱𝔥𝔢 𝔱𝔦𝔪𝔢 . . . 𝔦𝔫𝔱𝔬 𝔱𝔥𝔢 𝔱𝔢𝔪𝔭𝔩𝔢.   Print on to ye end of the 40. v.[1]

¶ Saint Matthias day.

. . . . .

Annunciation of the Virgin Mary.   192.   *i. Read*: The Annunciation Day of the
Blessed Virgin Mary.

. . . . .   *ii. Read*: The Annunciation of our
Lord to the Blessed Virgin Mary.

¶ Saint Markes day.

The Collect.

𝔄𝔩𝔪𝔦𝔤𝔥𝔱𝔦𝔢 𝔊𝔒𝔇 . . . 𝔱𝔥𝔶 𝔈𝔲𝔞𝔫𝔤𝔢𝔩𝔦𝔰𝔱 𝔖.   193.   *Read*: . . . thy blessed[2] Euangelist
𝔐𝔞𝔯𝔨𝔢 . . . 𝔬𝔲𝔯 𝔏𝔬𝔯𝔡.   S. Marke . . .

. . . . .

S. Philip and Iames day.   *Read*: . . . and S.[2] Iames day.

. . . . .

---

[1] FC: Print on to v. 41.   [2] FC *omits*.

either alter, or be left out, but be alwayes used immediatly before Advent Sunday, to which the Epistle and Gospel of that do expressly relate.

Cf. S II: In ye Order of Sarum, if there be more Sundayes after Trinity then xxv. it is appointed, that ye Service of ye 24. Sunday, shalbe repeated over againe, once, twice, or thrice, as ye Number of those Sundayes may be. So yt ye xxv. Sunday is always to be observed for ye Sunday next before Advent.

No. 188 is based on Part. 40; no. 189 draws on the existing rubric, SL, and no. 188. Wren is presumably referring to the use of the word 'Septuagesima'.

Adv.: On St Andrewes day.
[Almighty God, Who gavest such Grace unto thy Holy Apostle Andrew, that He] &c.

On St Thomas Day.
[Almighty and everliving God, Who for the more Confirmation of the fayth] &c.
. . . and the holy Ghost be all Honour and Glory now and for ever.

On the Conversion of St Paul.
[O God, Who hast taught all the world] &c.

190. **Adv.:** The Presenting of Xt in ye Temple, calld the Purification.
Cosin prefers the Latin forms 'Presentation', 'Manifestation'.

191. **Adv.:** Here wants an Epistle. Let it be Malach. 3. to the 6th verse.
The Gospell also would be set down, unto the end of the 40th vers.

Part. 41: At ye Purification there wants an Epistle proper to it selfe, which might be easily supplied.

Cf. S II: In ye Order of Sarum, the Epistle is Malachy 3.: *Haec dicit Dñus, Ecce Ego mitto Angelum meũ*, &c. usque ad — *Sicut anni antiqui dicit Dñus.*
Sarũ habet hoc ipsum Evang. & Cantic. Simeonis in fine.
The Sarum lections ended at v. 4 and v. 32 respectively.

192. **Adv.:** On St Matthias day.
[Almighty God, Who into the place of the Traytor Iudas didst choose] &c.
Th'Annunciation of our Lord to the B. Virgin Mary.
[. . . the glory of his Resurrection, for the merits of Jesus Xt our Lord. Amen.
Cf. no. 43 ('a Soloecisme').

193. **Adv.:** On St Marks Day.
[Almighty God, Who hast instructed thy Holy Church, wth the heavenly Doctrine of thy Holy Evangelist Mark, Give us grace,] &c.

Sarum: beatum Marcum evangelistam tuum.

❡ S. Barnabe Apostle.

The Collect.

𝕷𝖔𝖗𝖉 𝕬𝖑𝖒𝖎𝖌𝖍𝖙𝖎𝖊, 𝖜𝖍𝖎𝖈𝖍 𝖍𝖆𝖘𝖙 𝖊𝖓𝖉𝖚𝖊𝖉 𝖙𝖍𝖞 𝖍𝖔𝖑𝖞 𝕬𝖕𝖔𝖘𝖙𝖑𝖊 𝕭𝖆𝖗𝖓𝖆𝖇𝖆𝖘 𝖜𝖎𝖙𝖍 𝖘𝖎𝖓𝖌𝖚𝖑𝖆𝖗 𝖌𝖎𝖋𝖙𝖊𝖘 𝖔𝖋 𝖙𝖍𝖊 𝖍𝖔𝖑𝖞 𝕲𝖍𝖔𝖘𝖙: 𝖑𝖊𝖙 𝖚𝖘 𝖓𝖔𝖙 𝖇𝖊 𝖉𝖊𝖘𝖙𝖎𝖙𝖚𝖙𝖊 𝖔𝖋 𝖙𝖍𝖞 𝖒𝖆𝖓𝖎𝖋𝖔𝖑𝖉𝖊 𝖌𝖎𝖋𝖙𝖘, 𝖓𝖔𝖗 𝖞𝖊𝖙 𝖔𝖋 𝖌𝖗𝖆𝖈𝖊, 𝖙𝖔 𝖚𝖘𝖊 𝖙𝖍𝖊𝖒 𝖆𝖑𝖜𝖆𝖞 𝖙𝖔 𝖙𝖍𝖞 𝖍𝖔𝖓𝖔𝖚𝖗 𝖆𝖓𝖉 𝖌𝖑𝖔𝖗𝖞, 𝖙𝖍𝖗𝖔𝖚𝖌𝖍 𝕵𝖊𝖘𝖚𝖘 𝕮𝖍𝖗𝖎𝖘𝖙 𝖔𝖚𝖗 𝕷𝖔𝖗𝖉.

.   .   .   .   .

❡ S. Iohn Baptist.

.   .   .   .   .

❡ Saint Peters day.

The Collect.

𝕬𝖑𝖒𝖎𝖌𝖍𝖙𝖞 𝕲𝖔𝖉, 𝖜𝖍𝖎𝖈𝖍 𝖇𝖞 𝖙𝖍𝖞 𝕾𝖔𝖓𝖓𝖊 𝕵𝖊𝖘𝖚𝖘 𝕮𝖍𝖗𝖎𝖘𝖙 𝖍𝖆𝖘𝖙 𝖌𝖎𝖚𝖊𝖓[2] 𝖙𝖔 𝖙𝖍𝖞 𝕬𝖕𝖔𝖘𝖙𝖑𝖊 𝕾. 𝕻𝖊𝖙𝖊𝖗 𝖒𝖆𝖓𝖞 𝖊𝖝𝖈𝖊𝖑𝖑𝖊𝖓𝖙 𝖌𝖎𝖋𝖙𝖘, 𝖆𝖓𝖉 𝖈𝖔𝖒𝖒𝖆𝖓𝖉𝖊𝖉𝖘𝖙 𝖍𝖎𝖒 𝖊𝖆𝖗𝖓𝖊𝖘𝖙𝖑𝖞 𝖙𝖔 𝖋𝖊𝖊𝖉𝖊 𝖙𝖍𝖞 𝖋𝖑𝖔𝖈𝖐𝖊;

𝖒𝖆𝖐𝖊 𝖜𝖊 𝖇𝖊𝖘𝖊𝖊𝖈𝖍 𝖙𝖍𝖊𝖊 𝖆𝖑𝖑 𝕭𝖎𝖘𝖍𝖔𝖕𝖘 𝖆𝖓𝖉 𝕻𝖆𝖘𝖙𝖔𝖚𝖗𝖘 𝖉𝖎𝖑𝖎𝖌𝖊𝖓𝖙𝖑𝖞 𝖙𝖔 𝖕𝖗𝖊𝖆𝖈𝖍 𝖙𝖍𝖞 𝖍𝖔𝖑𝖞 𝖜𝖔𝖗𝖉, 𝖆𝖓𝖉 𝖙𝖍𝖊 𝖕𝖊𝖔𝖕𝖑𝖊 𝖔𝖇𝖊= 𝖉𝖎𝖊𝖓𝖙𝖑𝖞 𝖙𝖔 𝖋𝖔𝖑𝖑𝖔𝖜 𝖙𝖍𝖊 𝖘𝖆𝖒𝖊, 𝖙𝖍𝖆𝖙 𝖙𝖍𝖊𝖞 𝖒𝖆𝖞 𝖗𝖊𝖈𝖊𝖎𝖚𝖊 𝖙𝖍𝖊 𝖈𝖗𝖔𝖜𝖓𝖊 𝖔𝖋 𝖊𝖚𝖊𝖗𝖑𝖆𝖘𝖙𝖎𝖓𝖌 𝖌𝖑𝖔𝖗𝖞, 𝖙𝖍𝖗𝖔𝖚𝖌𝖍 𝕵𝖊𝖘𝖚𝖘 𝕮𝖍𝖗𝖎𝖘𝖙 𝖔𝖚𝖗 𝕷𝖔𝖗𝖉.

The Epistle. Act. 12. 1.

𝕬𝖙 𝖙𝖍𝖊 𝖘𝖆𝖒𝖊 𝖙𝖎𝖒𝖊 . . . 𝖕𝖗𝖆𝖞𝖊𝖗 𝖜𝖆𝖘 𝖒𝖆𝖉𝖊 𝖜𝖎𝖙𝖍= 𝖔𝖚𝖙 𝖈𝖊𝖆𝖘𝖎𝖓𝖌 𝖔𝖋 𝖙𝖍𝖊 𝖈𝖔𝖓𝖌𝖗𝖊𝖌𝖆𝖙𝖎𝖔𝖓 𝖚𝖓𝖙𝖔 𝕲𝖔𝖉 . . . 𝖔𝖋 𝖙𝖍𝖊 𝕵𝖊𝖜𝖘.

.   .   .   .   .

S. Iames the Apostle.[4]

.   .   .   .   .

❡ Saint Bartholomew Apostle.

The Collect.

𝕺 𝕬𝖑𝖒𝖎𝖌𝖍𝖙𝖞 𝖆𝖓𝖉 𝖊𝖚𝖊𝖗𝖑𝖆𝖘𝖙𝖎𝖓𝖌 𝕲𝖔𝖉 . . . 𝖙𝖔 𝖑𝖔𝖚𝖊 𝖙𝖍𝖆𝖙 𝖍𝖊𝖊 𝖇𝖊𝖑𝖊𝖊𝖚𝖊𝖉, 𝖆𝖓𝖉 𝖙𝖔 𝖕𝖗𝖊𝖆𝖈𝖍 𝖙𝖍𝖆𝖙 𝖍𝖊 𝖙𝖆𝖚𝖌𝖍𝖙, 𝖙𝖍𝖗𝖔𝖚𝖌𝖍 𝕮𝖍𝖗𝖎𝖘𝖙 𝖔𝖚𝖗 𝕷𝖔𝖗𝖉.

❡ S. Matthew Apostle.

The Collect.

𝕬𝖑𝖒𝖎𝖌𝖍𝖙𝖞 𝕲𝖔𝖉, 𝖜𝖍𝖎𝖈𝖍 . . . 𝖉𝖎𝖉𝖘𝖙 𝖈𝖆𝖑𝖑 𝕸𝖆𝖙𝖙𝖍𝖊𝖜 𝖋𝖗𝖔𝖒 𝖙𝖍𝖊 𝖗𝖊𝖈𝖊𝖎𝖙 𝖔𝖋 𝖈𝖚𝖘𝖙𝖔𝖒𝖊 . . . 𝖌𝖗𝖆𝖓𝖙 𝖚𝖘 𝖌𝖗𝖆𝖈𝖊 . . . 𝖙𝖔 𝖋𝖔𝖑𝖑𝖔𝖜 𝖙𝖍𝖞 𝖘𝖆𝖎𝖉 𝕾𝖔𝖓𝖓𝖊 𝕵𝖊𝖘𝖚𝖘 𝕮𝖍𝖗𝖎𝖘𝖙, 𝖜𝖍𝖔 𝖓𝖔𝖜 𝖑𝖎𝖚𝖊𝖙𝖍 𝖆𝖓𝖉 𝖗𝖊𝖎𝖌𝖓𝖊𝖙𝖍, &𝖈.

.   .   .   .   .

194.   Read: S. Barnabas Apostle.[1].

i. Read: O Lord Almightie, who didst endue thy blessed Apostle . . .
ii. Read: O Lord God Almightie, who didst endue thy Holy Apostle . . .
Delete , nor yet   Stet

195.   After Peters add: & St. Pauls (crossed out)

Add: & mad'st thy Apostle St Paul a chosen Vessell to beare thy Name before ye Gentiles, (crossed out)
i. Read: . . . all the Pastours, the Bishops of thy Church, & all other Ministers . . .
ii. Read: all Bishops and Pastours & other Ministers of thy Church[3]
Before receiue add: all

196.   Omitt this   (crossed out)
Or rather 2. Tim. iiii. 1. v. to ye 9th. (crossed out)
For congregation read: Church[4]

197.   i. Read: to loue that Gospel wch hee beleeued, and to preach the same, through Christ our Lord.
ii. For Gospel read: word

198.   Before Matthew add: ye holy Evangelist   (crossed out)
Delete said

---

¹ FC: S. Barnabas the Apostle.   ² FC: . . . didst giue . . .   ³ FC omits.
⁴ Also in the Gospel, and in the Epistle for S. James' day; FC does not alter in any of these places.

194. **Adv.:** On St Barnaby th' Apostle.
          [O Lord Almighty, Who didst endue thy holy Apostle Barnabas wth singular] &c.

   Sarum: beati Barnabae Apostoli tui.

   Part. 42: In ye Collect upon St. John Baptist's day, ye word *Penance* (wch is now abused by ye
          Papists) would be subject to no offence if it were altered into our ordinary word of
          Repentance, now more usuall with us then that of *Penance* is, & more consonant to the
          later Translation of our Bibles.

195. **Adv.:** On St Peters Day.
          [Almighty God, Who by thy Sonne Jesus Xt gavest unto thy Holy Apostle Peter many
          excellent gyfts, and commandedst him earnestly to feed thy flock, make we beseech
          thee the Bishops, the Pastors of thy Church among us, and all other ministers, diligently
          to preach thy holy word, and the people obediently to follow the same, that they may
          all in their severall Callings receive the Crown of everlasting Glory, through Jesus Xt
          our Lord. Amen.]
              '& St. Pauls': cf. no. 43. 'A chosen Vessell . . . Gentiles': Acts ix. 15. FC reads 'didst
              give', without support from DB. Sancroft may have adapted this from Adv., here or
              at no. 194, or from the BCP (e.g. St. Andrew's Day).

196.   *The suggested Epistle is appointed in Sarum for the Common of a Martyr. SL reads
              'Church' in all the three places where DB substitutes it, as does also Part. 69 (at no.
              307).*

197. **Adv.:** On St Bartholmew's day.
          [. . . Who gavest grace to thy holy Apostle Bartholmew truly to beleeve and to preach
          thy word, Grant we beseech thee unto the Church, to love that Gospell, wch he
          beleeved, and faythfully to preach the same, through Jesus Xt our Lord. Amen.]

198. **Adv.:** On St Matthewes Day.
          [Almighty God, Who by thy blessed Sonne didst call thy Holy Evangelist Matthew
          from the Receit of Custome, to be an Apostle, Grant us Grace to forsake all covetous
          desires, and inordinate love of Riches, and to follow thy Sonne Jesus Xt, Who liveth
          and reygneth wth Thee and the Holy Ghost, ever one God world wthout end. Amen.]

   Part. 42, cont.: On *St. Matthew's day*, there is in the Collect — *thy said Sonne*; it were better, if
          yt Word *said* were left out.

   Sarum: Beati Matthaei Apostoli tui et Evangelistae.

S. Michael and all Angels.

.   .   .   .   .

¶ S. Luke the Euangelist.

        The Collect.

𝕬lmighty 𝕲od, which calledst 𝕷uke the 𝕻hysician whose praise is in the 𝕲ospel; to be a 𝕻hysician of the soule: it may please thee . . . our 𝕷ord.

199.   *Bracket* whose praise is in the Gospel
    Read: . . . may it please thee . . .

        The Epistle. 2 Tim. 4. 5.

𝖂atch thou in all things . . . onely 𝕷ucas is with me. 𝕿ake 𝕸arke . . . withstood our words.

Bracket Take Marke . . . our words.[1]

.   .   .   .   .

¶ Simon and Iude Apostles.

200.   *Read*: S. Simon and S. Iude Apostles.

        The Collect.

𝕬lmighty 𝕲od, which hast builded thy 𝕮ongregation . . . our 𝕷ord.

For Congregation *read*: Church

.   .   .   .   .

¶ All Saints.

        The Collect.

𝕬lmighty 𝕲od . . . thy holy 𝕾aints . . . our 𝕷ord.

201.   *For* holy *read*: blessed

        The Gospel.

𝕵esus seeing the people . . . which were before you.

Here set a faire fleuron.

---

[1] FC *does not bracket*.

199. **Adv.:** On St. Michael.
    [Everlasting God, Who hast ordayned the Services of all Angels and Men] &c.

       On St Lukes Day.
    [Almighty God, Who calledst Luke the physitian, whose prayse is in the Gospell, to be physitian of the Soul, May it please Thee by] &c.
       The words 'whose praise is in the Gospel' are bracketed in the 1559 edition of the BCP.

200. **Adv.:** On St Simon and Iude.
    [O Almighty God, Who hast built thy Church upon the foundation of the] &c.

    SL: . . . thy Church . . .
       'Church': cf. also Part. 69 (at no. 307).

201. **Adv.:** On All Saynts Day.
    [Almighty God, Who hast knitt together thyne Elect, in one Communion and fellowshipp, in the mysticall Body of Thy Sonne Xt our Lord, Grant us grace so to follow thy Saynts in all virtuous and godly Living, that we] &c.
    to say [Holy Saynts] is a very improper speech.

¶ The order for the administration of
the Lords Supper or holy Communion.

Set here a faire Compartment.

Print this Title in faire Capitals on
the next page.

So many as intend to be partakers of the holy
Communion, shall signifie their names to the
Curate ouer night, or els in the morning afore the
beginning of Morning prayer, or immediatly
after.

202.   *i. For* ouer night . . . after *read*: two
dayes before at least.

ii. Read: some pt of the daye before at least.

iii. Read: at least some time ye day before.

And if any of those be an open and notorious
euill liuer, so that the Congregation by him is
offended, or haue done any wrong to his neighbours by word or deed: the Curat hauing knowledge thereof, shall call him, and aduertise him, in
any wise not to presume to the Lords Table,
vntill he haue openly declared himselfe to haue
truly repented and amended his former naughty
life, that the Congregation may thereby be satisfied, which afore were offended, and that he haue
recompensed the parties whom he hath done
wrong vnto, or at the least declare himselfe to be
in full purpose so to doe, as soone as he conueniently may.
The same order shall the Curate vse with those
betwixt whom he perceiueth malice and hatred
to reigne, not suffering them to be partakers of
the Lords Table, vntill he know them to be

203.   *For* open and notorious *read*: open,
notorious, & infamous
Stet as printed.

i. After presume *add*: to come

ii. For in any wise . . . Table *read*: that in
any wise he presume not to come to
the Lords Table

For whom he hath done wrong vnto
read: to whom he hath done wrong

202. **Adv.:** In the first Paragraph, those words [or immediately after] would now be left out; By-cause now in very few Parish Churches is there any space at all given between the Morning Prayer, and the Communion Service.

Part. 43: In ye first Rubrick before ye Administration of ye Holy Coṁunion, ye order appointed for *ye Coṁunicants to signifie their Names to ye Curate iṁediately after Morning Prayer,* seemes to Crosse ye Coṁon Custome in all or most places of Reading ye Morning Service, & ye Coṁunion Service both at one time. For if they be read at once, wthout any interṁission or due space of houres betweene them, what time or convenience can ye Coṁunicants have to give in their Names, or the Curate to take them? Here therfore a direction is wanting what space of time is to be allowed betweene these Two Services.

Exceptions: The time here assigned for notice to be given to the Minister is not sufficient.

Bishops: Conc. 5. That a longer time be required for signification of the names of the Com. and the words of the *Rubr.* be changed into these (at least some time the day before.)

Cf. S I: Wherupon is necessarily inferr'd a certaine distance of time betweene Morn. Prayer, & High Service. A rule wch is at this day duly observed in York & Chichester; but by negligence of Ministers and carelesnes of people wholy omitted in other Places.

and Lords: 11. In the Rubrique for the administration of the Lords Supper, whether this altera-tion to bee made, that such as intend to communicate shall signify their names to the Curat over night or in the morning before Prayers.

> *As with other Savoy Conference concessions, Wren and Cosin were already convinced of the desirability of a change.*

203. **Part. 44:** In ye 2d Rubrick there, it is not cleere whether ye Curate may refuse to give ye Coṁunion unto *an open & notorious Evill Liver,* nor who is to be accompted so *notorious;* wch therfore requires here some explanation for ye avoyding of disputes, doubts, & contentions at that time betweene such Coṁunicants & ye Curate, who otherwhiles challengeth yt power of Refusing or Admitting a Coṁunicant in that Case by vertue of this Rubrick, the rather because in ye Rubrick iṁediately following it is said, *That he shall use ye same order* wth those yt are in malice with one another, where he has power given him to Refuse ye *Obstinate Person.*

Cf. S I (from Andrewes): Our Law of England will not suffer ye Minister to iudge any man a Notorious offendour, but him, who is convicted by some Legall Sentence.

> *See also no. 409. The alterations by S are stylistic.*

reconciled. And if one of the parties so at variance, be content to forgiue from the bottome of his heart all that the other hath trespassed against him, and to make amends for that he himselfe hath offended, and the other party will not be per-swaded to a godly vnity, but remaine stil in his frowardnesse and malice: the Minister in that case ought to admit the penitent person to the holy Communion, and not him that is obstinate.

204. *After* reconciled *add*: Or if either of them refuse so to be, untill he hath certified his Ordinary therof (wch he shall doe without delay,) and have direction from him what in yt case ought to be done. (*crossed out*)

205. *Add*: Provided, yt every Minr so repelling any (as is specifyed either in this, or the next preceding[1] Rubrick) shall be obliged to give an account of ye same immediately after to ye Ordinary.

The bread & wine for ye Cõion shalbe provided by ye Curate, & ye Church-wardens at ye charges of the Parish.

The Table hauing at the Communion time a faire white linen cloth vpon it, shall stand in the body of the Church, or in the Chancell, where Morning prayer and Euening prayer be appointed to be said. And the Priest standing at the North side of the Table, shall say the Lords prayer, with this Collect following.

206.
  i. *After* Table *add*: being at all times decently covered, &
  Before body *add*: Chancell, or
  Print this in a faire Italick character
  ii. *Delete the whole Rubric and read*:
  The TABLE always standing in the midst at the upper part of the Chancell, or Church, where a Chancell is wanting, and being at all times decently covered with a carpet of Silk[2] shall also have at the Comunion time a faire white linnen cloth spread over it.
  And the Priest standing at the North End of ye Table shall say the Lords prayer
  OUR FATHER, who art &c"—but deliver us from Evill. Amen.
  Print it out at large.
  iii. *For* upper part *read*: upper end
  For or Church . . . wanting *read*: (or of the Church . . . wanting,)
  Delete decently
  For spread over it *read*: upon it with patin chalice &[3] other decent furniture meet for the high Mysteries there to be celebrated.
  iv. *For* End *read*: side or end

---

[1] FC: precedent.   [2] *Originally* a silke Carpet.   [3] patin chalice & *added subsequently*.

204. Adv.: The Third Paragraph is so set down, as that it may be a Snare, both to the Minister, and to the People. Yf it shall be thought fitt, it may go better thus, [Untill He know them to be reconciled: Or yf any One of them refuse to be, Untill he hath certified his Ordinary thereof, by the Churchwardens, or by himself, (wch shall be done wthout delay,) and have Directions from him, what to do in that Case.

205. Exceptions: We desire the Ministers power both to admit and keep from the Lords Table, may be according to his Majesties Declaration of the 25. *Octob.* 1660 . . .

Bishops: Conc. 6. That the power of keeping scandalous Sinners from the Communion, may be expressed in the *Rubr.* according to the 26. and 27. *Canons,* so the Minister be obliged to give an account of the same immediately after to the Ordinary.

Canon 27: Provided that every Minister so repelling any (as is specified either in this or in the next precedent Constitution) shall vpon complaint, or being required by the Ordinary, signify the cause thereof vnto him, and therein obey his order and direction.

> *S conflates the Bishops' Reply and Canon 27; FC is closer to the Canon in one word ('precedent'). The new rubric omits the qualification in the Canon: 'upon complaint'. 'The bread & wine . . .': transferred to this point from no. 280.*

206. Adv.: In the *4th* Paragraph, those words, [Or in the Chancell, where Morning Prayer and Evening Prayer be appointed to be sayd] are very ambiguous. Many Churches now have no Chancels: Also in the most that have, though the Desk for Reading the Prayers doth stand in ye Body of the church, yet they use to goe into the Chancell to Receive the Communion. Let it therfore be expressely here set down, what is intended, still keeping the use of the Chancels, where it may well be done: But leave nothing ambiguous.

> *ibid.* And the Preist standing at the North of ye Table, (the people all kneeling) shall begin wth the Lords Prayer, [Our Father, Who art in] &c.

Part. 45: In ye 4th Rubrick there, wch appoints ye *Table to be covered with a linnen cloth* onely, & *to stand in the Chancell or Body of ye Church, where Morng & Eveng Prayers are ordered to be said,* somewhat is wanting to make it agree with ye Injunctions of Q. Elizab. (still in force) & ye common practise of most Churches.

SL: The holy Table having at the Communion time a Carpet, and a faire white linen cloth upon it, with other decent furniture, meet for the high mysteries there to be celebrated, shall stand at the uppermost part of the Chancell or Church, where the Presbyter, standing at the north-side or end thereof, shall say the Lords prayer, with this Collect following for due preparation.

Injunctions (¶ For the Tables in the Churche): . . . And that the holy Table in euery Churche be decently made, and sette in the place where the aulter stode, and there commonly couered . . . sauyng when the Communion of the Sacrament is to be distributed; at whiche tyme, the same shalbe so placed in good sort within the Chaunsell . . . And after the Communion done, from tyme to tyme the same holy Table to be placed where it stode before.

Canon 82: . . . couered in time of Diuine Seruice with a carpet of Silke or other decent stuffe . . . and with a faire linnen cloth at the time of the administration . . .

> *Stage i follows Part. 45 in appealing to the Injunctions, whose phrases 'decently made . . . and there commonly covered' become 'at all times decently covered'. This stage was broken off incomplete, and a fresh start made.*

After Lords prayer *add*: with the Collect
following
For who art *read*: which art

¶ The Communion.

For The Communion *read*: The
Collect.

𝕬𝖑𝖒𝖎𝖌𝖍𝖙𝖞 𝕲𝖔𝖉, 𝖚𝖓𝖙𝖔 𝖜𝖍𝖔𝖒 . . . 𝖙𝖍𝖗𝖔𝖚𝖌𝖍
𝕮𝖍𝖗𝖎𝖘𝖙 𝖔𝖚𝖗 𝕷𝖔𝖗𝖉. 𝕬𝖒𝖊𝖓.

Then shall the Priest rehearse distinctly all the ten   207.
Commandements: and the people kneeling, shall
after euery Commandement, aske God mercy for
their transgression of the same, after this sort.

After Priest *add*: turning to the
people
Before kneeling *add*: still
For after *read*: in

Minister.

𝕲𝖔𝖉 𝖘𝖕𝖆𝖐𝖊 𝖙𝖍𝖊𝖘𝖊 𝖜𝖔𝖗𝖉𝖊𝖘 𝖆𝖓𝖉 𝖘𝖆𝖎𝖉, 𝕴 𝖆𝖒 𝖙𝖍𝖊
𝕷𝖔𝖗𝖉 𝖙𝖍𝖞 𝕲𝖔𝖉: 𝖙𝖍𝖔𝖚 𝖘𝖍𝖆𝖑𝖙 𝖍𝖆𝖚𝖊 𝖓𝖔𝖓𝖊 𝖔𝖙𝖍𝖊𝖗   208.
𝖌𝖔𝖉𝖘 𝖇𝖚𝖙 𝖒𝖊.

.   .   .   .   .   .

After thy God *add*: who brought thee out
of the land of Egypt, out of ye house of
bondage.

𝕽𝖊𝖒𝖊𝖒𝖇𝖊𝖗 𝖙𝖍𝖆𝖙 𝖙𝖍𝖔𝖚 𝖐𝖊𝖊𝖕 𝖍𝖔𝖑𝖞 𝖙𝖍𝖊 𝕾𝖆𝖇𝖇𝖔𝖙𝖍
𝖉𝖆𝖞 . . .

For Sabboth *read*: Sabbath

.   .   .   .   .   .

. . . 𝖜𝖊 𝖇𝖊𝖘𝖊𝖊𝖈𝖍 𝖙𝖍𝖊𝖊.

Then shall follow the Collect of the day, with one   209.
of these two Collects following for the King, the
Priest standing vp, and saying,

Read: Then shall follow one of
these two Collects for the King,
& the Collect of the Day, the
Priest standing as at first, and
saying,

Stage ii draws on SL ('the upper part', 'at the Communion time', 'a fair white linen cloth', 'the north end'); Canon 82 adds 'a carpet of silk'. 'Where a Chancel is wanting' is suggested by Adv., and 'at all times decently covered' is retained from stage i. An important addition, not found in any of the sources quoted above, is the word 'alwayes', relating to the position of the Table at the upper part of the Chancel; the Injunctions *regard this as the normal position, except at the Communion Service; SL directs this position for the Communion, which presumably implies 'and at other times also'; but this is the first explicit statement that the Table is to remain always 'where the altar stood', thus realizing Laud's ideal.*
Stage iii incorporates a further phrase from SL ('other decent furniture . . . celebrated') and adds the paten and chalice, perhaps after mentioning them in connexion with the manual acts.
Stage iv also goes back to SL for 'north side or end'. This phrase continued to arouse discussion, for in FC the original entry was 'at the North   of the table'. Sancroft evidently expected that either 'side' or 'end' would be chosen, but in the end both were retained, and he was forced to write 'sideorend' in the small space left.

207. **Adv.:** In the 1 Collect. [. . . through Jesus Xt our Lord.
  In the Rubrick there, thus,
  Then the Preist, turning his face towards the people, shall rehearse distinctly all the Ten Commandm.] &c.

  SL: Then shall the Presbyter, turning to the people, rehearse distinctly all the TEN COMMANDEMENTS: the people all the while kneeling . . .

  SL rather than Adv.

  Cf. S I (from Andrewes):
  The Priest after the Collect descends to ye dore of ye Septum, makes a low Adoration towards ye Altar. Then turnes to ye people; and standing in the dore, readeth ye x Commandemts (as from God) whiles they lie prostrate, to ye end, as to God speaking.

208. **Exceptions:** We desire,
  First, that the Preface prefixed by God himself to the ten Commandments may be restored.

  Bishops: Conc. 7. That the whole Preface be prefixed to the Commandments.

209. **Adv.:** In that Rubrick, thus,
  Then the Preist, at the Holy Table where he stood at first, leaving out the words [Let us pray] or else saying, [Let us pray for our Lord the King] shall say one of these following Collects, and after it shall say the Collect for the Day.

¶ 𝕷et 𝖚𝖘 𝖕𝖗𝖆𝖞.

𝕬lmig𝔥tie 𝕲o𝔡, w𝔥o𝖘e 𝕶ing𝔡ome i𝖘 euer=
la𝖘ting an𝔡 power infinite, 𝔥aue mercy 𝖚pon
t𝔥e w𝔥ole 𝕮ongregation, an𝔡 𝖘o rule t𝔥e
𝔥eart of t𝔥y c𝔥o𝖘en 𝖘eruant 𝕵ame𝖘 . . . worl𝔡
wit𝔥out en𝔡. 𝕬men.

210.   *For* the whole Congregation *read*:
           thy holy Church
        For Iames *read*: Charles
        Add: or.

𝕬mig𝔥ty an𝔡 euerla𝖘ting 𝕲o𝔡 . . . 𝕵e𝖘u𝖘
𝕮𝔥ri𝖘t our 𝕷or𝔡.

Immediatly after the Collects, the Priest shall
reade the Epistle, beginning thus:

𝕿𝔥e 𝕰pi𝖘tle written in t𝔥e 𝕮𝔥apter of

211.   *i. Read*: . . . the Priest or one ap-
           pointed, shall turne to ye people
           & reade the Epistle in the place
           assigned for it, beginning thus
        The Epistle is written in the Chapter
        of
        & ending thus
        Here endeth ye Epistle.
     ii. For one *read*: the Epistler

And the Epistle ended, he shall say the Gospel,
beginning thus:

212.   *i. Read*: . . . he, or one a Deacon that
           ministreth shall read ye Gospel
           saying first,

Part. 46: In ye Rubrick after ye X Comdts, it is appointed, *That then shall follow ye Collect of ye day, with one of ye Two Collects there specified for ye King, ye Priest standing up & saying, Almighty &c.* but whether ye Collect for ye King, or ye Collect for ye day shalbe first said, is not there determined; wch for the avoyding of dispute & diversity herein, should be further explayned. And ye Collect for ye day is alwayes most properly used together wth the Eple & Gospel, wherunto many times it relateth.

SL: Then shall follow one of these two Collects for the King, and the Collect of the day, the Presbyter standing up, and saying,

SL, expressing Part. 46 and Adv. (the latter supplying 'at first'). Brightman (I. ccxvii) regards this change as 'unhappy', and this opinion is fairly widespread among writers on the BCP; for example, Dom G. Dix (The Shape of the Liturgy, 660 n.), who appeared not to know the excellent reason given by Cosin for the new order. Cosin's own collects always 'relate' to the Epistle and Gospel (see nos. 145, 150, 162, 172).

210. **Adv.:** In that Collect for the King, thus,
[. . . have mercy upon thy Church, and so rule the hart of thy servant Ch: our king, that he knowing, whose minister He is] &c.
That the word [Governor] makes but a Diminution; and that ill use hath bin made of it in this Rebellious age, to take upon them to judg, how He governed, is too well known: The word [chosen] also hath bin pretended among the people, for their Rebellion, that they are the Choosers, & Makers of kings.
Betwixt these 2 Collects, set, Or. and there leave out the word [Governour] also.

SL: . . . thy holy Catholike Church . . .
SL rather than Adv.?

211. **Adv.:** Add to those Rubricks, [And when the Epistle is finished, he shall say, [So endeth the Epistle,] And when the Gospell [So endeth the holy Gospell.]

SL: Immediatly after the Collects, the Presbyter shall read the Epistle, saying thus: the Epistle written in the   Chapter of   at the   verse. And when he hath done, he shall say: Here endeth the Epistle.

1549: . . . the priest, or he that is appointed, shall reade the Epistle, in a place assigned for the purpose . . .

Advertisements: Item, *In the ministration of the holy Communion in cathedrall and collegiat churches, the principal minister shall vse a cope, with gospeller and epistoler agreablye,* and at all other praiers to be said at that Communion table, to vse no Copes but surplesses.
(The words in italics were underlined by Cosin in his own copy.)
1549, supplemented from SL, and possibly from S I:
Here the other Priest, or if there be none, He yt executes, descendeth to ye dore, adores, & then turning, readeth ye Eple & Gospell.
In Cathedrall Churches ye Epistoler is seldom a Priest. . . .
The author then goes on to quote the Advertisements. *The first sentence comes from Andrewes's Notes.*

212. **Adv.:** *see no. 211.*

Part. 47: At ye Reading of ye Gospel, there is no *Posture* appointed for ye people, wch gives many of them occasion to refuse ye Posture of *Standing*, as in all places & time hath bin

The Gospel written in the Chapter of

The holy Gospell is written in the
    Chapter of
And the people all standing up shall
    say,
Glory be to thee O Lord.
At ye end of the Gospell
He that readeth it shall say,
Here endeth the holy Gospel.
And the people shall answere,
Thanks be to thee, ô Lord.

ii. For or one a Deacon that ministreth
    read: or one appointed
    Before At ye end *add*: And

iii. For he, or one *read*: the priest or the
    Gospeller

And the Epistle and Gospel being ended, shall be
said the Creede.

213. *i. Read*: Then shall be said or sung
    this Creede, all still reverently
    standing up.

  ii. Read: Then shall be sung or said . . .[1]

I Beleeue in one God . . .

    .   .   .   .   .   .

the world to come. Amen.

New paragraphs at and in one Lord
Iesus Christ *and* And I beleeue in
the holy Ghost.

After the Creede, if there be no Sermon, shall
follow one of the Homilies already set foorth, or
hereafter to be set foorth by common authoritie.

214. *Read*: After the Creede shall follow
    ye Sermon, or one . . .
  For common *read*: publick
    (*both crossed out*)

After such Sermon, Homily, or Exhortation, the
Curate shall declare vnto the people, whether
there be any Holy-dayes, or Fasting-dayes the
weeke following,

215. *i. Read*: Which being ended, the
    Curate shall declare vnto the
    people what Holy-dayes, or Fast=
    ing-dayes are that weeke to be
    observed.

  ii. For that weeke *read*: the weeke fol-
    lowing

---

[1] FC: . . . said, or sung. . . .

accustomed. This therfore were requisite to be here added. Nor is there any order after ye Naming of ye Gospel for ye people to say *Glory be to Thee ô Lord*, as hath bin likewise accustomed, & was specially ordered in K. Edward's time, together with *Thanks be given to God*, at ye End of ye Gospel. For uniformitie, & ye advancemt of our devotions herein, that order would be fitly here renewed.

SL: And the Epistle ended, the Gospel shalbe read, the Presbyter saying: The holy Gospel is written in the   Chapter of   at the   verse. And then the people all standing up shall say: Glory be to thee, O Lord. At the end of the Gospel, the Presbyter shall say: So endeth the holy Gospel. And the people shall answer: Thanks be to thee, O Lord.

1549:   . . . the Priest, **or** one appointed to reade the Gospel . . . The Clearkes and people shal aunswere. Glory be to thee, O Lorde. The priest or deacon then shall reade the Gospel . . .

Advertisements: *see no. 211.*

> *Again SL and 1549, rather than Adv. or Part. Cf. also S I:*
> *When ye Gospell is named ye People are to answere Glory be to thee o Lord, wch was appointed in K. Edw. Service book, & is still used, howsoever it came to be left out here . . . If it had pleased the printer this might have stood still.*
> *'Thanks be given to God' appears to be peculiar to Cosin; cf. MS. Tanner 48 (1), a single sheet in Cosin's hand, written in December 1661:*
> *7. Before ye Gospel to be said or sung, 'Glory be to thee ô Lord.' And after it is ended, 'Thanks be given to the Lord.'*

213. **Adv.:**   Then shall be rehearsed by Him and them all, The Beleef, called the Nicen Creed.

Part. 48: At ye Nicen Creed, there is likewise no Posture of Standing specially here appointed: by reason of which omission many refuse to stand, though at ye other Creed of ye Apostles they are appointed to doe it, as here likewise they ought to doe; & at *Athanasius his Creed* besides; for all wch provision may be made in their severall places.

SL: And the Epistle and Gospel being ended, shall be said or sung this Creed, all still reverently standing up.

Cf. S I: Adorat, ascendit, et legit Symbolum Nicaenum, populo adhuc stante. (Andrewes)

> *It will be remarked that Andrewes's Notes have exerted a considerable influence on this part of the service, through Cosin and possibly through SL. Making the people stand for the Nicene Creed was one of the charges brought against Cosin by Peter Smart (Correspondence, I. 144).*

214. **Adv.:**   In the third Line, it should be, [. . . and the Sonne, is together worshipped and].
The first Rubrick there, to be thus,
After the Creed, immediately shall the Sermon begin: or yf there be no Sermon, One of the Homilies (already set forth, or hereafter to be set forth by Authority) shall be read by the Minister, out of the Pulpit.

1549: After the Crede ended, shall folowe the Sermon or Homely . . .
> *With the two sources above, compare Exceptions:*
> *We desire, that the preaching of the Word may be strictly injoyned, and not left so indifferent at the administration of the Sacrament . . .*

215.   *Stylistically improved and slightly more forceful.*

216. *i. Add*: & then shall notice be given of ye Coṁunion, & ye Banns of Matrimony published. And nothing els shalbe proclaymed or published in ye Church but by ye minister; nor by him any thing but what is prescribed in the Rules of this Booke, or injoyned by the Ordinary of ye Diocesse.

ii. After & then *add*: (if occasion be)
After published. *add*: & Briefs, Citations, or Excommunications read, if any be brought for yt purpose.

iii. Delete if any . . . purpose.
Delete els
For by the Ordinary of ye Diocesse *read*: by the King or by the Ordinary of ye place.

and earnestly exhort them to remember the poore, saying one or moe of these sentences following, as he thinketh most conuenient by his discretion.

217. *i. Read*: Then shall the Priest returne unto ye Lords Table, & begin the Offertory, and earnestly exhort the people to remember the poore, saying . . . discretion.

ii. Delete and earnestly . . . discretion.[1]

𝕷et your light so shine before men . . . Matth. 5.
𝕷ay not vp for your selues . . . Matth. 6.
𝖂hatsoeuer ye would . . . Matth. 7.
𝕹ot euery one that sayth . . . Matth. 7.
𝖅ache stood forth . . . Luke 19.
𝖂ho goeth a warfare . . . 1. Cor. 9.
𝕴f wee haue sowen . . . 1. Cor. 9.
𝕯oe yee not know . . . 1. Cor. 9.
𝕳e that soweth little . . . 2. Cor. 9.
𝕷et him that is taught . . . Galat. 6.
𝖂hile we haue time . . . Galat. 6.
𝕲odlinesse is great riches . . . 1. Tim. 6.
𝕮harge them which are rich . . . 1. Tim. 6.
𝕲od is not vnrighteous . . . Hebr. 6.
𝕿o doe good, and to distribute . . . Hebr. 13.
𝖂ho so hath this worlds good . . . 1. Iohn 3.
𝕲iue almes of thy goods . . . Tob. 4.
𝕭e mercifull after thy power . . . Tob. 4.
𝕳ee that hath pity vpon the poore . . . Prou. 19.
𝕭lessed is the man that prouideth . . . Psal. 41.

218. *i.* Print the first thirteene of these Sentences, at a distance from ye Six following; & those Six at a distance from the Six next after; & ye last (being the 26.) in a distance by it self.

The Sentences are numbered as follows to arrange them in a new order, including the additional Sentences at no. 219:
1, 2, 3, 4, 20, 14, 15, 16, 17, 18, 19, 5, 6, 7, 8, 21, 24, 25, 23, 22.
The resultant order is:

Let your light so shine . . .
Lay not vp for your selues . . .
Whatsoeuer ye would that men . . .
Not euery one that sayth . . .
Godlinesse is great riches . . .
Charge them which are rich . . .
God is not vnrighteous . . .
To doe good, and to distribute . . .
In processe of time . . .
Speak vnto the children . . .
Yee shall not appeare . . .
Give vnto the Lord yee families . . .
As Jesus sate . . .

Who goeth a warfare . . .
If wee haue sowen vnto you . . .
Doe yee not know . . .
He that soweth little . . .
Let him that is taught . . .
While we haue time . . .

---

[1] FC *restores:* saying . . . discretion.

216. **Adv.:** After such Sermon, or Homily, the Minister shall return agayn to the Table, and turning
toward the people, shall declare unto them, What Holydayes, and Fastingdayes will
be in that week following. He shall also then publish the Banes for Matrimony, and
signify the Contents of such Breefes as are brought to the Parish, for Collections, and
then he shall say, [Heare now the Monitions of the Holy Ghost, as it is written,]
naming the Chapter and Verse, whence it is taken, and reading One, or moe, as He
shall thinck meet in his discretion.

There wants an Order,

That no man shall publish any thing in the Church, but the Minister alone: And that He
make no Publication or Proclamation there of any thing, But what is prescribed by the
Rules of this Book, or enjoyned by his Ordinary.

*Cf. Canon 22 (quoted at no. 227), and no. 366. The rest is from Adv. Brightman (I. 651)
finds Presbyterian influence in iii.*

217. **Adv.:** *see no. 216.*

SL: . . . saying (for the offertory) one or moe . . .

BCP (Rubric after the Blessing, at no. 272): . . . the Offertory . . .

Cf. Cosin, *Visitation Articles,* 1626: 9. When the Sermon is ended, doth he *returne* unto the Holy
Table . . .?

218. **Adv.:** These Sentences now are all the same here, that were before, But the Order of their
standing is a little altred: To this purpose, that as they are now ordered, the Seaven
that stand first, will appeare to be in generall for All kind of Charitable Gyfts; The
seaven next to tend particularly to that, wch they calld Prosphoran in the Primitive
Church, that is, A Freewill Offring unto God: And the six last, to be especially for the
Eleemosyna, that is, our Almes deeds to the poor. Thus then set them,

Matth. 5. 16.	Matth. 6. 19.	Matth. 7. 21.
1. Tim. 6. 6.	1. Tim. 6. 17.	Heb. 6. 10.
Hebr. 13. 16.	Matth. 7. 12.	1. Cor. 9. 7.
1. Cor. 9. 11.	1. Cor. 9. 13.	2. Cor. 9. 6.
Gal. 6. 6.	Gal. 6. 10.	Luc. 19. 8.
1. Ioan. 3. 17.	Psal. 41. 1.	Prov. 19. 17.
Tobit. 4. 7.	Tobit. 4. 8.	

but let the words of every Sentence be set agayn down at larg, as they were before,
and the Texts in ye Marge.

Exceptions: Two of the sentences here cited are Apocryphal . . .

Bishops: . . . though some of the Sentences be Apocryphal, they may be useful.

*SL omits the two Apocryphal Sentences. Their removal here causes the alteration from
'Six' to 'fower'. If the existing Sentences are numbered 1–20 and the new ones (no. 219)
21–26, the various combinations and rearrangements may be tabulated thus:*
SL: *21, 22, 23, 26, 24, 2, 4, 25, 6, 7, 8, 9, 10, 13, 14, 15.*
This omits ten of the old Sentences; the order is biblical.

Adv.: *1, 2, 4, 12, 13, 14, 15; 3, 6, 7, 8, 9, 10, 11; 5, 16, 20, 19, 17, 18.*
*This only uses the old Sentences. They are arranged by subject-matter (see above).
The first two groups are in biblical order; in the third, the order is N.T., O.T.,
Apocrypha.*

Zache stood forth, and said . . .
Who so hath this worlds good . . .
Blessed be the man that prouideth . . .
Hee that hath pity . . .
Giue almes of thy goods . . .
Be mercifull after thy power . . .

Blessed be thou ô God for ever . . .

ii. Delete the Sentences

Giue almes of thy goods . . . *and* Be
mercifull after thy power . . .

For the six next after *read*: the fower
next after

219.   *Add these Sentences:*

9. Gen. 4. In processe of time, it
came to passe that Cain brought
of ye fruit of ye ground an offering
unto ye Lord; & Abel brought
also of ye firslings of his flock, &
of the fatt therof. And the Lord
had respect unto Abel, &[1] his
offering.

10. Exod. 25. Speak unto the children of Israel, that they bring me
an Offering. Of every one that
giveth willingly with his heart,
they shall take my Offring.

11. Deut. 16. Yee shall not appeare
before the Lord empty. Every
man shall give as he is able, &
according to the blessing of the
Lord thy God, wch he hath given
thee.

12. Psal. 96. Give unto the Lord
yee families of the people: give
unto the Lord glory & power;

Give unto the Lord ye glory due
unto his name; bring presents, &
enter into his Courts.

13. Mark. 12. As Jesus sate over
&   against the Tresurie,
Luke. 21. he beheld how ye
people cast mony into it; & many
that were rich cast in much. And
he saw also a certaine poore
Widdow, who cast in two Mites.
And he said; Of a truth I say unto
you, that this poore Widdow hath
cast in more then they all. For
they of their superfluity cast into
the Tresury of God, but she of
her penury hath cast in all the
living that she had.

---

[1] FC: . . . & unto his offering.

DB: *1, 2, 3, 4, 12, 13, 14, 15, 21, 22, 23, 24, 25; 6, 7, 8, 9, 10, 11; 5, 16, 20, 19, 17, 18; 26.*

This is the order of Adv., with no. 3 restored to the first group; five of the new Sentences are added to the first group; and the sixth is placed by itself at the end. Later, 17 and 18 were removed.

219. **S I** (Andrewes): Peculiar Sentences for ye Offertorie.

Gen. 4. 3. 4. *Identical with DB.*

Exod. 25. 2. *Identical with DB.*

Deut. 16. 16. 17. Three times in ye yeere shall all ye males appeare before ye Ld thy God, in ye place which he shall choose, & they shall not appeare before the Lord empty. Every man shall give according as he is able . . .
  Then as DB.

1 Chron. 29. 14. 17. All things come of thee o Ld. and of thine owne wee give unto thee. I have offred willingly in ye uprightnes of my heart, of all these things. Now also have I seene thy people, wch are found here to offer unto thee willingly with ioy. (Nehem. 10. 30.)

Ps. 96. 7. 8. Give unto the Ld. ye families of ye people, Give unto ye Ld. glorie & powre. Give unto ye Ld. ye glory of his name, bring an offring & enter into his Courts.

Mar. 12. 41. *As DB, except:* 'And many rich men', 'cast into ye offerings of God'. (Act. 24. 17.)

> *SL has only nos. 1–4, 6, and 7; the wording reproduces the A.V. exactly. Andrewes's version is adapted from older translations. DB follows SL's choice of Sentences, but in the main follows Andrewes's wording, though some phrases are from A.V., and some are peculiar to DB.*
>
> *In the first two Sentences DB exactly reproduces Andrewes's divergences from A.V. In the third Sentence DB is almost identical with SL, while Andrewes gives a differing extract with minor variants. Both Andrewes and SL have the Chronicles passage next, and here DB differs from both. In the Psalm Sentence, DB is close to Andrewes, which is a conflation of A.V. and the BCP version; SL has only one verse, from A.V. In the last new Sentence, DB again follows Andrewes closely, in his conflation of Mark and Luke; SL uses Mark only. Here, 'superfluity' is taken by DB from the 'Bishops' Bible', while 'Treasury of God' appears to be peculiar to DB.*

26. 1. Chron. 29. Blessed be thou ô
God for ever. Thine ô Lord is
ye greatnes & the glory. For all
that is in ye heaven & in ye
earth is thine. Both Riches &
Honour come of thee; & of thine
owne doe wee give unto thee.[1]
As for me, in ye uprightnes of my
heart I have willingly offred all
these things. And now have I
seene with joy thy people, who are
here present, to offer willingly
unto thee.

Then shall the Churchwardens, or some other by them appointed, gather the deuotion of the people, and put the same into the poore mans boxe,

220. i. Read: While the Priest distinctly
pronounceth some or all of these
Sentences for ye Offertory, the
deacon, or if no such be present,
one of the churchwardens shall
receive the devotions of the people
in a decent Basin provided for that
purpose, & reverently bring it[2]
to ye priest, who shall humbly
present the same before the Lord,
& place it upon the holy Table.
And after the Comunion is ended,
such Almes shalbe putt[3] into the
poore mens Boxe, or distributed
if present need require.

ii. After the devotions of the people
add: & ye Almes for the Poore
For such Almes ... distributed read:
they shall put the same Almes
into the poore mens Boxe, or
forthwith distribute it

iii. Read: While the Priest distinctly
pronounceth some of (or all) these
Sentences for ye Offertory, the
deacon, or if no such be present,
the churchwardens shall receive
ye Almes for the Poore & other
devotions of ye people in a decent
Basin provided for that purpose,
& reverently bring it to ye priest,
who shall humbly present & place
it upon the holy Table.

[1] FC: . . . we give thee.
[2] Originally them.
[3] such Almes shalbe putt is written over the original version, which is indecipherable.

220. Adv.: Now Divide this Rubrick, and set it thus,

Yf any Person have in his hart a Freewill Offring for God, let them cause it to be delivered in private to the Minister, wth their other accustomed Offrings, such as are then due from them.

As for the Devotion of the people to the Poor, the Churchwardens, or some appointed by them, shall presently after the Sentences go about, and gather it, and then shall bring it unto the Minister, by him to be placed on the Holy Table, till the Divine Service be finished, and then to be put into the Poor Mens boxe, or to be presently given, as need shall be.

After the Curate hath pronounced such of the Sentences, as he shall choose, he shall say,

Part. 45, cont.: And somewhat is also wanting for a direction when & where to sett ye *Bread & wine* for ye Comn upõ yt Table.

Part. 50: In ye Rubrick following ye Sentences at ye Offertorie, *ye Churchwardens, or some other by them appointed*, are ordered to *gather ye devotions of ye people, & to put ye same into ye poore-mens Boxe*; wch being seldome or never observed in most Churches, nor agreeing to divers Sentences (before sett downe) would be otherwise here Ordered or Explained. And ye *accustomed offerings to ye Curate* are here appointed *to be paid by every man or woman, After wch done ye Priest shall say*. &c. Wch, if it should be thus observed & at this time when they come to receive the Comunion, would breed a great disturbance in ye church, & take up more time, then can be allowed for yt purpose. Wherfore it is needfull yt some alteration were made of this Rubrick; & That the offrings or devotions of ye people then collected should be brought to ye Priest, & by him presented & layd upon ye Altar or Comunion Table for such uses as be peculiarly named in ye sentences then read by him.

SL: While the Presbyter distinctly pronounceth some or all of these Sentences for the offertory, the Deacon, or (if no such be present) one of the Church-wardens, shall receive the devotions of the people there present in a bason provided for that purpose. And when all have offered, hee shall reverently bring the said bason with the oblations therein, and deliver it to the Presbyter, who shall humbly present it before the Lord, and set it upon the holy Table. And the Presbyter shall then offer up and place the bread and wine prepared for the Sacrament upon the Lords Table, that it may be ready for that service. And then he shall say,

and vpon the offering dayes appointed, euery man and woman shall pay to the Curate the due and accustomed offerings.

Read: And vpon the offering dayes appointed, euery man and woman shall bring & pay to the Curate the due and accustomed offerings.

i. *Add*: And if there be a Comūnion, the Priest shall then offer up, & place ye Bread & Wine in a comly Paten & Chalice upon the Table, that they may be ready for the Sacrament, so much as he shall think sufficient.

ii. *Read*: And if there be a Comūnion, the Priest shall then offer up, & place upon the Table so much Bread & wine as he shall think sufficient.

¹After which done, the Priest shall say.

¶ Let vs pray for the whole state of Christs Church militant here in earth.

221.   i. *For* state *read*: estate
ii. *Read*: Let vs offer up our prayers & praises for the good estate of Christs Catholick Church.
And here the people shall kneele.

𝔄lmighty & euerliuing 𝔊od, which by thy holy 𝔄postle hast taught vs to make prayers and supplications, and to giue thankes for all men: we humbly beseech thee, most mercifully (to accept our almes, and) to receiue these our prayers,

[𝔍f there be no almes giuen vnto the poore, then shall the words (of accepting our almes) be left out vnsaid.]

which wee offer vnto thy diuine 𝔐aiesty, beseeching thee to inspire continually the vniuersall 𝔠hurch with the spirit of trueth, vnitie, and concord: and grant that all they that doe confesse thy holy 𝔑ame, may agree in the trueth of thy holy 𝔚ord, and liue in vnitie, and godly loue. 𝔚ee beseech thee also to saue and defend all 𝔠hristian 𝔎ings, 𝔓rinces, and 𝔊ouernours, and specially thy

222.   *Read*: . . . (to accept these our almes & Oblations, and) . . .
After almes *add*: or Oblations
Delete vnto the poore
After almes *add*: or Oblations

---

¹ FC: *new paragraph.*

1549: Than shall the minister take so muche Bread and Wine, as shall suffice for the persons appoynted to receiue the holy Communion, laiyng the breade vpon the corporas, or els in the paten . . . And puttyng ye wyne into the Chalice . . . And setting both the bread and wyne vpon the Alter . . .

Canon 84: The which almes and devotion of the people, the Keepers of the Keys shall . . . (as need requireth,) take out of the chest, and distribute the same . . .

> *i is closest to SL, which expresses the intention of Adv. and Parts. 45 and 50; 1549 and Canon 84 are also drawn upon. The increased prominence given to the Offertory is found on all hands:*

S I (from Andrewes):
They shold not pay it to ye Curate alone, but to God upon ye Altar.

Wren, *Particular Orders:* 18. . . . by him be reverently presented before ye Lord, & sett upon ye Table . . .

Taylor, *Collection of Offices:* Let him in an humble manner present it to God, laying it upon the Communion Table.

> *Wren has a rubric of this nature in Adv. after the* Sanctus *(see no. 238).*

221. **Adv.:** [Let us pray for the whole State] &c.
[Almighty and everliving God, who by thy] &c.

1549: Let us praie for the whole state of Christes churche.

> *For 'estate', see Adv. on no. 223. The words 'militant here in earth' are inconsistent with the passage added at no. 224, and are therefore omitted.*

222. **SL** (at no. 220): . . . the said bason with the oblations therein . . .

> *The meaning of the phrase 'alms and oblations' is fully discussed by Bp. J. Dowden (Further Studies, 191–213). His evidence includes two quotations from Wren (Order for the Consecration of Abbey Dore, 1635, and Particular Orders), who is probably responsible for the introduction of the word 'oblations', though the two words are found in conjunction in Jeremy Taylor's Communion Office:*
> *Lord accept the oblation and almes of thy people . . .*
> *The words 'vnto the poore' are deleted as applying only to the alms, and not to the oblations.*

seruant James our King, that vnder him we may be godly and quietly gouerned: and graunt vnto his whole Counsaile, and to all that bee put in authoritie vnder him, that they may truely and indifferently minister iustice, to the punishment of wickednes and vice, and to the maintenance of Gods true Religion and vertue. Giue grace (O heauenly Father) to all Bishops, Pastours, and Curats that they may both by their life and doctrine, set forth thy true and liuely word, and rightly and duely administer thy holy Sacraments: and to all thy people giue thy heauenly grace, and specially to this Congregation here present, that with meeke heart, and due reuerence they may heare and receiue thy holy Word, truely seruing thee in holines and righteousnes all the dayes of their life.

For Iames *read*: Charles

For Gods *read*: Christ's
(*crossed out*)
Read: . . . to all Pastours, Bishops, and Curats . . .[1]

223.　*Delete* and specially to this Congregation here present,

Add: [And wee commend especially unto thy mercifull goodnes this Congregation which is here assembled in thy Name, to celebrate ye Commemoration of ye most pretious death & Sacrifice of thy Sonne & our Saviour Jesus Christ,]
In margin: When there is no Communion, these Words thus inclosed [ ] are to be left out.

And we most humbly beseech thee of thy goodnes, O Lord, to comfort and succour al them which in this transitory life be in trouble, sorrow, neede, sickenesse, or any other aduersity:

224.　*Add*: And wee also blesse thy holy Name for all those thy Servants, who having finished their course in faith doe now rest from their labours. And wee yield unto thee most high praise & hearty thanks for the wonderfull grace & vertue declared in all thy Saints, who have bin the choyse Vessels of thy Grace, & the Lights of the World in their severall Generations; most humbly beseeching thee, that wee may have grace to

---

[1] FC: *no alteration.*

'Gods' is altered to 'Christ's' because the prayer is addressed to the Father. With 'all
Pastours . . .' cf. nos. 113 and 195.

Adv.: at the 2d line, thus,
Give grace, O heavenly Father, unto the Pastors of the Church the Bps, and unto all
other that are charged wth the Cure of Soules, that they may] &c.

223. **Adv.:** at the 7th line, leave out those words [And specially to this Congregation here present,]
The Prayer being ordayned for the whole Estate of Xts Church; And also when it is
used in small Families, and at Communions for the Sick, or otherwise, those words
are not so Proper.

SL and 1549 do not contain the words 'and specially to this Congregation here present' at
this point, but have an equivalent phrase at the end of the sentence.

SL: [And we commend especially unto thy mercifull goodnesse, the congregation which is
here assembled in thy name to celebrate the commemoration of the most precious
death and sacrifice of thy Son and our Saviour Jesus Christ.]
In the margin: When there is no Communion, these words thus inclosed [ ] are to be
left out.

1549: And especially we commend vnto thy merciful goodnes, thys congregacion whiche is
here assembled in thy name, to celebrate the commemoration of the most glorious
deathe of thy sonne.

DB is closer to SL than to 1549, except for 'this Congregation'; SL is probably preferred
because of the mention of Christ's sacrifice.

224. **Adv.:** But now it is to be well markt, What a proposall is made unto God in the beginning of
this Prayer: It is sayd, For 2 Things, First, To pray for all, and then, To give Thancks
for all. So they begin to pray, and go on wth it throughout: but That done, There's
an end, and No Thanksgiving. Of all Right, it would be added now agayn. For in the
Primitive Church, they ever had here a Commemoration, and Thanksgiving for the
Saynts. It was also here in this Prayer in Edw. VI Dayes. But in ye beginning of Qu.
Eliz. that the Vulgar might not thinck, they did either pray to the Dead, or for the
Dead, they chopt of the End of this prayer, Never thincking of ye Proposall made in
the beginning of it. Thanks be to God, there can be no pretence at all now, Why it
should not be restored.
But yf not, Let not God be flouted to his face, by the Church, but leave out those words
at first, [And to give thanks.]

Part. 51: In ye Beginning of *ye Prayer for ye State of Christ's Church militant*, there be these words,
(sett as Preface to what is intended to follow, & to have Relation thereunto,) *Which*
hast taught us to Give Thanks for all men; & accordingly, in the old forme of this prayer
sett forth in K. Edward's time, *such Thanks were given*, yt one part of the prayer might be
correspondent to ye other. But here in our forme, ye *Thanksgiving* is omitted, & yet
ye preface of *Giving Thanks* is suffered to stand still; being indeed forgotten to be put
out. Therfore it either now to be taken away, or els the former (or the like) Thanksgiving ought to be added unto the prayer: for otherwise wee say to God, (in effect)
that though *he hath taught us to give Thanks for all men*, yet wee thinke fitt to let it alone.

SL: *identical with DB.*

follow ye example of their stedfastnes in thy faith, & obedience
to thy holy Comandements, that
at the day of the generall Resurrection, wee and all they wch are[1]
of the mysticall Body of thy Sonne,
may be sett on his right Hand, &
heare that his most joyfull voyce,
"Come yee Blessed of my Father,
inherit the Kingdome prepared
for you from the foundation of the
World".

grant this, O Father for Jesus   Grant &c
Christs sake our onely Mediatour and
Aduocate, Amen.

Then shall follow this exhortation at certaine   225.   i. *Read*: When the Curate . . . holy
times, when the Curate shall see the people   Communion, he shall use this
negligent to come to the holy Communion.   Exhortation, upon ye Sunday
                                                         before he intendeth to celebrate
                                                         ye same.
                                                    ii. *Read*: . . . he shall use this Exhorta-
                                                         tion in the pulpit after the Sermon
                                                         or Homilie there ended, upon ye
                                                         Sunday or some Holyday before
                                                         he intendeth to celebrate ye same.

---

[1] *Originally* be.

1549: And here wee doe geue vnto thee moste high prayse, & heartie thankes, for the wonderfull grace and vertue, declared in all thy sainctes, from the begynninge of the worlde: and chiefly in the most glorious and most blessed virgin Mary, mother of thy sonne Iesu Christ our Lord and God, & in the holy Patriarches, Prophetes, Apostles and Martyrs, whose examples (O Lorde) and stedfastnes in thy faythe, and keping thy holye commaundementes, graunte vs to folowe. We commend vnto thy mercie (O Lorde) all other thy seruauntes, whiche are departed hence from vs, with the signe of fayth, and nowe do reste in the slepe of peace: Graunte vnto them, we beseche thee, thy mercy, and euerlasting peace, and that at the daye of the generall resureccion, we and all they whiche bee of the misticall body of thy sonne, maye altogether bee set on his right hand, and heare that his most ioyful voice: Come vnto me, O ye that be blessed of my father, and possesse the kingdome, whiche is prepared for you, from the begynning of the worlde: Graunte this . . .

> *SL is again the source (note the correction by S of the single tiny divergence); 1549 would have been quite unacceptable at that time. Part. 51 is based upon a very similar passage in S III, which is also used by L'Estrange, who recommends* 'some such clause as the Scotch Litturgy exhibiteth, as Eucharistical for the Saints departed in the faith'.

> *The fact that both Adv. and Part. deal with the point at such length suggests that neither was using L'Estrange's Alliance, and that Cosin had not the Advices before him when writing the Particulars.*

225. Adv.: Now for that Exhortation, It would be well considered, Whither it shall not now be quite left out, for divers Reasons.
    1. Yf the Parishioners do not Receive, as often as they ought by Law, they are lyable to censure for neglecting.
    2. [To stand by as Gazers & Lookers on] is now wholy out of use in all Parishes, And the Not-Communicants generally do use [to depart,] wthout bidding.
    3. Where all that would be Communicants, do not at the Beginning of this Service come up into the Chancell, (wch in most places they do not,) the Minister knowes not well, whither he shall have few Communicants, or no.
    4. It contradicts the former Rubrick made for certyfying of their Names, that would communicate, and now lets them know, They shall presently be admitted, yf they will come, So that there was no need to certifye their Names.
The Rubrick therfore may be thus,
[Warning shall be duly given for every Communion, by the Minister, upon the Sunday before, next after the Nicen Creed at Morning Prayer; And then, yf by their not having come to him to signify their Names, he do perceive to much negligence in them, He may take occasion in his Sermon, or at Reading the Homily to make some use of this Exhortation.]
But surely it will be better to omitt both it, and this Rubrick, and therfore I do not now point at some slipps in it.

Part. 52: The first & second *Exhortations* yt follow, are more fitt to be read some dayes before ye Comûnion, then at ye very same time when ye people are come to receive it. For first they yt tarry for yt purpose are not *negligent*, & they yt are *negligent*, be gone, & heare it not. Then 2ly they yt should *come to ye Minister for the quieting of their Conscience & Receiving ye Benefit of Absolution*, have not then a sufficient time to doe it. Wherfore requisite it is, that these *Two Exhortations* should be appointed to be read upon ye Sunday, or some other Holyday before.

We be come together at this time (dearely beloued brethren) to feede at the Lords Supper . . .

226.

Read: Dearely beloued brethren On — Day next, I doe intend by Gods grace to celebrate the Lords Supper

.   .   .   .   .   .

When God calleth you, bee you not ashamed to say you will not come? When you should returne to God, will you excuse your selfe and say, that you bee not ready?

For bee *read*: are

For bee *read*: are

.   .   .   .   .

Euen so it is your duety to receiue the Communion together in the remembrance of his death, as hee himselfe commanded. Now, if you will in no wise thus doe, consider with your selues how great iniurie you do vnto God, and how sore punishment hangeth ouer your heads for the same. And whereas you offend God so sore in refusing this holy banket, I admonish, exhort, and beseech you. that vnto this vnkindnesse yee will not adde any more: which thing ye shall doe, if yee stand by as gazers and lookers on them that doe communicate, and be not partakers of the same your selues. For what thing can this be accounted else, then a further contempt and vnkindnesse vnto God: Truely it is a great vnthankfulnesse to say nay, when yee be called: but the fault is much greater when men stand by, and yet will neither eate nor drinke this holy Communion with other. I pray you what can this be else, but euen to haue the mysteries of Christ in derision: It is said vnto all, Take ye, and eate, Take & drinke ye all of this, Do this in remembrance of me. With what face then, or with what countenance shall ye heare these words: what will this be else, but a neglecting, a despising and mocking of the Testament of Christ: wherefore rather then yee should so doe, depart you hence, and giue place to them that be godly disposed. But when you depart, I beseech you ponder

After death, *add*: & Sacrifice

Delete And whereas . . . them that be godly disposed.

Exceptions: If it be intended that these Exhortations should be read at the Communion, they seem to us to be unseasonable.

Bishops: Conc. 8. That the second Exhortation be read some Sunday, or Holy-day before the celebration of the Communion, at the discretion of the Minister.

Canon 22: *see no. 227.*

> *Another case of agreement between Wren, Cosin, and the Presbyterians. 'In the pulpit': i.e., rather than at this point in the service, when the Minister has returned to the altar (no. 217).*

226. **SL:**   . . . death and sacrifice . . .

> *The opening words are modified, and a long passage about 'gazing and looking' omitted, in accordance with the suggestions made by Adv. at no. 225.*

with your selues from whom yee depart. Yee
depart from the Lords Table, yee depart from
your brethren, and from the banquet of most
heauenly food. These things if ye earnestly
consider, yee shall by Gods grace returne to
a better minde: for the obtaining whereof we
shall make our humble petitions, while we
shall receiue the holy Communion.

For Yee depart . . . heauenly food.
　　read: when yee wilfully abstaine
　　from the Lords Table, & separate
　　from your brethren, who come to
　　feed on the banquet of that most
　　heauenly food.

And sometime shall this be said also at the discretion of the Curate.

Dearely beloued,

227.　　*Read*: When[1] the minister giveth
　　　warning for ye Celebration of ye
　　　holy Comunion, he shall always
　　　read this Exhortation following.

228.　i. *Add*: On — day next I purpose
　　　through Gods gracious assistance
　　　to offer unto all such as shalbe
　　　religiously & devoutly disposed,
　　　the most comfortable Sacrament
　　　of ye Body & Bloud of Christ, to
　　　be received of them in the remem-
　　　brance of his most fruitfull &
　　　glorious Crosse & Passion, where-
　　　by wee have obteyned remission
　　　of our sins, & be made partakers
　　　of the Kingdome of heaven, being
　　　therof assured if wee come to that
　　　Sacrament with hearty repentance
　　　for our Sinnes, with a stedfast
　　　faith in Gods mercy, & with an
　　　unfeyned purpose to obey him &
　　　offend no more. And forasmuch
　　　&c.
　　ii. *For* offer *read*: tender
　　　Delete most fruitfull & glorious
　　　For have obteyned *read*: obteyne
　　　Delete And forasmuch &c.

forasmuch as our duety is
to render to Almighty God our heauenly
Father most hearty thankes,

　　i. *Read*: Wherfore our duty is, so to
　　　come to those holy Mysteries; &
　　　further to render most hearty
　　　thanks unto almighty God our

---

[1] *Originally* And always when . . .

227. **Adv.:** Supposing the foregoing Exhortation to be quite left out, This Rubrick would now be
thus,
[When there is to be a Communion, the Curate shall give warning thereof at Morning
Prayer on the Sunday before, next after the Nicen Creed, and shall then (before he
proceed to ye Sentences) read this Exhortation following, [Dearely Beloved,] &c.

Exceptions and Bishops: *see no. 225.*

Canon 22: . . . Wee doe require euery Minister to giue warning to his Parishioners publiquely
in the Church at Morning prayer the Sunday before euery time of his administring
that holy Sacrament, for their better preparation of themselues . . .

Cf. Wren, *Particular Orders*: 8. That warning be given . . .; And that as soon as such warning is
given, The second of those 3 Exhortations . . . be treatably pronounced . . .

Cf. nos. 216 and 225.

228. **1549:** On   next, I do intende by Gods grace to offre to all suche as shalbe godly disposed,
the moste comfortable Sacrament of the body and bloud of Christe, to be taken of
them, in the remembraunce of his moste fruitfull and glorious Passion: by the whiche
passion, we haue obteigned remission of our sinnes, and be made partakers of the
kyngdom of heauen, whereof we bee assured and asserteigned, yf wee come to the
sayde Sacrament, with heartie repentaunce for our offences, stedfast faithe in Goddes
mercye, and earnest minde to obeye Goddes wyll, and to offend no more.

heavenly Father, & his blessed
Sonne our Saviour Jesus Christ,
for that, &c

ii. *For* so to come *read*: to come thus
prepared
Delete & his blessed . . . Christ,

for that he hath
giuen his Sonne our Sauiour Jesus Christ,
not only to die for vs, but also to be our
spirituall food and sustenance, as it is declared vnto vs, as well by Gods word as by
the holy Sacraments of his blessed body and
blood, the which being so comfortable a thing to
them which receiue it worthily, and so dangerous to them that will presume to receiue
it vnworthily:

i. *Delete* as it is . . . blood,
ii. Stet
Before holy *add*: same
iii. *Read*: in that holy Sacrament

i. *After* the which *add*: Sacrament
(*crossed out*)
Before comfortable *add*: divine &
holy, & so
ii. *Delete* holy, & so

After you *add*: in ye meane season
For the holy *read*: that holy

my duety is to exhort you to consider the dignity of the holy mystery, and the
great perill of the vnworthy receiuing thereof,
and to search and examine your owne con-
sciences, as you should come holy and cleane
to a most godly and heauenly feast, so that in
no wise you come but in the mariage garment
required of God in holy Scripture, and so
come and be receiued, as worthy partakers of
such a heauenly Table . . .

For as you should . . . Table *read*:
& that not lightly, nor after the
manner of dissemblers wth God,
but so[1] that yee may come holy
and cleane to such a heauenly
feast, in the mariage garment required by God in holy Scripture,
and be receiued, as worthy partakers of that holy Table.

·   ·   ·   ·   ·   ·

therfore if there be any of you, which by the
means aforesaid cannot quiet his owne conscience but requireth further comfort or
counsell, then let him come to me, or some
other discreete and learned Minister of Gods
Word,

i. *For* which . . . conscience *read*: who
cannot quiet his owne mind
herein
ii. *Read*: who by this means cannot quiet
his owne conscience herein

i. *For* Minister of Gods Word *read*:
Priest & Minister of God
ii. *Read*: Priest, ye Minr of Gs word

and open his griefe, that hee may receiue such ghostly counsell, aduice, and comfort: as his conscience may be relieued, and
that by the ministerie of Gods word he may
receiue comfort, and the benefite of absolution,
to the quieting of his conscience, and the
auoiding of all scruple and doubtfulnesse.

i. *Read*: and open his griefe, that by
the ministerie of Gods holy word
he may receiue the benefite of absolution, ghostly counsell, & advise,
to the quieting . . . doubtfulnesse.
ii. Stet: hee may receiue such ghostly
counsell, aduice, and comfort: as his
conscience may be relieued, and that
(*crossed out*)

---

[1] *Originally* they who.

Wherefore our duetie is to come to these holy misteries . . . The whiche Sacrament being so Diuine and holy a thing, and so comfortable . . . My duetie is to exhorte you in the meane season . . . and that not lyghtly nor after the maner of dissimulers with GOD: But as they whiche shoulde come to a moste Godly and heauenly Banket . . .

The passage in the text 'as it is declared . . . blood' was added in 1552. The intention of these additions and omissions is to restore the text of 1549, with minor modifications (e.g., footnote). The alterations in the passage on Absolution seem to be merely stylistic, except for the insertion of 'Priest', which follows SL: . . . Presbyter or Minister of Gods word . . .

Then shall the Priest say this exhortation.

𝔇earely beloued in the 𝔏ord . . .

.   .   .   .   .   .

Therefore, if any of you be a blasphemer of 𝔊𝔒𝔇, an hinderer, or slanderer of his word, an adulterer, or bee in malice, or enuie or in any other grieuous crime, bewaile your sinnes, and come not to this holy Table, lest after the taking of that holy Sacrament, the deuill enter into you, as hee entered into Judas, and fill you full of all iniquities, and bring you to destruction both of body and soule . . .

229.   *i. After* crime *add*: not having duly repented therof, learne to (*crossed out*)
     For come not *read*: presume not to come   Stet
   ii. Bracket the whole sentence.

.   .   .   .   .   .

And to the end . . . he hath instituted and ordained holy mysteries, as pledges of his loue, and continuall remembrance of his death, to our great and endless comfort . . . all the dayes of our life.

230.   *Before* holy *add*: these
     Before continuall *add*: for a
     Before his death *add*: Him & of (*crossed out*)
     Add: Amen.[1]

Then shall the Priest say to them that come to receiue the holy Communion.

𝔜ou that doe truely . . . his holy wayes: 𝔇raw neere,

and take this holy 𝔖acrament to your comfort, make your humble confession to 𝔄lmighty God, before this 𝔠ongregation here gathered together in his holy 𝔑ame, meekely kneeling vpon your knees.

231.   *i. Add*: with a true heart in full assurance of faith   (*crossed out*) Stet
   ii. Delete with a true heart
     For make *read*: making (*crossed out*)
     For before *read*: in   Stet

     Before meekely *add*: as you are now (*crossed out*)

---

[1] FC *in text.*

229. **Adv.:** That Rubrick to be thus,
  The Preist having ended the Prayer for the Militant Church, shall then begin this
  Exhortation following: Dearely beloved in the Lord, yee] &c.
  At the *17th* line, to avoyd unnecessary contention, put it thus [The Devill enter into you,
  as He entred into Iudas after the sopp, and fill you] &c.

  Part. 53: Likewise in ye *Third Exhortation* there be these words appointed to be read somewhat
  out of due time, *If any of you be a Blasphemer of God, a Hinderer or Slanderer of his word,
  an Adulterer, or be in Malice or Envy, or in any other grievous crime, Bewayle your sins, & come
  not to this Holy Table, Least after the taking of yt Holy Sacramt, ye divel enter you as he did
  into Judas &c.* For is any person who comes at yt time purposely to Receive ye Com̄-
  union, likely to discover himself (if he be guiltie) in the presence of all ye Congregation by Rising up & departing suddenly from it? Therfore this Clause were fitter to be
  omitted in this *Third Exhortation* & to be added to *ye Second*, a weeke or some dayes at
  least before the Com̄union is administred.

  1549: . . . except he be truely sory therefore . . .

  *The sentence referred to in Part. 53 is bracketed, but not omitted, or transferred to the
  Second Exhortation, as Cosin suggests. With 'presume not' cf. no. 203.*

230. **Adv.:** At the first line, put those words thus,
  [. . . He hath to our great and endless comfort instituted and ordayned these Holy
  Mysteries for Pledges of His Love, and for a continual Remembrance of Him, who
  Dyed for us. To him therfore] &c.

  'of Him & of his death': cf. no. 244, where Wren's reason for this change is expounded.

  BCP: Amen.

231. **Adv.:** The first Rubrick to be thus,
  Then shall the Preist say unto them that are come together for the Communion.
  You now truly and earnestly repenting you of your sinnes, and being in love & charity
  wth all men, intending by Gods assistance to lead a New life, and to follow the Commandments of God, and to walk frõ henceforth in His holy wayes, shall receive this
  holy Sacrament to your Comfort. Make therfore your humble Confession unto
  Almighty God, all meekely kneeling before him.

  Part. 54: In the next words wch *the Priest is to say unto them yt come to ye holy Com̄union*, they are
  invited *To draw neere*; And though in many places they use so to doe, where they are
  to remove from their Seates, & to approach neerer to ye Table in the church or chancell
  for ye Taking of ye Holy Sacramt; yet in other places, where ye Chapells are small, &
  the Com̄unicants so few, yt they are all fixed already in their severall places within ye
  chancell or church neere to ye Table before these words come to be read unto them,
  there will be no need to have them Remove, & therfore no need of any such words.
  For wch reason there would be a provision here made to yt purpose.

  *'Meekely kneeling upon your knees' is not superfluous if the communicants have only
  just drawn near; DB's addition 'as you are now' attempts to make the phrase appropriate, now that the practice of drawing near is less frequent. So also the substitution of
  'in this Congregation' for 'before . . .' The completion of the quotation from Hebrews
  (x. 22) may likewise be an attempt to suggest a spiritual drawing-near.*

Then shall this generall confession be made, in the name of all those that are minded to receiue the holy Communion, either by one of them or else by one of the Ministers, or by the Priest himselfe, all kneeling humbly upon their knees.

232. *For* one of them or else by *read*: a Deacon, or *(crossed out)*
Delete or by the Priest himselfe
For all *read*: both he & all the people
After knees *add*: & saying.

𝕬𝖑𝖒𝖎𝖌𝖍𝖙𝖞 𝕲𝖔𝖉 . . . 𝖜𝖊 𝖐𝖓𝖔𝖜𝖑𝖊𝖉𝖌𝖊 𝖆𝖓𝖉 𝖇𝖊𝖜𝖆𝖎𝖑𝖊 . . . 𝕵𝖊𝖘𝖚𝖘 𝕮𝖍𝖗𝖎𝖘𝖙 𝖔𝖚𝖗 𝕷𝖔𝖗𝖉. 𝕬𝖒𝖊𝖓.

233. *For* knowledge *read*: acknowledge

Then shall the Priest or the Bishop (being present) stand vp, and turning himselfe to the people, say thus.

234. *For* say thus *read*: pronounce this Absolution.

𝕬𝖑𝖒𝖎𝖌𝖍𝖙𝖞 𝕲𝖔𝖉 . . . 𝕵𝖊𝖘𝖚𝖘 𝕮𝖍𝖗𝖎𝖘𝖙 𝖔𝖚𝖗 𝕷𝖔𝖗𝖉. 𝕬𝖒𝖊𝖓.

Then shall the Priest also say.

❡ 𝕳𝖊𝖆𝖗𝖊 𝖜𝖍𝖆𝖙 𝖈𝖔𝖒𝖋𝖔𝖗𝖙𝖆𝖇𝖑𝖊 𝖜𝖔𝖗𝖉𝖘 . . . 𝕮𝖔𝖒𝖊 𝖛𝖓𝖙𝖔 𝖒𝖊 . . . 𝖙𝖍𝖊 𝖕𝖗𝖔𝖕𝖎𝖙𝖎𝖆𝖙𝖎𝖔𝖓 𝖋𝖔𝖗 𝖔𝖚𝖗 𝖘𝖎𝖓𝖓𝖊𝖘.

After which the Priest shall proceed, saying.

𝕷𝖎𝖋𝖙 𝖛𝖕 𝖞𝖔𝖚𝖗 𝖍𝖊𝖆𝖗𝖙𝖘.

Answere.

𝖂𝖊 𝖑𝖎𝖋𝖙 𝖙𝖍𝖊𝖒 𝖛𝖕 𝖛𝖓𝖙𝖔 𝖙𝖍𝖊 𝕷𝖔𝖗𝖉.

Priest.

𝕷𝖊𝖙 𝖛𝖘 𝖌𝖎𝖚𝖊 𝖙𝖍𝖆𝖓𝖐𝖊𝖘 𝖛𝖓𝖙𝖔 𝖔𝖚𝖗 𝕷𝖔𝖗𝖉 𝕲𝖔𝖉.

Answere.

𝕴𝖙 𝖎𝖘 𝖛𝖊𝖗𝖞 𝖒𝖊𝖊𝖙𝖊 𝖆𝖓𝖉 𝖗𝖎𝖌𝖍𝖙 𝖘𝖔 𝖙𝖔 𝖉𝖔𝖊.

Priest.

235. *Read*: Then shall the Priest turne to Gods Table & say.

𝕴𝖙 𝖎𝖘 𝖛𝖊𝖗𝖞 𝖒𝖊𝖊𝖙𝖊, 𝖗𝖎𝖌𝖍𝖙, 𝖆𝖓𝖉 𝖔𝖚𝖗 𝖇𝖔𝖚𝖓𝖉𝖊𝖓 𝖉𝖚𝖊𝖙𝖞 𝖙𝖍𝖆𝖙 𝖜𝖊𝖊 𝖘𝖍𝖔𝖚𝖑𝖉 𝖆𝖙 𝖆𝖑𝖑 𝖙𝖎𝖒𝖊𝖘, 𝖆𝖓𝖉 𝖎𝖓 𝖆𝖑𝖑 𝖕𝖑𝖆𝖈𝖊𝖘, 𝖌𝖎𝖚𝖊 𝖙𝖍𝖆𝖓𝖐𝖊𝖘 𝖛𝖓𝖙𝖔 𝖙𝖍𝖊𝖊, ✠ 𝕷𝖔𝖗𝖉 𝖍𝖔𝖑𝖞 𝕱𝖆𝖙𝖍𝖊𝖗, 𝕬𝖑𝖒𝖎𝖌𝖍𝖙𝖞 𝖊𝖚𝖊𝖗𝖑𝖆𝖘𝖙𝖎𝖓𝖌 𝕲𝖔𝖉.

232. **Adv.:** Now the *2d* Rubrick to be thus.
> Then shall this generall Confession be made in the Name of all present, either by One of them, or by One of the Ministers, Or by the Preist himself, all humbly kneeling.

Part. 55. In ye Rubrick before ye *Confession*, there wanteth a direction for ye people to say ye wordes of yt Confession after ye Minister; whereunto they are all invited by the words before *Make your humble Confession, meekely kneeling.*

SL: . . . by the Presbyter himself, or the Deacon, both he and all the people kneeling humbly upon their knees.

Exceptions: We desire it may be made by the Minister only.

Bishops: Conc. 9. That the general Confession at the Communion be pronounced by one of the Ministers, the people saying after him, all kneeling humbly upon their knees.

> *There is a general consensus of opinion in favour of the congregation joining in the Confession; cf. S I (Andrewes):*
> *The other Priest, (if there be a second) or He that executes descendeth to ye dore and there kneeling saith ye Confession, ye people repeating after him.*
> *and Lords:*
> *14. Whether the Rubrique is not to be mended, concerning the party that is to make his generall confession upon his knees, before the Communion, that it should be said only by the Minister and then at every clause repeated by the people.*

233. **Adv.:** in the 2d line of that Confession, let it be, [Maker of all the world, Iudg of all men] &c.
   SL (& **BCP** from 1559): . . . we acknowledge . . .
   > *Sanderson also amends this archaism.*

234. **Adv.:** Add here the Chapter and Verse to these Scriptures.
> After those Sentences of Scripture, let the Rubrick be,
> [The Preist standing agayn at the Table shall proceed and say,
> [Lyft up your Harts.]

   SL: . . . pronounce the absolution, as followeth.

235. **Adv.:** But at those words in the Last line, [It is very meet, right, and] he must mark, that on Trinity Sunday the words [Holy Father] must be left out.
   1549 (before the Prayer of Humble Access): Then shall the Priest turning hym to goddes boord . . . saye . . . this prayer following.
   > *Cf. Wren's rubric at no. 234.*

Here shall follow the proper preface, according
to the time, if there be any specially appointed:
or else immediatly shall follow.

For if there be any *read*: as is here
Stet

Therefore with Angels & Archangels, &c.

Proper Prefaces.

Vpon Christmas day, and seuen dayes after.

**Because thou didst giue Jesus Christ thine
onely Sonne to be borne as this day for vs . . .**

.   .   .   .   .   .

236.   *i. After* day *add*: (or time)
    ii. Read: (or as about this time)

Vpon Whitsunday, and sixe dayes after.

**Through Jesus Christ our Lord, according
to whose most true promise the holy Ghost
came down this day . . .**

**Whereby we are brought out of darkenesse
and errour . . .**

i. After down *add*: as at (*crossed out*)
ii. & iii. As on Christmas Day.
For are *read*: have bin

Vpon the Feast of Trinitie onely.

**It is very meete, right, and our bounden
duety, that wee should at all times & in all
places giue thankes to thee, O Lord, Al=
mighty and euerlasting God, which art one
God, one Lord, not one onely person, but
three persons in one substance. For that
which we beleeue of the glory of the Father,
the same we beleeue . . . inequalitie.**

237.   *Delete* onely[1]
    Delete It is very meete . . . euer-
    lasting God.

    Begin ye Prop. preface heere
i. For which art . . . substance *read*:
    who art one God, & one Lord, yet
    not one onely person, but three
    persons in one divine substance.
ii. Stet as printed, except who *for*
    which.

After which Prefaces, shall follow immediatly.

**Therefore with Angels . . . O Lord most
high.**

238.   *Read*: After which Prefaces, shall
    immediatly be sung or said.
    Add: Amen.

239.   *i. Add*:
    Here followeth the Consecration.
    When the Priest hath so ordered
    the Bread & Wine placed upon
    the Table, as that he may with the
    more ease & decency take them
    into his hands, standing up he
    shall say.
    Almighty God &c
    as in ye next page.

---

[1] FC: *not deleted.*

236. **Exceptions:** . . . First, we cannot peremptorily fix the Nativity of our Saviour to this or that particular day. Secondly, it seems incongruous to affirm the birth of Christ, and the descending of the holy Ghost to be *on this day*, for seven or eight daies together.

    Bishops: Conc. 4. That the words (this day) both in the Collects, and Prefaces, be used only upon the day itself, and for the following dayes, it be said (as about this time.)

        Cf. no. 148 (the Collect). Sanderson has 'to be born as at this time'.

    Adv.: In the 5th line read it,
        [Whereby we have bin brought out of darknes] &c.

237. **Adv.:** The next Rubrick to be thus,
    Upon Trinity Sunday and 6 dayes after.
        [. . . all places, give thanks unto Thee, O Lord Almighty, and everlasting God, Who art One God, and One Lord, and yet not One onely Person, but Three Persons in One Divine Substance: For that] &c.
    Now here wants a Proper Preface for the Presenting of Xt in the Temple, being among us so great a Festivall.
        'Onely' (after 'upon the Feast of Trinitie') is not in 1549.

238.   *On the singing or saying of 'Therefore with Angels . . .' by the people, see the interesting note in Brightman (I. ccxviii, referring to p. 687).*

239. **Adv.:** The last Rubrick on that Page would be thus,
    Here shall the Bread and Wine, wch is provided for that Communion, be in a decent manner presented by the Churchwardens or some other for them, unto the Preist, Who shall wth due Reverence set as much thereof in both kinds, as he shall conceive there will be then use of, upon the Lords board, (and the rest to remayn, ready at hand by him, yf need should be of it:) And then He kneeling down before the Table, shall in the Name of all Present say, [We do not presume to come to] &c.

ii. *Read*: Here followeth the Prayer of
Consecration.[1]

When the Priest standing before ye
Table, hath so ordered the Bread
& Wine, that he may with the
more readines & decency break
the Bread & take the Cup into his
hands, he shall say, as followeth.
Almighty God &c.
as in ye next page.[2]

iii. *After* break the Bread *add*: before
the people.

Then shall the Priest kneeling downe at Gods
Board, say in the name of all them that shall
receiue the Communion, this prayer following.

𝔚e doe not presume to come to this thy
𝔗able . . . graunt us therefore gracious
𝔏ord, so to eate the flesh of thy deare 𝔖onne
. . . and he in us. 𝔄men.

240.   *After* Lord *add*: in these holy
Mysteries   (*crossed out*)

Then the Priest standing vp, shall say as followeth.

241.   *For* Then . . . followeth *read*: The Prayer
of Consecration.

𝔄lmighty 𝔊od, our heauenly 𝔉ather, which
of thy tender mercy diddest giue thy onely
𝔖onne 𝔍esus 𝔠hrist to suffer death vpon the
𝔠rosse for our redemption, who made there
(by his one[3] oblation of himselfe once offered)
a full, perfect, and sufficient sacrifice, obla=
tion, and satisfaction for the sins of the whole
world, and did institute, and in his holy
𝔊ospel commaund us to continue a perpetuall
memory of that his precious death, vntill his
comming againe: 𝔥eare us, 𝔒 mercifull
𝔉ather, we beseech thee,

242.   *Before* continue *add*: celebrate &
(*crossed out*)
After death *add*: & Sacrifice[4]
Before beseech *add*: most humbly

---

[1] FC *adds*: What followes from hence to ye end of the distribution is somewhat otherwise methodiz'd
in ye paper B. & both left to censure. See after the next leafe. (See *Appendix B, p. 290.*)
[2] FC *places this rubric at no.* 241.
[3] FC: one (*for* owne *in text*).
[4] FC *omits here, but includes in Paper B.*

(*at no. 241*): This first Rubrick to be thus,

Then the Preist standing before the Table shall so order and set the Bread and the Wine, That while he is pronouncing the following Collect, he may readily take the Bread and break it, and also take the Cup, to poure into it, (yf he poure it not before,) and then he shall say,

[Almighty God our heavenly Father, Who of thy tender Mercy didst give] etc.

Part. 57: . . . to *take the Bread & Cup* into his hands, nor to *Break the Bread* before ye people . . .

SL: Then the Presbyter standing up, shall say the prayer of consecration, as followeth; but then during the time of consecration, he shall stand at such a part of the holy Table, where he may with the more ease and decency use both his hands.

S II: Which is a Posture of Reverence, & here ordered for ye Priest to use, that he may with ye more readines performe his office in Consecrating ye Elemts.

> *For an analysis of this entry, see the Introduction, pp. xviii–xix. The insertion of titles in the Scottish Liturgy was suggested by Laud (Works, VI. 457). Baxter also desired the manual acts to be visible; cf. his* Reformed Liturgy:
> *Then let the Minister take the bread and break it in the sight of the people.*
> *The Prayer of Humble Access is postponed to no. 267.*

240. **1549:** . . . and to drinke his bloude, in these holy Misteries . . .

> *The cancelling of this small restoration of the 1549 text is evidence of the extreme caution of the revisers.*

241. **SL:**   *see no. 239.*

   S II: The Prayer of Consecration. (*Title.*)

242. **Part. 56:** In ye Prayer of Consecration, where ye Priest saith — *to Continue a perpetuall memorie of that his pretious death* — here seemes to want — *& Sacrifice untill his Coming againe;* wch, if added, would be more Consonant to the Nature of yt Holy Action, & the words of the Catechisme following, made & sett forth for yt purpose.

   SL: . . . death and sacrifice . . . we most humbly beseech thee . . .

   1549:   . . . commaunde vs to celebrate a perpetuall memorye . . .

> *Cosin, as usual, introduces the idea of sacrifice, following SL; cf. S II:*
> *Ideò veteres Memorationem huic Sacramento peculiarem, Sacrificium memorativum, Precationem autem Oblationem appellare amant.*
> *A long note in English follows, on the sense in which the Communion is a sacrifice.*

𝔞𝔫𝔡 𝔤𝔯𝔞𝔲𝔫𝔱 𝔱𝔥𝔞𝔱 𝔴𝔢, 243. *Read*: and[1] by ye power of thy holy
𝔯𝔢𝔠𝔢𝔦𝔲𝔦𝔫𝔤 𝔱𝔥𝔢𝔰𝔢 𝔱𝔥𝔶 𝔠𝔯𝔢𝔞𝔱𝔲𝔯𝔢𝔰 𝔬𝔣 𝔅𝔯𝔢𝔞𝔡 𝔞𝔫𝔡 Word and Spirit vouchsafe so to
𝔚𝔦𝔫𝔢, blesse & sanctifie these thy Gifts
& Creatures of Bread & Wine,
that wee receiving them

𝔞𝔠𝔠𝔬𝔯𝔡𝔦𝔫𝔤 𝔱𝔬 𝔱𝔥𝔶 𝔖𝔬𝔫𝔫𝔢 𝔬𝔲𝔯 𝔖𝔞𝔲𝔦𝔬𝔲𝔯 244. *Before* his death *add*: Him, & to
𝔍𝔢𝔰𝔲𝔰 𝔆𝔥𝔯𝔦𝔰𝔱𝔰 𝔥𝔬𝔩𝔶 𝔦𝔫𝔰𝔱𝔦𝔱𝔲𝔱𝔦𝔬𝔫, 𝔦𝔫 𝔯𝔢𝔪𝔢𝔪= shew forth
𝔟𝔯𝔞𝔫𝔠𝔢 𝔬𝔣 𝔥𝔦𝔰 𝔡𝔢𝔞𝔱𝔥 𝔞𝔫𝔡 𝔭𝔞𝔰𝔰𝔦𝔬𝔫, 𝔪𝔞𝔶 𝔟𝔢 *New paragraph at* who
𝔭𝔞𝔯𝔱𝔞𝔨𝔢𝔯𝔰 𝔬𝔣 𝔥𝔦𝔰 𝔪𝔬𝔰𝔱 𝔟𝔩𝔢𝔰𝔰𝔢𝔡 𝔅𝔬𝔡𝔶 𝔞𝔫𝔡
𝔅𝔩𝔬𝔬𝔡: 𝔴𝔥𝔬 𝔦𝔫 𝔱𝔥𝔢 𝔰𝔞𝔪𝔢 𝔫𝔦𝔤𝔥𝔱 𝔱𝔥𝔞𝔱 𝔥𝔢𝔢 𝔴𝔞𝔰
𝔟𝔢𝔱𝔯𝔞𝔶𝔢𝔡,

𝔱𝔬𝔬𝔨𝔢 𝔟𝔯𝔢𝔞𝔡, 𝔞𝔫𝔡 𝔴𝔥𝔢𝔫 𝔥𝔢 𝔥𝔞𝔡 𝔤𝔦𝔲𝔢𝔫 245. *i. Add asterisks to* tooke *and* brake,
𝔱𝔥𝔞𝔫𝔨𝔢𝔰 𝔥𝔢 𝔟𝔯𝔞𝔨𝔢 𝔦𝔱, 𝔞𝔫𝔡 𝔤𝔞𝔲𝔢 𝔦𝔱 𝔱𝔬 𝔥𝔦𝔰 𝔡𝔦𝔰𝔠𝔦𝔭𝔩𝔢𝔰, *and a marginal note:*
𝔰𝔞𝔶𝔦𝔫𝔤, 𝔗𝔞𝔨𝔢, 𝔢𝔞𝔱, 𝔱𝔥𝔦𝔰 𝔦𝔰 𝔪𝔶 𝔅𝔬𝔡𝔶 𝔴𝔥𝔦𝔠𝔥 𝔦𝔰 At these words [tooke Bread] the
𝔤𝔦𝔲𝔢𝔫 𝔣𝔬𝔯 𝔶𝔬𝔲, 𝔡𝔬𝔢 𝔱𝔥𝔦𝔰 𝔦𝔫 𝔯𝔢𝔪𝔢𝔪𝔟𝔯𝔞𝔫𝔠𝔢 𝔬𝔣 𝔪𝔢𝔢. Priest is to take ye Paten into his
Hands;[2] at [brake it] he is to
break the Bread; & at [This is my
Body] to hold his hands over it.
ii. For to hold his hands over it *read*:
to lay his hand upon it.

246. *Before* giuen thankes *add*: blessed &
(*also below*) (*crossed out*) Stet

---

[1] Vouchsafe *originally stood before* by ye power.   [2] *Originally* hand.

243. **SL:** of thy almighty goodnesse vouchsafe so to blesse and sanctifie with thy Word and holy Spirit these thy gifts and creatures of bread and wine . . .

   1549: with thy holy spirite and worde vouchsafe to blesse and sanctifie those thy gyftes, and creatures of bread and wyne . . .

   This epiclesis may be adapted either from 1549 or SL, which are very similar; it is perhaps slightly closer to SL.

244. **Adv.:** At the *15th* line let it be,
   [. . . according to thy Sonne our Saviour Jesus Xts holy Institution, for a Remembrance of him by shewing his Death and Passion, may be Partakers of his most blessed Body] &c.
   This would be thus, 1°. bycause St Paules word is [καταγγέλλετε,] *1. Cor. 11. 26.* and 2°. bycause [εἰς τὴν ἐμὴν ἀνάμνησιν] being spoken by Xt, does most properly signify, [To put me in mind of you] Xt of Us, and not, Us in mind of Xt; For in that we do this, it appeares we are mindfull of him: It is not done therfore, onely to put ourselves in mind of him.

   Cf. no. 230. This theory does not seem to have been shared by Cosin.

245. **Adv.:** At the words, [Took bread, and when He had given thancks he brake it, and gave it,] the Preist shall take the bread, and break it: . . .
   There is twise, [Do this in remembrance of me] but, to take away all exception, let it be in both, [Do this for a Remembrance of me.]

   Part. 57: Againe, at the words there, *Hee tooke Bread & He Brake it, & He tooke ye Cup,* No direction is given to the Priest (as in K. Edward's Service-Booke there was, and as in most places is still in use,) to *take the Bread & Cup* into his hands, nor to *Break the Bread* before ye people; wch is a needfull Circumstance belonging to that Sacrament; & therfore for his better warrant herein, such a direction ought here to be set in ye margin of ye Booke.

   SL: At these words (took bread) the Presbyter that officiates is to take the Paten in his hand.

   1549: Here the prieste must take the bread into his hãdes.

   Exceptions: We conceive that the manner of the consecrating of the Elements is not here explicit and distinct enough: And the Ministers breaking of the bread is not so much as mentioned.

   Bishops: Conc. 10. That the manner of consecrating the Elements, may be made more explicit, and express; and to that purpose, those words be put into the Rub. [then shall he put his hand upon the Bread, & break it] then shall he put his hand unto the Cup.]

   The desire for an explicit direction of the manual acts is shared by Wren, Cosin, and the Presbyterians. Taylor also has a marginal rubric:
   The Minister at those words shall touch the Bread.

   The suggestion of Adv. and Part. 57 is carried out by a combination of SL and 1549, altered to conform to the words of the Bishops' Reply. The survival of the manual acts as a custom, though no longer directed by rubric, is attested by, e.g., S II and L'Estrange.

246. **1549:** . . . when he had blessed, and geuen thankes: he brake it . . .

   Cf. Sarum: . . . gratias agens, benedixit, fregit . . .

   1549 does not have 'blessed and' in the case of the cup, but Sarum does have 'benedixit' there also. Matthew and Mark have 'blessed' only for the bread; Luke and Paul have 'given thanks' only; none of them has 'blessed' for the cup.

𝕷ikewise after 𝕾upper he tooke the 𝕮up, and
when hee had giuen thankes he gaue it to
them, saying, 𝕯rink ye all of this, for this is
my 𝕭lood of the new 𝕿estament, which is
shed for you and for many for the remission
of sinnes:

       doe this as oft as ye shall drinke it,
in remembrance of me.

247.   *New paragraph at* Likewise
   Add an asterisk to tooke *and a*
    marginal note: At the[1] words
    [tooke the Cup] the Priest is to
    take the Chalice into his hands,[2]
    & at [This is my Bloud] he is[3] to
    lay his hand upon every vessel,
    (be it Chalice or Flagon) in wch
    there is Wine to be consecrated.

248.   *Add*: Amen.

249.   *i. Add*: If any Bread or Wine be
    afterwards wanting, he is to con-
    secrate the same, as is before
    appointed, beginning at the words
    [When Christ in ye same night &c]
    for ye blessing of the Bread; & at
    [Likewise after Supper &c] for the
    blessing of the Cup.
   ii. Delete afterwards
    For the same *read*: more
    For When *read*: Our Saviour
   iii. For he *read*: the preist
    For at the words *read*: with the words
    Omitt this here, & set it p. seq. ad. ⌗

250.   *Add*: Immediately after shall follow
    this Memoriall, or Prayer of
    Oblation.
    Wherfore O Lord &c, as in ye next
    page.
    (*see nos.* 263–7)

---

[1] *Originally* these; FC: these.   [2] *Originally* hand.   [3] he is *crossed out*.

247. **Adv.:** And also, at [took the Cup,] the Preist shall take it into his hand, and poure into it, yf he have not filld it ready before . . .

    SL: At these words (took the cup) he is to take the chalice in his hand, and lay his hand upon so much, be it in chalice or flagons, as he intends to consecrate.

    1549: Here the Priest shall take the Cuppe into his hãdes.

    Part. 57, Exceptions, and Bishops: *see no. 245.*

    Taylor: *Here he must touch or handle the Chalice.*

248. **Taylor:** *The people shall answer,* Amen.

    Cf. L'Estrange: Though all our Liturgies stand silent in it, yet may I not omit what here by the way doth offer it self as observable, viz. That at the close of the Eucharistical prayer, the ancient manner was for the people to contribute their Amen. . . .

        'Amen' is supplied in accordance with the rubric at no. 67.

249. **Adv.:** And yf afterwards there prove to be use for any more Bread or Wine, then that, Of wch he brake, and blessed at first, He shall use the very Form, and say over the words audibly, before he gives it.

    Part. 59: If there be any Consecrate Bread or Wine wanting for the Coũmunicating of ye people, here is no order (as there ought to be) for ye Consecrating of more, nor for ye words wch the priest shall use for yt purpose, as in ye first forme of ye Coũmunion set out in K. Edwards time, & in ye Canons of ye Church, is injoyned. This therfore should be here added.

    SL: . . . if there be want, the words of consecration may be repeated again, over more, either bread or wine: the Presbyter beginning at these words in the prayer of consecration (our Saviour in the night that he was betrayed, took, &c.)

        The direction in the Order of Communion *referred to above is:*
        Note, that if it doth so chaunce, that the wyne halowed and consecrate dooth not suffice or bee ynough for them that doe take the Communion, the priest after the firste Cup or chalice be emptied, may go again to ye aultare, and reuerentlie, and deuoutlie, prepare, and consecrate an other, and so the thirde, or more lykwise, begynning at these woordes. *Simili modo, postquam cenatum est,* and endyng at these wordes, *qui pro nobis & pro multis effundetur in remissionem peccatorũ,* and without any levacion or lifting vp.

        The Canon referred to is no. 21:
        . . . no Bread or Wine newly brought shall bee vsed: but first the words of Institution shall bee rehearsed when the sayd Bread and Wine bee present vpon the Communion Table.

        Although the verbal dependence of the new rubric upon these sources is slight, their influence can scarcely (in view of Part. 59) be dismissed as 'perhaps accidental' (Brightman, I. ccxx). Wren's suggested rubric is already found in substance in his Particular Orders *(no. 16).*

250. **Part. 61:** The *Prayer of Oblation* is here placed after ye *Participation* & distribution of ye Sacramt made to the people; wch in K. Edwards first Service Book, & in all other Ancient Liturgies is set before it, & next after ye *Prayer of Consecration.* If it were so ordered here, & ye *Prayer of Thanksgiving (Almightie & everliving God, wee most hartily Thank thee &c)* appointed to follow for ye Post-Coũmunion, it would be more Consonant both to former precedents, & the Nature of this holy Action.

Then shal the Minister first recciue the Communion in both kinds himselfe, and next deliuer it to other Ministers (if any be there present) that they may helpe the chiefe Minister, and after, to the people in their hands, kneeling. And when he deliuereth the Bread, he shal say.

251.   *i. Read:* Then shall the Priest that celebrateth, first receive the holy Cõmunion in both kinds himself, & next deliver the same to the Bishops, Priests, & Deacons (if any be present,) & after to the people in due order, into their hands, all humbly kneeling:

And when he receiveth the holy Bread himself; & when he delivereth it to any other, he shall say

The Body of our Lord &c.

ii. For he receiveth the holy Bread himself *read:* he himself receiveth the Sacrament of the Body of Christ

iii. Read: Then shall the Priest that celebrateth, receive the holy Cõmunion in both kinds, upon his knees, &[1] when he taketh the Sacrament of ye Body of Christ, he shall say,

The Body of our Lord Jesus Christ which was given for mee, preserve my Body & Soule unto

---

[1] *Originally* first saying . . .

SL: Immediatly after shall be said this memoriall or prayer of oblation, as followeth.

Part. 61 is based upon a note in S I:

In K. Edw. first Service Book This Prayer was set before ye delivery of ye Sacramt to the people, & followed imediately after ye Consecration; & certainly it was ye better & ye more naturall order of ye Two: neither doe I know, whether it were ye Printers negligence or no, thus to displace it. For ye Consecration of ye Sacramt being ever ye first, it was alwaies ye use in all Liturgies to have ye Oblation follow (wch is this) & then ye Participation, wch goes before, & after all, ye Thanksgiving, wch is here set next before Gloria in Excelsis. In regard wherof, I have alwaies observed my Ld. & Mr. Dr. Overall to use this oblation in its right place, when he had consecrated ye Sacramt, to make an offering of it (as being ye true publick Sacrifice of ye Church) unto God, yt by ye merits of Xρs death wch was now comemorated, all ye Church of God might receive mercy &c. as in this prayer: and when that was done he did comunicate ye people, & so end with the thanksgiving following herafter. If men wold consider ye nature of this Sacramt, how it is ye Xρians Sacrifice also, they cold not choose but use it so too. For as it stands here it is out of his place. We ought first to send up Xρ. unto God, & then he will send him downe unto us.

S II has a brief note in agreement with this. SL had already placed this prayer before the Communion, and is followed by DB. After the Prayer of Oblation come the Lord's Prayer and the Prayer of Humble Access (see nos. 263–7, and the Detached Note, p. 189). The addition of the title 'Prayer of Oblation' in SL, as also of 'Prayer of Consecration', was suggested by Laud; 'Humble Access' and 'Thanksgiving', which were not carried over into DB, were added by the Scottish bishops.

251. **Adv.:** The last Rubrick to be thus,

. . . and next deliver it in both kinds to other Ministers, (yf any be there present, that they may help the cheef Minister,) and after, to the people, into the hand of every one, kneeling. And when he taketh the Bread himself, and when he delivereth it to any other, he shall say . . .

This would be expressely put thus, Bycause it is a proper Prayer, and of Blessing, Whereby it is a sufficient reason, why every one should kneel, when they Receive.

Part. 58: In ye Priest's Taking of ye Sacramt to himself, there is no direction either for *his Kneeling* when he takes it, or for ye words wch he is then to say. Which is therfore needfull here to be added, least otherwise some contentious minister might say, yt He is not injoynd to *Kneele* in this Holy Action himself, nor to say any words at all when he takes ye Sacramt.

Part. 60: There wants likewise an order for ye People to continue Kneeling at their prayers & devotions (as is most meete) during all ye time of ye whole Action.

SL: Then shall the Bishop, if he be present, or else the Presbyter that celebrateth, first receive the communion in both kindes himself, and next deliver it to other Bishops, Presbyters and Deacons (if any be there present,) that they may help him that celebrateth; and after to the people in due order, all humbly kneeling. And when he receiveth himself, or delivereth the bread to others, he shall say this benediction.

The body of our Lord Jesus Christ, which was given for thee, preserve thy body and soul unto everlasting life.

everlasting life. Amen. I take &
eat this in remembrance that
Christ dyed for me, & I feed on
Him in my heart by faith wth
Thanksgiving.

And when he taketh ye Sacrament
of Christs Bloud, he shall say,

The Bloud of our Lord &c.

Then shall he stand up, & proceed
to deliver the holy Comunion
first to the Bishops, Priests, &
Deacons (if any be present,) in
both kinds; & after to the people
in due order, into the hands of all
humbly kneeling: (& so continuing[1] (as is most meet) at their
devotions & prayers[2] unto ye End
of ye whole Comunion.)

And when he delivereth the Sacrament of the Body of Christ to
any one, he shall say

The Body of our Lord &c,
as in ye next page.

iv. *For* in remembrance that Christ *read*: for
the remembrance of Christ who
After The Bloud of our Lord *add*: J. X.
wch was shed for me, preserve my
Body, & Soul into everlastg life.
Amen. I drink this for ye remembrance
of X, who shed his blood for me, &
am thankfull

𝕿𝖍𝖊 𝕭𝖔𝖉𝖞 𝖔𝖋 𝖔𝖚𝖗 𝕷𝖔𝖗𝖉 𝕵𝖊𝖘𝖚𝖘 𝕮𝖍𝖗𝖎𝖘𝖙, 𝖜𝖍𝖎𝖈𝖍
𝖜𝖆𝖘 𝖌𝖎𝖚𝖊𝖓 𝖋𝖔𝖗 𝖙𝖍𝖊𝖊, 𝖕𝖗𝖊𝖘𝖊𝖗𝖚𝖊 𝖙𝖍𝖞 𝖇𝖔𝖉𝖞 𝖆𝖓𝖉
𝖘𝖔𝖚𝖑𝖊 𝖎𝖓𝖙𝖔 𝖊𝖚𝖊𝖗𝖑𝖆𝖘𝖙𝖎𝖓𝖌 𝖑𝖎𝖋𝖊: 𝖆𝖓𝖉 𝖙𝖆𝖐𝖊 𝖆𝖓𝖉 𝖊𝖆𝖙𝖊
𝖙𝖍𝖎𝖘 𝖎𝖓 𝖗𝖊𝖒𝖊𝖒𝖇𝖗𝖆𝖓𝖈𝖊 𝖙𝖍𝖆𝖙 𝕮𝖍𝖗𝖎𝖘𝖙 𝖉𝖞𝖊𝖉 𝖋𝖔𝖗
𝖙𝖍𝖊𝖊, 𝖆𝖓𝖉 𝖋𝖊𝖊𝖉 𝖔𝖓 𝖍𝖎𝖒 𝖎𝖓 𝖙𝖍𝖎𝖓𝖊 𝖍𝖊𝖆𝖗𝖙 𝖇𝖞 𝖋𝖆𝖎𝖙𝖍,
𝖜𝖎𝖙𝖍 𝖙𝖍𝖆𝖓𝖐𝖊𝖘𝖌𝖎𝖚𝖎𝖓𝖌.

252.   *Before* thee *add*: [mee, or]
Similarly with thy *and* thine
For and take *read*: [I, or] Take
Before feed *add*: [I]
(*all crossed out*)

253.   *After* life *add*: And here each[3]
person receiving shall say, [Amen.]
Then shall the Priest adde, Take
& Eate &c.

---

[1] *Altered to* they shall, *then back to* so continuing.
[2] FC: their Prayers, & Devotions.   [3] *Originally* every.

1549: Then shall the Prieste . . . And when he deliuereth the Sacramēt of the body of Christ . . .
And the Minister deliuering the Sacrament of the bloud . . . vnto euerlasting lyfe . . .
(Rubric at the end of the service): . . . and there with deuout prayer, or Godlye silence
and meditacion, to occupy themselues.

Wren, *Particular Orders:* 15. . . . that the Minister repeat to every Communicant severally all the
words yt are appointed to be said at ye distribution of ye holy Sacrament.

> *The stages of drafting seem to run as follows:*
> *i. SL and Adv. ('into', 'any other').*
> *ii. 1549.*
> *iii. Parts. 58 and 60. Cf. no. 253 (for the 'Amen').*
> *iv. Adv. (at no. 254).*
>
> *The position of the minister was a long-standing subject of controversy; cf. S I:*
> *Kneeling here for all ye puritans obiection hath reference aswell to ye minister hims.*
> *as to ye people & other ministers;*
> *though earlier the author has written:*
> *The transposing of this after yt wch goes before, otherwise than it was in K. Edw.*
> *Book hath left ye priest to receive the Sacramt standing, there being no Rubric or*
> *appointmt to alter his gesture after this . . . But see the answer infra.*

252. **Adv.:** . . . wch was given for Me (or, Thee) preserve My (or Thy) Body and Soule into everlasting Life: . . .

In the words there following, [And take, and eat this,] that first word [And] is but the
Rubrick, to tell the Preist, that he must say this Sentence also, but not to say that word.
This was added at the beginning of Qu. Eliz:

> *These additions are crossed out as being superfluous after stage iii of no. 251.*

253. **Adv.:** Answer, by the Receiver,
Amen.

. . . The Church of Rome to gayne some Colour to their fancy of Transubstantiation,
next after these words, [The Body of our Lord Jesus Xt] put in [Amen] there: Now
though we approve not of that, yet there is no Reason, why it should quite be omitted.

SL: Here the partie receiving shall say, Amen.

Cf. S I (Andrewes): To this Prayer of the Priest Every Cōmunicant shold say Amen: and then,
& not before take the Sacramt of him;

and L'Estrange (on SL):
This order is a peece of Reformation, wherein the Church of Scotland stands single and
alone. I call it a peece of Reformation, because it is the reviving of a very ancient
custome.

> *Wickham Legg* (English Church Life, p. 61) *collects some examples of the saying of*
> *'Amen' at this point during the seventeenth century.*

254.   *For* in remembrance that Christ *read*: for
the remembrance of Christ who

And the Minister that deliuereth the Cup, shall   255.   *Read*: And when he delivereth the
say.   Cup to any[1] one, he shall say.

𝕿𝖍𝖊 𝕭𝖑𝖔𝖔𝖉 of our 𝕷𝖔𝖗𝖉 𝕵𝖊𝖘𝖚𝖘 𝕮𝖍𝖗𝖎𝖘𝖙 𝖜𝖍𝖎𝖈𝖍
𝖜𝖆𝖘 𝖘𝖍𝖊𝖉 for 𝖙𝖍𝖊𝖊, 𝖕𝖗𝖊𝖘𝖊𝖗𝖚𝖊 𝖙𝖍𝖞 𝖇𝖔𝖉𝖞 and   256.   *For* and drinke . . . thankfull *read*:
𝖘𝖔𝖚𝖑𝖊 into 𝖊𝖚𝖊𝖗𝖑𝖆𝖘𝖙𝖎𝖓𝖌 𝖑𝖎𝖋𝖊: and 𝖉𝖗𝖎𝖓𝖐𝖊 𝖙𝖍𝖎𝖘   And here each person receiving
in 𝖗𝖊𝖒𝖊𝖒𝖇𝖗𝖆𝖓𝖈𝖊 𝖙𝖍𝖆𝖙 𝕮𝖍𝖗𝖎𝖘𝖙𝖘 𝖇𝖑𝖔𝖔𝖉 𝖜𝖆𝖘 𝖘𝖍𝖊𝖉   shall say, [Amen.] Then the Priest
for 𝖙𝖍𝖊𝖊, 𝖆𝖓𝖉 𝖇𝖊 𝖙𝖍𝖆𝖓𝖐𝖋𝖚𝖑𝖑.   shall adde, Drinke this for the
                                                                  remembrance of Christ who shed his
                                                                  bloud for thee, and be thankfull.

257.   *i. Add*: If there be a deacon or other
Priest to assist ye chief Minister,
then shall he follow with the Cup;
& as ye chief Minister giveth the
Sacrament of the Body, so shall
he give ye Sacramt of the Bloud,
in forme before prescribed.

ii. Read: If there be another Priest or a
Deacon to assist . . .

258.   ⌗ If any Bread, or Wine be wanting. ut
pag. preced. ad notã ⌗

259.   *i. Add*: In the Comunion time shalbe
sung (where there is a Quire)
some or all these Sentences of
[2]holy Scripture following.
Sentences.[3] Rom. 11. 33. Ψ. 103. 1–5.
Luc. 1. 68, 74, 75. 1 Cor. 1. 30, 31.
Joh. 5. 13. Joh. 8. 31, 32. Matth.
24. 13. Luc. 12. 37, 40. Joh. 12.
35, 36. Rom. 13. 12, 13, 14.
1 Cor. 3. 16, 17. 1 Cor. 6. 20.
Joh. 15. 8, 12. Eph. 5. 1, 2. Rom.
8. 23. Apoc. 5. 12, 13.

---

[1] Originally *every*.   [2] FC omits holy.   [3] *FC gives the text of the Sentences in full (see p. 291).*

254. **Adv.:** But the words hereof (for they were then put in wth more Heat, then Head,) would of
right be thus,
[Take and eat this for a Remembrance of Christ, Who died for thee, and feed on Him
in thy hart by fayth wth thanksgiving.]
Cf. no. 244.

255. **Adv.:** The first Rubrick to be thus,
The Minister, when he taketh the Cup himself, or when he delivereth it to any one,
shall say,
[The bloud of our Lord Jesus Xt, wch was shedd for Me, (or Thee) preserve My
(or Thy) Body and Soul into everlasting Life.]

Canon 21: . . . to euery communicant seuerally.
Cf. Wren, Particular Orders (quoted at no. 251).

256. **Adv.:** Answer. Amen.
Preist.
Drinck this for a Remembrance of Xt, whose bloud was shedd for thee, and be thanckfull.
Yet let it now be well weyghed, whither it shall go so still, or be [And give Him thancks.]
For the Latin, out of wch it was turned for us, was [Et gratias age.] Also the verb in
Greek [εὐχαριστῆσαι,] from wch this Sacrament is rightly calld the Eucharist, signifies
not onely [Gratum esse,] to be Thankfull, but also [Gratias agere] to give Thanks.

SL: The bloud . . . unto everlasting life.
Here the party receiving shall say, Amen.

Sanderson has another variant:
in remembrance that Christ shed his precious blood for thee.

257. **1549:** If there be a Deacon or other Priest, then shal he folow with the Chalice: and as ye
Priest ministereth the Sacramēt of the body, so shal he (for more expedition) minister
ye Sacrament of the bloud, in fourme before written.

ii is a typical piece of editing by S.

258. *No. 249 is to be inserted here.*

259. **1549:** In the Communion tyme the Clearkes shal syng.
ii. O lambe of god that takeste awaye the synnes of the worlde: haue mercie vpon vs.
O lambe of god that takeste awaye the synnes of the worlde: graunte vs thy peace.

. . . . .

Sentēces of holy scripture, to be said or song euery daie one, after the holy Com-
munion, called the post Communion.
*Math. 16. Mar. 13. Luc. 1. Luc. 12. John. 4. John. 5. John. 8. John. 12. John. 14. John. 15.
Rom. 8. Rom. 13. I Cor. 1. I Cor. 3. I Cor. 6. Eph. 5.*
Cf. nos. 91 and 105 (Sentences at Mattins and Evensong).
*All the DB Sentences, except the first two and the last, are derived from 1549, which has
also three others which do not appear in DB: Math. 16, John 4, and John 14.
The DB Sentences are often longer than their 1549 models; in one case the Matthaean
version is preferred to the Marcan (Matt. xxiv. 13 = Mark. xiii. 13). DB has 'Rom. 8.
23', evidently in error for '8. 32': FC repeats the error here, but in Paper B, while*

> *ii. After* Quire *add*: O Lamb of God yt taketh away the sins of the world, have mercy upon us, & O L . . . grant us thy peace, together with

260.   *Add*: And where there is no Quire, let ye Comunicants make use of the same at their owne private & devout meditations. & let the priest, when he hath done the distribution read one or moe of them according to his discretion. (*crossed out*)

261.   *i. Add*: When all have comunicated, he that celebrateth shall returne to the Lords Table, & reverently place upon it what remaineth of ye Consecrated Elements, covering the same with a faire liñen cloth,[1] & then say one or moe of the Sentences above recited, according to his discretion, & after,

> The Lord be with you.
> Answere
> And with thy Spirit
> Priest
> Let us pray
> Almightie and [2]everliving &c.

ii. Delete one or moe . . . Spirit
iii. Stet: The Lord be with you . . . Spirit

Then shall the Priest say the Lords prayer, the people repeating after him euery petition. After shall be said as followeth.

262.   *Delete the whole Rubric.*[3]
Stet (*crossed out*)

✠ 𝕷𝖔𝖗𝖉 𝖆𝖓𝖉 𝖍𝖊𝖆𝖚𝖊𝖓𝖑𝖞 𝕱𝖆𝖙𝖍𝖊𝖗, 𝖜𝖊 𝖙𝖍𝖞 𝖍𝖚𝖒𝖇𝖑𝖊 𝖘𝖊𝖗𝖚𝖆𝖓𝖙𝖘

263.   *Read*: Wherfore O Lord & heavenly Father, according to ye institution of thy dearly beloved Sonne, our Saviour Jesus Christ, wee thy humble Servants doe celebrate, & make here before thy divine majestie with these thy holy Gifts the Memoriall wch thy Sonne hath willed & comanded us to make; having in remembrance his

---

[1] FC *ends at* cloth.   [2] *Originally* everlasting.   [3] FC: Our Father, &c. Print it out at large.

still giving the wrong reference, writes out the correct verse! Likewise FC repeats
'Joh. 5. 13.', but writes out part of verse 14. The order in 1549 is that of the Bible;
DB arranges the Sentences according to subject-matter.

260. **1549:** Where there are no clearkes, there the Priest shall saye all thinges appointed here for
them to syng.

. . . . . .

and there with deuout prayer, or Godlye silence and meditacion to occupy themselues . . .

Cf. nos. 251. iii and 217. The present rubric is superseded by no. 261.

261. **SL:** When all have communicated, he that celebrates shall go to the Lords table, and cover
with a fair linen cloth, or corporall, that which remaineth of the consecrated elements,
and then say this collect of thanksgiving, as followeth.

1549: The Lorde be with you.
The aunswere.
And with thy spirite.
The Priest.
Let vs praye.
Almightie and euerlyuynge GOD . . .

Cf. no. 260. FC ignores stage iii, and omits 'Let us pray', which was retained even in
stage ii, thus removing all the additions from 1549.

262. **Adv.:** The next Rubrick to be, thus,
When the Distribution is ended, the Preist standing at the Table, as he did at first,
shall beginn the Lords prayer, all the people devoutly saying it wth him; And here
shall be added,
[For thyne is the Kingdome, &c.]

The deletion of the rubric in the text is necessitated by no. 266, the Lord's Prayer being
now placed after the Prayer of Oblation.

263. **SL:** Wherefore O Lord and heavenly Father, according to the institution of thy dearly
beloved Son our Saviour Jesus Christ, we thy humble servants do celebrate and make
here before thy divine Majestie, with these thy holy gifts, the memoriall which thy
Son hath willed us to make, having in remembrance his blessed passion, mightie
resurrection, and glorious assension, rendring unto thee most hearty thankes for the
innumerable benefits procured unto us by the same. And we entirely desire . . .

1549: *Verbatim as above, except: . . . by the same, entyerely desyringe . . .*

Devotions (Prayers before the Sacrament, II): . . . thy humble seruants, who do now celebrate the memoriall which thy Sonne our Sauiour hath commanded to be made in

most blessed Passion & Sacrifice,
his mightie Resurrection, & his
glorious Ascension into Heaven;
rendring unto Thee most heartie
thankes for the innumerable benefits procured unto us by the same;
& wee entirely &c.

entirelp desire thp ﬀatherlp good=
nesse, mercifullp to accept this our sacrifice
of praise and thankesgiuing, most humblp
beseeching thee to graunt that bp the merites
and death of thp ﬦonne ﬦesus ﬦhrist, and   264.   *For* and through . . . Passion *read*:
through faith in his Blood, we and all thp   now represented unto[1] Thee, and
whole ﬦhurch map obtaine remission of our   through faith in his Blood, who
sinnes, and all other benefits of his ﬧassion.   maketh intercession for us at thy
                                                       right hand, we and all thy whole
                                                       Church may obtaine remission of
                                                       our sinnes, and be made par-
                                                       takers of all other benefits of his
                                                       Passion.

ﬡnd here we offer and present bnto thee, ﬠ
﬩ord, our selues, our soules and bodies, to
be a reasonable, holp and liuelp sacrifice
bnto thee, humblp beseeching thee, that all we   265.   *For* all we . . . fulfilled *read*: whoso-
which be partakers of this holp ﬦommunion,   ever shall be partakers of this
map be fulﬁlled with thp grace and heabenlp   holy Communion, may worthily
benediction.   receive ye most precious Body &
                                                       Bloud of thy Sonne Jesus Christ,
                                                       & be fulfilled

ﬡnd although we be bnworthp,
through our manifold sinnes, to offer bnto
thee anp sacrifice: pet we beseech thee to ac=
cept this our bounden dutp and seruice, not
weighing our merits but pardoning our
offences, through ﬦesus ﬦhrist our ﬩ord, bp
whom, and with whom, in the bnitp of the
holp ﬠhost, all honour and glorp be bnto thee,   266.   i. *Add*: Let us pray   (*crossed out*)
ﬠ ﬀather ﬡlmightp, world without end.   Stet (*crossed out*)
ﬡmen.   ii. *Read*: Then shall ye Priest adde, As
                                                          our Saviour Christ hath taught &
                                                          cõmanded us, wee are bold to say,
                                                          Our Father who &c
                                                          (& print it out at large)—deliver us
                                                          from Evill. Amen.
                                                      iii. *Delete* deliver us from Evill.

---

[1] *Originally* before.

remembrance of his most blessed Passion and Sacrifice . . . together with his mightie Resurrection from the earth and his glorious Ascension into Heaven . . .

> *At the only point where SL differs from 1549, DB follows SL. The Devotions make a sudden reappearance in DB after a long period of neglect, contributing a few words ('commanded', 'most blessed Passion and Sacrifice', 'Ascension into Heaven'). Cf. no. 264, especially the footnote.*

264. Devotions (ibid.): . . . that by the merits and power thereof now represented before thy diuine Maiestie, wee and all thy whole Church . . .

> *The original reading 'before' is faithful to the text of the Devotions. For the idea of representation, cf. S II:*
> *In Celebratione igitur Sacramenti Eucharistiae Deo Patri Filius suus, Filiique mors, quae verissimum est Sacrificium, a nobis representatur, & . . . offertur . . .*
> *This is part of a long quotation from Georg Calixtus's De Sacrificio Christi, the 1644 edition of which Cosin had acquired from some French friends while in exile. The relevant word 'representatur', however, has been added by Cosin himself, being an essential part of his eucharistic doctrine. See further the Introduction, p. xxiii.*
> *'Maketh intercession . . .': Rom. viii. 34.*

265. SL: whosoever shall be partakers of this holy communion, may worthily receive the most precious bodie and bloud of thy Son Jesus Christ, and be fulfilled . . .

1549: *Verbatim as above.*

266. SL: Then shall the Presbyter say: As our Saviour Christ hath commanded and taught us, we are bold to say,
Our Father which art in heaven . . . Amen.

1549: Let us praye.
As our sauiour Christe hath commaunded and taughte vs, we are bolde to say. Our father . . . And leade vs not into temptacion.

The aunswere.
But deliuer vs from euill. Amen.

> *i is from 1549, ii from SL, iii runs directly counter to the Directions to the Printer (p. 2), but cf. Adv. at no. 262. The transposition of 'taught' and 'commanded' is perhaps influenced by the Latin: 'praeceptis . . . et . . . institutione'.*

267.   *Add*: Then shall ye Priest kneeling
downe at God's Board, say in the
name of all them that are to
receive ye holy Communion this
prayer following.
Wee doe not presume &c,
as in the 3d page before.

268.   My LL. ye BB. at Elie house Orderd all
in ye old Method; thus. First ye prayer
of Address, We do not presume, wth
ye Rubrick When ye priest standg &c
ye prayer of Consecron unalterd (only
one for own & Amen at last) wth ye
marginal Rubrics. Then (ye Memorial
or prayer of Oblation omitted, & ye
Ld's prayer) follow ye Rubricks, &
Forms of Participation, & Distribution
to ye end of ye Rubrick, When all
have cõicated &c altogether as in this
book; only yt Rubrick, In ye Cõion
time shall be sung &c wth ye Sentences
following, wholly omitted. And yn
ye Lords prayer; ye Collect, O Ld, &
Heav. F. &c. &c to ye End.

Or this.

𝔄lmighty and euerlasting 𝔊od, we most
heartily thanke thee, for that thou doest
vouchsafe to feede us, which haue duely re=
ceiued those holy mysteries . . . world without
end. 𝔄men.

Then shall be said or sung.

269.   *Delete* Or this.

For euerlasting *read*: euerliving[1]
For doest vouchsafe *read*: hast
vouchsafed[2]
For those *read*: these

𝔊lory be to 𝔊od on high . . . 𝔚ee praise
thee . . .

𝔒 𝔏ord, the onely begotten 𝔖onne . . .

𝔉or thou onely art holy, thou onely art the
𝔏ord, thou onely 𝔒 𝔠hrist with the holy
𝔊host, art most high in the glory of 𝔊od the
𝔉ather. 𝔄men.

270.   *New paragraph.*

New paragraph.

New paragraph.
For holy Ghost *read*: most holy,
Eternall, & blessed Spirit   Stet

271.   *Add*: The finall Prayer
Almightie God who hast promised
to heare ye petitions &c.
as in ye next leaf.
(*crossed out*)

---

[1] FC *in text.*   [2] FC: *no alteration.*

267.   *The BCP rubric, transferred from after no. 239.*

268.   *For a discussion of the probable occasion of this 'order', see Appendix C (p. 296), and, at*
            greater length, an article in the Journal of Ecclesiastical History, *viii, No. 2 (1957),*
            188–92. The 'old Method' appears to include some new material. At least, the marginal
            notes for the manual acts, and the rubric 'When all have communicated', are specified;
            and presumably the rubrics nos. 249 and 257 are to be included also, and the alterations
            in the 'Forms of Participation'. Thus it is by no means a complete return to 1604, but
            an intermediate stage between that and the final version of DB. The version ultimately
            agreed upon represents a further step back towards 1604.

269. **Adv.:** In the 2d Prayer, put it thus,
            [. . . hartily thank thee, for that thou hast vouchsafed to feed us, (who of thy Grace
            have received these Holy Mysteries frō thee,) wth the spirituall food of the most
            pretious Body and Bloud of Thy Sonne] etc.

            'Or this' is now superfluous, as both prayers are to be said.
            'Everlasting' first appears in 1559; 1549 and 1552 both have 'euerliuing'.

    1549:   . . . thou hast vouchsafed . . . (*cf. Adv.*).

    BCP: . . . these holy mysteries . . .

270. **Adv.:** [. . . Thou onely O Xt, wth the most Holy, Eternall, and ever Blessed Spirit, art most
            high in the glory of God the Father. Amen.]

    Part. 62: At the *Gloria in Excelsis* wch is appointed to be *said* or *sung*, there is a question, whether
            the people are to say it after or wth the minister, or no. Where for the avoyding of
            any diversitie herin, some direction would be given.

            1549 has new paragraphs at these points; cf. no. 85.

271.   *Cf. nos. 92, 272, and 274.*

Then the Priest . . . shall let them depart with this blessing.

The peace of God . . . remaine with you alwayes. Amen.

Collects to be said after the offertorie, when there is no Communion, euery such day one, And the same may be said also as often as occasion shall serue, after the Collects either of Morning and Euening prayer, Communion, or Letanie, by the discretion of the Minister.

Assist vs mercifully, ☧ Lord . . . through Christ our Lord.

Graunt wee beseech thee . . .

Preuent vs, ☧ Lord . . .

Almightie God, the fountaine . . .

Almighty God, which hast promised to heare the petitions . . .

Vpon the Holy dayes (if there be no Communion) shall be said all that is appointed at the Communion, vntill the end of the Homily, concluding with the generall prayer **(for the whole estate of Christs Church militant here in earth)** and one or more of these Collects before rehearsed, as occasion shall serue.

And there shall be no celebration of the Lords Supper, except there be a great number to communicate with the Priest, according to his discretion.

And if there be not aboue twenty persons in the Parish, of discretion to receiue the Communion, yet there shall be no Communion, except foure or three at the least communicate with the Priest.

272.

273.

274.

275.

A fleuron.

Read: Collects to be said one or more at ye discretion of the minister, before ye finall Collect of Morning & Euening prayer, Litanie[1] or Comunion, as occasion shall serue: as also after the Offertorie or Prayer for ye estate of Christ's Church, when there is no Comunion celebrated.

Before Christ *add:* Jesus

Add: The finall Collect.
     ut supra.
     (*crossed out*)

Read: Vpon the Sundayes & other Holy dayes (if there be no Communion) shall be said all that is appointed at the Communion, vntill the end of the generall prayer for the good estate of Christs Catholick Church, concluding wth ye finall prayer Almightie God who hast promised to heare &c & the Blessing. (concluding *crossed out*)

i. *For* except . . . discretion *read:* except there be a sufficient number (yt is, foure or three at ye least) to communicate with the Priest.

ii. *Read:* except there be a sufficient number to communicate with the Priest, according to his discretion.

Delete the whole Rubric.   Stet

---

[1] *Originally* Comunion or Litanie.

272. **Adv.:** The Rubrick wch follows here after the Blessing, to be thus,
These Collects following, one or moe of them, at the discretion of the Minister, are to
be used, whither there be any Communion, or no, and are to be put in at the end of
Morning prayer, or Evening prayer, next before the Blessing be given.

SL: . . . every such day one or more.

Cf. nos. 92, 102, 104, and 124.

273. **Adv.:** In the first of these Collects,
[. . . through Jesus Xt our Lord. Amen.]

In the *2* last of these Collects,
[. . . Who knowest our necessities,] and
[. . . Who hast promised to heare the] etc.

Cf. no. 271 (for 'finall').

274. **Cf. S I:** Under wch Sundaies are comprehended, for certainly Sundaies are holydaies too. And
so it is but a peevish cavill of ye puritans to ask by what warrant men may read the 2d
Service upon Sundaies.

'The good estate . . .': cf. no. 221.

'Almightie God . . .': cf. no. 271.

275. **Adv.:** Here is a great Rubrick consisting of *3* Paragraphs. The formost whereof would be
divided: For the latter half of it, (wch was put in at first as a Barr against Private
Masses) is now become needless, & useless. Yet yf they will have it stand, Let it be
expressely set down, What is a good Number. Let it also be well considered, Whither
it be not very expedient now, to add a Caution against an overgreat Number; In
some Churches there coming about Easter, many Hundreths upon One day.

SL: . . . except there bee a sufficient number . . .

Cf. Wren, *Particular Orders*: 17. . . . that there may not come above 300 or (at the most) 400
Comunicants to one Comunion . . .

The first intention was to combine this and the following paragraph.

And in Cathedrall and Collegiate Churches, where bee many Priests and Deacons, they shall all receiue the Communion with the Minister euery Sunday at the least, except they haue a reasonable cause to the contrary.

276.   *After* Churches *add*: & Colledges,

For Minister *read*: Preist
After Sunday *add*: or once in a month
Delete except . . . contrary.

And to take away the superstition, which any person hath or might haue in the Bread and Wine, it shall suffice that the Bread be such as is vsually to be eaten at the Table with other meats, but the best and purest Wheat bread that conueniently may be gotten.

277.   *i. For* it shall . . . gotten *read*: the Bread shall be such as is vsual, yet the best and purest that conueniently may be gotten, though Wafer Bread shall not be forbidden, especially in such churches where it hath bin accustomed. The wine also shalbe of the best & purest yt may be had.
ii. After Wafer Bread *add*: (pure & wthout any figure set upon it)
iii. For the superstition *read*: all occasion of dissension, & superstition
For in the Bread *read*: concerning the Bread

And if any of the Bread and Wine remaine, the Curate shall haue it to his owne vse.

278.   *i. Before* Bread *add*: consecrated (*crossed out*)
ii. Read: If any of the Bread or Wine remaine unconsecrate, the Curate shall haue it to his owne vse: & if any remaine that was consecrate, it shall not be carried out of the

276. **Adv.:**   By this *2d* Paragraph it is presumed, that in Cathedrall, and Collegiate Churches, there is
a Communion every Sunday. But that Canon not having bin observed for very many
yeares: It is fit, that this be rectifyed, and that what Order shall herein be held, be now
expressed.

Part. 63: In ye fourth Rubrick after ye Cõmunion, *The priests & deacons of Cathedrall & Collegiate
churches are injoyned to receive the Cõmunion wth ye priest there, every Sunday at ye least.*
Questions are here moved, whether ye Church did not hereby intend to have the
Cõmunion administred in such places every day of ye week, or oftner then once in
the week *at least.* And whether the priest, who there waites in his weeke, ought not to
Cõmunicate oftner then every Sunday, or upon every Sunday *at the least.* Wch
Questions would be in this Rubrick determined by some few words added to it.

Lords: 17. Whether *Cathedrall and Collegiate* Churches shall be straitly bound to Celebrate the
Holy Communion every Sunday at the least, and might it not rather bee added *once
in a moneth.*

> *In view of Cosin's advocacy, here and elsewhere, of daily celebrations, this entry has been
> quoted as evidence that he was only acting as secretary to a committee. But the Lords'
> suggestion may well express Wren's views on the point, and Adv. supports it to
> a certain extent. It seems most probable, then, that Wren here overruled Cosin; the
> removal of the exceptive clause may have been a concession to him.*

277. **Adv.:**   [. . . in the Bread and Wine, It shall suffice, that the Bread, where it is not of fine Wafer,
pure, and wthout any Figure, or Print, be such as is usuall to be eaten] &c.
This would be put thus, Bycause in some places, (at Westminster, yf I remember
aright: and elsewhere,) playn Wafers have ever bin used.

Part. 64: In ye next Rubrick, it is said, That at ye Cõmunion *it shall suffice, yt The Bread be such, as
is usuall to be eaten, so it be ye best & purest yt may be gotten.* It is questioned here,
whether by vertue of this order any Church is restrayned from their Custome of using
Wafers at ye Sacramt, as in Westminster, & many other places they have bin alwayes
wont to doe. To avoyd dispute & contention herin, an order would here be annexed
for yt purpose.

SL: And to take away the superstition, which any person hath or might have in the Bread
and Wine, (though it be lawfull to have wafer bread) it shall suffice that the Bread be
such as is usuall: yet the best and purest Wheat Bread that conveniently may be gotten.

1549:   For auoyding of all matters and occasions of dissencion . . .

> *Part. 64 paraphrases a passage in S III, where Westminster is again cited as principal
> witness to the use of wafers, 'till the 17th of King Charles'. This makes less likely the
> suggestion that Adv. here depends on Part., or vice versa. Adv. alludes to the Eliza-
> bethan Injunctions:*
> *. . . that the said Sacramentall bread be made and fourmed playne, without any figure
> therevpon . . .*

278. **Adv.:**   What remayneth of the Bread of any Loaf, or Wafer, that was broken for the use of the
Communion, or of the Wine, wch was poured out, or had the Benediction, the Curate
shall after the Service is ended, take some of the Communicants to him, there to eat
and drinck the same. But all the rest in both kinds, the Curate shall have to his own use.
As this was set down before, much outcry was made against it.

Part. 65: It is likewise here ordered, *That if any of ye Bread & Wine Remaine, ye Curate shall have*

Church, but ye Priest & such
other of the Coɱunicants as he
shall then call unto him before ye
Lord's Table, shall reverently
eate and drinke the same.

iii. Before reverently *add*: there immediately after the Blessing

279. *i. Add*: [1]After the divine Service
ended, the money which was
offered shalbe divided, one half to
the Priest to provide him Books
of divinity, & the other half to be
imployed to some pious or charitable use for the decent furnishing
of the Church or ye relief of the
poore, to be presently distributed,
if need require, or put into the
poore-mans Boxe, at ye discretion
of the Priest & Churchwardens or
other Officers of the place, yt are
for that purpose appointed.

ii. Delete to provide him Books of
divinity, &
For to be presently *read*: among
whom it shalbe forthwith

The bread and wine for the Communion, shall   280.   *Delete the whole Rubric.*
bee prouided by the Curate and the Church-
wardens, at the charges of the Parish, and the
Parish shall bee discharged of such summes of
money or other dueties, which hitherto they
haue payed for the same by order of their houses
euery Sunday.

And note that euery Parishioner shall communi-
cate at the least three times in the yeere, of which
Easter to bee one, and shall also receiue the   281.   *For* to bee *read*: shall bee
Sacraments and other Rites, according to the   *Delete* and shall also . . . appointed.

---

[1] *Originally* At the end. . . .

it to his owne use. Wch words some Curates have abused & extended so farre, that they suppose, they may take all yt Remaines of the *Consecrate Bread & Wine it self,* home to their owne Houses, & there eat & drinke ye same with their other Common Meates; at least ye Roman-Catholicks take occasion hereby to lay this negligence & calumnie upon ye Church of England; wheras ye Rubrick only intends it of *such Bread & Wine* as Remaynes *Unconsecrate* of yt wch was provided for ye Parish, as appeareth by ye Articles of Inquiry hereabouts, in ye Visitations of divers Bpps. And therfore for ye better cleering of this particular, some words are needfull here to be added, wherby the Priest may be injoyned to consider ye number of ym wch are to Receive ye Sacramt, & to consecrate ye Bread & Wine in such a neere proportion, as shalbe sufficient for ym; but if any of ye consecrate Elemts be left, yt He & some others wth him, shall decently eate & drink ym in the church before all the people depart from it.

SL: And if any of the Bread and Wine remaine, which is consecrated, it shall be reverently eaten and drunk by such of the communicants only as the Presbyter which celebrates shall take unto him, but it shall not be carried out of the Church. And to the end there may be little left, he that officiates is required to consecrate with the least, and then . . . (*see no. 249*).

    S I, S II, and S III all interpret the rubric as referring to the 'unconsecrate' elements, and Part. 65 merely enlarges their arguments, perhaps also alluding to the SL rubric. Adv. summarizes SL.

    Stage i may have been an abortive attempt to follow SL, which ii defers until the unconsecrated elements have been dealt with. The source of the addition at stage iii has not been traced: it may be simply a more precise version of some of the earlier suggestions.

279. **SL:** After the divine service ended, that which was offered shall be divided in the presence of the Presbyter, and the Churchwardens, wherof one half shall be to the use of the Presbyter to provide him books of holy divinity: the other half shall be faithfully kept and employed on some pious or charitable use, for the decent furnishing of that Church, or the publike relief of their poore, at the discretion of the Presbyter and Churchwardens.

    The two halves are, respectively, the oblations and the alms. Cf. no. 220, and Dowden, Further Studies, p. 176.

280. *Transferred to the beginning of the service (no. 205).*

281. **Part. 66:** In ye last Rubrick there it is ordered & said, *That Every Parishioner shall Communicate at ye least 3 times in ye yeere* &c. *and shall also Receive ye Sacramts* &c. *according to ye order in this Booke appointed.* Where ye word *Sacraments* in ye *plurall number* being annexed to their *Coñunicating of ye Lords Supper,* (wch is *one Sacramt* already past & supposed to have bin taken by ye people, who are likewise already *Baptizd* in Another,) occasion is hereby given to thinke that the Church of England alloweth of *more Sacramts* then *Two:* but this being contrary both to the *Articles of Religion,* & ye *Catechisme* here following, it is requisite that in this place some explanation be made of ye word *Sacraments,* that there may be no difference betweene one place & another in our Bookes.

Part. 67: The like Explanation ought to be made of those words in ye *Act of Parliamt* sett at the beginning of this Booke, where in the 2d paragraph it is said, That all Ministers shall

order in this booke appointed. And yeerely at Easter, euery Parishioner shall reckon with his Parson, Vicar, or Curate, or his or their deputie or deputies, and pay to them or him all Ecclesiasticall dueties accustomably due, then and at that time to be payed.

282.   *i. For* And yeerely . . . be payed. *read*: And yeerely in Easter weeke, euery Parishioner shall reckon with the minister or his deputie, and pay to him all Ecclesiasticall dueties that are then accustomably due, to be payed for ye yeere past.

     ii. For in Easter weeke *read*: at Easter time

     iii. Stet *as printed.*

     A fleuron.

be bounden to say & use — *ye Celebration of ye Lords Supper*, (wch is one Sacramt) & *Administration of Each of the Sacraments*, (wch is more then One besides.

SL: . . . Easter shall be one . . .

> *DB avoids giving an 'explanation' of the word 'Sacraments' (Part. 66) by removing the entire clause.*

282. **Adv.:**   Make another Paragraph of it, at the 2d Line, and set it thus,

In Easter Week yearely every Parishioner, or one for him, shall reckon wth the Minister or his Deputy, and shall pay to him all Ecclesiasticall Duties accustomably due, as then, and at that time to be payd for the yeare past, unles they have payd for the same before.

Detached Note: The arrangement of the Communion Service
in the English Prayer Books.

As far as the first part of the service is concerned, SL and DB do not diverge at all in structure from 1552; as against 1549, all three discard the Introit Psalm, and transfer the *Gloria* to the end of the service. After the Offertory, DB follows SL exactly, but diverges from both 1549 and 1552. The various arrangements may be tabulated thus:

1549	1552	SL and DB
Sursum corda, &c.		
Prayer for the Church	Prayer for the Church	Prayer for the Church
	Exhortations	Exhortations
Prayer of Consecration		
Prayer of Oblation		
Lord's Prayer		
Invitation	Invitation	Invitation
Confession	Confession	Confession
Absolution	Absolution	Absolution
Comfortable Words	Comfortable Words	Comfortable Words
	Sursum corda, &c.	*Sursum corda*, &c.
Prayer of Humble Access	Prayer of Humble Access	
	Prayer of Consecration	Prayer of Consecration
		Prayer of Oblation
		Lord's Prayer
(Prayer of Humble Access)		Prayer of Humble Access
Administration	Administration	Administration
	Lord's Prayer	
	Prayer of Oblation *or*	
Prayer of Thanksgiving	Prayer of Thanksgiving	Prayer of Thanksgiving
	Gloria	*Gloria*
Blessing	Blessing	Blessing

Thus the arrangement in DB and SL is a compromise between 1549 and 1552. On the one hand, it follows 1552 in detaching the Prayer for the Church, and placing it, together with the penitential section (*Invitation* to *Comfortable Words*), before the *Sursum corda*. On the other hand, it juxtaposes the Prayer of Oblation with the Prayer of Consecration, following it with the Lord's Prayer, and restores the Prayer of Humble Access to its 1549 position immediately before the Communion.

¶ The ministration of Baptisme, to be vsed in the Church.

283.
   i. Before Baptisme *add*: Infants'
   ii. Read: The Administration of pub-lick Baptisme of Infants, to be vsed in the Church.
   iii. For Infants *read*: Children
      Print this on ye other page, & set a fayre Compartement before it.

It appeareth by ancient Writers, that the Sacrament of Baptisme in the olde time was not commonly ministred, but at two times in the yeere: At Easter, and Whitsuntide. At which times it was openly ministred in the presence of all the Congregation . . .
       Wherefore the people are to be admonished, that it is most conuenient that Baptisme should not be ministered but vpon Sundayes, and other holy dayes, when the most number of people may come together . . . Neuerthelesse (if necessitie so require) children may at all times be baptized at home.
When there are children to be baptized vpon the Sunday or Holy-day, the parents shall giue knowledge ouernight, or in the morning afore the beginning of Morning prayer, to the Curate.

284.
   i. For Baptisme . . . At which times *read*: Baptisme was not commonly ministred of old, but at Easter and Whitsuntide; When
   ii. Read: Baptisme was not in their time commonly celebrated, but at the yearly feasts of Easter and Whitsuntide; When
   iii. Stet as printed.
   Delete may

285.
   For may . . . home *read*: may & ought to be baptized upon any other dayes.

   After knowledge *add*: therof

And then the Godfathers, Godmothers, and people, with the children must be ready at the Font, either immediatly after the last lesson at Morning prayer, or else immediatly after the last lesson at Euening prayer, as the Curate by his discretion shal appoint.

286.
   i. Read: And then the people with the Godfathers & Godmothers (who shall be three at ye least for every child, & such, as have before received ye holy Comunion) must be ready with the children at the Font . . .
   ii. Read: And then the Godfathers & Godmothers (who shall be three for every child i.e. for a male child 2[1] godff. & 1. godm. & for a female 2[1] godmothers, & 1. godfather) and ye people, with the children must be ready at the Font . . .

---

[1] *The original figure is indecipherable.*

283. **1549:** Of the Administracion of publyke Baptisme . . .

i suggests that a Form of Baptism of Adults was already envisaged; ii brings the title into line with 1549.

284. *Stylistic improvement.*

285. **Adv.:** At the bottome of this first Rubrick for Baptism, set it thus,
[Nevertheless Children may at all times be baptized at home, yf necessity so require; And at the Church, on any other dayes.]

1549: . . . children ought at all tymes to be Baptised . . .

286. **Adv.:** In the next Rubrick, thus,
The Godfathers and Godmothers, (that is to say, for a Male-child, 2 Godfathers, and 1 Godmother, and no more, And for a Female, one Godfather, and 2 Godmothers:) and other people, wth the Child, or Children, must be ready at the Font, immediately after the Second Lesson] &c.

Canon 29: . . . before the said person so undertaking hath received the holy Communion.

i. *'Three at the least': cf. the Synod of Worcester, 1240: Masculum ad minus duo masculi et una mulier suscipiant.*
Three was the customary number in England, and the requirement 'at the least' (otherwise unknown) may be intended to guard against the Puritan dislike of sponsors.
ii. *This arrangement is first found in a Canon of the Council of York, 1195. For this, and other references, see D. S. Bailey, Sponsors at Baptism and Confirmation (London, 1952), 103. The phrase in Adv. 'three and no more' recalls Sarum:*
ultra tres amplius ad hoc nullatenus recipiantur.
Wren had already embodied it in his Particular Orders:
14. . . . yt ye Minister admitt but 2. Godfathers & one Godmother for a male child; & 2. Godmothers & one Godfather, for a female . . .
See also Procter and Frere, A New History of the Book of Common Prayer (London, 1901), 575, for a long note on sponsors.
At this point attention must be drawn to a concession by the Bishops which is ignored by DB (the only one so treated):
11. That if the Font be so placed as the Congregation cannot hear, it may be referred to the Ordinary, to place it more conveniently.

And then standing there, the Priest shal aske whether the children bee baptized or no. If they answere no: Then shall the Priest say thus.

287. *i. Read*: And the Priest, comming to the Font, & standing there, shal aske, & say.

Hath this Child beene already baptized, or no.

If they answere No:

Then shall the Priest proceed as followeth.

ii. Read: And the Priest, comming to the Font (wch is to be then repleishd wth pure water), & standing there, shal say.

Hath this Child (or if there be more, whether Hath any of them) beene already baptized, or no.

If they answere No:

Then shall the Priest proceed as followeth (varying his words according to the number).

iii. For whether Hath any of them *read*: Hath any one of these children

For (varying . . . number) *read*: (varying the forme, only[1] those words wch are requisite to expresse a difference of ye Sexe, or Number of ye children.)

𝕯earely beloued . . . hee will graunt to these children[2] that thing which by nature they cannot haue, that they may be baptized with water and the holy Ghost, and receiued into Christs holy Church, and be made liuely members of the same.

Then shall the Priest say.

288. *Before* these *add*: (this child, or)

After nature *add*: (He, or She, or)

Throughout the service the sign (.) is inserted before pronouns, to indicate that they are to be altered as required.[3] This sign has not been repeated below.

𝕷et us pray.

Almighty and euerlasting God, which . . . diddest sanctifie thy flood Jordan, and all other waters, to the mysticall washing away of sinne: We beseech thee for thine infinite mercies, that thou wilt mercifully looke vpon these children . . . through Jesus Christ our Lord. Amen.

289. *Add*: And here all ye Congregation shall kneele downe.

For thy *read*: the[4]

290. *For* We beseech . . . thou wilt *read*: Sanctifie, we beseech thee, this Fountaine of Baptisme, & (*crossed out*)

Almighty and immortall God . . . we call vpon thee for these infants, that they comming to thy holy Baptisme, may receiue remission of their sinnes by spirituall regeneration. Receiue them, (O Lord) as thou hast promised . . . So giue now vnto vs that aske . . . the heauenly washing . . . by Christ our Lord. Amen.

291. *For* comming *read*: being here brought   Stet

For Receiue them, (O Lord) as . . . So *read*: Receiue them, O Lord; & as . . . so

For the *read*: thy[4]

---

[1] *Originally* only where ye number.
[3] FC: *All pronouns are also underlined.*

[2] FC: persons (*Cosin*).
[4] FC: *in text.*

287. **Adv.:** In the first Rubrick, thus,
    The Preist shall first ask, whither the child, (or yf there be more, whither any of them)
    hath bin baptized already.

1549: The Priest . . . cuṁing into the church towarde the font . . .

Wren, *Particular Orders:* 14. That ye Font at Baptisme be filled wth cleane water.

An example of the tendency in DB to turn rubrics into forms of words.
i: 1549 and Adv. ii: Part. Orders and Adv. iii: Editorial.

288.   *Cf. Adv. on no. 307 ('He, or She'). Notice Cosin's alteration in FC, 'persons' for*
    'children', possibly an attempt to make the service suitable for adults as well as infants.
    If so, this entry must be very early; cf. no. 283. i.

289. **Adv.:** After the Preface, when the Preist sayeth, [Let us pray,] All the Congregation shall
    kneel down.
    [Almighty and everlasting God, Who of Thy great] &c.

BCP: . . . the flood . . .

290. **SL:** Sanctifie this fountain of baptisme, thou which art the Sanctifier of all things.
    SL borrowed this phrase from the 1549 form for blessing the water.

291. **BCP:** . . . thy heauenly washing . . .

Then shall the Priest say.
Heare the words of the Gospel written by S.
Marke, in the tenth Chapter.

292. *i. Add*: at ye 13. verse.
> Here ye Answere
> Glory be to thee ô Lord.

ii. For Here ye Answere *read*: Here ye people shall stand up, & say

iii. in ye new translon

At a certaine time . . . and blessed them.

293. *Add*: So endeth ye Holy Gospel.
> Answere
> Thanks be to thee ô Lord.

After the Gospel is read, the Minister shall make this briefe exhortation vpon the words of the Gospel.

Friendes you heare in this Gospel . . . and nothing doubting but that he fauourably alloweth this charitable worke of ours, in bringing these children[1] to his holy Baptisme: let vs faithfully and deuoutly giue thankes vnto him, and say,

Almighty and euerlasting God . . . now and for euer. Amen.

294. *i. For* fauourably alloweth *read*: approveth & favourably accepteth

ii. Read: favourably accepteth our obedience in

Then the Priest shall speake vnto the Godfathers and Godmothers in this wise.

Welbeloued friends, yee haue brought these children here . . . by you that be their sureties, that they will forsake the deuill and all his workes, and constantly beleeue Gods holy word, and obediently keepe his Commaundements.

295. *After* Then *add*: shall they all rise up, &   (*crossed out*)

After sureties *add*: (untill they come of age to take it upon themselves)
For forsake *read*: renounce

296. *i. Add*: Answere me therfore —

ii. Read: I demand therfore

Then shall the Priest demand of the Godfathers and Godmothers these questions following.

Doest thou forsake the deuill and all his workes . . . nor be led by them?

Answere.

I forsake them all.

Minister.

Doest thou beleeue in God the Father Almighty, maker of heauen and earth?

And in Iesus Christ his onely begotten Sonne . . . and from thence shall come againe

297. *After* Godmothers *add*: of every severall child yt is to be baptised, (*crossed out*)

i. For forsake *read*: in the name of this Child renounce

ii. Read: renounce
Read: And every one of them shall Answere, audibly.   (*crossed out*)
I renounce them all

298. *Add*: Doest thou in the name of this child professe this faith?

Add: Answere   I believe.
Read: Doest thou believe in Iesus Christ his onely begotten Sonne

---

[1] FC: persons (*Cosin*).

292. **Adv.:**   The first Rubrick, thus,
          Then shall they all stand up, and the Preist shall say,

  SL: Mark 10. 13.

              *Cf. no. 212. SL adds the verse number to the announcement of the Gospel in the Com-
              munion Service, where DB does not.*

293.   *'So endeth . . .' is SL's phrase at no. 212, where DB has 'Here endeth . . .'.*

294. **Adv.:**   In ye Exhortation after ye Gospell, thus.
              [. . . that he commanded the Children to be brought unto Him, expressely declaring,
              that though but Children, yet the Kingdome of God belongd unto them; That he
              blamed his own Disciples, that would then have kept thẽ frõ him; That he exhorteth
              all men] &c.
              [. . . For he embraced them in his Armes, as admitting them into his Church, whereof
              himself was the Head, (for wch end he did afterward institute this Sacrament of
              Baptism:) He layed his hands upon thẽ, and blessed them.]
              For the FC reading, see no. 288.

295. **Adv.:**   In the first line, thus,
              [. . . their Sureties, untill they come of age to take it upon themselves, That they will
              forsake the Devill and all his works, and constantly beleeve Gods holy word, and
              obediently keep his Commandments.]
              The direction to 'rise up' is superseded by no. 292. ii.
              'Forsake': cf. no. 297.

296. **Adv.:**   Answer me therfore,
              Doest thou forsake the Devill &c.
              'Demand' comes from the rubric following. Cf. no. 287.

297. **Adv.:**   The Sureties, in the childs name to answer,
              I forsake them all.

  Sarum: R̷. Abrenuncio.

              'In the name of this child': cf. Private Baptism, at no. 327.
              'Renounce': cf. Taylor:
              Dost thou abjure, and renounce, and promise to forsake the Devil . . . ?

298. **1552** (Private Baptism, at no. 328): Doest thou in the name of this childe professe thys fayth, to
          beleue in God . . . ?

  1549:   Ans. I beleue.
          Doest thou beleue in Iesus Christ . . . ?
              The triple affirmation of belief follows 1549.

at the end of the world to iudge the quicke and
the dead? . . . and euerlasting life after
death?

... and that from thence he shall
come againe . . . and the dead?
Add: Doest thou believe this?
Answere   I believe.
(*all crossed out*)[1]

Answere.

All this I stedfastly beleeue.

299.   *i. Add*:   Minister
Doest thou promise that thou wilt
obediently keep Gods holy will, &
Commandements, & walk in ye
same all the dayes of thy Life?
Answere
I promise & vow by God's grace so
to doe.

ii. For I promise . . . to doe *read*: I doe
promise.

Minister.

Wilt thou be baptized in this faith?

Answere.

That is my desire.

Then shall the Priest say.

O Mercifull God . . .

·   ·   ·   ·   ·   ·

. . . the world and the flesh. Amen.
Grant that whosoeuer is here dedicated . . .
world without end. Amen.

300.   *For* this faith *read*: in the faith wch
thou hast professed   (*crossed out*)

Read: Grant that they being here
dedicated . . .

Almighty euerliuing God . . . Regard, we
beseech thee, the supplications of thy Congregation,

301.   *For* Congregation *read*: Church

           and grant that all thy seruants
which shall be baptized in this water

302.   *i. For* all thy seruants which *read*: this
child (or these children who

ii. Read: these thy seruants or this thy servt
which[2]

303.   *After* water *add*: (wch we here blesse
in thy name, & dedicate to this
holy action)   (*crossed out*)

                          may
receiue the fulnesse of thy grace, and euer
remaine in the number of thy faithfull and
elect children, through Jesus Christ our
Lord. Amen.

---

[1] *Question-marks are added at the end of each clause.*   [2] FC: these thy seruants (or this Child).

299. **BCP** (Catechism): And thirdly, that I should keepe Gods holy will and commandments, and walk in the same all the dayes of my life.
They did promise and vow . . . and by Gods help so I will.
(Baptism, at no. 295): . . . that they will . . . obediently keepe his Commaundements.

The third promise from the Catechism, bringing the present passage into line with the answer 'They did promise and vow three things in my name.' 'Obediently' comes from the end of the Priest's address at no. 295. Sanderson has a question similarly based on the third promise.

300. *Cf. no. 298.*

301. **Adv.:** At the *16th* line, thus,
[. . . all Nations, and baptize them in the name of the Father, and of the Sonne, and of the Holy Ghost, regard, we beseech thee the supplications of thy Church,]

SL: . . . thy Church . . .

302. **Adv.:** . . . and grant, that all thy Servants, (or, yf but one, this thy servant,) wch shall be baptized &c.

Part. '68': In ye prayer wch is used for Blessing ye Water in the Font, before ye Children (then brought to ye Church) be Baptized in it, there is this Expression, *Grant that All thy Servants wch shalbe baptized in this Water may receive &c* where *All thy Servants* cannot be said when there is but *one child* brought to ye Font for that purpose. And therfore those words would be better changd into these, *Grant that This Child (or These Children) wch shall now be baptized &c.*

ii shows S following Adv. in preference to Part. FC combines i and ii.

303. **SL:** (which we here blesse and dedicate in thy name to this spiritual washing)

Cf. no. 290. 'Action' is a favourite word of Cosin's: see, for example, his Confirmation address (Works, V. 526) and no. 250.

Then shall the Priest take the childe in his hands, and aske the name: and naming the childe, shall dip it in the water, so it be discreetly and warily done, saying.

304. *Read*: Then shall the Priest take the childe into his hands, & say to ye Godfathers & Godmothers,
    Name this child
And then audibly naming it after them,[1] (if they certifie him, that the child is able,) he shall dip it in the water discreetly and warily, saying.

N. 𝔍 baptize thee in the 𝔑ame of the 𝔉ather, and of the 𝔖onne, and of the holy 𝔊host. 𝔄men.

And if the child be weake, it shall suffice to powre water vpon it, saying the foresaid words.

305. *For* And *read*: But
For vpon it *read*: vpon the face of it (*crossed out*)
Read: N I baptize thee &c

N. 𝔍 baptize thee in the 𝔑ame . . . holy 𝔊host. 𝔄men.

Then the Priest shall make a Crosse vpon the childes forehead, saying.

306. i. *Read*: Then the Priest at the words [doe signe him] wch follow, shall make a crosse vpon the childes forehead, saying.
ii. *Read*: Then the Priest shall say.

𝔚ee receiue this childe into the 𝔠ongregation of 𝔠hrists flocke, and doe signe him with the signe of the 𝔠rosse, in token that hereafter he shall not be ashamed to confesse the 𝔉aith

of 𝔠hrist crucified, and manfully to fight vnder his banner, against sin, the world and the deuill, and to continue 𝔠hrists faithfull souldier and seruant vnto his liues end. 𝔄men.

307. i. *For* the Congregation of Christs flocke *read*: the Church of Christ
ii. *Stet as printed; add*:
[Then ye Priest shall make a Crosse upon the child's forehead, & adde]
For and manfully *read*: but constantly *Stet*
Delete to

---

[1] *Originally* as they shall answere.

304. **Adv.:** In the first Rubrick, thus,
         Then shall the Preist take every Child in his hands, and yf they certify him, that the
         Child is strong enough, asking the Name, and audibly naming it, he shall dipp it in the
         water, discreetly and warily, and shall say,
            [N. I baptize thee in the Name] &c.

          Cf. no. 287 (rubric into form of words).

305. **Adv.:** In the next Rubrick, thus,
         But yf the Child be weak, it shall be sufficient to poure water on ye forehead, to run
         upon the face of it, and to say,

   1549: N. I Baptise thee. &c.

          Taylor has 'to sprinkle water on the face', another example of the general agreement in
          matters of practice.

306. **Adv.:** In the next Rubrick, thus,
         Then the Preist shall make a cross on the Childs forehead, after that he hath sayd,

          i is superseded by no. 307. ii.

307. **Adv.:** [Having now baptized this Child into Xt, and thereby received it into Xts Church, and
         the Congregation of his flock, We do signe it wth the sign of the Cross, ✠ (here
         delivering back the child) in token that hereafter He, (or She) shall not be ashamed to
         confesse the fayth of Xt crucified, against sinne, the world, and the Devill, and to
         continue Xts spirituall Souldier, and faythfull Servant unto His (or Hir) lives end.]
       As this went before, (manfully to fight under his Banner) it offended many, bycause it
       appertaynes not naturally, to ye Female Sexe. The last ArchBp. varied frõ it, Baptizing
       ye Princess Royall.

  Part. '69': At Signing ye Child wth ye Signe of ye Crosse, it is said, *Wee Receive this Child into*
         ye Congregation of Christ's Flock, wch word *Congregation* both here & in many other
         places of ye Booke is a new word, never used by any Former Liturgie, or ancient
         Writer in ye Church. It were therfore requisite, for ye avoyding of that Exception
         wch ye Roman-Catholicks wth some advantage to themselves take against it, that
         where ever *this word* is found in ye whole Book, (as in *divers Collects* & in *ye Gospel*
         upon *St. Peters* day it is), it may be altered, & be putt into the old usuall Expression of
         the word, (yt is) *Church of Christ.*

  SL: . . . into the Church of Christ . . .

         SL or Part. '69' rather than Adv.
         'The last ArchBp.' is Laud, who baptized the Princess Royal on 4 November 1631. This
         description suggests that Juxon had not yet been elevated to the see of Canterbury when
         Wren wrote, though it is not entirely inconsistent with the existence of an Archbishop
         at the time of writing.

308.   i. *Add*: And then he shall deliver back
          the child; & if there be more
          children then one, he shall baptize
          & signe every one of them in the
          same manner
      ii. *After* baptize *add*: receive
     iii. *Delete the whole Rubric.*

Then shall the Priest say.

𝔖eeing no𝔴, dearel𝔂 belo𝔲ed bret𝔥ren, t𝔥at
t𝔥ese c𝔥ildren be regenerate and graffed into
t𝔥e bod𝔂 of 𝔠𝔥rists congregation, let 𝔲s gi𝔲e
t𝔥anks 𝔲nto 𝔊od for t𝔥ese benefits, and 𝔴it𝔥
one accord make our pra𝔂ers 𝔲nto 𝔄lmig𝔥t𝔂
𝔊od, t𝔥at t𝔥e𝔂 ma𝔂 lead t𝔥e rest of t𝔥eir life
according to t𝔥is beginning.

309.   *For* be *read*: are
       For congregation *read*: Church
       Before giue *add*: therfore[1]
       Before God *add*: almightie
       Delete for these benefits   Stet
       For Almighty God *read*: him
       Add: (all kneeling)
       Print it out at large.

Then shall be said.

𝔒ur 𝔉at𝔥er 𝔴hic𝔥 art in 𝔥ea𝔲en, &c.

Then shall the Priest say.

𝔚ee 𝔂eeld t𝔥ee heart𝔂 t𝔥anks . . . to incorporate 𝔥im into t𝔥𝔂 𝔥ol𝔂 𝔠ongregation . . . t𝔥e
𝔴hole bod𝔂 of sinne, t𝔥at as 𝔥ee is made partaker of t𝔥e deat𝔥 of t𝔥𝔂 𝔖on, so 𝔥e ma𝔂 bee
partaker of 𝔥is resurrection, so t𝔥at finall𝔂
𝔴it𝔥 t𝔥e residue of t𝔥𝔂 𝔥ol𝔂 𝔠ongregation, 𝔥e
ma𝔂 be in𝔥eritour of t𝔥ine e𝔲erlasting kingdome, t𝔥rough 𝔠𝔥rist our 𝔏ord. 𝔄men.

310.   *For* Congregation *read*: Church   Stet
       For that *read* & that
       For so he may *read*: he may be also
       For so that *read*: also that
       For Congregation *read*: Church

At the last end, the Priest calling the Godfathers
and Godmothers together shall say this exhortation following.

311.   i. *Read*: Then shall the Priest say to
          the Godfathers and Godmothers
          this Exhortation following.
      ii. *Read*: Then all standing up the
          Priest shall say . . .

𝔉orasmuch as t𝔥ese c𝔥ildren ha𝔲e promised
b𝔂 𝔂ou to forsake t𝔥e de𝔲ill and all 𝔥is 𝔴orks,
to bele𝔢ue in 𝔊od, and to ser𝔲e 𝔥im:

312.   i. *For* promised . . . serue him *read*:
          severally covenanted & promised
          by you their Sureties to renounce
          the deuill and all his works, to
          beleeue in God, and to keep his
          duty
      ii. *Delete* severally
          Stet: to serue him

                                     𝔂ou
must remember t𝔥at it is 𝔂our parts and
duties to see t𝔥at t𝔥ese infants be taug𝔥t, so
soone as t𝔥e𝔂 s𝔥all bee able to learne, 𝔴hat
a solemne bo𝔴e, promise, and profession

       For parts and duties *read*: part &
       dutie

---

[1] *FC omits.*

308. **Adv.:**   . . . here delivering back the child . . .
        Add also this Rubrick,
            Yf there be moe Children then One, both ye Baptism itself, and this Sentence shall be
            repeated upon every One.

309. **Adv.:**   The first Rubrick here, to be thus,
            After all the Children are baptized, and delivered to their freinds, the Preist shall say,
            [Seing now, Dearly beloved, that these Children are regenerate, and graffed into
            the Body of Xts Church, Let us give thanks,] &c.

        and here, to [Our Father, Who art in Heaven,] etc. let be added,
            [for thyne is the Kingdome,] &c. to be sayd wth the Preist by all Present.
          Cf. no. 307; several of the alterations are editorial.

310. **Adv.:**   In that Prayer, thus,
            [. . . and to incorporate Him, (Hir, or Them) into thy Holy Church: And humbly we
            beseech thee] &c.
            [. . . with the residue of thy holy Church, He may be Inheritor of thy everlasting
            kingdome through Jesus Xt our Lord. Amen.
          Cf. no. 307.

311.
          'Standing up' follows 'kneeling' in no. 309.

312. **Adv.:**   That last Rubrick, to be thus,
            Last of all the Preist, directing his speech particularly, unto the Godfathers, & God-
            mothers shall say,
            [Forasmuch as these Children severally have Covenanted, and by you their Sureties
            promised to forsake the Devill] &c.
            [. . . all other things, wch a Xtian ought to know,] leaving out the word, [man.]

    Part. '70': In ye Exhortation to ye Godfathers &c, it is appointed, yt *ye Children shalbe taught ye
    Creed, ye Pr̃ nr̃ & ye X Comts in the English Tongue.* But suppose (as it falls often out)
    yt children of strangers, wch never intend to stay in England, be brought there to be
    Baptized; shall they also be exhorted & injoyned to learne those principles of Religion
    in ye *English Tongue* only? It would be freer from Exception if these words were thus
    expressed, — *in ye vulgar Tongue yt they shall use.*

they haue made by you. And that they may
know these things the better, ye shall call
vpon them to heare Sermons, and chiefly you
shall prouide that they may learne the Creed,
the Lords prayer, and the ten Commande=
ments in the English tongue, and all other

things which a Christian man ought to know
and beleeue to his soules health, and that
these children may be vertuously brought vp
to leade a godly and a Christian life, re=
membring alwayes that Baptisme doeth represent vnto vs our profession, which is, to
follow the example of our Sauiour Christ,
and to be made like vnto him . . . in all vertue
and godlinesse of liuing.

The Minister shall command that the children
bee brought to the Bishop to be confirmed of
him, so soone as they can say in their vulgar
tongue, the Articles of the Faith, the Lords
prayer, and the ten Commandements, and be
further instructed in the Catechisme set foorth for
that purpose, according as it is there expressed.

Before made *add*: here
Delete call vpon them to heare
Sermons, and chiefly you shall
Stet

For the English *read*: their vulgar[1]
(*crossed out*)
Delete man
For health, and *read*: health; And
Before vertuously *add*: the more
(*crossed out*)
For remembring always *read*: yee
shall call upon them at due time
hereafter [2]to frequent ye divine
Service, & to heare Sermons in the
Church putting them in remem-
brance Stet

313.   i. *Read*: Then shall he adde & say
Furthermore I require you, to take
care that these children bee
brought to the Bishop to be confirmed by him, so soone as they
can say in the[3] vulgar tongue, the
Articles of the Faith, the Lords
prayer, and the Ten Commandements, and be sufficiently instructed in the Catechisme wch
is set foorth by publick authority
for that purpose.
Print this in ye black character.
ii. *For* and be sufficiently . . . that purpose
read: and are further instructed in the
Church Catechisme set foorth for that
purpose, according as it is there
expressed.

314.   *Add*: Then shall the minister return
from ye font, & proceed in ye
Service as is before appointed.
(*crossed out*)
i. *Add*: And that no man may think
ut infra init. Catechisme[4]
ii. *For* And . . . think *read*: It is certain by
H. Script. &c.
A Compartement.

---

[1] English *is underlined but not crossed out.*
[2] to heare Sermons *originally came first.*
[3] FC: *no alteration.*
[4] FC: *i.* And that no man may thinke, as at ye end of ye Preface in Confirmation (*Cosin*).
      ii. It is certain by God's word &c as at . . .

Part. '71': There also it is said, — *And all other Things wch a Christian Man ought to know &c.* But suppose it be a *Woman*, or a *female child*: therfore yt word *Man* were better left out, & ye word *Christian* only would then remaine indefinite; as likewise ye words *His* & *Him* (many times used in this forme of Administering Baptisme) ought rather to be changed into *this child*, yt they may referre either to *Male* or *Female*.

> *Sanderson also omits 'man'. Cosin has not followed the quotation from Lyndwood which he entered in S II:*
> *Haec dictio non solum masculum, sed etiam feminam comprehendit.*
> *'Frequent': cf. Cosin's Confirmation Address* (Works, *V. 526*), *ad fin.:*
> *And the frequenting of it may doe much good.*
> (*The correct reading is 'frequenting', not 'frequency', some editors having misunderstood the abbreviated ending 'tg'.*)
> *The other alterations are stylistic.*

313. **Adv.:** At the end of the Exhortation, this Rubrick to be sett,
> Yf Baptism at any time be administered not in the Church, or there, not in the Time of the Divine Service, then let the Close of all here be, wth the Blessing, [The Grace of our Ld Jesus] &c.;
[The Preist alwaies adding, thus,
> In the Name of Xt, and of his Church, I charge you the Sureties, to see to it carefully, that these Children be brought to the Bishop to be Confirmed, as soon as they can say] &c.
Then this Rubrick to follow,
> For wch purpose, the Arch-Bps and Bishops are required, by themselves, or some other Bishop in their stead, once in every Third yeare (at the furthest) to solemnize Confirmation through theire Dioceses: And all the Time between, to cause their Clergy to be diligent and faythfull in Catechizing, according to this Book, and to the Canon of the Church in that behalf.

> *A further case of rubric turned into form of words. 'Publick authority': cf. no. 214.*

314.
> *i.e., with the last Canticle and the rest of Morning or Evening Prayer.*
> *For i and ii, cf. nos. 341–3. i already has the alteration 'may' (no. 341. i); ii is no. 341. ii, quoted inaccurately. Cosin's entry in FC also has 'may', so that it must have been made between stages i and ii of no. 341. Sancroft has made his correction accurately in FC, though not in DB ('H. Script.').*

❡ Of them that are to be baptized in priuate houses in time of necessitie, by the Minister of the *Parish, or by any other lawful Minister, that can be procured.*

The Pastors and Curates shal often admonish the people, that they deferre not the baptisme of Infants any longer then the Sunday or other Holy day next after the child be borne, vnlesse vpon a great and reasonable cause declared to the Curate, and by him approoued.

And also they shall warne them, that without great cause and necessitie, they procure not their children to be baptized at home in their houses. And when great need shall compell them so to doe, then Baptisme shalbe administered on this fashion.

First, let the lawfull Minister, and them that be present, call vpon God for his grace, and say the Lords prayer if time will suffer.

And then the child being named by some one that is present, the said lawfull Minister shall dip it in water or powre water vpon it, saying these words.

𝕹. 𝕴 𝕭apti𝔷e thee in the 𝕹ame of the 𝕱ather, and of the 𝕾onne, and of the holy 𝕲host. 𝕬men.

315.   *i. Read:* ❡ The Ministration of Private Baptisme of Children in Houses, when Necessitie shall so require. Print this Title on a new page.
       ii. Delete when . . . require.

316.   *i. Read:* The Ministers in every parish shall in their Exhortations to the people often admonish them, that they deferre not the Baptisme of their Children any longer then the first or second Sunday (or other Holy day falling betweene) next after their Birth, vnlesse . . . approoued.

       ii. Read: The Ministers in every parish shall in their Exhortations often admonish the people that they deferre not . . .

       Before great *add:* like

       For And *read:* But
       Before great *add:* such   (crossed out)

317.   *i. Read:* First, a decent Basin filled wth pure water being provided, let the Minister of ye parish [1](or in his absence any other lawfull Minister that can be procured) standing by it, together with them that be present, call vpon God for his grace,[2] saying, Sanctifie, ô Lord this fountaine of Baptisme, adding the Lords prayer & so many of the Collects appointed to be said before in the forme of publick Baptisme, as ye time & present exigence will suffer.
       ii. Read: First, let the Minister of ye parish (or . . . procured) with them that be present, call vpon God for his grace, & say the Lords prayer . . . suffer.

318.   *Delete* said lawfull
       Delete dip it in water or

---

[1] standing by it *originally stood here.*   [2] FC *omits* for his grace.

315.   *The title is assimilated to that of Public Baptism (cf. no. 283). 'By the Minister . . .' is*
       transferred to no. 317.

316. **Adv.:**   That last Rubrick on this page, to goe thus,
       All Ministers in every place where they are to officiate, shall in their exhortations to
       the People often admonish them, that they deferr not to have their Children Baptized,
       any longer, then the First, or the Second Sunday, or other Holyday falling between,
       next after the Birth of their Children, Unless upon a great] &c.

   Part. '72': In the first Rubrick there ye *Cause and Necessitie* of Baptizing in private houses, ought
       to be expressed, as *When ye child is in suddaine danger of death, & not likely to live so long
       a time yt it may be brought to Publick Baptisme in ye Church*; least otherwise every one
       take upon them to be judge of this *Cause & Necessitie* at their pleasure.

       ii is a typical improvement by S.

317. **Part. '73':** In ye next Rubrick, ye *Lawfull Minister* is appointed in this urgent Cause to Baptize
       ye child, wch was added by *King James* his direction only in ye Conference at Hampt.
       Court, to avoyd ye Baptizing by *Midwives* or *Others* yt were no *lawfull Ministers*
       ordeyned for yt purpose. This alteration was well, but it wanteth the force *of a Law*,
       according to ye *Act of Uniformity* prefixed to ye Booke.

   Part. '74': It is not here said what shalbe done in this Case when *a Lawfull Minister* cannot be
       found, or whether ye child ought to be Baptized againe or no, when only a *Midwife*
       or some *other such* hath baptized it before.

       *Cf. nos. 220 ('a decent Basin'), 287. ii ('filled with pure water'), 315 ('any other lawfull
       Minister . . .'), and 299 ('Sanctifie . . .').*

318. **Adv.:**   At the end of ye first Rubrick, leave out those words [Dip it in Water, or.]

   Cf. Lords: 21. In private Baptisme, the rubrique mentions that which must not be done, *that
       the Minister may dip the child in water being at the point of Death.*

319. 　*i. Add*: Then the Minister shall make
　　　a Crosse upon the child's fore-
　　　head, saying
　　　Wee receive this Child into the
　　　Church of Christ.
　　　And all kneeling downe shall give
　　　thanks unto God, & say
　　　Wee yield thee hearty thanks most
　　　mercifull Father, that it hath
　　　pleased thee to regenerate this
　　　Infant, with thy holy Spirit, to
　　　receive him for thine owne child
　　　by adoption, & to incorporate him
　　　into thy holy Church. And wee
　　　humbly beseech thee to grant
　　　that he being dead unto sinne &
　　　living unto God, now made par-
　　　taker of ye death of thy Sonne, he
　　　may be also of his Resurrection,
　　　& that finally with ye residue of
　　　thy Saints he may inherit thine
　　　everlasting Kingdome, through ye
　　　same Jesus Christ our Lord.
　　　Amen.
　　　The Grace of our Lord Jesus
　　　Christ, &c. Amen.

　ii. Read: Then the Minister shall say
　　　Wee receive this Child into the
　　　Church of Christ, & make a Crosse
　　　upon the child's forehead.
　　　Then all kneeling downe the
　　　Minister shall give thanks unto
　　　God, & say
　　　Wee yield thee . . . thy holy Church.
　　　And wee humbly beseech thee to
　　　grant that as he is now made par-
　　　taker of ye death of thy Sonne, so
　　　he may be also . . . our Lord.
　　　Amen.
　　　Delete The Grace . . . Amen.
　　　For lawfully *and* sufficiently *read*:
　　　well and rightly　Stet
　　　New paragraph.

And let them not doubt, but that the child so
baptized is lawfully and sufficiently baptized, and
ought not to be baptized againe.
　　　　　　　　　But yet neuer-
thelesse, if the childe which is after this sort
baptized, doe afterward liue, it is expedient that
it be brought into the Church, to the intent that
if the Priest or Minister of the same Parish did
himself baptize that child, the Congregation may
be certified of the true forme of Baptisme by him
priuatly before vsed:

320. 　*i. For* it is expedient . . . Church, *read*:
　　　it shall be brought by the God-
　　　fathers & Godmothers into the
　　　parish church[1] on a Sunday or
　　　other Holyday within three
　　　months following,

　ii. For within . . . following *read*: as[2] soon as
　　　conveniently may be

---

[1] FC: . . . into the parish church by the Godfathers & Godmothers . . . 　　　[2] FC: soe soone as . . .

319. Part. '75': It is not here ordered, whether ye child thus suddenly baptizd, shall have ye *Signe of ye Crosse* made upon it, neither then, nor when it is appointed to be afterwards brought into the church; wch for the avoyding of all Scruple & question in this case ought here to be supplyed.

> *Cf. no. 306.*
>
> *This prayer is an adaptation of that at no. 310. Notice 'living unto God' for 'living unto righteousness'; the omission of 'and being buried with Christ in his death, may crucify the old man, and utterly abolish the whole body of sin'; 'now made' for 'that he is made'; 'Saints' for 'Congregation'; etc. These alterations are suggested by the occasion.*

320. Adv.:   In the next Rubrick, thus,

> ... doe afterwards live, It is hereby required, that it be brought on a Sunday, or Holyday at the time of Divine Service, into the Parish Church, (And yf wthin 3. Moneths it be not brought, the Churchwardens are hereby required to present unto the Ordinary the Parents, or Guardians, in whom the defalt lies;) to this intent, that] &c.
>
> Yf this may thus be set, Nothing will better provide against Private Baptism, then this.

Part. '76': Nor is it ordered, at what *distance of time* the child shalbe brought into ye church after it is thus privately baptizd.

321.   *i. Add*: saying;

I certifie you that [1]according unto ye due & prescribed order of the Church in case of Necessitie, I administred Private Baptisme to this child; who being borne in originall sinne &c.

ii. For saying; *read*: In wch case he shall say thus;

After Necessitie *add*: at such a time, & in such a place, & before divers witnesses, I &c

After sinne &c. *add*: ut infr` ad not. ⌗[2]

Or if the child were baptized by any other lawfull Minister, that then the Minister of the Parish . . . shall . . . examine them further, saying,

322.   *New paragraph.*
Print it at distance
Delete Or
For were *read*: was   Stet
Delete that

For the *read*: this[3]

𝔅𝔂 𝔴𝔥𝔬𝔪 𝔴𝔞𝔰 𝔱𝔥𝔢 𝔠𝔥𝔦𝔩𝔡𝔢 𝔟𝔞𝔭𝔱𝔦𝔷𝔢𝔡?
𝔚𝔥𝔬 𝔴𝔞𝔰 𝔭𝔯𝔢𝔰𝔢𝔫𝔱 𝔴𝔥𝔢𝔫 𝔱𝔥𝔢 𝔠𝔥𝔦𝔩𝔡𝔢 𝔴𝔞𝔰 𝔟𝔞𝔭𝔱𝔦𝔷𝔢𝔡?
𝔄𝔫𝔡 𝔟𝔢𝔠𝔞𝔲𝔰𝔢 𝔰𝔬𝔪𝔢 𝔱𝔥𝔦𝔫𝔤𝔰, 𝔢𝔰𝔰𝔢𝔫𝔱𝔦𝔞𝔩𝔩 𝔱𝔬 𝔱𝔥𝔦𝔰 𝔖𝔞𝔠𝔯𝔞𝔪𝔢𝔫𝔱, 𝔪𝔞𝔶 𝔥𝔞𝔭𝔭𝔢𝔫 𝔱𝔬 𝔟𝔢𝔢 𝔬𝔪𝔦𝔱𝔱𝔢𝔡 𝔱𝔥𝔯𝔬𝔲𝔤𝔥 𝔣𝔢𝔞𝔯𝔢 𝔬𝔯 𝔥𝔞𝔰𝔱𝔢 𝔦𝔫 𝔰𝔲𝔠𝔥 𝔱𝔦𝔪𝔢𝔰 𝔬𝔣 𝔢𝔵𝔱𝔯𝔢𝔪𝔦𝔱𝔦𝔢: 𝔱𝔥𝔢𝔯𝔢𝔣𝔬𝔯𝔢 𝔍 𝔡𝔢𝔪𝔞𝔫𝔡 𝔣𝔲𝔯𝔱𝔥𝔢𝔯 𝔬𝔣 𝔶𝔬𝔲.
𝔚𝔦𝔱𝔥 𝔴𝔥𝔞𝔱 𝔪𝔞𝔱𝔱𝔢𝔯 𝔴𝔞𝔰 𝔱𝔥𝔢 𝔠𝔥𝔦𝔩𝔡𝔢 𝔟𝔞𝔭𝔱𝔦𝔷𝔢𝔡?
𝔚𝔦𝔱𝔥 𝔴𝔥𝔞𝔱 𝔴𝔬𝔯𝔡𝔰 𝔴𝔞𝔰 𝔱𝔥𝔢 𝔠𝔥𝔦𝔩𝔡𝔢 𝔟𝔞𝔭𝔱𝔦𝔷𝔢𝔡?
𝔚𝔥𝔢𝔱𝔥𝔢𝔯 𝔱𝔥𝔦𝔫𝔨𝔢 𝔶𝔬𝔲 𝔱𝔥𝔢 𝔠𝔥𝔦𝔩𝔡𝔢 𝔱𝔬 𝔟𝔢 𝔩𝔞𝔴𝔣𝔲𝔩𝔩𝔶 𝔞𝔫𝔡 𝔭𝔢𝔯𝔣𝔢𝔠𝔱𝔩𝔶 𝔟𝔞𝔭𝔱𝔦𝔷𝔢𝔡?

Delete And[4]

Delete such[4]

---

323.   *Add*: To every one of these Questions must Answere be directly given by them that bring the child.

For the answeres . . . the child *read*: their answeres
For not he *read*: he not

And if the Minister shal find by the answeres of such as bring the child, that all things were done as they ought to be: then shall not he Christen the childe againe, but shall receiue him as one of the flocke of the true Christian people, saying thus.

For of the true *read*: of true

𝔍 𝔠𝔢𝔯𝔱𝔦𝔣𝔦𝔢 𝔶𝔬𝔲, 𝔱𝔥𝔞𝔱 𝔦𝔫 𝔱𝔥𝔦𝔰 𝔠𝔞𝔰𝔢 𝔞𝔩𝔩 𝔦𝔰 𝔴𝔢𝔩𝔩 𝔡𝔬𝔫𝔢, 𝔞𝔫𝔡 𝔞𝔠𝔠𝔬𝔯𝔡𝔦𝔫𝔤 𝔲𝔫𝔱𝔬 𝔡𝔲𝔢 𝔬𝔯𝔡𝔢𝔯 𝔠𝔬𝔫𝔠𝔢𝔯𝔫𝔦𝔫𝔤 𝔱𝔥𝔢 𝔟𝔞𝔭𝔱𝔦𝔷𝔦𝔫𝔤 𝔬𝔣 𝔱𝔥𝔦𝔰 𝔠𝔥𝔦𝔩𝔡𝔢, 𝔴𝔥𝔦𝔠𝔥 𝔟𝔢𝔦𝔫𝔤 𝔟𝔬𝔯𝔫

---

[1] *After* I certifie you that, *Cosin first wrote* I pri, *then* this child, *then as above.*
[2] *See no. 324.*
[3] *And below.*
[4] FC: *not deleted.*

321.   *Cf. no. 287 (rubric into form of words).*

                    The service is to continue from no. 324, omitting what comes between.

322.   *The section from this point to no. 324 is to be transferred to the end of the service: see
                    no. 333.*

323. **Adv.:** Let a Rubrick at the bottome be,
                    To every one of these Questions shall Answers be directly given, by those that bring
                    the Child, as farr as they know.

in originall sinne, and in the wrath of God, is now by the lauer of regeneration in Baptisme, receiued . . . on this wise.

At a certaine time . . .

. . . . . .

and blessed them.

324. *After* sinne *add*: # &c. as is before prescribed to ye End of ye Exhorton. v.p.abhinc 3m. not. ♣[1]

In ye new transl'on

After the Gospel is read, the Minister shall make this exhortation vpon the wordes of the Gospel.

Friends, you heare in this Gospel . . . that he hath giuen vnto him the blessing of eternall life, and made him partaker of his euerlasting kingdome.

325. *For* that he hath giuen *read*: & as he hath promised in his holy word, will give (*crossed out*) Stet
For made *read*: make

Wherefore we being thus perswaded of the good will of our heauenly Father, declared by his Sonne Jesus Christ towards this infant, let vs faithfully and deuoutly giue thankes vnto him, and say the Prayer which the Lord himselfe taught,[2] and in declaration of our faith, let vs recite the Articles contained in our Creede.

326. *i. Read*: Wherfore after this promise made by Christ, who will most surely keep & performe the same, this Infant for his part must also faithfully promise by you yt be his Sureties, that he will forsake ye divel & all his works, & constantly believe Gods holy word, & obediently keep his Commandements. Answere me therfore.
ii. For forsake *read*: renounce
For Answere me *read*: I demand

Here the Minister with the Godfathers and Godmothers, shall say.

Our Father which art in heauen, &c.

Then shall the Priest demand the name of the childe, which being by the Godfathers and Godmothers pronounced, the Minister shall say.

Doest thou in the name of this childe forsake the deuill and all his workes . . . and not to follow and be led by them?

Answere.

I forsake them all.

327. *Read*: Then shall the Priest demand of the Godfathers and Godmothers these Questions following.
For forsake *read*: renounce
Read: . . . so that thou wilt not follow nor be led by them?
And every one of them shall
Answere, audibly.
I renounce them all.

Minister.

Doest thou in the name of this Childe, professe this faith, to beleeue in God . . .

. . . . . .

And doe you in his name beleeue in the holy Ghost . . . the remission of sinnes, resurrection, and euerlasting life after death?

Answere,

All this I stedfastly beleeue.

328. *Read*: . . . this faith? Doest thou beleeue in God . . .
Then as no. 298.
Read: And doest thou beleeue in the holy Ghost . . .
For resurrection *read*: the resurrection of the flesh[3]
Then as no. 299.

[1] FC: ∞ &c. as before. But if &c. ut infra ad ♁.

[2] *Add*: us.

[3] *Altered to* Body.

324. **Adv.:** [. . . concerning the Baptizing of this Child, Who, being born in Original Sinne, and in the Wrath of God, by the laver of Regeneration in Baptism hath bin received into the Number of the Children of God, and of the Heyres of] &c.

   The note in the text applies only to the section nos. 322–4, which is to be transferred to the end of the service.

325.   *Taken from the address to the godparents which follows in Public Baptism (at no. 295): 'hath promised in his Gospel'. The form for Baptism of such as are of Riper Years also has 'in his holy Word'.*

326.   *From the same source as no. 325. Cf. also no. 296 ('I demand').*

   Adv.: The first Rubrick, thus,
   Here shall they all kneel down, and shall say wth the Minister, [Our Father, Who art in Heaven] &c., adding also, [for thyne is the Kingdome] &c.
   Then standing up againe, the Preist shall demand the name of the Child] &c.

327.   *Cf. no. 297.*

328.   *Cf. nos. 298 and 299.*

   BCP: . . . the resurrection of the flesh . . .

𝕷et 𝖚s pra𝖞.

329. *i. Read:* Then shalbe said, (all kneeling)

Let us pray.
Our Father, which art in heaven,
&c — from Euill. Amen.
print it at large.
ii. Add: And this Collect.
Alm. & everl. G. &c.

𝕬lmightie and euerlasting 𝕲od . . . that he
ma𝖞 . . . continue th𝖞 seruant, and attaine th𝖞   330.
promise, through the same our 𝕷ord 𝕵esus
𝕮hrist th𝖞 𝕾onne, who liueth and reigneth
with thee in the vnitie of the same hol𝖞 𝕾pirit
euerlasting. 𝕬men.

For attaine thy promise *read*: truly
performing in his owne person ye
promises & professions that have
been here made in his name, may
finally attaine thy heavenly promise   *Stet as printed*
For euerlasting *read*: now & for euer

Then shall the Minister make this exhortation to   331.
the Godfathers and Godmothers.

Read: Then all standing up the
Minister shall make . . .

𝕱orasmuch as this 𝕮hilde hath promised b𝖞
𝖞ou, to forsake the deuill and all his workes,
to beleeue in 𝕲od, and to serue him . . .

For by you, to forsake *read*: by you
his Sureties, to renounce
Before to beleeue *add*: stedfastly
Before to serue *add*: duly
(*both crossed out*)
Then as no. *312.*

.   .   .   .   .   .

. . . godlinesse of liuing.

And so foorth, as in Publique Baptisme.

332. *i. Read:* Then shall he adde & say[1]
Furthermore I now[1] require you
print it out at large
ii. After you *add*: to take care &c ut supr.
in publ. Baptism.

333. *i. Add:* ❡ If the Child was baptised &c.
ut sprà ad hanc notam ·?· usque
ad ²originall sinne &c ut supra
usque ad finem.
ii. For was *read*: were

But if they which bring the infants to the Church,
doe make such vncertaine answeres to the Priests
questions . . . then let the Priest baptize it in forme
aboue written, concerning Publique Baptisme,
sauing that at the dipping of the childe in the
Font, he shall vse this forme of words:

For infants *read*: infant

For written . . . Baptisme *read*: prescribed for Publique Baptisme of
children

𝕴f thou be not alread𝖞 bapti𝖟ed, 𝕹. 𝕴 bapti𝖟e
thee . . . 𝕬men.

A fleuron.

---

[1] FC *omits* & say *and* now.
[2] *Originally* ad finem. FC: If the Child were Baptised by any other &c. ut supr. usq. ad — original
sinne printed out at large; and then an &c. wth as above prescribed to ye end of the Exhortation.

329.   *Cf. the Adv. rubric on the recitation of the Lord's Prayer at no. 326.*

330.   *Cf. no. 312 (there, 'made by you').*

331. **Adv.:** The same Mutations, and Additions to be made here at this Exhortation, as are set downe
before, in the Publike Baptism.

       Cf. no. 311. ii.

332. **Part. '77':** At ye End of this Forme of Baptisme, it is said, *And so forth as in Publick Baptisme,*
where there is nothing more added, then what is here printed at large. This therfore
seemes to be an Error of ye Printer.

       Cf. no. 313.

333.   *i.e., nos. 322, 323, and 324 are to be placed here.*

334.   *i.*   A Catechisme.[1]

       ii.   Print in a new Leafe.

           The Forme of Baptisme to such as are of perfect age, or come to the yeeres of discretion & are able to render an accompt of their faith, & undertake for themselves.

       iii.   *Read*: The Ministration of publick Baptisme to such as are of perfect age, or come to the yeeres of discretion.[2]

¶ The order of Confirmation, or laying on of handes vpon children Baptized, and able to render an account of their Faith, according to the Catechisme following.

335.   *i.*   *Read*: The order of Confirmation, or Imposition of handes vpon those that are Baptized, and come to yeers of discretion.

           Set this Title & Preface after the Catechisme.

       ii.   *Delete the whole title.*

336.   *Add*: The Preface.

       This to be placed in Confirmation, at this Mark. & to be printed in ye black letter.

To the ende that Confirmation may be ministred to the more edifying of such as shall receiue it (according to Saint Pauls Doctrine, who teacheth that all things should be done in the Church to the edification of the same) it is thought good that none hereafter shall be Confirmed, but such as can say in their mother tongue the Articles of the Faith, the Lords prayer, and the tenne Commaundements,

337.   *i.*   *For* should be done . . . but such as *read*: should be done to edification) the Church hath thought good to order, that none [3]shall bee Confirmed, but such as the Ministers of the severall parishes have first instructed and examined in the Catechisme following, & shall testifie & undertake for them, that they

       ii.   *For* the Ministers . . . that they *read*: are come to yeers of discretion &   *(crossed out)*

            and can also answere to such questions of this short Catechisme, as the Bishop (or such as hee shall appoint) shall by his discretion appose him in. And this order is most conuenient to bee obserued for diuers considerations.

338.   *i.*   *For* such questions . . . him in. *read*: such other questions as in the prescribed Catechisme are conteyned, wherein the Bishop (or such as hee shall appoint) may at their discretion examine & appose them.

---

[1] FC: A Catechisme (*Cosin, crossed out*). A forme.

[2] FC *adds*: as in the Order, & forme prepared for that purpose. v. pap. BB.   [3] FC *keeps* hereafter.

334.   'The Forme of Baptisme to such as are of perfect age' was allotted to a Committee of
        Convocation on 18 May 1661, and unanimously approved on 31 May (Cardwell,
        Synodalia, II. 641–2.). The catchword 'A Catechisme' must have been inserted before
        this date, as also in FC. For stage iii, cf. the title of Private Baptism (no. 315). FC
        included the Form as 'Paper BB' (no longer extant). Stages ii and iii were presumably
        entered after 31 May.

335.   'Years of discretion': cf. no. 339.
        See nos. 354 and 355. Cf. also no. 287.

336.   As no. 335. The transfer of this section (nos. 336–40) is a notable improvement.

337.   Cf. the rubric at no. 364. Also S I:
        It has bin thought more expedient by the Church, yt children shold be first able to give
        an accompt of their Faith . . . Fathers and Godfathers & Curates, & others yt have the
        care of young children might hereby take occasion to instruct them in yt profession of
        faith & religion which they had made for them in their baptisme.

338.   Cf. no. 350.

           ii. Delete prescribed
           Delete wherein . . . appose them.

First, because that when children come to the   339. *i. Read*: First, that children being
yeeres of discretion, and haue learned what their   now come to the age of reason &
Godfathers and Godmothers promised for them   discretion, & having learned . . .
in Baptisme, they may then themselues with their   *Delete* then
owne mouth . . . confirme the same . . . haue   *ii. For* age of reason & *read*: yeeres of
assented vnto.

Secondly, forasmuch as Confirmation is
ministred to them that be baptized . . .   340. *For* them that *read*: such as

by the frailtie of their owne flesh . . .   *Read*: by their owne frailtie Stet

sundry kindes of sinne.

Thirdly, for that it is agreeable with the usage . . .

to them that were of perfect age . . .   *Read*: to them who were of com-
to the will of God.   petent age Stet

And that no man shall thinke that any detriment   341. *i. For* shall *read*: may
shall come to children by deferring of their
Confirmation, he shall know the trueth; that it is   *For* he shall know the trueth *read*:
certaine by Gods word, that children being bap-   till yeeres of discretion as is before
tized haue all things necessary for their saluation,   determined; let him know for a
and be vndoubtedly saued.   trueth
                   ii. Delete And that . . . trueth; that
                   Before necessary *add*: then
                   (*crossed out*)

           342. *i. Add*: if they dye before they com-
                  mitt actuall sinne
               ii. Add: though they be not confirmed

           343. ¶ Set this before at ye end of
                  Baptisme.
                  Print it in an Italick letter.
                  (*crossed out*)

339. **Adv.:** First, that the Children being now come to some yeares of discretion, and having bin
taught, what theire Godfathers, and] etc.

340. **Adv.:** in the *12* Line, [. . . against all the Temtations of Sinne, and] etc.

in the *18* line, [. . . the Church in times past, By wch Confirmation was ordinarily
ministred to them that were of grown age, That they being instructed] etc.

341. **Adv.:** Then let that Paragraph be divided, and set thus,
And that none may thinck, that any detriment shall come to Children by deferring
their Confirmation till yeares of some understanding in them, Let them know for
a Truth, that it is certayn by Gods Word,] etc.

BCP (1549, 1552, 1559): . . . he shall know for truth . . .
The first part of the rubric is deleted as being incongruous with no. 342. i.

342. **Exceptions:** These words are dangerous, as to the misleading of the vulgar, and therfore we
desire they may be expunged.

Bishops: Conc. 13. That the words of the last Rubr. before the Catechism, may be thus altered,
(that children being baptized have all things necessary for their salvation, and dying
before they commit any actual sins, be undoubtedly saved, though they be not
Confirmed.]
*Stage i is entered by Cosin and diverges slightly from the words of the thirteenth con-
cession, so was probably entered before the conclusion of the Savoy Conference. On
the other hand it agrees with the text of the Bishops' Reply, at the point where the
Exception is answered, in reading 'actual sin' rather than 'any actual sins' (as in the
Concession, above).*

343.   *i.e., at no. 314.*

¶ A Catechisme, that is to say, An in-   344.
struction to bee learned of euery childe,[1]
before hee be brought to be Confirmed
by the Bishop.

For that is to say *read*: or[1]
After instruction *add*: in the prin-
ciples of Christian Religion,
(*crossed out*)
For bee *read*: be

Question.

𝔚𝔥𝔞𝔱 𝔦𝔰 𝔭𝔬𝔲𝔯 𝔫𝔞𝔪𝔢?

.   .   .   .   .

𝔉𝔦𝔯𝔰𝔱, 𝔱𝔥𝔞𝔱 𝔍 𝔰𝔥𝔬𝔲𝔩𝔡 𝔣𝔬𝔯𝔰𝔞𝔨𝔢 𝔱𝔥𝔢 𝔡𝔢𝔲𝔦𝔩𝔩 . . .

For forsake *read*: renounce

𝔗𝔥𝔢 𝔰𝔞𝔪𝔢 𝔴𝔥𝔦𝔠𝔥 𝔊𝔬𝔡 𝔰𝔭𝔞𝔨𝔢 . . . 𝔍 𝔞𝔪 𝔱𝔥𝔢
𝔏𝔬𝔯𝔡 𝔱𝔥𝔶 𝔊𝔬𝔡, 𝔴𝔥𝔦𝔠𝔥 𝔥𝔞𝔲𝔢 𝔟𝔯𝔬𝔲𝔤𝔥𝔱 𝔱𝔥𝔢𝔢
𝔬𝔲𝔱 . . .

For which haue *read*: who

.   .   .   .   .

𝔐𝔶 𝔡𝔲𝔢𝔱𝔶 𝔱𝔬𝔴𝔞𝔯𝔡𝔰 𝔊𝔬𝔡 𝔦𝔰, 𝔱𝔬 𝔟𝔢𝔩𝔢𝔢𝔲𝔢 𝔦𝔫 𝔥𝔦𝔪,   345.
𝔱𝔬 𝔣𝔢𝔞𝔯𝔢 𝔥𝔦𝔪, 𝔞𝔫𝔡 𝔱𝔬 𝔩𝔬𝔲𝔢 𝔥𝔦𝔪 𝔴𝔦𝔱𝔥 𝔞𝔩𝔩 𝔪𝔶
𝔥𝔢𝔞𝔯𝔱, 𝔴𝔦𝔱𝔥 𝔞𝔩𝔩 𝔪𝔶 𝔪𝔦𝔫𝔡𝔢, 𝔴𝔦𝔱𝔥 𝔞𝔩𝔩 𝔪𝔶 𝔰𝔬𝔲𝔩𝔢,
𝔞𝔫𝔡 𝔴𝔦𝔱𝔥 𝔞𝔩𝔩 𝔪𝔶 𝔰𝔱𝔯𝔢𝔫𝔤𝔱𝔥. 𝔗𝔬 𝔴𝔬𝔯𝔰𝔥𝔦𝔭 𝔥𝔦𝔪, 𝔱𝔬
𝔤𝔦𝔲𝔢 𝔥𝔦𝔪 𝔱𝔥𝔞𝔫𝔨𝔢𝔰, 𝔱𝔬 𝔭𝔲𝔱 𝔪𝔶 𝔴𝔥𝔬𝔩𝔢 𝔱𝔯𝔲𝔰𝔱 𝔦𝔫
𝔥𝔦𝔪, 𝔱𝔬 𝔠𝔞𝔩𝔩 𝔲𝔭𝔬𝔫 𝔥𝔦𝔪, 𝔱𝔬 𝔥𝔬𝔫𝔬𝔲𝔯 𝔥𝔦𝔰 𝔥𝔬𝔩𝔶
𝔑𝔞𝔪𝔢 𝔞𝔫𝔡 𝔥𝔦𝔰 𝔴𝔬𝔯𝔡: 𝔞𝔫𝔡 𝔱𝔬 𝔰𝔢𝔯𝔲𝔢 𝔥𝔦𝔪 𝔱𝔯𝔲𝔢𝔩𝔶
𝔞𝔩𝔩 𝔱𝔥𝔢 𝔡𝔞𝔶𝔢𝔰 𝔬𝔣 𝔪𝔶 𝔩𝔦𝔣𝔢.

i. Before to beleeue *add*: I.
After in him *add*: to put my whole
trust in him
For To worship him *read*: II. To
honour & worship him with ye
outward reverence of my body
Delete to put my whole trust in him
Before to honour *add*: III.
ii. For honour & worship *read*: serve &
worship
iii. Delete all alterations except ii.[2]

.   .   .   .   .

𝔚𝔞𝔱𝔢𝔯: 𝔴𝔥𝔢𝔯𝔢𝔦𝔫 𝔱𝔥𝔢 𝔭𝔢𝔯𝔰𝔬𝔫 𝔟𝔞𝔭𝔱𝔦𝔷𝔢𝔡 𝔦𝔰 𝔡𝔦𝔭𝔭𝔢𝔡   346.
𝔬𝔯 𝔰𝔭𝔯𝔦𝔫𝔨𝔩𝔢𝔡 𝔴𝔦𝔱𝔥 𝔦𝔱, In the Name of the
Father, and of the Sonne, and of the Holy Ghost.

Before baptized *add*: is
Delete is dipped . . . with it

.   .   .   .   .

𝔜𝔢𝔰: 𝔱𝔥𝔢𝔶 𝔡𝔬𝔢 𝔭𝔢𝔯𝔣𝔬𝔯𝔪𝔢 𝔱𝔥𝔢𝔪 𝔟𝔶 𝔱𝔥𝔢𝔦𝔯 𝔖𝔲𝔯𝔢=   347.
𝔱𝔦𝔢𝔰, 𝔴𝔥𝔬 𝔭𝔯𝔬𝔪𝔦𝔰𝔢 𝔞𝔫𝔡 𝔟𝔬𝔴 𝔱𝔥𝔢𝔪 𝔟𝔬𝔱𝔥 𝔦𝔫 𝔱𝔥𝔢𝔦𝔯
𝔫𝔞𝔪𝔢𝔰: 𝔴𝔥𝔦𝔠𝔥 𝔴𝔥𝔢𝔫 𝔱𝔥𝔢𝔶 𝔠𝔬𝔪𝔢 𝔱𝔬 𝔞𝔤𝔢, 𝔱𝔥𝔢𝔪=
𝔰𝔢𝔩𝔲𝔢𝔰 𝔞𝔯𝔢 𝔟𝔬𝔲𝔫𝔡 𝔱𝔬 𝔭𝔢𝔯𝔣𝔬𝔯𝔪𝔢.

i. Read: It is sufficient, that their
Sureties doe promise . . .
ii. Read: Though they cañot in their
owne persons performe them,[3]
yet It is sufficient, that their
Sureties doe promise . . .
iii. Read: Because they promise ym both by
their Sureties: wch &c

.   .   .   .   .

. . . 𝔞𝔫𝔡 𝔟𝔢𝔢 𝔦𝔫 𝔠𝔥𝔞𝔯𝔦𝔱𝔶 𝔴𝔦𝔱𝔥 𝔞𝔩𝔩 𝔪𝔢𝔫.   348.

Add: The Curate of every Parish &c
as after Confirmation.

---

[1] FC: *no alteration*.   [2] FC: *no alteration at all*.   [3] FC: perform them in their owne persons.

344. **Adv.:** The following Title to be this,
> The Catechisme, that is to say, A form to be dayly used and continued, in Publike, and Private, for the first Institution of Children, to instruct them in the Principles of Xtian Religion; and therfore to be learnt by every One, before they be brought to be Confirmed by the Bishop.

The Title here, and throughout, to be,
> [The Institution of Children, cald the Catechisme.]

In the Beleef,
> [. . . His onely Sonne, our Lord, Who was conceived.

Part. '78': *All ye Questions & Answers* (after ye Lords Prayer) *concerning the Sacraments* were added by ye order of *King James* given in the Conference at Hampton Court. They want only ye Confirmation of *a Law*, wthout wch the Minister is in danger of ye penaltie sett downe in the *Act of Uniformitie.*

> *Adv.* ('*every One*') *and FC* ('*person*') *are again allowing for the baptism of adults.*

345. **Canon 18:** And likewise, when in the time of Diuine Seruice the Lord Jesus shall be mentioned, due and lowly reuerence shall be done by all persons present, as it hath been accustomed: testifying by their outward Ceremonies and Gestures . . .

Adv.: In the midst of that *2d* Answer, thus,
> . . . to all my Betters. All wch I do also acknowledg to be a part of my Duty towards God, in whose place They are. Also to hurt nobody] etc.

This is requisite to be thus put in: Inasmuch as the *V* Commandment is indeed a Branch of that, wch Xt calls the first Great Commandment. And it hath bin lately taught,
> [That they were indeed by Gods Commandment obliged to the King, but yet onely as by their Duty to their Neighbour, wch is, to love Him, as Themselves, but then Themselves in the first place, And let Him be destroyed, nay, Destroy Him, rather then They should perish.]

346. *Stylistic improvement.*

347. **Exceptions:** We desire . . . that it be not asserted, that they perform these by the promise of their Sureties . . .

Bishops: Conc. 12. That those words [yes they do perform them, &c.] may be altered thus: [because they promise them both, by their Sureties, &c.

> *The phrase had already attracted Cosin's attention before it was included in the Savoy concessions.*
> *With ii, cf. no. 330.*

348. *i.e., no. 364.*

So soone as the children can say in their mother
tongue the Articles of the Faith, the Lords prayer,

the tenne Commandements, and also can answere
to such questions of this short Catechisme as the
Bishop (or such as he shall appoint) shall by his
discretion appose them in:

then shall they bee
brought to the Bishop by one that shall bee his
Godfather, or Godmother, that euery childe may
haue a witnesse of his Confirmation. And the
Bishop shall confirme them on this wise.

349.   Set this at ye mark [after Con-
         firmation. (*crossed out*)
         After children *add*: are come to a
         competent age, &

350.   i. *For* answere . . . short *read*: render
          an accompt of their knowledge in
          this
        ii. *Read*: answere to such questions as are
          contained in this short
       iii. *Read*: answere the other questions of
          this short

351.   *For* as the Bishop . . . them in *read*:
         (wch shall be testified by the
         Ministers of ye severall parishes,)
         Stet as printed.

352.   *For* brought *read*: presented Stet
353.   *For* by one . . . Confirmation *read*:
         in some Church that he shall
         appoint; & every one shall have
         a Godfather, or Godmother, as
         a witnesse of their Confirmation.

         Delete And the Bishop . . . this wise.

         Add: And whensoever ye Bp shall give
         knowledge &c as after Confirmation.[1]

[1] FC *adds*: See the Paper C inserted after ye next leave, where this yt followes is sett together, & faire written. *Nos. 345–55 are deleted entirely. Paper C is not extant.*

349.   *i.e., at no. 364. 'Competent', cf. no. 340; S III defines it as 'between fourteen and sixteen years of age', also referring to 'the old Competentes'.*

350. **Canon 61:** . . . none may be presented to the Bishop for him to lay his hand vpon, but such as can render an account of their Fayth, according to the Catechisme . . .

Cf. no. 338.

351.   *Cf. no. 337.*

352. **Canon 61:** *see no. 350.*
353. **Adv.:**   At the *4th* line, thus,
. . . that every Child may have One, both to put him in mind of Gods Blessing in his Confirmation, and also to be his Witnes, that he hath bin confirmed.

Part. '79': The *place* whereunto the children shalbe brought for their Confirmation is left to *the appointmt of ye Bishop.* If the *place* were ordered here to be none but *the church,* & there the Office to be done wth the *Morng* or *Eveng Prayer* annexd, it would avoyd the offensive Liberty yt herein hath bin comonly taken, to *Confirme* children in the streets, in the high wayes, & in the common fields, wthout any sacred solemnitie.

'As after Confirmation' : *i.e., no. 364,* ad fin.

¶ Confirmation, or laying on of handes.

354.   *i. Read*: The Order of Confirmation, or Imposition of Hands upon those that are Baptized & come to ye yeeres of discretion.

  ii. For Imposition *read:* laying on

355.   *i. Add*: Upon ye day appointed, after Morning or Evening Prayer is ended, the Bishop shall goe to the Lords Table, & all that are to be then Confirmed being placed & standing in order before him, neere unto the same, He, or his Chaplaine, or some other Minister appointed by him, shall read this Preface following

To the end that Confirmation, &c. as before ye Catechisme usque ad —

to the will of God

Answere me therfore,

Doe you here in the presence of God, & of his holy Church renew the solemne promise & vow that was made in your name at your Baptisme, ratifying & confirming the same in your owne persons, & acknowledging your selves bound to doe all those things which your Godfathers & Godmothers then undertooke for you.

And every one shall audibly answere.

I doe.

Minister

Doe you renounce[1] ye divel & all his works?

Answere

I renounce them all.

Minister

Doe you[2] renounce ye vaine pomp & glory of the world, wth all the covetous desires of ye same?

Answere

I renounce them all.

Minister

Doe you[2] renounce ye wicked desires of the flesh, so yt you will[3] not follow nor be led by them?

---

[1] *Originally* Doest thou forsake . . .   [2] *Originally* Doest thou . . .
[3] *Originally* . . . thou wilt . . .

354.   *Cf. no. 335. 'Yeeres of discretion': BCP, at no. 339. 'Imposition' is used by Cosin in his
              Confirmation address, and by both Ministers and Bishops at the Savoy Conference.*

355. **Adv.:**   Then Another Rubrick, after the Title, thus,
              At the end of the Communion Service, next before the Blessing, The Bishop having
              all those, that shall then be admitted unto Confirmation, kneeling before him, shall,
              by himself, or some Minister appointed by him, begin thus,
                 Our help is in the Name of the Lord.
                    Answer.
              Who hath made heaven and Earth] etc.

Part. '79':   *see no. 353 (N.B. 'with the Morning or Evening Prayer annexed').*
                 *'Answere me' is not corrected to 'I demand', as it is at no. 296. For the first question, cf. the
                 Marriage Service: 'in the sight of God, and in the face of his congregation'; 'promise
                 and vow' and 'in your name' come from the Catechism; 'ratifying and confirming the
                 same' is from the Preface; 'in their own persons', cf. nos. 330 and 347; 'bound to doe'
                 is from the Catechism. It is a striking example of DB's habit of using BCP material.*

                 *For the next four questions, cf. nos. 297–9. The original reading 'forsake' was presumably
                 a slip of the pen, as it only occurs in one question; but it will be noticed that the
                 reference is to no. 299. i ('grace so to doe'), not ii. The amalgamation of the questions
                 in stage ii brings this passage even closer to the Baptism Service.*

Answere

I renounce them all.

Minister

Doe you believe in God ye father almightie, &c, as in publick Baptisme usque ad — grace so to doe.

Minister, or the Bp.

Almightie God, who hath given you the will to promise & undertake all these things, grant you also power & strength to performe ye same, that he may accomplish the good work which he hath begun in you, through Jesus Christ our Lord. Amen.

Then shall they all kneele, & the Bp standing at the Lords Table shall proceed & say

Our help &c.

ii. After I doe *read*:

Minister

Doe you renounce the divel & all his works, ye vaine pomp & glory of the world, wth all the covetous desires of ye same; ye wicked desires of the flesh, so yt you will not follow nor be led by them?

Answere

I renounce them all.

Minister

Doe you believe . . .

𝕺ur helpe is in the 𝕹ame of the 𝕷ord.

·   ·   ·   ·   ·   ·

Answere.

And let our cry come vnto thee.

¶ Let us pray.

Almightie and euerliuing God . . . the Spirit of thy holy feare. Amen.

356.   *After* feare *add*: now & for ever

The prayer after the questions is taken from the Ordering of Priests, omitting the clause about 'the latter day': this is retained in the FC Ordinal, but omitted in the later stages of revision.

356. **Adv.:** [Almighty and everliving God, Who didst heretofore vouchsafe to regenerate these thy Servants by Water and the Holy Ghost, and didst give unto them forgivenes of all their sinnes, We humbly beseech thee, That they having now by the Blessing of thy Grace attayned unto some knowledg of thee, Thou wouldst strenghthen them wth the Holy Ghost the Comforter, and dayly increase in them Thy Manifold Gyfts of Grace, The Spirit of Wisdome, and of Understanding, the Spirit of Counsell and of Ghostly Strenght, the Spirit of Knowledg and of true Godlines, and fulfill them O Lord wth the Spirit of thy Holy Feare, now and for ever. Amen.]

357. *Add*: Then shall the Chaplaine or
the Curate of the place read the
Epistle.
Acts. viii. v. 12. to the 18. v.
And the Gospel.
S. Luke. ii. v. 40. to ye end of ye
chapter. (*crossed out*)

Then the Bishop shall lay his hand vpon euery   358.
childe seuerally, saying,

𝕯efend, 𝕺 𝕷ord this childe with thy heauenly
𝕲race . . . thy euerlasting 𝕶ingdome. 𝕬men.

Read: Then all of them in order[1]
kneeling before the Bishop, He
shall lay his hands vpon the head
of euery one seuerally, saying,
Defend, O Lord this thy childe (or
servant) with thy heauenly
Grace . . .

359.   i. *Add*: The Lord be with you
Answ. And with thy Spirit
Read: The Bishop.
Let vs pray.
And[2] all kneeling downe
Our Father &c
ii. *For* The Bishop *read*: The Bishop shall say
After &c *add*: at large

Then shall the Bishop say,
        ¶ 𝕷et vs pray.

𝕬lmightie and euerliuing 𝕲od . . . acceptable
vnto thy 𝕸aiestie, wee make our humble sup=   360.
plications vnto thee for these children[3] . . .
they may obtaine the euerlasting life . . .
world without end. 𝕬men.   361.

Before Maiestie *add*: divine
After children *add*: (or thy servants)
Delete the

Add: O almighty Ld & everlasting
God, vouchsafe wee beseech thee
to direct &c.
Prevent us o Lord &c.
as in ye end after ye Com̃union.

362.

Then the Bishop shall blesse the children, saying
thus:

Read: Then the Bishop shall give
them this Blessing, all humbly
kneeling before him. Stet

𝕿he blessing of 𝕲od 𝕬lmighty . . . remaine
with you for euer. 𝕬men.

363.   *Add*: And there shall none be admitted &c. ut infrà. p. seq.

---

[1] *Originally* orderly.   [2] *Originally* And then . . .   [3] FC: these thy children . . .

357. *The Epistle is that for Tuesday in Whitsun Week, beginning two verses earlier: the added verses deal with baptism. The A.V. chapter-heading runs: 'Peter and John come to confirm . . . the church.' 'To the 18 v.' means, of course, 'to the end of v. 17'.*

The Gospel is that for Epiphany I, starting one verse earlier: the additional verse includes the words 'waxed strong in spirit'.

The inclusion of these lections is curious in the absence of any direction that the Communion should follow. Indeed the service may take place after Evening Prayer (see no. 355), while Wren envisaged it following the Communion (Adv. at no. 355). The original intention may have been to remodel the service on the lines of the Ordinal; cf. no. 355.

358. **Adv.:** Then the Bishop shall lay his hand upon every One severally, and shall say,

[Defend O Lord [this Child] thy servant wth thy Heavenly Grace, that He may continue Thyne for ever, and may dayly increase in thy Holy Spirit more & more] etc.

359. **1549:** The peace of the Lorde abide with you.

Aunswere. And with thy spirit.

360. **Adv.:** [Almighty and everliving God, Who makest us both to will, and to do those things, that be good and acceptable unto thy Divine Matie, We make our humble supplications unto Thee for these thy Servants, Upon whom We after the Example of the Holy Apostles, have layed] etc. . . .

Who wth Thee and the Holy Ghost liveth and reygneth ever one God, world wthout end. Amen.]

361. *The second and fourth Collects at the end of the Communion.*

Cf. Adv. at no. 355 ('next before the Blessing'), and also at no. 272.

362. **Adv.:** Then the Bishop, they all still kneeling before him, shall bless them, and dismiss them thus,

[The Blessing of God Almighty] etc.

363. *i.e., no. 365.*

The Curate of euery Parish . . . shall . . . instruct   364.   Set this at ye end of the Catechisme.
. . . so many children of his Parish sent vnto him
as the time will serue, and as hee shall thinke   *Delete* the time will serue, and as
conuenient, in some part of this Catechisme.

And all Fathers, Mothers, Masters and Dames,   *Bracketed with the previous Rubric*
shal cause their children, seruants and prentises . . .   *for transference to the end of the*
for them to learne.   *Catechism.*
                                             Add: So soone as the children &c,
                                             as after ye Catechisme.
                                             New paragraph.

                And whensoeuer the Bishop   *For* before *read*: unto
shall giue knowledge for children to be brought
before him to any conuenient place for their   *Delete* to any conuenient place
Confirmation, then shall the Curate of euery   *After* writing *add*: with his hand
Parish, either bring or send in writing the names   subscribed thereunto
of all those children of his Parish which can say   *For* which can say . . . Catechisme.
the Articles of the Faith, the Lords prayer, and   *read*: whom he doth then present
the ten Commandements, and also how many of   to the Bishop as fitt to be con-
them can answere to the other questions con-   firmed. And if the Bp. approveth
teined in this Catechisme.   them, he shall Confirme them in
                                             manner following.
                                             The Order of Confirmation &c.
                                             v. supr

And there shall none be admitted to the holy   365.   *Read*: And there shall none be ad-
Communion, vntill such time as he can say the   mitted unto the holy Communion
Catechisme, and be confirmed.   or unto Matrimony, vntill such
                                             time . . . confirmed.
                                             Add: or be ready, & desirous to be con-
                                             firmed
                                             A fleuron

364.   *'Set this . . .': i.e., at no. 348.*

'So soone as . . .', cf. no. 349.

'And whensoeuer . . .', cf. no. 353. The alterations to this rubric are designed to secure better preparation and more solemn performance.

Adv.:   At the 2d line, . . . send in writing a Certificate (setting his own Name thereunto,) of the Names of all those Childrē] etc.

Exceptions: We desire that none may be confirmed, but according to his Majesties Declaration. *Viz.* That Confirmation be rightly and solemnly performed by the information, and with the consent of the Minister of the place.
The reference in the Exceptions *is to the Declaration of 25 Oct. 1660, § V (Cardwell,* Conferences, *293).*

365. **Adv.:** In the next Paragraph of that Rubrick,
And there shall none be admitted unto the Cõmunion, or unto Mariage, Untill such time as they can say the Catechism, and be known to have bin Confirmed.

Exceptions: We desire that Confirmation may not be made so necessary to the holy Communion, as that none should be admitted to it, unless they be confirmed.

Bishops: Conc. 14. That to the Rubr. after Confirmation, these words may be added (Or be ready, and desirous to be Confirmed.]

¶ The forme of solemnization of Matrimonie.

First, the Banes must be asked three seuerall
Sundayes or Holy dayes in the time of seruice,
the people being present after the accustomed
maner.

Print this upon ye next page.

366.   *i. Add*: unlesse the Bp shall upon just
            cause dispense therewith
            (*crossed out*)
       ii. Read: First, the Banns of all yt are
            to be marryed together must be
            published in ye church three
            seuerall Sundayes or Holy dayes
            in the time of seruice, immediately
            after ye Creed that followeth the
            Gospel, the Curate saying after
            the accustomed maner,

            I publish the Banns of Marriage
            betweene N. & M. If any of you
            know cause or just impediment,
            why these Two should not be
            joyned together in holy Matri-
            mony, you are to declare it, This
            is ye first (second or third) time
            of asking.
       iii. Before seruice *add*: divine
            For N. & M. *read*: N. of   & M. of
            For after ye Creed . . . Gospel *read*: before
            ye Sentences for ye Offertory

367.   *i. Add*: The Impediments of Marriage
            are, Precontract, or a Suit de-
            pending   thereupon,   Consan-
            guinity or Affinity within the
            degrees prohibited by ye Lawes of
            God, & this Realme, Sentence of
            divorce from a partie yet living,
            want of competent yeeres, in-
            struction in ye Catechisme, Con-
            firmation, & such like.
       ii. For instruction in ye Catechisme *read*:
            consent of Parents in Minours, & of
       iii. Delete the whole note.

366. **Adv.:** In the next Rubrick, being for Mariage, thus,

The Banes shall first be published on three severall Sundayes or Holydaies, by the Minister, at the same time, when he is to declare, what Holydayes fall.

Part. '80': In ye first Rubrick, the Minister is injoyned not to *Celebrate Matrimonie unlesse the Banes have bin first published 3 severall times,* where to secure him from the penalty conteyned in the Act of Uniformitie, it were requisite that this Exception be added, *& unlesse there bee a Dispensation or Licence granted by the Bishop in some speciall or urgent cause, to Celebrate ye Marriage without yt publishing of the Banes,* or by *other Lawes* yet in force it is permitted him to doe.

S I: Hae duae personae N. & N. volunt contrahere mr̃imoniũ. Si quis est qui noverit aliquod impedimentum esse inter has personas, quod mr̃imoniũ inter eos impediat, illud denunciet. Et de hoc admonemus primò, secundò, tertiò, & peremptoriè infrà talem terminũ N.

BCP: . . . into the which holy estate these two persons present, come now to be ioyned. Therfore, if any man can shewe any iust cause, why they maye not lawfully be ioyned together . . .

. . . if either of you doe knowe any impediment why ye may not be lawfully ioyned together in Matrimonie, that ye confesse it . . .

. . . if any man doe allege and declare any impediment . . .

i: cf. no. 368. Part. '80' is drawn upon before Adv.

ii: the form of banns is a combination of the Latin form with phrases from other parts of the service in a typical DB cento.

iii delays the banns until after the sermon, in accordance with no. 216.

367. **Part. '82':** The *Impediments* of Matrimonie, or ye *Just Causes* why any Persons may not be joyned together, are not here specified. For want wherof, or a direction at least yt should be given to seeke ym in the knowne Table set out for yt purpose, & in other Bookes of ye Law, ye Curate is comõnly ignorant of them, & unable to give any resolution herein either to himself or others whom it may concerne.

Canon 102: . . . First, that . . . there is not any impediment of precontract, consanguinity, affinity, or other lawfull cause to hinder the said marriage. Secondly, that there is not any controuersie or suit depending . . . touching any contract . . .

Canon 99: No persons shall marry within the decrees prohibited by the Lawes of GOD, and expressed in a Table set foorth by authority in the yeare of our Lord GOD, 1563 . . .

Lords: 25. Whether none hereafter shall have licences to marry, nor be asked their banes of Matrimony, that shall not bring with them a Certificat from their Ministers that they are *instructed in their Catechisme.*

S I gives a list of the Canon Law impediments. S III has a note, on which Part. '82' is based:

These Words referred to the common known Impediments: But because some of them

And if the persons that should be maried, dwell
in diuers Parishes, the Banes must be asked in
both Parishes: and the Curate of the one Parish
shall not solemnize Matrimonie betwixt them,
without a certificate of the Banes being thrice
asked, from the Curate of the other Parish.

368.   *i. For* should *read*: are to
       For Banes *read*: Banns

       For Banes *read*: Banns
       Add: And none shalbe married till
       their Banns be thrice thus pub-
       lished, unlesse[1] a lawfull dis-
       pensation to ye contrary be pro-
       cured. Neither shall any persons
       under ye age of 21 yeers com-
       plete, be married without ye ex-
       presse consent[2] of their Parents,
       if they be living, or otherwise of
       their Guardians or Governors;
       nor in any other Place.
       No Minister[3] shall celebrate any
       Marriage but publickly in ye
       parish Church or Chappell, where
       one of the parties dwelleth; nor
       at other times then betweene the
       Houres of 8. & 12. in ye fore-
       noone.
       And here is to be noted that by
       ye Ecclesiasticall Lawes of this
       Realme, there be some times in
       the yeere, when Marriage is not
       ordinarily solemnized.
     ii. For Parents . . . Place. *read*:
       Parents or Guardians.
    iii. Delete the whole entry.

At the day appointed for solemnization of
Matrimonie, the persons to be married shal come
into the body of the Church with their friends
and neighbours. And there the Priest shall say
thus.

369.   *After* day *add*: & time

       Delete body of the   Stet

370.   *i. For* And there . . . thus *read*: And
       when Morning prayer is ended
       they shall come into the midst
       of the church, & there standing
       together (ye man on the right
       hand & the woman on the left)
       the Priest[4] shall come to them &
       say thus.

---

[1] *Originally* unlesse the Bishop.
[3] *Originally* No Marriage.

[2] consent *is added by S.*
[4] *Originally* before the Priest.

were taken off by Law; and for that there was no new Law made, concerning the Degrees of Consanguinity and Affinity, (which Bucer urged very earnestly,) therfore Archbishop Parker set forth a Table to that purpose; for before his time, there was no Rule but what the Canon Law prescribed, with reference to the Law of God, which was made a Statute Law here in the time of K. Henry 8.
'Confirmation': cf. no. 365. For ii, see no. 368.

368. **Part. '81':** It is not here ordered, At what time of the service this forme of Marriage shalbe celebrated. Nor at what time of the yeere (according to other Lawes) the solemnization of Matrimony is prohibited.

Canon 100: No children vnder the age of one and twenty yeeres complete, shall contract themselues, or marry without the consent of their Parents, or of their Guardians and Gouernours, if their Parents bee deceased.

Canon 102: . . . Lastly, that they shall celebrate the said Matrimony publikely in the Parish Church or Chapell where one of them dwelleth, and in no other place, and that betweene the houres of eight and twelue in the forenoone.
Cf. no. 366. i. S I has the Roman rules for non-solemnization of matrimony.

369. *Cf. no. 370.*

370. **Adv.:** In the last Paragraph there, thus,
At the Day appointed for the Solemnizing of Matrimony, as soon as the Letany is ended, and before they goe to ye Comunion Service, the Persons to be maried shall come into the Body of the Church] etc.

Part. '81': *see no. 368.*

S II (from Sarum): Vir autem stet a dextra mulieris, mulier autem a sinistris viri.
'The midst of the church': cf. no. 109. Despite Adv., the service is regarded as taking the place of the Litany.

ii. *Read*: And there standing together
    (ye man . . . left) the Priest shall
    say thus.

𝖉earelp beloued friends, we are gathered to-   371.   *Delete* friends
gether here in the sight of God, and in the
face of his Congregation to iopne together   i. *For* Congregation *read*: Church
this man and this woman in holp Matrimonp,   ii. *Read*: this Congregation
which is an honourable estate instituted of
God in Paradise, in the time of mans inno-   *Delete* in Paradise
cencie . . . and therefore is not to be enter-   *After* not *add*: by any
prised, nor taken in hand unaduisedlp . . .
like bruite beastes that haue no vnderstand-   *Delete* like . . . vnderstanding   Stet
ing, but reuerentlp . . . duelp considering the   *For* duely considering *read*: with
causes for which Matrimonie was ordeined;   due consideration of   Stet
One was the procreation of children, to be   *Before* One *add*: Wherof[1]
brought vp in the feare and nurture of the   (*crossed out*)
Lord, and praise of God. Secondlp, it was   *For* praise of God *read*: to the praise
ordained . . . that such persons . . . might   of his holy Name.
marry, and keepe themselues vndefiled mem-   *For* and *read*: that such as be
bers of Christs body. Thirdlp,[2] for the   married might live chastly in
mutuall societie . . .   Matrimony, &   (*crossed out*)
                        into the which holp   *For* into the which *read*: Into which
estate . . . Therefore if anp man can shew   *Delete* man   Stet
anp iust cause or impediment . . . for euer   *For* any iust *read*: a iust
holde his peace.

And also speaking vnto the persons that shall be   372.   *Read*: Then speaking directly vnto
married, hee shall say.   the persons that stand before him
                                                            to be married, hee shall say.
                                                            Stet as printed.

𝕴 require and charge pou[3] . . . that if either   *Delete* doe
of pou doe know anp impediment . . . that pee   *For* that yee *read*: yee doe now
confesse it . . . Matrimonie lawfull.

At which day of marriage . . . vnto such time as   *For* vnto *read*: vntill
the trueth be tried. If no impediment be alledged,   *New paragraph.*
then shall the Curate say vnto the man.

N. Wilt thou haue this woman . . .

·   ·   ·   ·   ·

𝕴 will.
Then shall the Minister say.

Who giueth this woman to be married to this
man?

And the Minister receiuing the woman at her   373.   i. *Read*: And the Minister . . . shall
father's or friend's hands, shall cause the man to   cause the man & the woman to
take the woman by the right hand, and so either   joyne their right hands, and to
to giue their troth to other, the man first saying.   say after him.

---

[1] FC: First, it was ordained for . . . (*Cosin*).
[2] FC: Thirdly, it was ordained for . . . (*Cosin*).   [3] FC: you both (*Cosin*).

371. **Adv.:**   Dearly beloved, we are here come, in the sight of God, and in the face of his Church, to joyn together, this] etc.

   1549:   . . . that suche persons as be maryed, might liue chastly in matrimonie, and kepe them-selues . . .

   Sanderson: . . . instituted in the state of man's innocency . . . if any of you can show any just cause . . .

> *The two correspondences with Sanderson (omission of 'in Paradise' and 'man') may be coincidental. Here begins a series of minor alterations in FC made in Cosin's hand, and not copied from DB.*

372. **Adv.:**   The first Rubrick, thus,
   Then speaking directly unto the Persons, that stand before him, to be married, he shall say,

   Sanderson: And more especially I charge you both . . . if either of you know . . . that you pre-sently confess it . . .

> *Three further correspondences with Sanderson: the first (addition of 'both') is only with FC; the second (omission of 'doe') is trivial; the third (addition of 'presently' where DB has 'now') is not close. The sudden appearance of five correspondences in a short space is impressive until they are analysed; even so, this is the best evidence to be found of Sanderson's collaboration in DB, or of the use of his manuscript.*

I. N. take thee N . . . till death vs depart, according to Gods holy ordinance: and thereto I plight thee my troth.

Then shall they loose their hands, and the woman taking againe the man by the right hand, shall say.

I. N. take thee N . . . I giue thee my troth.

Then shal they againe loose their hands, and the man shall giue vnto the woman a Ring, laying the same vpon the booke with the accustomed duety to the Priest and Clerke. And the Priest taking the Ring shall deliuer vnto the man to put it vpon the fourth finger of the womans left hand. And the man taught by the Priest shall say.

With this Ring I thee wed, with my body I thee worship,

            and with all my worldly goods I thee endow: In the name of the Father, and of the Sonne, and of the holy Ghost. Amen.

ii. *Read*: Then shall they give yr troth to each other in this manner. The Minister . . . shall cause the man wth his right hand to take the woman by her right hand, and to say after him, as followeth:

374.   *For* depart *read*: doe part

i. *Read*: . . . hands, and joyning them againe as before, the woman shall say after the Priest;
ii. *Read*: . . . hands, and the woman wth her right hand taking the man by his right hand, shall likewise say after the Priest;

375.   *After* Ring *add*: & other tokens of spouseage, as gold or silver, or bracelets. (*crossed out*)

        After man *add*: holding the Ring there, &

376.   i. *For* with . . . worship *read*: & receive thee into ye holy & honourable Estate of Matrimonie; I doe thee Honour,
        ii. *Delete*: & receive . . . Matrimonie   q

Then the man leauing the Ring vpon the fourth finger of the womans left hand, the Minister shall say,

¶ Let vs pray.
☩ Eternall God . . . through Jesus Christ our Lord. Amen.

    .   .   .   .   .   .

377.   i. *After* hand *add*: they shall both kneele, &
        ii. *Read*: . . . kneele downe, and

373. **Adv.:** ... (and so either to give their troth to other) the Man first saying, (And so the Woman afterward, as the Minister shall teach them,) I N. take] etc.

Part. '83': The *Man & Woman* are appointed to take each other *by ye right hand*: it should be also, each other *wth ye same Right Hand.*

Part. '83' may have occasioned the change, but did not suggest the form it took.

374. **Exceptions:** This word depart is here improperly used.

Bishops: Conc. 16. That those words (til death us depart) be thus altered (till death us do part.) *The alteration to 'doe part' had already been made by Cosin.*

375. **1549:** ... a ring, and other tokens of spousage, as gold or siluer ... (*in the Collect following*): ... after bracellets and Jewels of gold geuen ...

S III: And some marvel it is, that those Words, *and other Gifts of Gold and Silver*, should be taken out of the Book in the fifth of K. Edward, whenas Bucer liked them so well: But it is a general Custom still to observe this Order in the North part of the Kingdom.

The S III passage is also paraphrased by L'Estrange, being one of a number which show that he had access to these notes (see Intro., p. xx, note). The custom rests on Gen. xxiv. 22.

376. **Part. '84':** The Words here used by the *Man* to the *Woman* when he saith (*With my Body I thee worship, & with all my worldly Goods I thee endow*) ye former being not (as ye phrase is now usually understood) so consonant to Religion or reason, & ye latter not so agreeable to Law or Custome, require some Consideration, yt they may be explayned.

Exceptions: This word (worship) being much altered in the use of it, since this form was first drawn up. We desire some other word may be used instead of it.

Bishops: Conc. 15. That those words (with my body I thee worship) may be altered thus: (with my body I thee honour.)

L'Estrange and Sparrow have each a long note on the word 'worship', which they explain as equivalent to 'honour'. There was evidently a general desire for this change. '& receive thee ...': cf. the Preface (at no. 371).

377. **Adv.:** In the *2d* Rubrick, thus,
Then leaving the Ring upon the womans finger, they shall both kneel down, and the Preist standing before them, shall lay his hand upon both their Heads, and then shall say,

[O Eternall God, Creator and] etc.

𝔉orasmuch as 𝔑. & 𝔑 . . . 𝔍n the 𝔑ame of the 𝔉ather,[1] of the 𝔖onne, and of the holy 𝔊host. 𝔄men.

.   .   .   .   .

𝔊od the 𝔉ather . . . life euerlasting. 𝔄men.

Then the Minister or Clerkes going to the Lords Table, shall say or sing this Psalme following.

378. *i.* *Read*: Then shall they all goe into the Quire, the Minister & Clerkes saying or singing this Psalme following.

ii. *Read*: . . . Clerkes singing or saying . . .

iii. *Stet as printed, except & clerkes for or . . .[2]*

Beati omnes. Psal. 128.

𝔅lessed are they that feare . . .

.   .   .   .   .

world without end. 𝔄men.

Or this Psalme.
Deus misereatur. Psal. 67.

𝔊od be mercifull vnto vs . . .
𝔗hat thy way may bee knowne vpon the earth . . .[3]
let all the people praise thee.
. . . 𝔄s it was in the beginning, is now, &c.[4]

The Psalme ended, and the man and the woman kneeling afore[5] the Lords Table, the Priest standing at the Table, and turning his face toward them, shall say,

𝔏ord haue mercy vpon vs.

379. *Add*: Answ. Lord &c.

Answere.

Read: Minister.

𝔠hrist haue mercy vpon vs.

Add: Answ. Christ &c.

Minister.

𝔏ord haue mercy vpon vs.

Add: Answ. Lord &c.
(*all crossed out*)
Print it out at large.

¶ 𝔒ur 𝔉ather which art in heauen, &c.
𝔄nd leade vs not into temptation.

Answere.

Delete Answere.

𝔅ut deliuer vs from euill. 𝔄men.

Minister.

𝔒 𝔏ord saue thy seruant . . .

.   .   .   .   .

𝔄nd let our cry come vnto thee.

---

[1] FC: . . . and of the Sonne . . . (*Cosin*).   [2] FC: *no alteration.*
[3] FC: . . . vpon earth . . . yea, let all (*Cosin*).   [4] FC: *Printed at large* (*Cosin*).
[5] FC: before (*Cosin*).

378. **Adv.:** The *2d* Rubrick, thus,
   Then the Minister and Clarks going unto the Lords Table, the married Couple also following the Minister, and kneeling where He shall appoint them, This Psalm shall be sayd.

   1549: Then shall they goe into the quier, and the ministers or clarkes shall saye or sing, thys Psalme folowyng.

   S III: In the second of K. Edw. it was, *Going into the Choir and singing.*

379. **Adv.:** When the Psalm is ended, the Preist, as he stands at the Holy Table, but turning his face towards the married Couple, shall say,

   [Ld have mercy upon us.]

   Answer, by ye Clarks & the people,

   [Xt have mercy upon us.] etc.

   Our Father, Who art in Heaven, hallowed] etc. . . .

   For thyne is the Kingdome, the Power] etc.

   > Minister.

   O Lord save thy Servant, and thyne Handmayd.

   > Answer.

   Who put their trust in thee] etc.

   > *Cf. no. 86. Notice, above (in* Deus misereatur) *and below, further minor alterations in FC in Cosin's hand.*

Minister.

☩ God of Abraham . . . in their mindes[1] . . .
Christ our Lord. Amen.

     .   .   .   .

☩ Mercifull Lord . . . Christ our Lord.
Amen.

☩ God, which by thy mighty power hast made
all things of nought,[2] . . . that this woman
may be louing and amiable to her husband . . .   380.   *Delete* and amiable   Stet
Christ our Lord. Amen.

Then shall the Priest say.

Almighty God, which at the beginning . . .
your liues end. Amen.

Then shall begin the Communion. And after the   381.   i. *Read*: Then shall begin the Com-
Gospel shalbe said a Sermon, wherein ordinarily   munion, if any be that day ap-
(so oft as there is any mariage) the office of a man   pointed. And after the Gospel
and wife shall be declared, according to holy   & Creed, shalbe said a Sermon,
Scripture. Or if there be no Sermon, the Minister   wherein it is expedient that the
shall reade this that followeth.   office of man and wife be declared,
                                          according to holy Scripture. And
                                          if there be no such[3] Sermon &
                                          declaration, the Minister shall
                                          reade this that followeth.
                           ii. *Delete* if any . . . appointed.
                             Delete & declaration.

All yee which be married . . . as the Lord doth   382.   In ye new translon
the Congregation . . . dismayed with any   *For* Congregation *read*: Church[4]
feare.

The new married persons, the same day of their
marriage, must receiue the holy Communion.   383.   *Add*: unto which ye Minister is now
                                          to proceed, reading the Offertory
                                          &c according to ye forme pre-
                                          scribed.
                                          (*crossed out*)

---

[1] FC: *For* mindes *read*: hearts (*Cosin*).
[2] FC: *For* mighty *read*: almighty; *for* nought *read*: nothing (*Cosin*).
[3] FC *omits* such.   [4] *Also below.*

380. **Adv.:** In the Third Prayer on that Page, there is [Wch] three times, when it should be [Who.] [Almighty God, Who at the beginning didst create our] etc.

Part. '85': The like Consideration is to be had of those words where the Minister saith & prayeth, *That ye Woman may be amiable as Rachel, wise as Rebecca* &c wch are not so fitt for all Persons.

381. *Editorial. The omission of 'if any . . . appointed' is necessary because it conflicts with the rubric at no. 383.*

382. **Adv.:** In the beginning of the Exhortation,
 [All yee, Who are married, or Who intend to take the holy state of Matrimony upon you] etc.
 To every place of Scripture following let the Chapter and Verse be set in the Margen.
 Three times on this Page, change the word [Congregation] into [Church] and in the 4th place, leave it quite out.

383. **Adv.:** To the first Rubrick add, thus,
 [. . . holy Communion; Unto wch the Minister is now to proceed.
 Yet it must be remembred, That this Injunction [On the same day] does playnely thwart a cheef Reason that is commonly rendred, for The times of Mariages prohibited. But let this stand, and let that Order of Prohibiting be rectifyed.
 Cf. Adv. at no. 370, and also no. 41, where Cosin takes the opposite view.

¶ The order for the visitation of the sicke.

Set this in a new page.

384. *i. Add*: When any persons be dangerously sick, notice shalbe given therof to ye minister of ye Parish, And

ii. For be dangerously *read*: is

The Priest entring into the sicke persons house, shall say.

After Priest *add*: with his Clark (*crossed out*)

¶ Peace be to this house, and to all that dwell in it.

When he commeth into the sicke mans presence, he shall say kneeling downe.

Remember not Lord our iniquities . . . angry with us for euer.

385.   *Add*: Answ. Spare us good Lord. Minister. Let us pray.

Lord haue mercy vpon vs . . .
. . . deliuer vs from euill, Amen.

As no. 379.

Minister.

O Lord saue thy seruant.

Answere.

Which putteth his trust in thee.

See no. 288.

· · · · · ·

And let our cry come vnto thee.

Minister.

O Lord looke downe from heauen . . . Christ our Lord. Amen.

Heare vs Almighty and most mercifull God . . . in life euerlasting.

Add: through Jesus Christ our Lord. Amen.

· · · · · ·

Dearely beloued, know this . . . that leadeth vnto euerlasting life.

Take therefore in good woorth . . . there is a count to be giuen . . . as a Christian man should, or no.

386.   *Read*: there is an account to be giuen . . .

Here the Minister shall rehearse the Articles of the faith, saying thus.

Doest thou beleeue in God the Father Almightie, &c.

As it is in Baptisme.

Print it out at large.
Read: And ye sick person shall answere.
All this I stedfastly believe

384. **Cosin,** *Visitation Articles,* 1626: 34. Whether doth your Minister having notice given him visit
      ye Sick . . .?

      Possibly an echo of Cosin's parochial experience.

Sarum: . . . cum suis ministris . . .

385. **Adv.:**   On this page [Wch] is twise, for [Who] and once upon the next page.

      The response is that made at the corresponding point in the Litany.
      This treatment of the Lesser Litany and the Lord's Prayer is common to all the occasional
      offices in DB.

      Pronouns are marked throughout the service for variation according to sex.

386. **Adv.:** In the bottome of that page, set in the Margen, Hebr. 12. 6.

      BCP: . . . an account . . .

      'All this I stedfastly believe' : cf. Public Baptism, at no. 299.

Then shall the Minister examine . . . when they be in health.

These words before rehearsed, may be said before the Minister begin his prayer, as he shall see cause.

Delete the whole sentence.   Stet

The Minister . . . toward the poore.

Here shall the sicke person make a speciall confession, if he feele his conscience troubled with any weighty matter. After which confession, the Priest shall absolve him after this sort.

387.   *After* absolue him *add*: if he shall humbly[1] & heartily desire it,
For after this sort *read*: saying

Our Lord Jesus Christ . . . and of the holy Ghost. Amen.

¶ And then the Priest shall say the Collect following.
¶ **Let us pray.**

✠ **Most mercifull God . . . but take him unto thy fauour, thorow the merits of thy most dearely beloued Sonne Jesus Christ. Amen.**

388.   i. *For* take *read*: remove
ii. *Read*: strengthen him with thy Bl. Spirit; & when thou art pleased to take him hence, take[2]
For unto *read*: into[3]

Then shall the Minister say this Psalme. In te Domine speraui. Psal. 71.

389.   *After* say *add*: these words of (crossed out)
print it all

In thee, ✠ Lord, haue I put my trust . . .
. . . .

Verses 3, 6, 9, 16, 18–22 crossed out. Stet

Cast me not away in the time of age . . .
. . . .

For age *read*: my affliction[3]

As it was in the beginning, &c.

Adding this.
✠ **Sauiour of the world . . . we beseech thee, ✠ God.**

Then shall the Minister say.

The Almighty Lord . . . through whom thou mayest receiue health . . . our Lord Jesus Christ. Amen.

For thou mayest *read*: wee may[3]

390.   *Add*: Unto God's gracious Protection & Mercy wee committ thee. The Lord blesse thee & keep thee. The Lord make his face shine upon thee, & be gracious unto thee. The Lord lift up his countenance upon thee, and give thee Peace, both now & for evermore. Amen.

---

[1] *An indecipherable word has been crossed out* (. . . ly;? truly).
[2] *Written hastily and copied neatly; originally* . . . wth . . . Sp. . . . wn . . . pleas'd . . .
[3] FC: *no alteration.*

387. **Adv.:** At the end of that Rubrick, set it thus,
        . . . the Preist shall absolve him, yf he perceive, that he doth humbly and hartily desire it, after this sort,
   After the Absolution, the Preist shall kneel down, and say,
        O most mercifull God, Who according to the multitude of thy Mercies doest so put away the sinnes etc.
       This and the following entry are made from Adv. by S.

388. **Adv.:** At the ending of that prayer, thus,
        [. . . impute not unto him his former Sinnes, but strenghthen him by the comforts of Thy blessed Spirit, and when it pleaseth thee to take him frõ hence, take him unto thy favour, through the Merits] etc.

389.   *The verses to be omitted from Psalm 71 are inappropriate to the occasion, and their omission makes the psalm more suitable in length.*

   Adv.: In the 2d line, thus,
        O Saviour of the world, save us: Thou, Who by thy Cross & pretious bloud hast redeemed us, help us we beseech thee, Blessed Lord God.

390. **Adv.:** Then shall he say, over the Sick,
        The Almighty Lord, Who is a most strong Tower,] etc. . . . . the Name of our Lord Jesus Xt; Unto whose Grace and Mercy we humbly now committ thee, wayting his blessed pleasure, and ascribing unto him, wth the Father and the Holy Ghost, all Honor Prayse and Glory, now and for ever. Amen.

   Taylor (A form of prayer at the Visitation of the Sick):
        The Lord blesse you and keepe you; The Lord make his face to shine upon you, and be gracious unto you. The Lord lift up the light of his countenance upon you and give you peace.
       Cf. no. 414.

391. *Add*: If any sick persons desire[1] the prayers of the Church in publick, they are to send their names in writing to the Curate, who im̄ediately before the finall Collect of Morning or Evening Service shall declare the same, & use the forme above prescribed, beginning at these words[2] O Lord save thy Servant &c, unto the Exhortation, & ending with these two last prayers, The Almightie Lord &c. Unto God's gracious protection &c. (*crossed out*)

The Communion of the sicke.

Forasmuch as all mortall men . . . signifying also how many be appointed to communicate with him:

392. *i. Add*: (wch shalbe two or three at the least)
ii. Read: . . . three or two . . .

and hauing a conuenient place in the sicke mans house, where the Curate may reuerently Minister, and a good number to receiue the Communion with the sicke person, with all things necessary for the same, he shall there minister the holy Communion.

393. *i. Read*: and [3]a conuenient place in the sicke mans house being prepared, where the Curate may reuerently Minister, He shall celebrate the Holy Sacrament in the forme prescribed for the same, beginning at ye Confession, Almighty God father of our Lord Jesus Christ &c.
ii. After house *add*: wth all things necessary
For where *read*: that
iii. For being *read*: so
For He shall . . . Christ &c. *read*: He shall there celebrate the Holy Communion in the forme prescribed.

The Collect.

𝕬lmighty euerliuing 𝕲od . . . and whensoeuer his soule shall depart from the body . . . Christ our Lord. Amen.

Read: but however, when his soule shall depart from his body   Stet

The Epistle.

𝕸y sonne, despise not the chastening . . . whom hee receiueth.

ye new translon

---

[1] *Originally* person desireth.   [2] *Originally* from.   [3] FC: and hauing a conuenient place . . .

391. **Adv.:** Also, before we pass to [ye Order for Visiting the Sick,] here wants a breef Form of Publike Prayer, to be appointed for the Churches use, when such as are sick do send their Names, desiring to have the Prayers of the Church. Here therfore let such a Form be set down; Wth this Order, that it be used by him that Officiates, when there is Occasion. At Morning prayer next after the Nicen Creed, or at Evening prayer, next after the Second Lesson; So that the Preacher be not disturbed therewth, to require it of him, before, or after his Sermon.

> *The form now prescribed consists of the Suffrages with the two prayers following (at no. 385), the prayer 'The Almighty Lord . . .' (at no. 389), and the Aaronic Blessing (no. 390).*
> *Cf. Wren, Particular Orders: 9. That when any need is, the sick by name be prayed for, in the Reading Desk, and no where else, at ye close of the first Service (except it be in the afternoone, & then to be don immediatly after ye Creed:) using only those 2 Collects, wch are set down in ye Service book For ye Visitation of ye Sick . . .*

392. **Adv.:** In the Rubrick following, instead of [a good Number] put it, [And three, or foure to receive the Comunion] etc.

SL: . . . at least two or three . . .

> *Cf. no. 275 ('foure or three at the least').*

393. **Part. '86':** The Collect Eple & Gospell is here especially ordered; but what part of the publick order at the Comunion is to be used & what omitted (as some part of it seemes needfull to be,) is not here said.

1549: But before the curate distribute the holy Communion: the appoynted generall confession muste bee made in the name of the communicantes, the curate adding the absolucion with the comfortable sentences of scripture folowing in the open Communion: and after the Communion ended, the Collect. Almightie and euerliuyng God, we moste hartely thanke thee, &c.

> *1549 is evidently the model here, and in no. 394.*

Adv.: In the first Line,
[. . . Maker of Mankind, Who doest correct] etc.
[. . . shall depart from the Body, that it may be wthout spott presented unto thee, through] etc.
In the Margen, add the Verses of those Citations for th'Epistle, and Gospell.

The Gospel.

𝔙erily, berily 𝕴 say bnto you . . . from death bnto life.

ye new transl.

¶ At the time of the distribution of the holy Sacrament, the Priest shall first receiue the Communion himselfe, and after minister vnto them that are appointed to communicate with the sicke.

394.   *Add*: & last to ye sick person.

¶ But if a man . . . with his mouth.

¶ When the sicke person is visited, and receiueth the holy Communion all at one time, then the Priest for more expedition, shall cut off the forme of the visitation at the Psalme, **𝕴n thee, 𝕺 𝕷ord, haue 𝕴 put my trust,** and goe straight to the Communion.

Delete the whole Rubric. Stet
Delete all

¶ In the time of Plague, Sweat, or such other like contagious times of sickenesses, or diseases, when none of the Parish or neighbours can be gotten to communicate with the sicke in their houses, for feare of the infection, vpon speciall request of the diseased, the Minister may onely communicate with him.

395.   *i. Read*: Neverthelesse, in the time of Plague . . .
         After diseases *add*: & at other times,

         Delete for feare of the infection
         After diseased *add*: for the better peace & quiet of his mind
         For onely *read*: alone
       ii. Stet as printed, except alone *for* onely.[1]
         A fleuron

¶ The order for the buriall of the dead.

396.   *Add*: Here is to be noted, that the Office ensuing is not to be used for any that dye unbaptizd, or excommunicate, or have laid violent hands upon themselves.

The Priest meeting the corpes at the Church stile, shall say, or else the Priest and Clerkes shall sing, and so go, either into the Church, or towards the graue.

397.   *i. Read*: The Priest meeting the corpes at the Churchyard Gate, shall goe before it, & say, . .
       ii. Read: The Priest & Clerks meeting the corpes at the Churchyard Gate and going before it either into the Church, or towards the graue, shall say, or sing:

𝕴 am the resurrection . . .

    •   •   •   •   •

𝔅lessed be the name of the 𝕷ord.

398.   *Add*: If there be any divine Service to be read, or Sermon to be made at this time, the Corps shalbe conveniently[2] placed in the middle of the Church, till they be ended. (*crossed out*)

---

¹ FC: *no alteration.*   ² *Originally* decently.

394. 1549: . . . and then to the sicke person.

395. Part. '87': In ye last Rubrick there, no leave is given to Comunicate the sick person wthout other companie but in the times of Contagious sicknes, when none can be procured to comunicate wth him. If there might be here some further indulgence given in case the sick person doth so earnestly desire the Sacramt yt he cannot be in a quiet state of mind wthout it, it may be delivered to him by the Minister though there be no contagion in the sicknes, when others cannot be gotten to comunicate wth him, it would be to the greater satisfaction both of him & the minister, who is here restrayned to yt case only.

    BCP (1552, 1559) & SL: . . . alonely . . . (*cf. stage ii*).

        Cosin's proposal was presumably thought inconsistent with no. 392.

396. Canon 68: . . . (except the party deceased were denounced excommunicated *maiori excomunicatione,* for some grieuous and notorious crime, and no man able to testify of his repentance,) . . .

    S II: Pagani enim, & nondum Baptizati, illi etiam qui violentam sibi mortem quoquo modo intulerunt, aut in Excomunicatione mortui sunt, ad Sepulturam Ecclesiasticam non admittuntur.

    S III: For those that depart not in the Lord (says Bucer) i.e. in the Communion of the Church, (as they that are Excommunicated or Unchristned) are not to be buried by the Priest, in this Publick Form.

        This note is written in a very neat hand, which suggests that it was either composed at leisure or copied from some other source not as yet traced, rather than drafted at the time of entry.

397.   *'Stile' is presumably regarded as an archaism.*

398.   *This rubric presumably reflects contemporary practice. Cf. Adv. on no. 402; and Wren, Particular Orders: 23. . . . Sermons . . . are permitted at Funeralls.*

When they come to the graue, while the corps is made ready to be layde into the earth, the Priest shall say, or the Priest and Clerkes shal sing.

𝕸𝖆𝖓 𝖙𝖍𝖆𝖙 𝖎𝖘 𝖇𝖔𝖗𝖓𝖊 𝖔𝖋 𝖆 𝖜𝖔𝖒𝖆𝖓 . . .
𝕴𝖓 𝖙𝖍𝖊 𝖒𝖎𝖉𝖘 𝖔𝖋 𝖑𝖎𝖋𝖊 . . .
𝖄𝖊𝖙 𝕺 𝕷𝖔𝖗𝖉 𝕲𝖔𝖉 𝖒𝖔𝖘𝖙 𝖍𝖔𝖑𝖞 . . .
𝕿𝖍𝖔𝖚 𝖐𝖓𝖔𝖜𝖊𝖘𝖙 𝕷𝖔𝖗𝖉 𝖙𝖍𝖊 𝖘𝖊𝖈𝖗𝖊𝖙𝖘 . . . 𝖙𝖔 𝖋𝖆𝖑𝖑 𝖋𝖗𝖔𝖒 𝖙𝖍𝖊𝖊.

Then while the earth shall be cast vpon the body by some standing by, the Priest shall say.

𝕱𝖔𝖗𝖆𝖘𝖒𝖚𝖈𝖍 𝖆𝖘 𝖎𝖙 𝖍𝖆𝖙𝖍 𝖕𝖑𝖊𝖆𝖘𝖊𝖉 𝕬𝖑𝖒𝖎𝖌𝖍𝖙𝖞 𝕲𝖔𝖉 . . . 𝖎𝖓 𝖘𝖚𝖗𝖊 𝖆𝖓𝖉 𝖈𝖊𝖗𝖙𝖆𝖎𝖓𝖊 𝖍𝖔𝖕𝖊 𝖔𝖋 𝖗𝖊𝖘𝖚𝖗𝖗𝖊𝖈𝖙𝖎𝖔𝖓 𝖙𝖔 𝖊𝖙𝖊𝖗𝖓𝖆𝖑𝖑 𝖑𝖎𝖋𝖊, 𝖙𝖍𝖗𝖔𝖚𝖌𝖍 𝖔𝖚𝖗 𝕷𝖔𝖗𝖉 𝕴𝖊𝖘𝖚𝖘 𝕮𝖍𝖗𝖎𝖘𝖙, 𝖜𝖍𝖔 𝖘𝖍𝖆𝖑𝖑 𝖈𝖍𝖆𝖓𝖌𝖊 𝖔𝖚𝖗 𝖛𝖎𝖑𝖊 𝖇𝖔𝖉𝖞, 𝖙𝖍𝖆𝖙 𝖎𝖙 𝖒𝖆𝖞 𝖇𝖊 𝖑𝖎𝖐𝖊 𝖚𝖓𝖙𝖔 𝖍𝖎𝖘 𝖌𝖑𝖔𝖗𝖎𝖔𝖚𝖘 𝖇𝖔𝖉𝖞 . . . 𝖆𝖑𝖑 𝖙𝖍𝖎𝖓𝖌𝖘 𝖙𝖔 𝖍𝖎𝖒𝖘𝖊𝖑𝖋𝖊.

Then shall be said or sung.

𝕴 𝖍𝖊𝖆𝖗𝖉 𝖆 𝖛𝖔𝖎𝖈𝖊 𝖋𝖗𝖔𝖒 𝖍𝖊𝖆𝖚𝖊𝖓 . . . 𝖋𝖗𝖔𝖒 𝖙𝖍𝖊𝖎𝖗 𝖑𝖆𝖇𝖔𝖚𝖗𝖘.

Then shall follow this Lesson, taken out of the xv. Chapter to the Corinthians, the first Epistle.

𝕮𝖍𝖗𝖎𝖘𝖙 𝖎𝖘 𝖗𝖎𝖘𝖊𝖓 𝖋𝖗𝖔𝖒 𝖙𝖍𝖊 𝖉𝖊𝖆𝖉 . . . 𝕱𝖔𝖗 𝖍𝖊 𝖒𝖚𝖘𝖙 𝖗𝖊𝖎𝖌𝖓𝖊 𝖙𝖎𝖑𝖑 𝖍𝖊 𝖍𝖆𝖚𝖊 𝖕𝖚𝖙 𝖍𝖎𝖘 𝖊𝖓𝖊𝖒𝖎𝖊𝖘 𝖚𝖓𝖉𝖊𝖗 𝖍𝖎𝖘 𝖋𝖊𝖊𝖙 . . . 𝖞𝖔𝖚𝖗 𝖑𝖆𝖇𝖔𝖚𝖗 𝖎𝖘 𝖓𝖔𝖙 𝖛𝖆𝖎𝖓𝖊 𝖎𝖓 𝖙𝖍𝖊 𝕷𝖔𝖗𝖉.

The Lesson ended, the Priest shall say.

𝕷𝖔𝖗𝖉 𝖍𝖆𝖚𝖊 𝖒𝖊𝖗𝖈𝖞 𝖚𝖕𝖔𝖓 𝖚𝖘. . . . 𝖉𝖊𝖑𝖎𝖚𝖊𝖗 𝖚𝖘 𝖋𝖗𝖔𝖒 𝖊𝖚𝖎𝖑𝖑. 𝕬𝖒𝖊𝖓.

The Priest.

𝕬𝖑𝖒𝖎𝖌𝖍𝖙𝖞 𝕲𝖔𝖉, 𝖜𝖎𝖙𝖍 𝖜𝖍𝖔𝖒 𝖉𝖔𝖊 𝖑𝖎𝖚𝖊 . . . 𝖆𝖓𝖉 𝖎𝖓 𝖜𝖍𝖔𝖒 𝖙𝖍𝖊 𝖘𝖔𝖚𝖑𝖊𝖘 . . . 𝖙𝖔 𝖉𝖊𝖑𝖎𝖚𝖊𝖗 𝖙𝖍𝖎𝖘 𝕹. 𝖔𝖚𝖗 𝖇𝖗𝖔𝖙𝖍𝖊𝖗 . . . 𝖎𝖓 𝖙𝖍𝖞 𝖊𝖙𝖊𝖗𝖓𝖆𝖑𝖑 𝖆𝖓𝖉 𝖊𝖚𝖊𝖗𝖑𝖆𝖘𝖙𝖎𝖓𝖌 𝖌𝖑𝖔𝖗𝖞. 𝕬𝖒𝖊𝖓.

The Collect.

𝕺 𝕸𝖊𝖗𝖈𝖎𝖋𝖚𝖑𝖑 𝕲𝖔𝖉 . . . 𝖔𝖚𝖗 𝕸𝖊𝖉𝖎𝖆𝖙𝖔𝖚𝖗 𝖆𝖓𝖉 𝕽𝖊𝖉𝖊𝖊𝖒𝖊𝖗. 𝕬𝖒𝖊𝖓.

---

399.   *Read*: Then all going in decent manner to the grave, while . . . Stet

New paragraph.
New paragraph.
New paragraph.

400.   *See no. 288.*
  i. *For* in sure . . . resurrection *read*: in hope of our generall & joyfull resurrection
  ii. *Read*: in sure and certaine hope of resurrection
  iii. *Read*: in hope of a resurrection[1]

ye new translon
For haue *read*: hath

401.   *After* ended *add*: they shall all kneele downe, &
As no. 379.

For in *read*: with
Delete N.
After glory *add*: through Jesus Christ our Lord.

402. i. *Add*: Then shall ye Priest use this Blessing   The Blessing of God almighty, ye Father, Sonne, & holy Ghost, be wth you all now & evermore. Amen.
  ii. *For* use *read*: let ye people depart wth
  iii. *Read*: The Grace of our Ld. J. X. & the love of G. & ye fellowship of ye Holy Ghost be with us all evermore. Amen.
A fleuron

---

[1] FC *omits* a; *adds* q.

399. **Adv.:** Twise on this Page, [Wch] is put for [Who.]

400. **Exceptions:** These words cannot in truth be said of persons living and dying in open and notorious sins.

    Bishops: Conc. 17. That the words (sure and certain) may be left out.

> *Pronouns are marked, as at no. 288.*
> *Cosin had altered 'sure and certain' before the Savoy concessions, and Sanderson has 'in hope of resurrection', so that this is evidently another case of general agreement. This makes the return to the text in stage ii even harder to account for. Note that Cosin in stage i substitutes adjectives already applied to the resurrection elsewhere in the BCP, viz. in the Collect at no. 402 and that for Easter Even (the latter new in DB).*

401. **Adv.:** at the first line, this Rubrick,
> The Lesson being ended, they shall kneel down, and the Preist shall say,
> [Ld have mercy upon us.]

402. **Adv.:** Yf the Buriall were not after the Second Lesson, in the time of Divine Service, then it shall here be closed wth,
> [The Grace of our Ld Jesus Xt] etc.

> *i is probably quoted from memory; ii restores the text of the rubric in the Communion Service (at no. 271), though not that of the Blessing itself. iii is paralleled by both Sanderson and Taylor; the latter refers to it as 'the usual benediction', which need not mean 'usual at the end of the Burial Service', but only 'usual at the end of any service'.*

¶ The thankesgiuing of women after Childbirth, commonly called, The Churching of women.

¶ The woman shall come into the Church, and there shall kneele down in some conuenient place, nigh vnto the place where the Table standeth, and the Priest standing by her, shall say these words, or such like, as the case shall require.

403.　i. *Read*: The woman a month after her delivery being recovered shall upon some Sunday or other Holyday come decently vayled into the parish Church, and at ye beginning of the Comunion Service shall kneele down in some conuenient place appointed unto her by the Minister before the Holy Table; at which he standing shall thus direct his speech to her.

ii. *Delete* upon some Sunday or other Holyday　Stet

Forasmuch as it hath pleased . . . and pray.

¶ Then shall the Priest say this Psalme.

I haue lifted up mine eyes . . .

· · · · ·

world without end. Amen.

404.　i. *Add*: Or Psalme. 127.
Except ye Lord build ye house &c
ii. *Read*: Or this Psalm. Ps. 127. Except ye Lord build ye house. &c.
Print it out at large.

Lord haue mercy upon us.

· · · · ·

deliuer us from euill. Amen.

Minister.

O Lord saue this woman thy seruant.

· · · · ·

And let our cry come unto thee.

Minister.

405.　*Add*: Let us pray.
As no. 379.

¶ Let us pray.

Delete Let vs pray.　Stet

O Almighty God, which hast deliuered . . . may both faithfully liue, and walke in her uocation, according to thy will, in this life present, and also may be partaker of euerlasting glory in the life to come, through Jesus Christ our Lord. Amen.

406.　i. *Read*: may both live religiously and duely walke in her Christian uocation, according to thy will, in this life present, and also in ye life to come may be partaker of euerlasting glory, through . . .
ii. *Stet as printed.*
iii. Read: . . . and duely walke . . . .

403. **Adv.**: The first Rubrick there, to be thus,
   The Woman decently vayled, shall at the beginning of the Communion Service be
   appointed where to kneel, not farr from the holy Table, at wch the Preist standing shall
   thus direct his speech to hir,
   [Forasmuch as it hath pleased] etc.

   Part. '88': The title of *Thanksgiving* was here added by the King's autoritie only at the Conference in Hampton Court, & wants a Confirmation of a Law.

   Part. '89': In ye Rubrick there, the words *or such like as the Case shall require*, seeme to give too
   much liberty to the Minister, to alter & adde at his pleasure. He were better to be
   confined yt an uniformity herin might be observed.

   Part. '90': The woman is not appointed in what Habit she shall come to church for this purpose,
   nor in what time after her recovery, wch for the avoyding of questions & too much
   liberty herin taken, requires here to be duly ordered.

   Cf. Wren,   Particular Orders: *10. . . . being vayled according to ye custome . . .*
   There is abundant evidence for the custom of veiling, which is derived from Canon Law.

404. **SL**:   Or else Psalme the 27.
   It is possible that this is a misprint for '127', but Ps. 27 is not unsuitable.

405.   *The transposition of 'Let us pray' assimilates this section to the corresponding portion of
   Morning and Evening Prayer.*

406. **Adv.**: Here also is [Wch] twise, instead of [Who.]
   Lett that Collect be thus closed,
   [. . . live and walk in hir Xtian Vocation, according to thy holy will in this present
   Life, and also in the Life to come may be made Partaker of everlasting Glory, through
   Jesus Xt our Lord. Amen.]

The woman that commeth to giue her thankes, must offer accustomed offerings: and if there be a Communion, it is conuenient that she receiue the holy Communion.

407. i. *Read*: The Priest here goeth on to the Communion Service, and if there be a Communion, it is conuenient that the woman doe receiue it. She must also offer the Offerings accustomed at such times to be given in that Church.

ii. Stet[1]

iii. *For* the holy Communion *read*: it.[2]

¶ A Commination against sinners, with certaine Prayers to be vsed diuers times in the yeare.

408. i. *Read*: A Commination, or Denouncing of God's Anger & Judgments against sinners, with certaine Prayers to be vsed after it[3] on the first day of Lent, & other times of publick & solemne fasts.

ii. *For* fasts *read*: fasting

¶ After morning Prayer . . . the Priest shall goe into the Pulpit, and say thus.

𝔅rethren, in the 𝔓rimitiue 𝔠hurch, there was a godly discipline, that at the beginning of 𝔏ent, such persons as were notorious sinners,

409. *For* were notorious sinners *read*: stood convicted of notorious Sinnes

were put to open penance, and punished in this world, that their soules might be saued in the day of the 𝔏ord, and that others admonished by their example, might be the more afraid to offend. 𝔍n the stead whereof, vntill the said discipline be restored againe, (which thing is much to be wished). . . . (in your presence) . . . the curse of 𝔊od to be due. 𝔠ursed is the man . . .

410. *For* punished *read*: did humbly submitt themselves to undergoe punishment Stet
For In the stead *read*: In stead

Delete thing
Read: . . . (in the presence of you all) . . .

.   .   .   .   .   .

Answere.

𝔞men.

---

[1] FC: . . . offer the accustomed offerings.   [2] FC: *No alteration.*   [3] FC *omits* after it.

407. **Adv.:** The Rubrick following to be this,

> The Preist here proceedeth to ye Communion Service. And yf there be a Communion, it is convenient that the woman do receive it. She must also offer the Offerings accustomed in that Parish.

> *Wren's influence is predominant throughout this service.*

408. **Adv.:** The Title, thus,

> A Denouncing of Gods Iudgments against Sinners, cald the Commination, wth certayn Prayers to be used after it.

> Then the Rubrick, thus,

> On the first day of Lent, after Morning Prayer, where it useth to be divided from the rest of the Divine Service, the people being assembled agayn by the Ringing of a Bell, the Publike Supplication (cald the Letany) shall be sayd, Wch ended, the Preist, before the Communion Service, going into the Pulpit, shall say thus,

Part. '91': This is appointed to be used at *divers times in ye yeere*, but those times are not specified. For want wherof few know when to read it, & some read it not at all.

Cf. 1549: The firste daie of Lente commonly called Ash-Wednisdaye.

SL: . . . to be used divers times in the year, and especially on the first day of Lent, commonly called, Ashwednesday.

S III: In the second of Edw. upon *Ashwednesday* . . .

409. **Adv.:** [Brethren, in the Primitive Church there was a Godly Discipline, that on the first Day of Lent, such Persons as stood convicted of Notorious Offenses, were put to open Pennance, and] etc.

> *Cf. no. 203; and S III:*

> *But this was never done, but when the Crime was notorious, and the Church had taken Offence at any Man's Doings that were openly Evil, and declared by the Judge to be notorious and scandalous.*

410. **SL:** . . . did humbly submit themselves to undergo punishment . . .

Adv.: In the next Paragraph,

> [. . . it is thought meet, that on this day of our generall Humiliation, in the presence of you all, should be read the generall Sentences] etc.

Minister.

𝔑ow seeing that all they be accursed (as
the Prophet Dauid beareth witnesse) . . .
Psal. 119. (remembring the dreadfull Iudge-
ment hanging ouer our heads and being
alwaies at hand) . . .

· · · · · ·

for his infinite mercy.

Then . . . the Priest and Clearkes kneeling (where
they are accustomed to say the Letanie) shall say
this Psalme, *Miserere mei Deus.*

𝕳aue mercy vpon me, 𝕆 God . . .

· · · · ·

𝕬s it was in the beginning, is now, &c.

𝕷ord haue mercy vpon vs.

· · · · ·

deliuer vs from euill. Amen.

Minister.

𝕆 Lord saue thy seruants.

· · · · ·

And let our cry come vnto thee.

¶ 𝕷et vs pray.

𝕆 Lord wee beseech thee . . . Iesus Christ
our Lord. Amen.

𝕆 Most mightie God . . . wearied with the
burden of our sinne. Thy propertie is to haue
mercie . . . which meekely knowledge our
uilenesse . . . So make haste to helpe vs . . .
our Lord. Amen.

Then shall the people, say this that followeth,
after the Minister.

𝕿urne thou vs, 𝕆 good Lord, . . . looke
upon us.

411. *To* Psal. 119. *add*: 21.

For at hand *read*: ready to fall
upon us
Add: Amen.

412. *For* Letanie *read*: Litanie

Add: Let us pray
As no. 379.

413. *For* sinne *read*: sinnes[1]
After is *add*: always
For knowledge *read*: acknowledge
Before So *add*: And

Delete comma after people.

414. *Add*: through ye Merits & Mediation
of thy blessed Sonne Jesus Christ
our Lord. Amen.

Minister.

The Lord blesse us & keep us.
The Lord lift up the light of his
Countenance upon us, & give us
peace, now and for evermore.
Amen.

---

[1] FC *in text.*

411. **Adv.:** At the 6th Line. Shall not the mention of David be here omitted? For though the phrase
of [Going astray] be in Psal. 119. 176, yet there's no mention at all of any Accursing.
At the *11th* Line: In what, [Being alwayes at hand] is not the same wth [Hanging over
our heads] it is less than it, and should not be added unto it.
Add the Verses to all these Citations, and so on the page before.

The allusion in 'going astray' (to Ps. 119. 21) is correctly taken by DB.

412. **Adv.:** In that Rubrick, thus,
The Preist, being come from the Pulpit, and he wth the Clarks kneeling, where they
sayd the Supplication, shall say this Psalme.
The 7th Line:
[Who put their trust in thee.]
The end of the first prayer,
[Through Jesus Xt our Lord, Amen.]
from thence to the end, there is [Wch] six times, for [Who].

Cf. no. 405.

413. 'Alwayes': *cf.* **BCP,** Prayer of Humble Access.

SL: ... and so ...

414. **BCP** (Prayer in time of war): through the merits of thy onely sonne Jesus Christ our Lord.

*Cf. Jeremy Taylor, at no. 390. Brightman (I. ccxii) can see no reason for shortening the
Aaronic Blessing, but it seems to have been an accepted practice, however unjustifiable.*

415.   *Add*:   Then   shall   follow   ye
          Coṁunion Service.   (*crossed out*)
          A fleuron

THE Psalter or Psalmes of Dauid, after
the Translation of the Great BIBLE,

Pointed as it shall be sung or said in Churches.

¶ Imprinted at London by Robert Barker, Printer
to the Kings most Excellent Maiestie.

                          1620.
¶ *Cum Priuilegio.*

416.   *i.* Here place
          The TABLE for the Order of ye
          PSALTER to be said or sung
          daily at Morning & Evening
          Prayer.

Dayes of the Month	Psalmes for Morning.	Psalmes for Evening.
1	1.2.3.4.5.	6.7.8.
2		
3		

       ii. *Read*: A TABLE for the Order of
             ye PSALMES to be sung or said
             at Morning and Evening Prayer...
      iii. *After 3 add*: &c. vid. retrò.[1]

Moneth. The j. day.
¶ THE PSALMES OF DAVID.

Beatus vir qui not abijt. Psal. j.

𝕭𝖑𝖊𝖘𝖘𝖊𝖉 𝖎𝖘 𝖙𝖍𝖊 𝖒𝖆𝖓 𝖙𝖍𝖆𝖙 𝖍𝖆𝖙𝖍 𝖓𝖔𝖙 𝖜𝖆𝖑𝖐𝖊𝖉 𝖎𝖓
𝖙𝖍𝖊 𝖈𝖔𝖚𝖓𝖘𝖆𝖎𝖑𝖊 𝖔𝖋 𝖙𝖍𝖊 𝖚𝖓𝖌𝖔𝖉𝖑𝖞, 𝖓𝖔𝖗 𝖘𝖙𝖆𝖓𝖉 𝖎𝖓 𝖙𝖍𝖊   *For* stand *read*: stood[2]
𝖜𝖆𝖞 𝖔𝖋 𝖘𝖎𝖓𝖓𝖊𝖗𝖘: 𝖆𝖓𝖉 𝖍𝖆𝖙𝖍 𝖓𝖔𝖙 𝖘𝖎𝖙 𝖎𝖓 𝖙𝖍𝖊 𝖘𝖊𝖆𝖙𝖊   *i.* *For* sit *read*: sitten
𝖔𝖋 𝖙𝖍𝖊 𝖘𝖈𝖔𝖗𝖓𝖊𝖋𝖚𝖑𝖑.   *ii.* *Read*: satt[3]

        ·   ·   ·   ·   ·   ·

---

   [1] FC *gives the Table in full, and also the note about Ps. 95 (see no. 35).*
   [2] FC *in text.*
   [3] FC: *No alteration.*

415. **Adv.:** A Rubrick to be set at the bottome,
These prayers being finished, they are to go on to the Communion Service.
This is implied in the introductory rubric.

Adv.: The Psalter follows. The Title Page whereof saies, [It is after the Translation of the Great
Bible.] Whereas we have now, (and had thē) another Translation after that, and a
greater Bible.

416.   *Cf. no. 34.*

... and the way of the ungodly shall perish.　417.

i. Add: Glory be to ye Father &c. [& so print it at ye end of every psalme, & every portion of ye 119. psalme.]

ii. After Father &c. *add*: As it was in ye beg. &c

Confitebor tibi. Psal. 9.

11 ℗ praise the Lord which dwelleth in Sion ...　418.

Who for wch (when it is personall) & so correct it all along — through ye whole Psalter.[1]

Si vere vtique. Psal. 58.

8 ... so let indignation uexe him, euen as a thing that is raw.

i. Read: so let indignation soare uexe him, & as that which is raw.

ii. Read: so let indignation suddenly uexe him, euen as that which is raw.[1]

Laudate Dominum. Psal. 150.

6 Let every thing that hath breath: praise the Lord.

Add: Glory be to the Father &c. here print it out. *(crossed out)*
A faire fleuron

Certaine godly prayers to be vsed for sundry purposes.　419.

These are no part of ye Comon Prayer Booke, but added by ye printer & in ye next Edition are to be omitted.[2]

Imprinted at London by *Robert Barker* and *Iohn Bill*, Printers to the Kings most Excellent Maiestie.

ANNO 1620.

Cum priuilegio Regiae Maiestatis.

---

[1] FC: *No alteration.*
[2] FC: Omitt all that follows to the End, being noe authorized part of the Comon prayer booke.

417.   *Cf. no. 76, and the* Directions to the Printers.

418.   *Cf. Adv. on no. 69.*

          It is not clear why Cosin chose this particular verse (58. 8) out of the whole Psalter for alteration; nor why he made these alterations, for they do not follow any of the other versions.

419. **Adv.:** After the Psalter, there are divers pages, inscribed [Godly Prayers to be used] etc.
      To be used in private, perhaps they meant. But by what Authority? Though many of thẽ are not amiss: and the rest may soon be amended. But why are they joyned here, more then many Hundreths of other Prayers?
      Yf it were the Printers boldnes alone, He should not dare to have done such a Thing, for feare of his Priviledg.

      Cf. H. Burton, quoted in Appendix C (p. 293).

THE ORDINAL

THE FORME AND MANNER OF
MAKING and Consecrating BISHOPS,
PRIESTES and Deacons.

420.   *For* MAKING and Consecrating *read*:
        MAKING, Ordeyning, and Conse-
        crating of

Imprinted at London by ROBERT BARKER,
Printer to the Kings Most Excellent Maiesty: and
by the Assignes of IOHN BILL.
                   Anno. 1634.

For ROBERT BARKER, Printer *read*: the
        Printers
Delete and by . . . BILL.

THE PREFACE.

It is evident vnto all men . . . there hath beene
these orders . . . except hee were first called . . .
and also by publique prayer . . . admitted thereunto. . . . no man . . . shall execute any of them,
except hee bee called . . . And none shall be
admitted a Deacon, except hee bee twenty one
yeeres of age at the least. . . . as hereafter followeth.

421.   *For* hath *read*: have[1]
        Read: But every one was first called[2]
        After and *add*: was

        For except *read*: untill[1]
        q three
        Add: & hath bin confirmed.

The Forme and Manner of Ordering of Deacons.

First, when the day appointed . . . in their
vocation.

After the exhortation ended, the Archdeacon or
his Deputie, shall present such as come to the
Bishop to bee admitted, saying these words.

422.   *Read*: . . . present to the Bishop sitting
        in his Chaire neare ye Lord's Table,
        all such as are to bee admitted
        Deacons, saying these words.

Reverend Father in God . . .

     •   •   •   •   •

and think them so to be.

And the Bishop shall say vnto the people.

**Brethren, if there be any of you . . . ad-
mitted to the same, let him come foorth . . . or
impediment is.**

For the same *read*: that Office

And if any great crime or impediment be
obiected . . . the party accused shall trie himselfe
cleare of that crime.

For trie himselfe cleare *read*: cleare him-
        selfe

Then the Bishop . . . with the prayers.

The Letanie and Suffrages.

     •   •   •   •   •

---

[1] *Cosin in the margin, Sancroft in the text.*
[2] *Originally* But that he ought to be. . . .

420. **Adv.:** The Manner of Ordering, Making, and Consecrating Bishops, Preists, and Deacons.

Wren explains the omission of 'Form' and the addition of 'Ordering' in a separate 'Rationale' (see p. 289).

Cf. Directions to the Printers and no. 3.

421. **Adv.:** The Preface.

It is evident to all men, diligently reading Holy Scripture, & antient Authors, that from the Apostles time, there have bin these Orders of Ministers in the Church of Xt, Bishops, Preists, & Deacons; Wch Offices were evermore had in such reverend estimation, That no man might ever presume to execute any of them by his own private Authority, But that he was first to be called, tried, examined, & known to have such Qualities, as were requisite for ye same, And also by Publike Prayer, wth imposition of hands, to be approved, & admitted thereunto.

And therfore, to the intent, that these Orders should be continued, and reverently used & esteemed in this Church of England, It is required, that no man, (not being then at the present, Bishop, Preist, nor Deacon,) doe execute any of them, Untill he be called, tried, examined, & admitted by the Church, according to this Forme here prescribed. It is also required, that every man who is to be consecrated unto the Order of a Bishop, be fully Thirty years of age; And every man, who is to be admitted to be a Preist, be full Foure & Twenty yeares old; And none shall be admitted to be a Deacon, except he be Twenty & One yeares of age at the least.

Some passages in ye close of the Preface are here omitted; But they are afterwards inserted in their due place; so that (in the whole) there is not any part of the Old Rubrick omitted in this new Order of the Book.

Notice Cosin making entries in FC. Adv. is totally lacking for the Ordering of Deacons and the Ordering of Priests (which it places after the Consecration of a Bishop).

422. *Cf. no. 355, and the rubric at no. 425.*

From all sedition and priuy conspiracy, from
all false doctrine and heresie, from hardnesse
of heart, and contempt of thy word and Commandment.

423.

Read: From all open Rebellion, &
sedition; from all conspiracy, &
treason; from all false doctrine
heresie, & schisme; from . . .[1]

·   ·   ·   ·   ·   ·

We sinners . . . thy holy Church vniuersally
in the right way.

For vniuersally *read*: vniuersall

We beseech thee to heare . . .

That it may please thee to blesse and preserue our gracious Queene Mary . . .

See ye note here made in ye Letanie
after Morng Prayer.

·   ·   ·   ·   ·

That it may please thee, to illuminate . . .
accordingly.

Add: That it may please thee to bless
these thy servants, to be admitted to
ye Order of Deacons [or Priests] & to
poure thy grace upon ym, yt they may
duly execute yr Office to ye edifying
of thy Church, & ye glory of thy H.
Name.
We beseech thee &c.

That it may please thee to blesse and keepe
the Magistrates . . .

For the *read*: all the subordinate

·   ·   ·   ·   ·

Our Father which art in heauen, &c.
But deliuer vs from euill. Amen.

Print it out at large.

The Versicle.

Delete The Versicle.

O Lord deale not with vs after our sinnes.

Answere.

Delete Answere.

Neither reward vs after our iniquities.

In ye Rom. lrs.

·   ·   ·   ·   ·

The Versicle.

Delete The Versicle.

O Lord let thy mercy be shewed vpon vs.

Answere.

Delete Answere.

As we doe put our trust in thee.

Let vs pray.

We humbly beseech thee . . . our Lord. Amen.

Almightie God . . . life euerlasting. Amen.

Then shall bee said also this that followeth.

---

[1] *Cosin in the margin, Sancroft in the text.*

423. **Adv.**: Yf in the edition of ye Liturgy, any word or passage in ye Letany shall be otherwise put, then was before, it would here be so put also.

> *Cf. nos. 110, 111, 112, 114, 116, 117. There are minor differences between the corrections at these numbers and those made here. The Embertide suffrage is adapted from the equivalent suffrage in the Consecration of a Bishop (no. 436).*

Almighty God, which by thy diuine proui=
dence . . . and profit of the congregation . . .   424.   *Read*: and ye benefit of thy Church
now and for euer. Amen.

Then shall be sung or said the Communion of the   *For* Communion *read*: Service for
day, sauing the Epistle shall be read out of   the Communion
Timothie, as followeth.   *After* sauing *add*: that
Likewise must the Ministers . . . receiued   1 Tim. iii. 8. in ye new Translation.
vp in glory.

Or else this out of the sixth of the Acts.
Then the twelue . . . vnto the faith.   Acts vi 2.
                                                                  the new translation.
And before the Gospel, the Bishop sitting in a   425.   *For a read*: his
chaire, shall cause the Oath of the Kings supre-
macie . . . to be ordered.

                .   .   .   .   .

Then shall the Bishop examine euery one of
them . . . following.

                .   .   .   .   .

Doe you thinke that yee truly be called . . .   *For* truly be *read*: are truly

                .   .   .   .   .

                The Bishop.
It appertaineth to the office of a Deacon in
the Church, where he shall be appointed, to   *After* appointed *add*: to serve[1]
assist the Priest . . .

        .   .   .   .   .

they may bee relieued by the Parish, or other   *For* by the Parish . . . almes *read*: wth the
conuenient almes: will you do this gladly and   Alms of the Parish, or other good
willingly?   people:
                Answere.
I will so doe by the helpe of God . . .

                The Bishop.
Will you reuerently obey . . . them to whom   *Read*: them to whom is cõmitted ye
the gouernement and charge is committed   governemt, & charge over you
ouer you . . .?

                .   .   .   .   .

Then the Bishop laying his hands seuerally vpon
the head of euery of them, shall say,   *For* euery of them *read*: euery one
Take thou authority to execute the office of   of them humbly kneeling before
a Deacon . . . In the name of the Father, the   him,
Sonne, and the holy Ghost. Amen.   *Read*: . . . of the Father, & of the Sonne,
                                                                    and of the holy Ghost. Amen.
Then shal the Bishop deliuer to euery of them the
New Testament, saying,
Take thou authoritie to read the Gospell . . .   *Read*: . . . if thou be thereunto ap-
if thou be thereto ordinarily commanded.   pointed by lawfull Authority.

---

[1] *Originally* to serve, that he assist. . . .

424. Adv.: The Translation of the Epistles & Gospells is now put as was enjoyned under K. Iames. *'Benefit of thy Church': cf. no. 132.*

425. *Editorial.*

Then one of them, appointed by the Bishop, shall reade the Gospel of that day.

Then shall the Bishop proceed to the Communion . . . with the Bishop.

426. *For* to *read*: in

The Communion ended, . . . shall be said this Collect following.

𝕬𝖑𝖒𝖎𝖌𝖍𝖙𝖞 𝕲𝖔𝖉 . . . 𝖙𝖍𝖆𝖙 𝖙𝖍𝖊𝖞 . . . 𝖒𝖆𝖞 𝖘𝖔 𝖜𝖊𝖑𝖑 𝖚𝖘𝖊 𝖙𝖍𝖊𝖒𝖘𝖊𝖑𝖚𝖊𝖘 . . . 𝖜𝖔𝖗𝖑𝖉 𝖜𝖎𝖙𝖍𝖔𝖚𝖙 𝖊𝖓𝖉. 𝕬𝖒𝖊𝖓.

For vse *read*: behave

And here it must bee shewed vnto the Deacon . . . (except for reasonable causes it bee otherwise seene to his Ordinary) . . . to the Order of Priesthood.

For shewed *read*: declared

For seene to *read*: appointed by

The forme of Ordering of Priests.

Vid infr ad ⚊ When &c.

When the exhortation is ended, then shall follow the Communion. And for the Epistle, shall bee read out of the twentieth Chapter of the Actes of the Apostles, as followeth.

427. *Delete the whole Rubric.* **A.**

Act. 20. 17.

𝕱𝖗𝖔𝖒 𝕸𝖎𝖑𝖊𝖙𝖔, 𝕻𝖆𝖚𝖑 𝖘𝖊𝖓𝖙 𝖒𝖊𝖘𝖘𝖊𝖓𝖌𝖊𝖗𝖘 𝖙𝖔 𝕰𝖕𝖍𝖊𝖘𝖚𝖘, 𝖆𝖓𝖉 𝖈𝖆𝖑𝖑𝖊𝖉 𝖙𝖍𝖊 𝕰𝖑𝖉𝖊𝖗𝖘 𝖔𝖋 𝖙𝖍𝖊 𝕮𝖔𝖓𝖌𝖗𝖊𝖌𝖆𝖙𝖎𝖔𝖓: . . . 𝖙𝖔 𝖌𝖎𝖚𝖊, 𝖙𝖍𝖊𝖓 𝖙𝖔 𝖗𝖊𝖈𝖊𝖎𝖚𝖊.

For Congregation *read*: Church

Or else this third Chapter, of the first Epistle to Timothie.

Read: Or else when on the same day some are to be ordeined Deacons, & some Priests this third Chapter . . . **B.**

𝕿𝖍𝖎𝖘 𝖎𝖘 𝖆 𝖙𝖗𝖚𝖊 𝖘𝖆𝖞𝖎𝖓𝖌 . . .

This when Deacons and Priests are made both in one day.

Delete This when . . . one day.

. . . 𝖗𝖊𝖈𝖊𝖎𝖚𝖊𝖉 𝖚𝖕 𝖎𝖓 𝖌𝖑𝖔𝖗𝖞.

After this shall be read for the Gospel, a piece of the last Chapter of Matthew, as followeth.

For a piece *read*: part
Before Matthew *add*: S. **C.**

𝕵𝖊𝖘𝖚𝖘 𝖈𝖆𝖒𝖊 𝖆𝖓𝖉 𝖘𝖕𝖆𝖐𝖊 𝖚𝖓𝖙𝖔 𝖙𝖍𝖊𝖒 . . . 𝖙𝖍𝖊 𝖊𝖓𝖉 𝖔𝖋 𝖙𝖍𝖊 𝖜𝖔𝖗𝖑𝖉.

Matth. 28. 18.

Or else this that followeth, out of the tenth Chapter of Iohn.

Joh. 10. 2.

𝖁𝖊𝖗𝖎𝖑𝖞, 𝖇𝖊𝖗𝖎𝖑𝖞 . . . 𝖆𝖓𝖉 𝖔𝖓𝖊 𝖘𝖍𝖊𝖕𝖍𝖊𝖗𝖉.

Or els this, of the xx. Chapter of Iohn.

Joh. 20. 19.

426. *Editorial.*

427. *The whole of this section is to be transferred to the end of no. 429; hence the letters A, B, C, DD. Brightman (I. ccxxiii) suggests, with much probability, that the Service is thus assimilated to the Ordering of Deacons in order to facilitate the conferring of both orders at one service.*

𝕮𝖍𝖊 𝖘𝖆𝖒𝖊 𝖉𝖆𝖞 𝖆𝖙 𝖓𝖎𝖌𝖍𝖙 . . . 𝖙𝖍𝖊𝖞 𝖆𝖗𝖊 𝖗𝖊𝖙𝖆𝖎𝖓𝖊𝖉.

Add: Or else Luke, 12.   v. 35. to v. 48.
Lett your loines be girded &c.   DD
Print it out at large.

When the Gospel is ended, then shall be sayd or sung.

428.   as tis corrected   pap. E.

𝕮𝖔𝖒𝖊 𝖍𝖔𝖑𝖞 𝕲𝖍𝖔𝖘𝖙 𝖊𝖙𝖊𝖗𝖓𝖆𝖑𝖑 𝕲𝖔𝖉 . . . 𝖚𝖓𝖙𝖔 𝖙𝖍𝖊 𝖜𝖔𝖗𝖑𝖉𝖘 𝖊𝖓𝖉. 𝕬𝖒𝖊𝖓.

And then the Archdeacon shall present vnto the Bishop, all them that shall receiue the order of Priesthood that day; . . . 𝕻𝖗𝖎𝖊𝖘𝖙𝖍𝖔𝖔𝖉.

☩ Begin heere.
Read: When the exhorton[1] is ended, the Archdeacon or in his absence one appointed in his stead shall present . . .

Cum interrogatione & responsione, vt in ordine Diaconatus.

Delete Cum . . . Diaconatus.

Add: Bishop.
Take heed, that the persons, whom ye present unto us, be apt, & meet, for their learning, & godly conversation to exercise their Ministery duely, to the honour of God, & the edifying of his Church.
The Archdeacon shall Answer.
I have enquired of them, & have also examined them: & think them soe to be.

And then the Bishop shall say to the people,

𝕲𝖔𝖔𝖉 𝖕𝖊𝖔𝖕𝖑𝖊, 𝖙𝖍𝖊𝖘𝖊 𝖇𝖊 𝖙𝖍𝖊𝖞 . . . 𝖉𝖊𝖈𝖑𝖆𝖗𝖊 𝖙𝖍𝖊 𝖘𝖆𝖒𝖊.

And if any great crime or impediment be obiected, Vt supra in Ordine Diaconatus, usque ad finem Letaniae, cum hac Collecta.

429.   *For* Vt . . . Collecta *read*: the Bishop shall surcease from ordering that person, untill such time, as the party accused shall cleare himselfe of that Crime.
Then the Bishop, (com̃ending such, as shall be found meet to be ordered, to ye Prayers of the Congregation) with ye Clerks, & people present shall sing, or say the Litanie wth the praiers, as followeth.
O G. the Father of heaven
     as before to —
life everlasting. Amen.
Then shall be said also this that followeth.

[1] *Originally* exhorton, or Sermon.

Luke xii. 35–48 is the Sarum Gospel for the Common of Many Confessors, and also for various Saints' Days.

428. **Adv.:** Yf there be a more elegant Translation of [Veni Creator] it would here be put in, instead of ye old ⟨. . . . . . .⟩. I heare, that at ye Ks Coronation, there was another.

> *Transferred to the end of no. 431; see above. 'Pap. E' is not now to be found, but its readings are probably reproduced in the Convocation Book. The indecipherable word in Adv. might be 'rigmarole': if so, it is much earlier than the O.E.D. date for the first appearance of this word (1736). As Brightman (I. cxcii) shows, it cannot be the coronation of Charles II that is referred to, but quite possibly may be that of Charles I. 'In his absence': cf. the Ordering of Deacons (at no. 422).*

429. *Cf. nos. 424 ('Service for the Communion') and 427 (Epistles and Gospels).*

Almighty God . . . and profit of thy Congregation . . . world without end. Amen.

Read: and the benefitt of thy Church . . .
Add: Then shall be sung, or said the Service for the Comunion of the day, & for the Epistle shalbe read out of &c. as before ad not. A.
Or else, when on ye same day &c. ad not. B.
After this shall be read for the Gosp. &c as before ad not C. usq. ad DD.
Print them all heere at large.

Then the Bishop shall minister . . . set forth in the order of Deacons . . . as hereafter followeth.

430.   *For* order *read*: ordering

You haue heard, brethren, aswell in your priuate examination, as in the exhortation, and in the holy Lessons taken out of the Gospel, and of the writings of the Apostles, of what dignity, and of how great importance this office is (whereunto yee be called.) And now wee exhort you in the Name of our Lord Iesus Christ, to haue in remembrance into how high a dignity, and to how chargeable an office yee be called;

After exhortation *add*: wch was now made to you
For and of the *read*: and the

For be *read*: are
After now *add*: againe

For chargeable . . . called *read*: weighty an Office, & charge ye are called
After say, *add*: to be

           that is to say, the messengers, the watchmen, the Pastours and the Stewards of the Lord; to teach, to premonish, to feede, and prouide for the Lords family; to seeke for Christs sheepe that be dispersed abroad, and for his children which bee in the middest of this naughty world, to bee saued through Christ for euer.

For which *read*: that
For to *read*: that they may

Haue alwayes therefore . . . and also of the horrible punishment . . . either of errour in Religion, or for uiciousnesse in life.

Delete of
For of *read*: for

Then, forasmuch as your office is both of so great excellencie, and of so great difficultie, ye see with how great care and study yee ought to apply your selues, aswell that you may shew your selues kind to that Lord, who hath placed you in so high a dignity, as also to beware, that neither you your selues offend, neither be occasion that other offend . . . all worldly cares and studies.

Delete aswell
For kind *read*: dutifull & thankfull

For neither be *read*: nor be an
For other *read*: others
Before apply *add*: will

Wee haue good hope, that . . . you apply your selues wholly to this one thing, and draw all your cares and studies this way, and to this end. And that you will continually pray for the heauenly assistance of the holy Ghost from God the Father, by the mediation of our onely Mediatour and Sauiour Iesus Christ, that by daily reading and weighing of the Scriptures, ye may so waxe riper and

For for the heauenly . . . Christ *read*: to God the Father by the Mediation of our only Saviour Jesus Christ for ye Heavenly assistance of his Holy Spirit

Delete so

430.
431. } *Mostly editorial, with restorations of the true BCP readings.*
432.

stronger in your ministery. And that yee may so endeauour your selues from time to time, to sanctifie the liues of you and yours, and to fashion them after the rule and doctrine of Christ: And that ye may be wholsome and godly examples and patternes for the rest of the congregation to follow: & that this present congregation of Christ here assembled, may also vnderstand your mindes and wils in these things: and that this your promise shall more moue you to doe your duties, ye shall answere plainely to these things, which we in the name of the congregation shall demand of you touching the same.

For the liues of you and yours *read*: your owne lives, & the lives of those, yt belong to you
Delete And

For congregation *read*: people
For & *read*: And

For shall *read*: may ye

For the congregation *read*: God, & of his Church

. . . . . .

Will you then giue your faithfull diligence . . . as this Realme hath receiued the same . . . obserue the same?

431.

Before Realme *add*: Church, &

. . . . . .

Will you be diligent to frame . . . examples and spectacles to the flocke of Christ?

For spectacles *read*: patterns

Answere.

I will apply my selfe, the Lord being my helper.

After selfe *add*: thereunto

. . . . . .

Will you reuerently obey your Ordinarie, and other chiefe Ministers, vnto whom the gouernment and charge is committed ouer you . . . their godly iudgements?

For the gouernment . . . ouer you *read*: is comitted the governement, & charge over you.

Answere.

I will so doe, the Lord being my helper.

Then shall the Bishop say,

Almightie God . . . vntill the time hee shall come at the latter day, to iudge the quicke and the dead.

After time *add*: when

After this, the Congregation shall bee desired secretly in their prayers, to make humble supplications to God for the foresaid things: for the which prayers, there shall be a certaine space kept in silence.

After make *add*: their
For the foresaid *read*: all these
For a certaine . . . silence *read*: silence kept for a certaine space.
Add: After wch shall be sung, or said, Come Holy Ghost &c. as before.
print it at large heere.

That done, the Bishop shall pray in this wise.

Let vs pray.

Almightie God and heauenly Father, which

431.   *The new position of* Veni Creator *is derived from the Consecrating of a Bishop.*

of thy infinite loue, and goodnesse towards
vs, hast giuen to vs thy onely and most deare
beloued Sonne Jesus Christ to be our
redeemer and author of euerlasting life . . . to
the same office and ministerie of saluation
of mankinde . . . by the same thy Sonne, our
Lord Jesus Christ . . . world without end.
Amen.

When this prayer is done . . . saying.

Receiue the holy Ghost . . . Amen.

The Bishop shall deliuer to euery one of them the
Bible in his hand, saying,

Take thou authority to preach the word of
God, and to minister the holy Sacraments in
this Congregation, where thou shalt be so
appointed.

When this is done, the Congregation shall sing
the Creed; and also they shall goe to the Communion; which all that receiue Orders, shall take
together, and remaine in the same place where
the hands were layd vpon them, vntill such time
as they haue receiued the Communion.

The Communion being done . . . shall be said
this Collect.

Most mercifull Father . . . that they may bee
clad about with all iustice . . . through Jesus
Christ our Lord. Amen.

And if the Order of Deacons and Priesthood be
giuen both vpon one day, then shall all things at
the holy Communion be vsed as they are appointed at the ordering of Priests, Sauing that for
the Epistle, the whole third Chapter of the first
to Timothie shall be read, as it is set out before in
the order of Priests. And immediately after the
Epistle the Deacons shall be ordered. And it shall
suffice the Letany to be said once.

---

432. *Delete* towards vs
      For deare *read*: dearly

      Before author *add*: the
      For of saluation *read*: for the saluation
      For the same . . . Christ *read*: the merits
         of the same Jesus Christ thy blessed
         Sonne

      For in *read*: into

      For this *read*: the
      For so *read*: thereunto

      For also . . . Communion *read*: the Bishop
         shall goe on in the Service of the
         Communion
      For the hands *read*: hands

      For clad . . . iustice *read*: cloath'd with all
         righteousnesse

433. *Read*: And if on the same day the Order
      of Deacons be given to some, & the
      Order of Priesthood to others; the
      Deacons shall be first presented, &
      then ye Priests in ye forme before sett
      downe: and it shall suffice, that the
      Litanie be once said for both. Then
      begins the Communion Service; in wch
      the Epistle shall be the whole 3. cap.
      of 1 Tim; Imediately after wch, they,
      yt are to be made Deacons shall take
      the Oath of Supremacy, be interro-
      gated, & then ordain'd, as is above
      prescribed. Then one of them having
      read the Gospel (wch shall be one of
      those fower appointed before in this
      Office) they, yt are to be made Priests
      shall likewise every one take the Oath
      of Supremacy, & then be interrogated,
      & ordeyned, as is before directed.

433.   *The new version makes fully explicit what was before implicit.*

The Forme of Consecrating of an Archbishop, or Bishop.

434.

Before Consecrating *add*: ordeyning, &

At the Communion.

435.

Add: Service

The Epistle

This is a true saying . . . of the euill speaker.

1 Tim. 3. 1.
ye new translation.
& soe in ye gospel.
Joh. 21. 15.

The Gospel.

**Jesus said to Simon Peter, Simon
Johanna . . . feed my sheepe.**

Or else out of the tenth Chapter of Iohn: as
before in the order of Priests.

For Iohanna *read*: sonne of Jonas (*thrice*)

Read: Or else this. Joh. 10. 2. Verily,
verily I say unto you &c.
as before in the ordering of Priests
Print it out at large.
Before Creed *add*: Nicene   (*crossed out*)
Before ended *add*: are

After the Gospel and Creed ended: first the
elected Bishop shall bee presented . . . the
Bishops that present him, saying,

**Most reuerend Father in God, we present
vnto you this godly and well learned man to
be consecrated Bishop.**

436.

For consecrated Bishop *read*: ordeined
consecrated a Bishop.

Then shall the Archbishop demand the Kings
mandate, for the consecration, and cause it to bee
read. And the Oath touching the knowledge of
the Kings Supremacie, shall be ministred to the
persons elected, as it is set out in the order of
Deacons. And then shall bee ministred the Oath
of due obedience vnto the Archbishop, as followeth.

For knowledge *read*: acknowledgement

For out *read*: downe
After shall *add*: also
After ministred *add*: to them

The Oath . . .

**. . . doe professe and promise all due
reuerence and obedience to the Archbishop
and to the Metropoliticall Church of N. and
to their successors . . . Jesus Christ.**

q

Then the Archbishop shall mooue the Congregation present, to pray; saying thus to them,

**Brethren, it is written . . . or euer that he
did chuse . . . or euer they laid hands vpon,
or sent forth Paul and Barnabas . . .
or that we admit and send forth . . . the holy
Ghost hath called him.**

For or euer that *read*: before
Read: before they laid hands vpon Paul
and Barnabas & sent them forth.
For or that *read*: before

And then shall be said the Letanie, as afore in the
order of Deacons.

For afore *read*: before

And after this place, **That it may please thee to
illuminate all Bishops, &c.** he shall say.

For place *read*: suffrage

434. Adv.:   The Forme of Ordering or Consecrating of an Arch-Bishop, or Bishop.
              See the 'Rationale' (p. 289).

435. Adv.:   *The Divine Service for that day, is to be proceeded in by the Preist, & the Deacon, (but omitting*
              the Letany,) untill they have read the Epistle, & the Gospell, & the Nicen Creed.
              The Deacon reads The Epistle, 1 Tim. 3. 1.
              This is a true saying . . . & the snare of the Devill.[1]
              [So endeth the Epistle.]
              The Holy Gospell is read by the Preist, Ioan. 21. 15.
              Jesus sayth to Simon Peter . . . Feed my Sheep.[1]
              [So endeth the Holy Gospell.]
              The Nicen Creed followeth, [I beleeve in one God, the Father, etc.]
              After the Creed is ended, The ArchBishop, & his Suffragans take their chayres before the Holy
              Table; and then two of them, bring the Bishop Elect, (having put on a Rochet onely over his
              gown) & present him unto the ArchBishop of their Province, or some other Bishop appointed by
              Commission, The Presenters saying,
              Most Reverend Father in God, we present unto you this godly & well learned man to
              be consecrated Bishop.

436.   *'Ordeined consecrated': see the 'Rationale' (p. 289).*

   Adv.:   *Hereupon the ArchBp shall demand the Kings Mandate for the Consecration, & cause it to be*
              read: wch done, He shall also require the Oath of the Ks Supremacy to be taken by him, who
              is to be ordered, as followeth,
              I A.B. do utterly testify . . . & the Contents of this Book.[2]
              [Next, the Oath of due obedience unto the ArchBp. shall be taken by ye Person Elected, as
              followeth,]
              In the Name of God, Amen . . . through Jesus Xt.[2]

---

[1] *Written out in full, in the A.V. rendering.*   [2] *Written out in full from the Book of Common Prayer.*

Concluding the Letanie in the end, with this prayer.

Almighty God, giuer of all good things ... world without end. Amen.

Then the Archbishop sitting in a chaire, shall say to him that is to bee consecrated.

Brother, for as much as holy Scripture, and the old Canons commandeth, that we should not be hasty in laying on of hands, and admitting of any person to the gouernment of the Congregation of Christ, which he hath purchased with no lesse price then the effusion of his owne blood: afore I admit you to this administration, whereunto ye are called, I will examine you in certaine articles, to the end the Congregation present, may haue a triall and beare witnesse how ye be minded to behaue your selfe in the Church of God.

. . . . .

Are you perswaded that the holy Scriptures containe sufficiently all doctrine, required of necessitie for eternall saluation, through the faith in Jesus Christ? And are you determined with the same holy Scriptures ... to teach or maintaine nothing ... but that you shall be perswaded may be concluded and proued by the same?

. . . . .

Be you ready with all faithfull diligence ... to the same?

. . . . .

Will you deny all vngodlinesse and worldly lusts, and liue soberly, righteously, and godly in this world ... hauing nothing to lay against you?

. . . . .

Will you maintain and set forward ... by the ordinance of this Realme?

Then shall be sung or sayd, Come holy Ghost, &c. as it is set out in the order of Priests.

That ended the Archbishop shall say.

. . . . .

Almighty God ... thy onely and most deare beloued Sonne Jesus Christ to be our Redeemer and Author of euerlasting life ... and making perfect his Congregation ... thy Gospel, and glad tidings of reconcilement to God ...

Delete in the end

437.   *For* a *read*: his

For commandeth *read*: command
Delete of
For the gouernment of the Congregation *read*: government in the Church

For afore *read*: before

After end *add*: that

Delete the

For with *read*: out of
After that *add*: which

For be *read*: are

Before world *add*: present
For lay *read*: say

Before Realme *add*: Church, &

As in ye Ordg of Priests.
Print it out at large.

438.   *For* deare *read*: dearly

Before Author *add*: the
For Congregation *read*: Church
Before glad *add*: the
For reconcilement to God *read*: reconciliation with thee

437. *Editorial.*

map at the last bee receiued into ioy, through Jesu Christ our Lord . . . Amen.

Before ioy *add*: everlasting
For Iesu *read*: Iesus

Then the Archbishop and Bishops present, shall lay their hands vpon the head of the elected Bishop, the Archbishop saying,

After Bishop *add*: humbly kneeling before the Lord's Table

Take the holy Ghost, and remember that 439. thou stirre vp the grace of God, which is in thee, by imposition of hands: for God hath not giuen vs the spirit of feare but of power, and loue, and sobernesse.

After Ghost *add*: by whom the Office, & Authority of a Bishop is now comitted unto thee:

For sobernesse *read*: of a sound mind.

Then the Archbishop shall deliuer him the Bible, saying,

Giue heed vnto reading . . . that the increase comming thereby . . . the immarcessible crowne of glory, through Jesus Christ our Lord. Amen.

After increase *add*: of piety
For immarcessible *read*: neverfading

Then the Archbishop shall proceed to the Communion, with whom the new consecrated Bishop, with other shall also communicate. And for the last Collect . . . shall be said this prayer.

For to the Communion *read*: in the Communion Service
For with other *read*: (with others)

Most merciful Father . . . world without end. Amen.

Imprinted at London by ROBERT BARKER, 440. Printer to the Kings most Excellent Maiestie: And by the Assignes of IOHN BILL.
Anno 1634.

For ROBERT BARKER, Printer *read*: the Printers
Delete And by . . . BILL.

438. **Adv.:** . . . before the Holy Table . . .

439. **Burnet,** *History of the Reformation*, Part II, p. 144:
> For there was then no express mention made in the words of Ordaining them, that it was for the one, or the other Office: In both it was said, *Receive thou the Holy Ghost in the name of the Father*, &c. But that having been since made use of to prove both Functions the same, it was of late years altered, as it is now [1683].

Prideaux, *Validity of the Orders of the Church of England:*
> p. 9. The alterations, or rather explanatory Additions made in our Ordinal in the Year 1662, were not inserted out of any respect to the controversie we have with the Church of *Rome*, but only to silence a cavil of the Presbyterians . . . So those explanatory words were inserted, whereby the distinction between a Bishop and a Priest is more clearly and unexceptionably expressed . . .
>
> p. 42. (*After quoting Burnet*) Thus far Dr. *Burnet*; and he having published it within twenty years after the thing was done, when so many were alive that were Members of Convocation when the alteration was made, and especially Dr. *Gunning* and Dr. *Peirson*, who I understand were the prime advisers of it, it is impossible he could want true information in this particular . . .

> > *Wren, however, in his 'Rationale' (q.v.), does not rule out the controversy with the Church of Rome. The phrase was further altered in the Convocation Book, and it is this version to which Burnet and Prideaux more particularly refer.*

440.   *Cf.* Directions to the Printers *and no. 3.*

> **Adv.:** Any change of words in ye book is very sparingly done, & such they are, as the reasons thereof will appear by the very reading of them . . . For instead of [Congregation] the word [Church] is restored; And instead of [Wch] having in propriety of speech a relation onely to Things, is put [who] when it relates unto Persons, to God, or to Man. Also, where the Mood is Indicative, instead of [Bee] wch properly belongs not but to ye other Moods, is put [are.]

APPENDIX A

The Portions of Wren's Advices not Included in the Notes

Advizing Thus But Submitting all to the ⟨Judgment⟩[1] Of Our H. Mother,
the Church of England.

IT is God alone, that can bring Light out of Darknes.

Never could there have bin an Opportunity so offenseles on the Churches part, for amending the Book of Common Prayer, As now, When it hath bin so long disused, that not One of Five Hundeth is so perfit in it, as to observe alterations: And they who are likeliest to pry into it, do know themselves to have bin the Causers of it. Yf, therefore, upon the Loud Clamors wch for these 15 yeares have bin taken up (in generall Termes) against the Book, By the severall Factions, (Who would have no set Formes, That They Themselves might be bound to none; that desire All Religion should hang on their Lips, as well for Praying, as for Preaching; That liked not to have the Kings Authority somuch asserted, and so often prayed for, as in the Liturgie it is; Nor would have the B^ps at all:) It may now please the King of his Grace to all, By Proclamation, or how else he shall please, to make it lawfull for every man, of such a Quality, in every County, Att such places, and w^thin so many Dayes (wch need not be many, after 15 yeares praeparation,) to bring in under their Hands, in termes beseeming, What Particulars soever they would except against in the Book, and the Reasons, To be delivered to such, as His Matie shall appoint in every County to receive the same: Also, that they who Receive the same, shall keep a perfit Note of every such [1]. . . . the day when, and the Parties, from whom they Receive the same, and then shall presently under their own Hands and seals, transmit the same into ye Chancery: Where all such Exceptions shall be viewed, and judged of, By those whom His Majesty shall think fit to appoint in his own stead; and these Alterations being by them so admitted as thereby to make perfit that Form of Common Prayer, the Book shall come forth, for publike Use, as the former Book did.

This would be done, wth as much Expedition, as may be; wth a Command, that none of the Old Editions shall in the mean while be required in the Churches. But by this way, those Amendments, whereof there is need, may be inserted: And nothing shall redound to the Dishonour of the Church, under wch it was so long used, and not amended before.

Toward this Reforming,

1. One Generall Rule would be, That every Word throughout, (as much as can be) should be commonly understood. The ayming whereat in the Compilers of the Old Book, was very commendable, though it was but slenderly observed, bycause Latin Termes were then so much in use, and one Course, wch they took therein, was not so well advized, As having produced that, wch is now a Blemish, and cals for an Amendment: When using a

---

[1] Indecipherable.

Word not perfitly understood in our Language, they joyned another to it to expound it, As [Erred and Strayed,] Perils, and Dangers] Vanquish and Overcome] King and Governor] Bishop and Pastor.] But now 'tis grown, to be but an idle Repetition; And in some, the latter word is less understood, or lyable to more misconstruction, then the former.

2. Another Rule would be, That whatsoever is not very perfit and right, be it never so small, should now be set right, to prevent all after quarrels; yet all care now to be had, that, in setting it right, it be done wth as little Alteration as well may bee. But the more it is now condescended to the mending of the smaller things, though some but merely verball, The less scruple will be made of altering some other things, that may seem to be of a greater Consequence.

3. A third Rule would be, Bycause no Language but at first is more unperfect, and impolished, and in every Age (of 70 yeares) admitts much variation, That heed be now taken to this, It being so long since the former Book was composed, that the Errors thereof have now by use corrupted the Language. There is one little Word wch crept into our Prayers, at the Translation of ye Letany into English, under *K. Hen. VIII*, for the use of the Army then going to Bulloyn, wch from thence hath spread itself, and hath infected many of ye Collects, and the Prayers, wch have bin used since, and yet is a very Soloecisme: That the word [Which] wch doth onely belong unto Things w^thout Life, or w^thout Reason, should be used also instead of [who,] and be the Relative for Persons, Humane or (much less) Divine. It began therfore then, w^th [Our Father, wch art in heaven] instead of, [Our Father, Who art in heaven.] The altring whereof, yf it may seem strang at first to unskilfull eares, yet will it not be a Nine dayes Wonder; But for ever after a Right expression in all our addresses unto God.

Some other Rules, fit to observe, will fall in, by the way as we goe on.

In these Advises, I goe by that Edition, (wch I onely now have,) of the Book of Common Prayer, in *4to*, Printed, *A^o. 1639.*

Unto every Page whereof I have added the Number, untill I came unto ye Epistles and Gospels, wch I cite by the Day.

At the Order also for ye Communion, I return again to sett the Pages thereof, and to make my Notes by those Numbers. But in this Part, there was a Mistake, the *15th* Page being sett twise: wch I hope will be pardoned.

The *40* first pages of this Book contayn nothing but Kalendars, and Rubricks or Rules, and other Praeambles. But in that they are set in the Front of this book, it is fitt, that they be reviewed also.

·   ·   ·   ·   ·

Now, in all these Notes of mine, where [etc.] is set, the meaning is, to goe on Verbatim, as it is now in ye book of Common Prayer, untill a New Note come. [But let not ye Printer use it.]

·   ·   ·   ·   ·

What Advices, for other exceptions and alterations shall be brought, and what shall bee therein ordred,

let the Church of Engl: consider,

Unto whom all herein is humbly submitted.

·   ·   ·   ·   ·

(The Note which follows is placed at the end of the Ordinal.)

Rationale.

The Reasons of the small variation made in the Title of this Book, are

1. Bycause [Form, & Manner] in effect are both ye same.

2. Bycause ye words [Ordering & Ordination] in an Act that is confined to Persons, are much more proper, then is the word [Consecrating,] wch may be applyed unto Dead or Inanimate things, To Bread, & Wine, to Places, & Times.

3. Bycause the Church from the beginning hath used it, by ye word of [Holy Orders] onely to signify these Spirituall Functions.

4. Bycause, when we have used the word [Ordring] for Preists, & Deacons, then to use the word [Consecration] alone for B^ps, As it is suspected, to relish a little too much of the Pomp of ye Church of Rome, So hath it bin abused in way of argument, by 2 contrary Factions; Both by ye Canonists, thereby to draw Episcopacy to a dependency wholy on the Pleasure, and Power of ye Papacy, as but his Comissioners; and also by ye Aërian Faction, from thence to pretend, that Episcopacy is not a distinct Order in ye Church of Christ, but onely a Degree, in nature no otherwise above Presbytery, then as Archiepiscopacy is above Episcopacy. By ye very same Paralogism also, this Faction hath made their Deaconry to be in itself nothing else but a Laicall Faculty, that thereby they may give a litle more colour to their Lay Presbytery.

The reasons of transposing these Formes now, & setting that for Bishops first, are

1. Bycause this is consonant both to ye Title of the former Book, & also to ye words of ye Preface, where it is twise so put.

2. Bycause the Institution of X^t himself was so: For in ye beginning He gave unto His Apostles, *Matth. 28.* all plenary Power over His Church, by them to be derived to their Successors & Substitutes unto ye worlds end, & this was Episcopacy, being *Specialis Potestas, ad omnes Actus Sacros*; Afterward, the Apostles (by ye guidance of the Holy Spirit) found cause by way of Distribution to Ordayn Partiary Powers also, & so by them were introduced the Orders of Preisthood, & of Deaconry.

3. Bycause the doing of this will conduce to some prevention of error in those, who being little able to judg, and reading first, (as the book of Ordination now hath it) what is sayd in ye Ordring of Preists, are easily mistaken, when in that wch followes for ye Ordring of B^ps they find so little difference (to their apprehensions) & thereby run into a surmise, That there is little or no need of ye latter of these, or (at the best) that by ye Institution of both they are but One Order, & in some small Degree onely differing.

4. Bycause this order accords wth the example of our Liturgy, wch hath set ye Comunion Service before that of Baptismes & Confirmation.

.   .   .   .   .   .

APPENDIX B

Paper B from the Fair Copy

ANOTHER Method of the Consecration, Oblation, Addresse, & Distribution.

(239)   When the Priest, standing before the Table, hath soe ordered the Bread, & wine, that he may with the more readines, & decency breake the Bread before the People, & take yᵉ Cup into his hands, he shall say the Prayer of Consecration, as followeth.

(241) Almighty God, our Heavenly Father, who of thy tender mercie didst give thine only sonne Jesus Christ, to suffer death upon the Crosse for our Redemption; who made there (by his one oblation of himselfe once offered) a full, perfect, & sufficient Sacrifice, oblation, & satisfaction, for the Sinns of the whole world; & did institute, & in his holy Gospel com̃and us to continue a perpetuall Memory of that his precious
(242) Death, & Sacrifice untill his coming againe: Heare us, ô Mercifull Father, wee most
(243) humbly beseech thee; & by the power of thy holy word, & spirit vouchsafe soe to blesse, & sanctifie these thy gifts, & creatures of Bread, & Wine, that wee receiving them according to thy Sonne our Saviour Jesus Christ's holy Institution, in re-
(244) membrance of Him, & to shew forth his Death, & Passion, may be partakers of his most blessed Body, & Bloud
(245)   Who in the same night, that he was betraied, ¹tooke Bread, & when he had blessed,
(246) & given thanks, he ¹brake it, & gave it to his disciples, saying, Take, Eat, ¹This is my Body, wᶜʰ is given for you; Doe this in remembrance of me.
(247)   Likewise after Supper he ¹tooke the Cup, and when he had given thanks, he gave it to them, saying, Drink ye all of this; for ¹This is my Bloud of the New Testament, wᶜʰ is shed for you, & for many for the Remission of Sinnes: Doe this, as oft, as ye
(248) shall drink it, in remembrance of me. Amen.

(250)   Im̃ediately after shall follow this Memoriall, or Prayer of Oblation.

(263)   Wherfore, o Lord, & Heavenly Father, according to the Institution of thy dearely beloved Sonne, our Saviour Jesus Christ, wee thy humble servants, doe celebrate, & make heere before thy divine Majesty, with these thy holy gifts the Memoriall, wᶜʰ thy sonne hath willed, & com̃anded us to make; having in remembrance his most blessed Passion, & Sacrifice, his mighty Resurrection, & his glorious Ascension into heaven; rendring unto thee most heartie thanks for the iñumerable benefits, procured unto us by the same. And wee entirely desire thy Fatherly goodnes, mercifully to accept this our Sacrifice of Praise, & Thanksgiving; most humbly beseeching thee to
(264) grant, that by the Merits, & Death of thy Sonne Jesus Christ, now represented unto thee, & through faith in his Bloud, who maketh Intercession for us at thy right Hand,

---

¹ Marginal notes as at nos. 245 and 247.

wee, & all thy whole Church may obtaine Remission of our Sinns, & be made partakers of all other Benefits of his Passion. And heere wee offer, & present unto thee,
ô Lord, ourselves, our soules, & bodies, to be a reasonable holy, & lively Sacrifice

(265) unto thee; humbly beseeching thee, that, whosoever shall be partakers of this holy
Comunion, may worthily receive the most precious Body, & Bloud of thy Sonne
Jesus Christ, & be fulfilled with thy Grace, & Heavenly Benediction. And although
wee be unworthy, through our manifold sinnes, to offer unto thee any Sacrifice; Yet
wee beseech thee, to accept this our bounden duty, & service, not weighing our
Merits, but pardoning our offences, through Jesus Christ our Lord, By whom, & w^{th}
whom in the Unity of the Holy Ghost all honour, & glory be unto thee, O Father
Almighty, world without end. Amen.

(266)   Then shall the Priest adde,
As our Saviour Christ hath taught, & comanded us, wee are bold to say
Our Father, wch art &c — from evill. Amen.
     Print it at large.

(267) Then shall the Priest, kneeling downe at God's board, say in the Name of all them,
that are to receive the holy Comunion, this Prayer following.

We doe not presume, to come to this thy Table, ô mercifull Lord, trusting in our
owne righteousnesse, but in thy manifold, and great mercies. Wee be not worthy soe
much as to gather up the crumbs under thy Table. But thou art the same Lord, who's
property is allwaies to have mercy. Grant us therfore, Gracious Lord, soe to eat the
flesh of thy deare Sonne Jesus Christ, & to drink his bloud; that our sinfull bodies may
be made cleane by his body, & our soules washed through his most precious blood;
& that wee may evermore dwell in him, & he in us. Amen.

(251) Then shall the Priest, that celebrateth, receive the holy Comunion in both kinds
upon his knees, &c. as in the booke. Only next before ye Rubric When all have
comunicated &c shall this Rubric be inserted.

(259) In the Comunion time shall be sung (where there is a Quire)
O Lambe of God, y^t takest away the Sins of ye world, Have mercy upon us.
O Lambe of God, y^t takest away the Sins of ye world, Grant us thy peace.
wth some, or all these Sentences of Scripture following.
Rom. 11. 33. Oh the depth of ye Wisd. & Knowl. of God! how incomprehensible
are his Judgm^{ts}, & his waies past finding out!
Ps. 103. 1. Praise the L^d. O my Soule; & all that is w^{th}in me, praise his H. Name.
 2. Praise the L^d. ô my Soule; & forgett not all his benefits.
 3. Who forgiveth all thy sinne: & healeth all thine infirmities.
 4. Who saveth thy life frō destruction; & crowneth thee wth mercy &
lov^g kindnes.
 5. Who satisfieth thy mouth wth good things; & feedeth thee wth ye bread
of Heaven.

Luc. 1. Blessed be ye Ld G. of Isräel; for he hath visited, & redeemed his people. Therf. being saved frõ our enemies: let us serve him wthout feare.

In holines, & right'ness before him: all the daies of our Life.

1 Cor. 1. 30. Christ Jesus is made of G. unto us: Wisd. & Right'ness & Sanctifi^{on}, & Redemtion.

        31. That acc: as it is written: He y^t glorieth sh^d glory in the L^d.

Joh. 5. 13. Behold thou art made whole: Sin no more least a worse th. happen unto thee.

Joh. 8. If ye continue in my word; then are ye my disciples indeed.

        And ye shall know the Truth: & the Truth shall make you free.

Mat. 24. 13. Whosoever shall endure unto ye end: the same shall be saved.

Luc. 12. Happy are those serv^{ts}: whõ y^r L^d, w^n he cometh, shall find so doing.

Luc. 12. 40. Be ye therfore ready also: for ye Son of M. cometh at an hower w^n ye think not.

John. 12. 35. Yet a little while is ye light with you: walk, while you have ye light, lest darkn. come upon you.

        36. While ye have light beleeve in ye light: y^t ye may be ye children of light.

Rom. 13. 12. The night is far spent ye day is at hand: let us therfore cast of ye works of darkness & let us put on ye armor of light.

        13. 14. Let us walk honestly, as in ye day: putting on ye Ld Jesus Christ.

1 Cor. 3. Know ye not, y^t ye are ye Temples of G.: & y^t ye Sp. of G. dwelleth in you.

        If any one defile ye Temple of G. him shall G. destroy.

1 Cor. 6. Ye are bought wth a price: therfore glorify G. in y^r bodies, & in y^r Spirits, for they belong to G.

John 15. Heerein is the F. glorified: that ye beare much fruit.

        This is X^s Com^{dt}, y^t wee love another: even as he hath loved us.

Eph. 5. Be wee followers of G. as deare childr. & walk in love: even as X. loved us, & gave hims. an offer^g, & a sacrif. of a sweet savour unto G. for us.

Rom. 8. 23.[1] He y^t spared õ his own Son, but delivered him up for us all: how shall he not wth him also freely give us all things.

Apoc. 5. 12. Worthy is ye Lamb, y^t was slain, to receive power, & riches, & wisd. & strength, & honour, & glory, and blessing.

        13. Blessing, honor, glory, & power, be unto him y^t sitteth upon ye throne: & unto ye Lamb for ever & ever.

---

[1] The reference is copied accurately from no. 259, but the text that follows is Rom. 8. 32.

APPENDIX C

The Date of DB

IN a manuscript catalogue of the Cosin Library at Durham, dating probably from 1669 or 1670, DB is described thus:

> Common Prayer Booke with my MS Notes in the Margent made for Variations in the last new Liturgy.

This, no doubt, represents the final purpose of the book, and the occasion of the majority of the entries; but some scholars have argued that the book was begun much earlier, and in particular that it was connected with the Lords' Committee of 1641. The account given above assumes that the vast bulk of the entries was not made until 1660–1, a view which rests on the following grounds.[1]

The *terminus post quem* for any entry is 1620, the date of the Psalter bound up with the Prayer Book. There is also some evidence that Cosin did correct the text of the Book of Common Prayer for the press in his early days of prominence. A note on the Ornaments Rubric in his 'Second Series' tells us:

> The word *ALL* here, had bin divers yeeres omitted in the Editions of this Booke, contrary to the true Copie of it, sett forth in ye first yeere of Q. Eliz.: (wch was done either by the negligence of the Printer or upon designes) untill K. Charles ye I. in the first yeere of his Reigne comãnded it to be restored, & sent me to his Printing House to see it done; ever since which time it hath so continued. (*Works*, v. 231.)

Again, H. B(urton), in *A Tryall of Private Devotions* (London, 1628), an attack on Cosin's *Devotions*, writes in the introductory Epistle:

> I haue seene in the great Printing house at London a cast[2] *Seruice-booke* wherein this our author (as if he would correct *Magnificat*) hath in sundry places noted with his owne hand (as they say) where and how he would haue the *Seruice booke* altered, how hee would haue the names of some Saints dayes changed, and redde letters put for the blacke, as if hee would canonize more holidaies for you to obserue. And throughout the booke, where he finds the word *Minister* he would haue it cancelled, and Priest put instead thereof. . . .
>
> And in conclusion, for those priuate godly prayers in the end of the reading *Psalmes*, he thinks them fitter to be omitted, then added. And why? . . . because, saith he, they were not at first put into the Seruice booke, when it was established by Act of Parliament, but afterwards.

Finally, a letter from Cosin to Laud, of June 1628, includes this passage:

> The Accusations w[ch] they bring ag[t] me about *altering of y[e] Common Prayer Book*, your Lo[p] can best tell how peevish & vayne they be; specially if you have called for That Booke from y[e] King's

---

[1] For a detailed discussion of the various theories, see *Journal of Ecclesiastical History*, vol. vi, no. 1, pp. 60–72.

[2] I.e. 'cast-off'; or, as Dr. A. I. Doyle has suggested to me, 'projected'.

Printer, wch they say I have so magisterially noted. Some marginall directions indeed I wrote at the instant request of Bill & Norton to be a help to y^m in ye amending of such faults & omissions in their severall volumes, for wch they had bin a little before schooled by your Lo^p upon warrant & com̃and from his Matie. Notes for other Alterations I made not, unlesse it were here & there for ye beautifying of ye Book wth sundry characters & fairer l^res y^n before, or for ye printing of the Pater nr at large. There were divers false & misnamed *Lessons noted, wch in ye gr^t Book they have not yet amended, and in the Calendar, where they begin to reckon the Kalends of or before every Month, they have let ye name of ye month stand still in ye same character & in ye same order wth ye Saints dayes, as if Februarie and Hilarie were sainted both alike.

*As, The i. Lesson at Evensong upon ye day of Circumcision. &. The, 1 Lesson at Mattins upon ye day of Epiphanie. ye first of these ending where it shold begin; & ye 2d. most improperly set for a proper Lesson. being ye xl. whereas it shold be ye lx. of Esay. by wch transposition of one letter, ye people in many Churches are told of S. John Baptist, when they shold heare of ye Gentils coming to Christ. (*State Papers, Domestic: Charles I*, cviii. 75.)

DB contains all the alterations here specifically mentioned: 'all' is restored to the Ornaments Rubric (no. 57); the Conversion of St. Paul and St. Barnabas are added to the list of 'Holy dayes' (no. 46), and entered in the Kalendar in red letters (no. 43); Priest is sometimes substituted for Minister (nos. 68, 86, 251, 276); and at the beginning of 'Certaine godly prayers' (no. 419) we find the comment:

These are no part of ye Com̃on Prayer Booke, but added by ye printer & in ye next Edition are to be omitted.

Numerous wrong readings are corrected; there are many directions such as 'Sett here a faire Compartement'; and the *Pater noster* often has the comment 'Print it out at large.' The lessons mentioned are altered (no. 31), and the names of the months are removed from the column of the Kalendar containing the Saints' days (no. 43).

In view of all this, it is tempting to identify DB immediately with the 'cast *Seruice-booke*'. There are, however, no traces of its having been used by printers; and Cosin has made no entries of 'a fleuron', and the like, after the end of the Baptism Service, which can hardly have been the case with the book used by the printers. It is also possible to suppose that Cosin at the same time entered the corrections into another copy for his own use. In FC many of the corrections have already been made by the printer, and if better printed copies were available in 1661, it is hard to see why Cosin should then go to the trouble of entering all the corrections afresh in an inferior text. On the other hand, the corrections are such as he would be able to enter from memory at any date in his life, and it cannot be regarded as more than a possibility that he made some entries in DB about 1626 or 1627.

This concludes the external evidence for an early date; of internal evidence there is nothing of value to be derived from the content of the entries; and little can be built upon differences in Cosin's handwriting. James Parker comments that the rubric which now stands at the head of the Burial Service (no. 396) 'is written in by Bishop Cosin in a very fine, and probably his early, handwriting'. It is true that this is probably the neatest example of Cosin's writing to be found in DB; but when it is compared with indubitably early specimens, such as the 'First Series' of Notes, also preserved at Durham, or the Parish Register of Brancepeth, where Cosin was rector from 1626, it appears much less 'fine'. In general, it is extremely hazardous to base arguments upon Cosin's handwriting; even in his later years, when his sight had deteriorated, he was still capable of small and neat lettering, side by side with hurried, sprawling characters. There are no examples in DB of the minute hand which he employed in the 'First Series' (this in itself is evidence against a very early date), and, apart from that, handwriting must be ruled out as a reliable source of chronological evidence.

The most decisive argument is derived from the sources used in DB, especially Wren's *Advices* and Cosin's *Particulars*. The *Advices* were probably put together by degrees during Wren's imprisonment, as references to the working of the Kalendar in 1648, 1651, and 1654 seem to indicate; but they must have been finally written down in 1660, for he alludes to '15 yeares praeparation', which must be reckoned from January 1645, when the Prayer Book was suppressed. The fact that Wren had access to only one Prayer Book must indicate that he was still in prison, but his suggestion of a royal proclamation shows that the Restoration must have been very close at hand. In fact, Wren was released on 15 March 1660, but was not allowed to resume possession of his palace until the King had returned; in the intervening time he lived in lodgings, and the writing-out of the *Advices* may be safely assigned to this period, i.e. April–May 1660. Cosin's *Particulars* cannot be conclusively dated from internal evidence, but they are described in the catalogue quoted above as:

Common Prayer Booke. Particulars therein that were considered, explained & corrected before the last edition, made & written by John L^d. B^{pp}. of Durham 1660. MS. fol.

This is a fuller title than that of the manuscript itself:

Particulars to be considered, explayned and corrected in ye Book of Comon Prayer.

Also the words 'to be' have been altered to 'that were'. But the long version may well be authentic, and have been taken from an outside sheet of the manuscript now lost. In its present state the manuscript consists of 14 sheets, the title being written at the top of the *recto* of the first sheet, and Particular No. 1 following immediately after. This suggests that originally there were 16 sheets, the first bearing the title as given in the catalogue, though in the future tense. If this was so, the date 1660 may be accepted with confidence. Cosin was consecrated on 2 December 1660, so that the *Particulars* were probably completed in December or shortly before. A correspondent addressed him as Lord Bishop of Durham as early as October, and in November he was signing himself as 'Jo. Dunelm. electus', so that the title may well have been written before his consecration.

Thus both *Advices* and *Particulars* may be assigned with high probability to 1660. Since entries taken from them (and such entries form a high proportion of the total) are always the first to be made at any particular point, it follows that many of the entries cannot have been made before 1660. Likewise the abundant use of material from SL suggests that DB is not connected with the projected revision of 1641, when that book was decidedly under a cloud, and its use would have been tactless in the extreme. By 1660 its stock had risen sufficiently for it to have been reprinted by L'Estrange, and it may have seemed to provide a practical way of reintroducing the ideas of 1549. Thus the evidence points to 1660 as the earliest possible date for the bulk of the entries, though it is not impossible that a few were made many years before.

On the other hand, the date of completion of the entries can be fixed with some precision. Last among the entries in order of time come the concessions granted at the Savoy Conference. Fifteen of the seventeen appear in DB, while two are ignored. Four which had already been suggested by Cosin or Wren appear in DB at an early stage; but each of the remaining eleven is the last entry at the point where it occurs, and was entered by Sancroft. The Bishops' *Reply*, in which these concessions were announced, was handed to the Presbyterian commissioners about 12 June 1661. It is not likely that the concessions were entered immediately, or indeed before the end of the conference; but it can be saidwith certainty that DB, though probably nearing completion, was still incomplete in the middle of June 1661. On the other hand, it is likely that the entry of the concessions was not long delayed after the end of the conference (25 July), since further concessions not specified in the Bishops' *Reply* are introduced in the Convocation Book, but not in DB. If DB was still being compiled when they were decided upon, they would surely have appeared in it.

These changes were entered by Sancroft, whose writing invariably appears at the final stage of any entry; it is clear that Cosin handed the book over to him towards the end of the process of compilation. The date of the change-over can be fixed within fairly narrow limits, the occasion being, in all probability, Cosin's departure for Durham. The exact date of his departure is not known, but he had reached Durham by 17 August, and it may be assumed that Sancroft had taken over by 10 August. He must have finished his work some days before making the Fair Copy, to allow time for the copying; and FC must have been complete before it was reviewed by the bishops, for it still includes the proposed rearrangement of the Canon on the lines of SL, with a new note that it is 'left to censure'; but this rearrangement was rejected by 'My LL. yᵉ BB. at Elie house'. This phrase may refer either to the Convocation Committee appointed on 21 November 1661, or to the informal consultations with Wren and Sheldon for which Cosin was recalled to London at the beginning of November. In favour of the latter, it may be pointed out that the Convocation Committee, though directed to meet at Ely House, agreed to meet *in hac domo pro praesenti*. On the other hand, it is possible that the committee had begun meeting at Ely House by the time they reached the Communion Service.

But whichever meetings are meant, FC must have been complete before they began. If it had not been transcribed until after the meetings, Sancroft would not have needed to copy out in full the Canon 'otherwise methodiz'd'. Hence FC must have been complete by 21 November, or even 1 November; and, *a fortiori*, work on DB must have ended by then. To sum up: DB has no connexion with the revision projected in 1641, though some of the entries could have been made as early as 1627. The bulk of the entries derive from Wren's *Advices*, written in the spring of 1660, and Cosin's *Particulars*, completed in December of the same year. Wren and Cosin in the winter and spring of 1660–1 systematically worked through DB with their respective lists of suggestions, together with the Scottish Liturgy and other sources. This process may have been repeated, at some points more than once. Their draft alterations and additions were entered by Cosin into DB, and into FC for part of the Ordinal. On leaving for Durham in early August 1661, Cosin handed over both books to Sancroft, who carefully revised the whole of DB, greatly reducing the number of suggestions, and then copied out the final state into FC, also completing the revision of the Ordinal. The result was submitted to 'my Lords the Bishops at Ely House' in November 1661.

APPENDIX D

The Fair Copy

FC PRESENTS two interesting features: first, a number of variants from the final text of DB; and secondly, suggestions for the revision of the Ordinal. Little attention has been paid to the former; but, when examined, they fall into the same groups as are found in Sancroft's entries in DB: notably, further improvements in the wording of the rubrics, new directions to the printer, and tacit suppression of suggestions made in DB, to the number of twenty-eight cases in the last category. There is also one marked divergence: whereas DB proposes quite definitely to rearrange the Canon, FC leaves it as it stands, and gives the proposed rearrangement as Paper B, '& both left to censure' (no. 239, note). All this indicates that FC is not a mere copy, but a continuation of the same process of revision visible in Sancroft's entries in DB (see the Introduction, p. xxi).

There are also nearly thirty entries[1] made by Cosin in the main body of FC: many are corrections of errors in transcription made by Sancroft, but some are not found in the text of DB at all. Ten minor alterations for which DB provides no parallel were made in the Marriage Service. Another group of four suggests that the 'Form for the Baptizing of Adult persons' had not yet been projected when the entries were made: in the Baptism Service the word 'persons' is substituted for 'children', and at the end of the service 'A Catechism' is written in as a catchword; Sancroft subsequently altered it to 'A Forme'. One entry also reproduces the first draft of DB (no. 314), and has to be altered by Sancroft. Why these fourteen corrections were made here, and not in DB, remains unexplained. Some were accepted by Convocation, some were not.

The corrections made in the Ordinal of FC are not copied from DB, for that has no Ordinal. Theories of a separate original, now lost, are pure conjecture: it is most probable that FC is, for the Ordinal, the first stage of revision. In favour of this suggestion, it may be pointed out that the *Particulars* do not deal with the Ordinal at all; nor do Cosin's 'First' and 'Third Series' of Notes; while the 'Second Series' only contains a few transcriptions, mainly from a work by P. Aerodius, none of which were drawn upon for FC. Evidently Cosin had little interest in the Ordinal. Nor do the entries in FC show any signs of the use of the Ordinal of 1550, while SL had no Ordinal to draw upon at all. Thus, of all the main sources of DB, only the *Advices* were used for the Ordinal. There was therefore no occasion for the detailed comparison of sources carried on throughout DB; all that was needed was to work through the text with the *Advices*. This Cosin appears to have begun to do. It is not generally known that there are twenty entries in his hand in the FC Ordinal, covering the Preface and the Ordering of Deacons, but going no further; about half are taken from the *Advices*; and the Litany is altered to the final form of DB. Thus the Ordinal was already in part revised before the transfer to Sancroft. Unfortunately most of the portion of the

See nos. 9, 17, 30, 31, 67, 68, 114, 167, 288, 294, 296, 314, 334, 344, 353, 371, 372, 376, 378, 379, 421, 423, 424, 425, 426.

Advices relating to the Ordinal is lost, so that we cannot estimate how many of the changes are due to Wren, but the vast majority are small verbal changes such as abound in the *Advices*, or might have been introduced by Sancroft himself. There is only one change of importance, the slight rearrangement of the Ordering of Priests, which may have been recommended by Wren. At any rate, there is no reason to suppose that FC does not represent the first stage in revising the Ordinal. A further argument in favour of this hypothesis is provided by the Convocation Book, in which the Ordinal is subjected to a thorough-going revision, comparable in extent to the most detailed parts of DB, and more extensive than the treatment given in Convocation to any other part of the Prayer Book. Evidently the Ordinal was regarded as needing special attention, and this presumably because FC was only a first draft.

APPENDIX E

The Connexion of Wren and Cosin with the Scottish Liturgy

THE frequent use made in DB of SL raises the question whether Wren and Cosin had any share in the making of the latter book. Dr. G. Donaldson's book *The Making of the Scottish Prayer Book of 1637* has thrown a great deal of light on the previously obscure circumstances of its compilation. It is now quite clear that Wren was only called in at the eleventh hour, when printing had already begun, to advise upon some proposals made by Bishop Wedderburne of Dunblane. But even if similarities between *Adv.* and SL occur, it is as possible that Wren was influenced by SL as that SL was influenced by him. The one case where his active participation in the wording of SL seems highly probable is at the Offertory (Donaldson, p. 307), where the Christ Church book originally read:

While the presbyter treatably pronounceth . . .

The unusual word 'treatably' was replaced by 'distinctly', but it is noteworthy that it also occurs in Wren's *Particular Orders* issued in the same year (1636):

8. That warning be given. . . . And that as soon as such warning is given, The second of those 3 Exhortations . . . be treatably pronounced.

Wren has a partiality for obscure words, and it seems clear that he took some part in the drafting of SL, however small.

Cosin's participation is alleged by Robert Baillie, who alludes to it in his *Letters and Journals* (Donaldson, p. 79) and in *The Canterbvrians Self-Conviction* (Donaldson, p. 80, as expanded by Fuller). Yet it is difficult in his case also to prove influence either way. Of the parallels cited by Donaldson, the great majority are from Cosin's *Particulars* of 1660, and are open to the same alternative explanations as the parallels with *Adv.* The parallel with Cosin's *Devotions* (Donaldson, p. 271) is only found in the editions after 1662. Of Cosin's earlier works, the *Second Series of Notes* offers no point of contact with SL, while the *First Series* has ten, two of which were more probably derived directly from 1549, and four more from Andrewes's *Notes*, which the Scottish bishops were using independently (e.g. their suggestion of his Offertory Sentences). The remaining four are too slight to *prove* a connexion with Cosin, though it is far from impossible that he should have suggested them to Laud and Wren (see nos. 31, 43, 49, 93). The *Third Series* adds nos. 92 and 277, and two more corrections of lessons. The date of this series is unknown, so little can be built on it.

A definite link seems to be afforded by Cosin's letter to Laud about faults in the printing of the Prayer Book (see App. C, p. 293) of which the note on the Kalendar in the Christ Church book (Donaldson, p. 262) reads like a quotation. In this letter Cosin also points out errors in the lessons for the Circumcision and the Epiphany, which were corrected in SL. It is quite conceivable that Laud, having kept this letter, should have made use of it on this occasion. If so, two of the points of contact quoted above from Series I and III are already accounted for, and the connexion becomes slighter than ever.

To sum up, the verdict in Cosin's case must be 'Not proven', though it is quite probable that he made unofficial suggestions, and that his letter was used; but it is equally probable that his name was drawn into the propaganda against the book as that of a prominent and unpopular Laudian.